LONGMAN
KEYSTONE

D

Anna Uhl Chamot

John De Mado

Sharroky Hollie

PEARSON
Longman

LONGMAN
KEYSTONE **D**

Pearson Education, One Lake Street, Upper Saddle River, NJ 07458

Staff credits: The people who made up the Longman Keystone team, representing editorial, production, design, manufacturing, and marketing, are John Ade, Rhea Banker, Liz Barker, Danielle Belfiore, Don Bensey, Virginia Bernard, Kenna Bourke, Anne Boynton-Trigg, Johnnie Farmer, Maryann Finocchi, Patrice Fraccio, Geraldine Geniusas, Charles Green, Henry Hild, David L. Jones, Lucille M. Kennedy, Ed Lamprich, Emily Lippincott, Tara Maceyak, Maria Pia Marrella, Linda Moser, Laurie Neaman, Sherri Pemberton, Liza Pleva, Joan Poole, Edie Pullman, Monica Rodriguez, Tania Saiz-Sousa, Donna Schaffer, Chris Siley, Lynn Sobotta, Heather St. Clair, Jennifer Stem, Siobhan Sullivan, Jane Townsend, Heather Vomero, Marian Wassner, Lauren Weidenman, Matthew Williams, and Adina Zoltan.

Smithsonian American Art Museum contributors: Project director and writer: Elizabeth K. Eder, Ph.D.; Writer: Mary Collins; Image research assistants: Laurel Fehrenbach, Katherine G. Stilwill, and Sally Otis; Rights and reproductions: Richard H. Sorensen and Leslie G. Green; Building photograph by Tim Hursley.

Text design and composition: Kirchoff/Wohlberg, Inc.

Text font: 11.5/14 Minion
Acknowledgments: See page 468.
Illustration and Photo Credits: See page 470.

Library of Congress Cataloging-in-Publication Data
Chamot, Anna Uhl.
    Longman keystone / Anna Uhl Chamot, John De Mado, Sharroky Hollie.
        p. cm. -- (Longman keystone ; D)
    Includes index.
    ISBN 0-13-158258-5 (v. D)
    1. Language arts (Middle school)--United States. 2. Language arts (Middle school)--Activity programs. 3. Language arts (Secondary)--United States. 4. English language--Study and teaching. I. Demado, John II. Hollie, Sharroky III. Title.
    LB1631.C4466 2008
    428.0071'2--dc22
                                            2007049279

ISBN-13: 978-0-13-158258-3
ISBN-10: 0-13-158258-5

Printed in the United States of America
11 12 13 14 15 V057 16 15 14 13 12

About the Authors

Anna Uhl Chamot is a professor of secondary education and a faculty advisor for ESL in George Washington University's Department of Teacher Preparation. She has been a researcher and teacher trainer in content-based second-language learning and language-learning strategies. She co-designed and has written extensively about the Cognitive Academic Language Learning Approach (CALLA) and spent seven years implementing the CALLA model in the Arlington Public Schools in Virginia.

John De Mado has been an energetic force in the field of Language Acquisition for several years. He is founder and president of John De Mado Language Seminars, Inc., an educational consulting firm devoted exclusively to language acquisition and literacy issues. John, who speaks a variety of languages, has authored several textbook programs and produced a series of music CD/DVDs designed to help students acquire other languages. John is recognized nationally, as well as internationally, for his insightful workshops, motivating keynote addresses, and humor-filled delivery style.

Sharroky Hollie is an assistant professor in teacher education at California State University, Dominguez Hills. His expertise is in the field of professional development, African-American education, and second-language methodology. He is an urban literacy visiting professor at Webster University, St. Louis. Sharroky is the Executive Director of the Center for Culturally Responsive Teaching and Learning (CCRTL) and the co-founding director of the nationally acclaimed Culture and Language Academy of Success (CLAS).

Reviewers

Sharena Adebiyi
Fulton County Schools
Stone City, GA

Jennifer Benavides
Garland ISD
Garland, TX

Tracy Bunker
Shearer Charter School
Napa, CA

Dan Fichtner
UCLA Ed. Ext. TESOL Program
Redondo Beach, CA

Trudy Freer-Alvarez
Houston ISD
Houston, TX

Helena K. Gandell
Duval County
Jacksonville, FL

Glenda Harrell
Johnston County School Dist.
Smithfield, NC

Michelle Land
Randolph Middle School
Randolph, NJ

Joseph E. Leaf
Norristown Area High School
Norristown, PA

Ilona Olancin
Collier County Schools
Naples, FL

Jeanne Perrin
Boston Unified School Dist.
Boston, MA

Cheryl Quadrelli-Jones
Anaheim Union High School Dist.
Fullerton, CA

Mary Schmidt
Riverwood High School
Atlanta, GA

Daniel Thatcher
Garland ISD
Garland, TX

Denise Tiffany
West High School
Iowa City, IA

Lisa Troute
Palm Beach County School Dist.
West Palm, FL

Dear Student,

Welcome to **LONGMAN**

KEYSTONE

Longman Keystone has been specially designed to help you succeed in all areas of your school studies. This program will help you develop the English language skills you need for language arts, social studies, math, and science. You will discover new ways to use and build upon your language skills through your interactions with classmates, friends, teachers, and family members.

Keystone includes a mix of many subjects. Each unit has four different reading selections that include literary excerpts, poems, and nonfiction articles about science, math, and social studies. These selections will help you understand the vocabulary and organization of different types of texts. They will also give you the tools you need to approach the content of the different subjects you take in school.

As you use this program, you will discover new words, use your background knowledge of the subjects presented, relate your knowledge to the new information, and take part in creative activities. You will learn strategies to help you understand readings better. You will work on activities that help you improve your English skills in grammar, word study, and spelling. Finally, you will be asked to demonstrate the listening, speaking, and writing skills you have learned through fun projects that are incorporated throughout the program.

Learning a language takes time, but just like learning to skateboard or learning to swim, it is fun! Whether you are learning English for the first time, or increasing your knowledge of English by adding academic or literary language to your vocabulary, you are giving yourself new choices for the future, and a better chance of succeeding in both your studies and in everyday life.

We hope you enjoy *Longman Keystone* as much as we enjoyed writing it for you!

Good luck!

Anna Uhl Chamot
John De Mado
Sharroky Hollie

Learn about *Art* with the
Smithsonian American Art Museum

Dear Student,

At the end of each unit in this book, you will learn about some artists and artworks that relate to the theme you have just read about. These artworks are all in the Smithsonian American Art Museum in Washington, D.C. That means they belong to you, because the Smithsonian is America's collection. The artworks were created over a period of 300 years by artists who responded to their experiences in personal ways. Their world lives on through their artworks and, as viewers, we can understand them and ourselves in new ways. We discover that many of the things that concerned these artists still engage us today.

Looking at an artwork is different from reading a written history. Artists present few facts or dates. Instead, they offer emotional insights that come from their own lives and experiences. They make their own decisions about what matters, without worrying if others agree or disagree. This is a rare and useful kind of knowledge that we can all learn from. Artists inspire us to respond to our own lives with deeper insight.

There are two ways to approach art. One way is through the mind—studying the artist, learning about the subject, exploring the context in which the artwork was made, and forming a personal view. This way is deeply rewarding and expands your understanding of the world. The second way is through the senses—letting your imagination roam as you look at an artwork, losing yourself in colors and shapes, absorbing the meaning through your eyes. This way is called "aesthetic." The great thing about art is that an artwork may have many different meanings. You can decide what it means to you.

This brief introduction to American art will, I hope, lead to a lifetime of enjoyment and appreciation of art.

Elizabeth Broun
The Margaret and Terry Stent Director
Smithsonian American Art Museum

Glossary of Terms

You will find the following words useful when reading, writing, and talking about art.

abstract a style of art that does not represent things, animals, or people realistically

acrylic a type of paint that is made from ground pigments and certain chemicals

background part of the artwork that looks furthest away from the viewer

brushstroke the paint or ink left on the surface of an artwork by the paintbrush

canvas a type of heavy woven fabric used as a support for painting; another word for a painting

composition the way in which the different parts of an artwork are arranged

detail a small part of an artwork

evoke to produce a strong feeling or memory

figure the representation of a person or animal in an artwork

foreground part of the artwork that looks closest to the viewer

geometric a type of pattern that has straight lines or shapes such as squares, circles, etc.

mixed media different kinds of materials such as paint, fabric, objects, etc. that are used in a single artwork

oil a type of paint that is made from ground pigments and linseed oil

paintbrush a special brush used for painting

perception the way you understand something you see

pigment a finely powdered material (natural or man-made) that gives color to paint, ink, or dye

portrait an artwork that shows a specific person, group of people, or animal

print an artwork that has been made from a sheet of metal or a block of wood covered with a wet color and then pressed onto a flat surface like paper. Types of prints include lithographs, etchings, aquatints, etc.

symbol an image, shape, or object in an artwork that represents an idea

texture the way that a surface or material feels and how smooth or rough it looks

tone the shade of a particular color; the effect of light and shade with color

watercolor a type of paint that is made from ground pigments, gum, and glycerin and/or honey; another word for a painting done with this medium

Contents

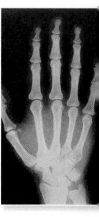

Contents

How are growth and change related? 70

UNIT 3

Contents

How can we tell
what's right? **134**

 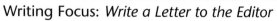

UNIT 4

 THE BIG QUESTION

Can we think with the heart? 196

Contents

UNIT 5

What can we learn from **times of war?**..**264**

UNIT 6

What makes animals so amazing?

UNIT

1

What is light?

THE BIG QUESTION

2

This unit is about light and the absence of light. You'll find out what light is and how it behaves. You'll read stories showing different ways in which light is important to us. Reading, writing, and talking about this topic will give you practice using academic language and help you become a better student.

READING 1: Myth
- "Grandmother Spider Brings the Sun" by Geri Keams

READING 2: Science Article
- "Light"

READING 3: Short Story
- "A Game of Light and Shade" by Arturo Vivante

READING 4: Social Studies Article
- From *The Eye of Conscience* by Milton Meltzer and Bernard Cole

Listening and Speaking

At the end of this unit, you will play a **description guessing game**.

Writing

In this unit you will practice **descriptive writing**. Describing things means telling what things look, sound, feel, smell, or taste like. After each reading you will learn a skill to help you write a descriptive paragraph. At the end of the unit, you will use the skills to help you write a descriptive essay.

QuickWrite
In your notebook, write the word *Light* at the top of a page. What things do you associate with light? List as many ideas as you can. Then share your ideas with a partner.

Visit *LongmanKeystone.com*

What You Will Learn

Reading

■ Vocabulary building:
*Literary terms,
dictionary skills,
word study*

■ Reading strategy:
Predict

■ Text type:
Literature (myth)

Grammar, Usage, and Mechanics
Order of adjectives

Writing
Describe a character

THE BIG QUESTION

What is light? Light often represents different things in literature. For example, it might stand for knowledge or hope. Why do you think this is so? Can you think of some other examples? Discuss with a partner.

BUILD BACKGROUND

In this unit you will read a myth called **"Grandmother Spider Brings the Sun."** Myths are fictional tales that explain how things in nature came to be or describe the actions of gods or heroes. People probably created myths as a way of explaining things they didn't understand about the world around them.

Different ancient cultures each had their own myths. People told these myths to their children generation after generation. Because myths were passed down orally, or by word of mouth, we say that they are part of the oral tradition. Luckily for us, many myths have been written down.

The myth you are about to read comes to us from the Native American people known as the Cherokee. It explains some facts about the natural world in an amusing way.

▲ A Cherokee storyteller and his audience

Learn Literary Words

As part of the oral tradition, "Grandmother Spider Brings the Sun" is written exactly the way a storyteller would tell it. It is a story that we should listen to as well as read.

Because this story is meant to be heard, it includes words that imitate sounds. For example, the word *Whoosh!* is used when a character in the story throws water on something burning. *Whoosh!* is a word that sounds like the noise made by water putting out a fire. We call the use of words that imitate sounds **onomatopoeia**. Other examples of onomatopoeia include the words *buzz*, *click*, *jingle*, *bang*, and *boom*.

Another way storytellers appeal to your sense of hearing is by using **repetition**. Repetition is using words more than once. For example, in the story you are about to read, the character Coyote says, "Calm down, calm down, calm down." Repetition can show that a character is emotionally excited—nervous, happy, or angry. When listeners hear that a character is excited, they are more likely to get involved in the story. Repetition can also be used for emphasis, or to show importance. Finally, repetition helps to create humor.

Literary Words

onomatopoeia
repetition

Practice
Workbook
Page 1

Work with a partner. Take turns reading the lines below aloud. Identify the examples of onomatopoeia and repetition. In your notebook, write a sentence using onomatopoeia. Then write a sentence using repetition.

> The frog jumped into the pond with a loud splash.
>
> "Please, please, please don't chase me anymore," cried the frightened rabbit.
>
> There was nothing to do but listen to the pitter-patter of the rain.
>
> The coyote raised his head and howled.
>
> After the game was over, the little girl cheered, "I won! I won! I won! I won!"

A coyote howling ▶

Learn Academic Words

Study the **red** words and their meanings. You will find these words useful when talking and writing about literature. Write each word and its meaning in your notebook. After you read "Grandmother Spider Brings the Sun," try to use these words to respond to the text.

Academic Words

author
culture
text
tradition

author = someone who writes a book, story, article, or play	➡	Geri Keams is the **author** who retold the story you are about to read.
culture = the art, literature, music, beliefs, and practices of a particular group of people	➡	Myths in the Cherokee **culture** include animal characters.
text = the words in a printed piece of writing	➡	Colorful illustrations go with the **text** of this story.
tradition = a belief, custom, or way of doing something that has existed for a long time	➡	Telling stories is a Cherokee **tradition**.

Practice  Workbook Page 2

Work with a partner to answer these questions. Try to include the **red** word in your answer. Write the sentences in your notebook.

1. Who is your favorite **author**?
2. Which celebrations are common in your home **culture**?
3. Do you prefer reading **text** with or without illustrations?
4. What **tradition** is important to you and your family?

▲ Three generations of Cherokee women weave baskets.

Word Study: Compound Words

A compound word is made up of more than one word. Some compound words are written as one word, as in *sunshine*. Some are written as two words, as in *peanut butter*. Some are written with hyphens between the words, as in *mother-in-law*.

Practice  **Workbook** Page 3

Work with a partner. Combine words from column A with words from column B to form compound words. Write the words in your notebook. Use a dictionary to find out whether the words are written as one word or two. None of these words is hyphenated.

A	B
1. any	brush
2. every	plane
3. high	mower
4. grand	school
5. some	cycle
6. tooth	one
7. air	father
8. motor	thing
9. lawn	body

▲ A Cherokee man and his granddaughter

READING STRATEGY   PREDICT

Predicting as you read helps you keep focused. It also helps you understand a text better. Before you read, predict, or guess, what the story will be about. You can also make new predictions as you're reading. To predict, follow these steps:

- Pause from time to time and think about what will happen next.
- Look for clues in the story and illustrations.
- Think about your own experiences and what you already know.
- If you discover your prediction was not correct, make a new one.

As you read "Grandmother Spider Brings the Sun," stop from time to time and check to see if your prediction was correct. Did you learn anything new that made you want to change your prediction?

 **Workbook** Page 4

Set a purpose for reading This myth is about light. What is a traditional Cherokee explanation for where light came from?

Grandmother Spider Brings the Sun

A Cherokee myth retold by Geri Keams

A long time ago it is said that half the world had the sun, but the other side of the world was very dark. It was so dark that all the animals were always bumping into each other and getting lost.

Wolf lived on this side of the world. He was tired of everybody bumping into him and asking him for directions, for you see, Wolf could see in the nighttime.

Wolf gathered all the animals together in a big cave. He got up in front of them and crossed his arms, and he said, "I am tired of everybody bumping into me and asking me for directions."

"I have an idea," he said. "I think we should go to the other side of the world and ask them for a piece of their sun. I think if we're nice, they'll give us a piece."

Another animal jumped up. This was Coyote, known as the trickster because he lies and cheats and steals.

Coyote said, "No, no, no, no, no! I don't think we should be so nice! If they're so nice, how come they haven't *offered* us a piece of their sun?"

The other animals nodded in agreement.

"I have a better idea," Coyote said. "I think we should sneak over there and just *steal* a piece."

"*Steal* a piece!" said Wolf. "What are you talking about, Coyote?"

"Calm down, calm down, calm down," Coyote said. "We're not going to steal a *big* piece. We'll only take a *little* piece. They'll never even miss it."

And that is what they decided to do.

Then all the animals began asking, "Who is going to go to the other side of the world? How will they get there?" Everybody had an idea, but none seemed quite right.

Then from the back of the room came a small voice. "Hey, I'll go! I'll go!"

Wolf said, "Who is that? Come down here. I can't see you."

Down to the front of the room came a little round animal with chubby cheeks. He was shy and quiet. He stood up in front of all the animals, and as he looked at all those hundreds of eyes looking back at him, he got kind of scared.

He looked out over the crowd of animals and he said in his timid voice, "Hi. M-m-m-my name is Possum. I think I can go to the other side of the world. You see, I've got these long, sharp claws, and I think I can dig a tunnel. And when I go *all* the way to the other side of the world, I'll take a piece of the sun and I'll hide it in my big, bushy tail."

And Wolf said, "Oh, a tunnel! That's the best idea yet!"

BEFORE YOU GO ON

1. What method do the animals decide upon to get part of the sun?

2. What makes Possum qualified for the task?

On Your Own
Do you think Coyote's idea is better than Wolf's? Why or why not?

9

So Possum went to the big wall of dirt at the back of the cave, stuck in his sharp claws, and began to dig and dig and dig and dig, faster and faster and faster and faster. Possum disappeared inside the tunnel, and soon he had gone all the way to the other side of the world.

Now, Possum had never seen the sun, so when he popped out on the other side, the light hit his eyes, and he was blinded. His eyes got all squinty and he rubbed them with his dirty fists, saying, "Hey! I can't see!" Well, you know, Possum's eyes have been squinty and ringed with dirt ever since.

Possum struggled over to the sun, took a little piece, and put it inside his big ol' bushy tail. Then he turned around and came running back down the tunnel.

Possum ran faster and faster and faster and faster. Something started to get hot inside his tail, but Possum kept running, faster and faster.

That something got hotter, and Possum kept running faster, and he soon ran into the room where all the animals were waiting. They all saw smoke coming out of his tail, and they screamed, "Possum! Your tail! Your tail!" and threw water on him. *Whoosh! Whoosh! Whoosh!* The light was gone.

When the smoke had cleared, Wolf looked up and said, "Oh, no, Possum! Look at your tail! It's all skinny!"

And you know, Possum's tail has been this way ever since.

Wolf said, "We still don't have any sun. What are we going to do now?"

A loud voice from the back of the room said, "Send me! I'll go!"

Down to the front stormed a large bird with long black feathers all over his body, and a crown of feathers on top of his head. He held his head high and stuck his chest out as he marched importantly past the other animals. You see, this bird was a show-off. He thought he was the most beautiful bird alive.

He stood up in front of all the animal people and he said, "It's me, Big Bad Buzzard. I'll go to the other side of the world and it won't take me long at all, but I wouldn't be so dumb as to hide the light in my tail. I'm gonna hide it in my beautiful crown of feathers."

Buzzard jumped into the tunnel and soared through the darkness, and it didn't take long at all until he came out on the other side.

Buzzard took a little piece of sun, put it inside his crown of feathers, turned around, and soared back down the tunnel faster and faster and faster and faster. As he came down the tunnel, something started to get hot on top of his head.

Buzzard soared faster and faster, and something got hotter and hotter.

Faster he soared, and soon he came into the room where all the animals were waiting. They looked up, and they saw smoke coming from Buzzard's head. "Oh, no! Buzzard! Your head! Your head!" They got water and *Whoosh! Whoosh! Whoosh!* The light went out.

Wolf looked up and said, "Buzzard! You're bald!"

✔ **LITERARY CHECK**
*What effect does the **repetition** of the word* faster *have here?*

10

All of Buzzard's feathers crackled and fell down to the ground. Big Bad Buzzard got so shy and quiet that he ran and hid in the back of the room. And you know, Buzzard has been bald ever since, and he still doesn't like anybody looking at him.

Wolf said, "Possum's burned his tail off and now Buzzard's bald, and we still don't have any sun. What are we going to do now?"

A tiny voice from up above said, "Send me, I'll go! Hey, send me, I'll go! I'll go!"

Wolf looked all around, but he couldn't tell where the voice was coming from. "Who is that? Where are you? Come down where I can see you."

Down from the corner of the ceiling squeaked the tiny voice: "Send me e e e e e e e!"

And right there in front of Wolf landed a tiny spider. The spider looked up and Wolf looked down, and Wolf said, "Oh, no! Not you, Grandma! You can't go to the other side of the world. You're too old—and besides that, you're too slow!"

Well, this was Grandmother Spider. She had done many things to help the animals in her long life. She crossed her little arms and said, "I know I'm old. You don't have to tell me I'm old. But I want to help my people one more time. I need a piece of clay about so big, and you'll get me a piece, won't you, son?"

Wolf went and got Grandmother Spider a piece of clay, and she sat in the middle of the room and began to chant. Soon she had worked the clay into a little bowl.

---

chant, sing words on one tone

✔ **LITERARY CHECK**
*Which word in the first sentence is an example of **onomatopoeia**?*

BEFORE YOU GO ON

1. Did you predict the first two animals would fail? Explain.

2. Why does Grandmother Spider "cross her little arms"?

On Your Own
How do you think Grandmother Spider will use the bowl? What does this say about her?

11

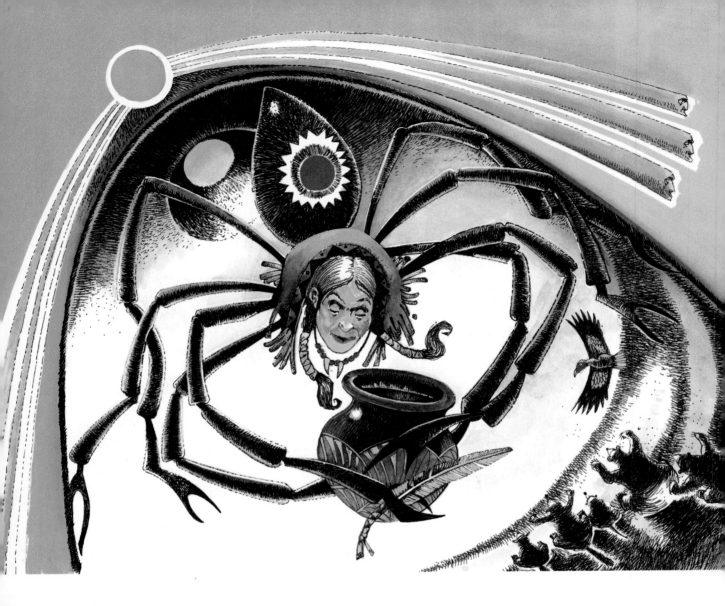

She picked up that beautiful clay bowl and disappeared inside the tunnel. They say it took Grandma Spider a long, long, long, long time to get to the other side of the world.

The Sun Guards were out now. They knew somebody was trying to steal some of their sun, and they stood in a tight circle around it. They weren't going to let anybody through.

The Sun Guards were mean-looking monsters. They had fire coming out of their heads. They had fire coming out of their mouths: *Hissssss!* And they held their weapons, ready for a fight.

But Grandmother Spider was so tiny that they didn't even see her. She sneaked between them, went up to the sun, took a little piece, put it in her clay bowl, and sneaked back past the Sun Guards.

✔ **LITERARY CHECK**

*How does the author use **repetition** to stress Grandmother Spider's slowness in this sentence?*

12

She came back down the tunnel *very* slowly. It took her a long, long, long, long time to get to her side of the world. And as she got closer, something happened. The light inside her bowl began to grow. The little rays stretched out of the bowl.

As she came out of the tunnel into the cave, that ball of light was growing. She could hardly even carry it.

All the animals came running to help Grandmother Spider: blind Possum and bald Buzzard, Wolf and Coyote and Bear and Deer and all the others. But that ball of light just kept getting bigger and bigger and bigger and bigger, and it got so big that the animals had to squeeze it out of the cave, and as it squeezed out into the world it bounced up into the sky: *Boingggg!*

It is said that from that day on, whenever Grandmother Spider would spin her web, the shape of the sun would be at the center. And you see, Grandmother Spider spins her web that way to this very day.

ABOUT THE **AUTHOR**

Geri Keams is an author, storyteller, and actress. Born and raised in the Navajo Nation in Arizona, Keams grew up herding sheep and weaving rugs with her grandmother. Also a storyteller, Keams's grandmother taught her grandchildren the importance of preserving and sharing the stories of Native American peoples. Keams tells Native American stories in order to encourage others to explore these cultures and to help keep them alive.

✔ **LITERARY CHECK**
*Which word in this paragraph is an example of **onomatopoeia**?*

BEFORE YOU GO ON

1. Why doesn't Grandmother Spider fear the Sun Guards?
2. What explanation does this myth give for the shape of a spider web?

On Your Own
What does this myth suggest about the importance of age and size?

Review and Practice

READER'S THEATER

Act out the following scene in small groups.

Buzzard: What a bad, bad day I had! I took a piece of sun and zoomed back down the tunnel. I felt so good. But then I felt something hot on top of my head. Suddenly I heard, "Buzzard! Your head! Your head!" Then *Whoosh! Whoosh! Whoosh!* The fire went out, and I was soaking wet. Now, as you can see, I'm bald. My beautiful feathers are gone! Please don't look at me.

Possum: You call that bad? As soon as the light hit my eyes, I was blinded. But even though I could hardly see, I took a piece of sun and ran back down the tunnel. I felt something getting hot inside my tail, but I kept running, faster and faster. Then I heard, "Possum! Your tail! Your tail!" And someone threw water on me. *Whoosh! Whoosh! Whoosh!* When the fire went out, my tail was all skinny. My big bushy tail is naked. And my eyes are all squinty!

Wolf: At least we have sunlight now, and we can all see where we're going!

Possum: You mean everyone *except me* can see.

Wolf: Well, yes, I guess you're right, Possum.

COMPREHENSION

Workbook Page 5

Right There

1. Why is Wolf tired of the darkness? What does he propose the animals do?

2. What does Coyote say is wrong with Wolf's idea?

Think and Search

3. How does Buzzard's character change in the story?

4. According to Cherokee myth, why do certain animals look the way they do?

5. Which character does the author wish you to respect the most? Explain your answer.

6. What does the author do to make the story sound as though it is being told by a storyteller?

On Your Own

7. To this day, when the Cherokee people make clay bowls, it reminds them of Grandmother Spider's journey. What items in your culture remind you of a story in your culture's history?

8. What other myths do you know that explain how some part of the natural world came to be?

DISCUSSION

Discuss in pairs or small groups.

- Why do you think the tradition of oral storytelling still survives?

- **What is light?** Having sunlight will change how the animals live. It will bring them warmth and the ability to see things more clearly. In what ways does the light in this story represent more than just physical comfort and convenience? How is light important to you in your life?

RESPONSE TO LITERATURE

Write a paragraph that explains in a creative way why a certain animal looks or behaves the way it does. For example, you might tell how the giraffe got its long neck or how the elephant got its trunk. When you have finished, read your paragraph aloud to the class.

▲ A Native American woman

Grammar and Writing

Order of Adjectives

We often use more than one adjective to describe a noun. The adjectives must be placed in a certain order according to type. The chart below shows the different types of adjectives and their correct order.

Adjectives					Noun
Opinion	Size	Age	Color	Material	
beautiful		new		clay	bowl
	big		brown		bear
favorite		old		wool	scarf
	long		black		feathers

Right: Grandmother Spider made a **beautiful new clay** bowl.
Wrong: Grandmother Spider made a clay beautiful new bowl.

Right: In the cave was a **big brown** bear.
Wrong: In the cave was a brown big bear.

Right: She always wore her **favorite old wool** scarf.
Wrong: She always wore her old wool favorite scarf.

Right: Buzzard was proud of his **long black** feathers.
Wrong: Buzzard was proud of his black long feathers.

Practice  Workbook Page 6

Work with a partner. Use each group of words to write sentences with more than one adjective. Use the chart above to help you place the adjectives in the correct order. Write the sentences in your notebook.

1. old / long / yellow **raincoat**
2. rubber / black / ugly **boots**
3. new / green / tiny **leaves**
4. huge / brick / red **building**
5. clear / plastic / large **bottle**

▲ A Native American clay bowl

16

WRITING A DESCRIPTIVE PARAGRAPH

Describe a Character

At the end of this unit, you will write a descriptive essay. To do this, you'll need to learn some of the skills authors use in descriptive writing. To describe a character, you give details about the character's physical traits, or how the character looks. For example: *Buzzard has long black feathers all over his body.* You also give details about the character's traits, or how the character thinks and acts. For example: *Buzzard thinks he is the most beautiful bird alive.*

Physical traits	Character traits

Here is a model of a paragraph that describes Possum, a character from the story you just read. The writer has described Possum's physical traits and character traits. Before writing, the writer listed his ideas in a T-chart.

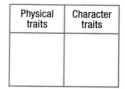

Evan Arbogast

Possum

Possum is a character in "Grandmother Spider Brings the Sun." He is a little round animal with cute chubby cheeks. Though shy and quiet, Possum bravely volunteers to go to the other side of the world to steal a piece of the sun. He plans to use his sharp claws to dig a tunnel and his bushy tail as a hiding place for the piece of sun. He speeds through the long dark tunnel, but as soon as he pops out, the bright light blinds him. But does that stop him? No. Possum manages to get a bit of the sun, but his tail catches fire. His friends put out the fire, and they end up with no sun. But Possum's valiant efforts do pay off because Grandmother Spider is able to use the tunnel he dug to retrieve a piece of the sun.

Practice **Workbook Page 7**

Write a paragraph describing a character you know from a story, a movie, or a TV show. Give details that describe the character's physical traits and character traits. Before you write, list your ideas in a T-chart like the one above. When you use more than one adjective to describe a noun, make sure that the adjectives are in the correct order.

Writing Checklist

IDEAS:
- ☑ I described the character's physical traits and character traits.

CONVENTIONS:
- ☑ My adjectives are in the correct order.

What You Will Learn

Reading

- Vocabulary building: *Context, dictionary skills, word study*
- Reading strategy: *Skim*
- Text type: *Informational text (science)*

Grammar, Usage, and Mechanics
Adverb clauses of time

Writing
Describe an object

THE BIG QUESTION

What is light? What do you know about light? Where does it come from? How do you use it every day? What are some of the main sources of light?

In your notebook, make a K-W-L-H chart like the one below. Work in small groups. Complete the first column with information you know about light. Use the questions above as a guide. Then complete the second column with what you want to know about light. When you've finished reading the text, you can complete the third column with the new information you've learned. Complete the fourth column by telling how you learned the new information.

K What do I **know**?	W What do I **want** to know?	L What did I **learn**?	H **How** did I learn it?

BUILD BACKGROUND

"Light" is a science article that tells what light is and how it behaves. Have you ever seen waves moving across the ocean? Different kinds of energy can move through air, water, and even solid materials in the form of waves. In this article you will read about electromagnetic waves. These are the waves that make up light. The article explains how light waves travel and what happens when light waves reflect off objects. It also explains how mirrors work.

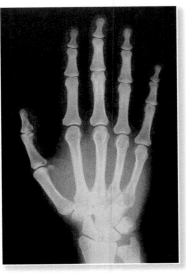

▲ X rays are one kind of electromagnetic wave.

Learn Key Words

Read these sentences. Use the context to figure out the meaning of the **red** words. Use a dictionary to check your answers. Then write each word and its meaning in your notebook.

1. A **concave** mirror curves inward and makes an image seem larger.

2. The side mirrors on a car are **convex**. They curve outward and make other cars reflected in them seem closer and smaller than they really are.

3. We cannot see through walls because they are **opaque**.

4. A **translucent** object, such as a sheet of notebook paper, allows some light to pass through it.

5. It is possible to see through a window because the glass is **transparent**.

6. Because radio waves are longer than X rays, we say they have a longer **wavelength**.

Practice  **Workbook** Page 8

Key Words
concave
convex
opaque
translucent
transparent
wavelength

Write the sentences in your notebook. Choose a **red** word from the box above to complete each sentence. Then take turns reading the sentences aloud with a partner.

1. A _____ mirror curves outward and makes objects appear smaller.

2. Because a leaf is _____, we can see light coming through it.

3. X rays have a shorter _____ than radio waves.

4. A _____ mirror makes the reflected image appear larger than it is.

5. A brick wall is _____, so light does not pass through it.

6. Clear plastic is an example of a _____ material.

This plastic bag is transparent. ▶

19

Learn Academic Words

Study the **red** words and their meanings. You will find these words useful when talking and writing about informational texts. Write each word and its meaning in your notebook. After you read "Light," try to use these words to respond to the text.

energy = usable power	⮕	Light and heat are forms of **energy**.
interpret = explain or decide what something means	⮕	Your brain will **interpret** different wavelengths of light as different colors.
transmit = pass something through	⮕	You can **transmit** light through glass.
virtual = able to be seen but not real	⮕	What you see in a mirror is a **virtual** image.
visible = able to be seen	⮕	Light waves are the only electromagnetic waves that are **visible**.

Practice  **Workbook** Page 9

Work with a partner to rewrite the sentences. Use the **red** word in each new sentence. Then write the sentences in your notebook.

1. When you see yourself in the mirror, you are looking at this kind of image. (**virtual**)
2. Sunlight gives us light and heat. (**energy**)
3. Light waves can be seen. (**visible**)
4. The brain will see the longest wavelengths of visible light as the color red. (**interpret**)
5. You can pass light through water. (**transmit**)

▲ The still water acts as a mirror.

Word Study: Words with /əl/ spelled -le and -el

Many words end with the /əl/ sound that you hear at the end of the word *pickle*. This sound is often spelled *le* or *el*. Here are some examples.

-le	-el
visible	angel
brittle	camel
little	bagel
fickle	vessel
ample	gravel
nimble	scalpel

Practice

Workbook Page 10

Work with a partner. Copy the chart above into your notebook. Say a word from the chart, and ask your partner to spell it aloud. Then have your partner say the next word. Continue until you can spell all of the words correctly. Then use a dictionary to look up the meaning of each word. Add to the chart any new *-le* or *-el* words you find in the reading.

READING STRATEGY SKIM

Skimming a text helps you get a general understanding of what the text is about. To skim a text, follow these steps:

- Look at the title and any visuals. What do they tell you?
- Read the first paragraph quickly. Then read the first sentence of the paragraphs that follow.
- Now read all the paragraphs quickly. Don't stop at words you don't know—skip over them.
- After you skim the text, try to summarize what you learned before you go back and read it again more carefully.

As you read "Light," skim the text quickly to see what it's about. Think about the subject and what you already know about it. What more do you think you will learn?

Workbook Page 11

Set a purpose for reading What is light and how does it behave?

Light

How Does Light Travel?

Light travels from the sun to Earth in waves. These waves, called electromagnetic waves, are a form of energy that can travel through space. We talk about electromagnetic waves in terms of the length of the wave, or wavelength.

The electromagnetic spectrum is the name for the whole range of electromagnetic waves. It is organized by wavelength, from the longest electromagnetic waves to the shortest. The longest waves in the spectrum are radio waves. Then come microwaves, infrared rays, visible light, ultraviolet rays, X rays, and gamma rays. (See Figure 1.)

▲ Colors in a soap bubble

---

electromagnetic waves, waves that form when an electric field couples with a magnetic field; the waves that make up light

When white light passes through a prism, it separates into colors. ▼

Visible light is the only part of the electromagnetic spectrum that people can see. Visible light is just a small part of the electromagnetic spectrum. It is located between infrared rays and ultraviolet rays. Visible light is a mixture of all the colors we can see in a rainbow: red, orange, yellow, green, blue, and violet. When our eyes take in different wavelengths of light, we see different colors. We see the longest wavelengths of visible light as red. We see the shortest wavelengths as violet.

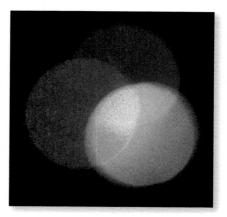

▲ Colors in visible light

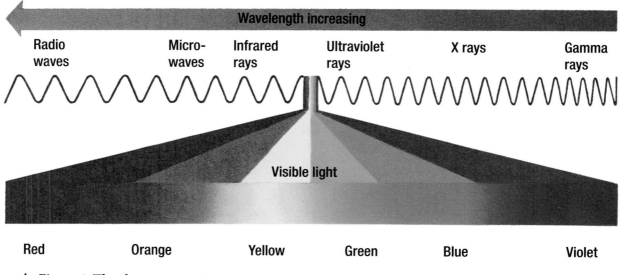

▲ Figure 1. The electromagnetic spectrum

What Happens When Light Strikes Objects?

When light strikes an object, the light can be reflected, or bounced off the object. The light might also be absorbed, or taken in by the object. Or the light can be transmitted, or passed through the object.

Objects that you cannot see through, such as wood and metal, are called opaque. When light strikes an opaque object, the light is either reflected or absorbed. You cannot see through an opaque object because light cannot pass through it. A glass object is transparent. When light strikes it, the light is allowed to pass through. As a result, you can see through the glass object.

BEFORE YOU GO ON

1 Which electromagnetic waves have the longest wavelength? The shortest wavelength?

2 What happens when light strikes an opaque object?

On Your Own
What are some transparent objects you use every day?

23

▲ Spools of thread

▲ A glass and bottle containing milk

▲ A frog behind a leaf

Other objects are translucent. When light strikes them, only some light passes through. When you look through a translucent object, you can see something behind it, but you cannot see the details clearly. Look at the pictures above. Which objects are opaque? Which are transparent? Which is translucent?

What Is Reflection?

All objects reflect some light. This means that light bounces off the objects. However, different objects reflect light in different ways.

Some objects allow you to see a reflection—or image—of something. For example, when you look at a mirror or a pool of water, you can see a reflection of yourself.

Other objects do not do this. For example, when you look at a wool sweater or a painted wall, you see only the object itself. What you see when you look at an object depends on how its surface reflects light.

To show how light travels and reflects, we can use straight lines to represent light rays. When parallel rays of light hit a smooth, or even, surface, all the rays are reflected at the same angle. This is called regular reflection. For example, when you look at a mirror, you see your own reflection. The light rays from your body hit the smooth surface of the mirror and are reflected regularly. (See Figure 2.)

▲ Your image in a mirror is caused by rays of light that reflect regularly from the mirror.

---

parallel, two lines that stay the same distance apart and never touch

When parallel rays of light hit a bumpy, or uneven, surface, each ray is reflected at a different angle. This is called diffuse reflection. Most objects reflect light diffusely because their surfaces are not completely smooth. For example, a wall may look smooth. But if you look carefully, you will see that its surface has many small bumps. These bumps cause the light to scatter, or to be reflected at different angles. (See Figure 3.)

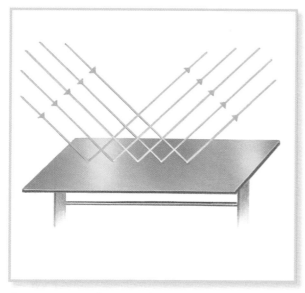

▲ Figure 2. When parallel rays of light strike a smooth surface, the reflection is regular.

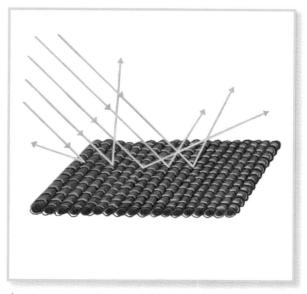

▲ Figure 3. When parallel rays of light strike an uneven surface, the reflection is diffuse.

How Do Mirrors Work?

A mirror is a sheet of glass that has a smooth, silver-colored coating on one side. Glass is transparent, so light passes through it. However, the silver coating behind the glass is opaque. When light rays pass through the glass, they hit the smooth surface of the silver coating and all the rays are reflected regularly. The result is that you see an image in the mirror. An image is a copy of an object and is formed by reflected rays of light.

Mirrors can have a flat or curved shape. The shape of a mirror determines how the image will look. An image in a mirror can be the same size as the object, or it can be larger or smaller—depending on the mirror's shape.

BEFORE YOU GO ON

1 What happens when light strikes the surface of a translucent object?

2 Which occurs more often—diffuse reflection or regular reflection? Why?

On Your Own
Have you ever seen your reflection in things other than mirrors? Explain.

A plane mirror has a flat surface. When you look into a plane mirror, you see an image that is the same size as you are. Your image appears to be the same distance behind the mirror as you are in front of it. The image you see in a plane mirror is called a virtual image. Virtual images are right side up, or upright. *Virtual* means something you can see but does not really exist. You can't reach behind a mirror and touch your image.

Figure 4 shows how a plane mirror forms a virtual image of a dancer. Light rays reflected from the dancer strike the mirror. (The green and orange arrows show light rays from the top and bottom of the dancer.) The mirror reflects the rays toward the dancer's eyes. The brain assumes that the reflected rays have reached the eyes in a straight line.

The rays are reflected, but the brain interprets the rays as if they had come from behind the mirror. The dashed lines show the points from which the rays appear to come. Since the dashed lines appear to come from behind the mirror, this is where the dancer's image appears to be located.

---

assumes, thinks that something is true; imagines

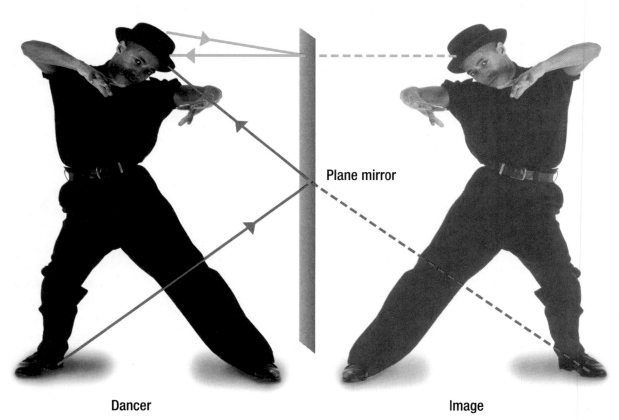

Plane mirror

Dancer   Image

▲ Figure 4. A plane mirror forms a virtual image.

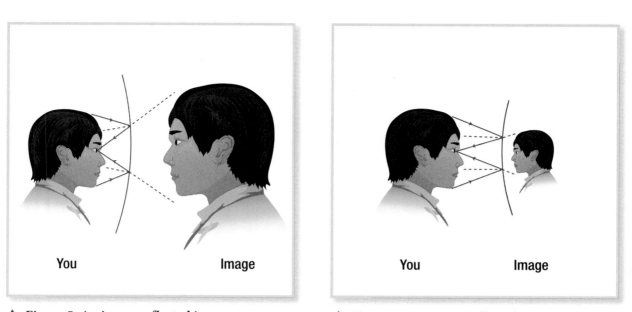

▲ Figure 5. An image reflected in a
concave mirror

▲ Figure 6. An image reflected in a
convex mirror

Curved mirrors behave as though they were many, many little flat mirrors placed side by side, each at a slight angle to the one next to it. Unlike plane mirrors, curved mirrors create reflected images that are not the same size as the object being reflected. The images also appear farther away from or closer to the mirror than the object really is.

A concave mirror has a surface that curves inward. When you look into a concave mirror, the image you see of yourself appears larger than you really are. It also appears farther away from the mirror than you are actually standing. (See Figure 5.)

A convex mirror has a surface that curves outward. When you look into a convex mirror, the image you see is smaller than you are. And it appears closer to the mirror than you really are. (See Figure 6.)

Concave and convex mirrors are both useful in their own ways. Because concave mirrors enlarge the image, people use them when they are putting on makeup or shaving. Concave mirrors are also used as reflectors in flashlights and headlights. Convex mirrors let you see a large distance and a wide field of view, so they are used as rearview mirrors in cars and buses. They are also used as security mirrors in stores.

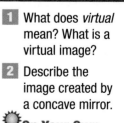

BEFORE YOU GO ON

1 What does *virtual* mean? What is a virtual image?

2 Describe the image created by a concave mirror.

On Your Own
What kind of objects create the darkest shadows? Why?

27

Review and Practice

COMPREHENSION

Workbook
Page 12

Right There

1. What are six different kinds of electromagnetic waves?
2. Which color of visible light has the shortest wavelength?

Think and Search

3. Why are convex mirrors used as security mirrors in stores?
4. Why are concave mirrors used as shaving and makeup mirrors?

Author and You

5. Do you think the author of this article would agree with this statement: "The image you see in a mirror exists only in your brain"? Why or why not?
6. If light did not reflect off objects, would we be able to see anything? Why or why not?

On Your Own

7. How would life be different if there were no mirrors? Explain.
8. As you go about your day, notice ways in which we use transparent materials. Keep a list and share it with a partner.

IN YOUR OWN WORDS

Imagine you are teaching someone about light and how it behaves. Tell this person five important facts that you learned by reading "Light." Write your ideas in your notebook and read them aloud to a partner. Then listen to your partner's ideas.

DISCUSSION

Discuss in pairs or small groups.

- What kinds of electromagnetic waves do you use every day?
- **What is light?** This article explains more about how light behaves (for example, what happens when it strikes an object) than what light is. Why do you think this is so?

> **Listening TIP**
>
> Look at each speaker as he or she speaks.

It is often easier to read a text if you understand the difficult words and phrases. Work with a partner. Choose a paragraph from the reading. Identify the words and phrases you do not know or have trouble pronouncing. Look up the difficult words in a dictionary.

Take turns pronouncing the words and phrases with your partner. If necessary, ask your teacher to model the correct pronunciation. Then take turns reading the paragraph aloud. Give each other feedback on your reading.

EXTENSION

Workbook
Page 12

The painting *Portrait of Giovanni Arnolfini and His Wife* uses a mirror in an interesting way. Look at the detail of the painting below. You can see the bride and groom's backs, and two other people, reflected in the mirror. Look again at the mirror. Would you say it is flat, concave, or convex? Why?

▲ *Portrait of Giovanni Arnolfini and His Wife*, Jan van Eyck, 1434

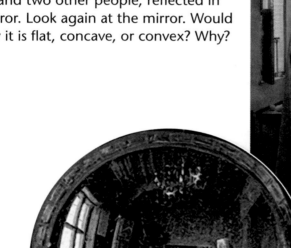

▲ A detail of the mirror in the painting

Grammar and Writing

GRAMMAR, USAGE, AND MECHANICS

Adverb Clauses of Time

Adverb clauses of time express *when*. An adverb clause of time begins with a time expression, such as, *after, before, when, until, while, since,* and *whenever*. When an adverb clause begins the sentence, use a comma. When an adverb clause finishes the sentence, there is no need for a comma.

Adverb clause at beginning	Adverb clause at the end
When light strikes an object, the light bounces off.	The light bounces off **when light strikes an object.**
When you look in the mirror, you see your reflection.	You see your reflection **when you look in the mirror.**

Other frequently used time expressions appear in the chart below.

Time Expressions	Example Sentences
after	She brushed her hair **after she saw her reflection**.
before	**Before they turned on the lights,** they couldn't see anything.
since	I haven't seen him **since he left this morning**.
until	We stayed there **until the next day**.
whenever	**Whenever I leave home,** I turn off the lights.
while	**While I was looking out the window,** I heard the doorbell ring.

Practice
Workbook
Page 13

Create a sentence using each of these time expressions: *after, before, since, until, when, whenever,* and *while*. Share these sentences with a partner.

WRITING A DESCRIPTIVE PARAGRAPH

Describe an Object

You have described a character. Now you will describe an object. Writers describe by using words that tell how things look, sound, feel, smell, or taste. These words are called sensory details.

Sensory details	
Sight	
Hearing	
Touch	
Smell	
Taste	

To describe a mirror, you might use the words *flat*, *smooth*, and *shiny*. The words *flat* and *smooth* appeal to the sense of touch. The word *shiny* appeals to the sense of sight.

The paragraph below describes a kaleidoscope. The writer included sensory details in his description. Before writing, he listed his ideas in a sensory-details chart like the one above.

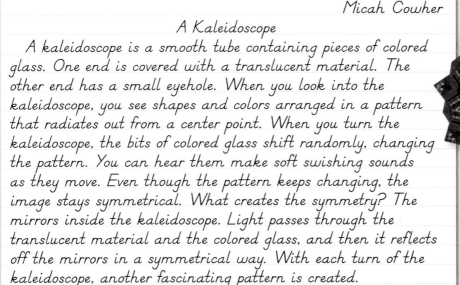

Micah Cowher

A Kaleidoscope

A kaleidoscope is a smooth tube containing pieces of colored glass. One end is covered with a translucent material. The other end has a small eyehole. When you look into the kaleidoscope, you see shapes and colors arranged in a pattern that radiates out from a center point. When you turn the kaleidoscope, the bits of colored glass shift randomly, changing the pattern. You can hear them make soft swishing sounds as they move. Even though the pattern keeps changing, the image stays symmetrical. What creates the symmetry? The mirrors inside the kaleidoscope. Light passes through the translucent material and the colored glass, and then it reflects off the mirrors in a symmetrical way. With each turn of the kaleidoscope, another fascinating pattern is created.

Practice

Workbook Page 14

Write a paragraph describing an object. Choose an object that you can describe by appealing to at least two senses. You can choose a man-made object, such as a quilt or a work of art. Or you can choose a natural object, such as a tree or a flower. List your ideas in a sensory-details chart like the one above. Be sure to use adverb clauses of time correctly.

Writing Checklist

WORD CHOICE:
☑ I used details that appeal to the reader's senses.

SENTENCE FLUENCY:
☑ I used adverb clauses correctly.

What You Will Learn

Reading
- Vocabulary building: *Literary terms, word study*
- Reading strategy: *Visualize*
- Text type: *Literature (short story)*

Grammar, Usage, and Mechanics
Prepositions of place

Writing
Describe a place

THE BIG QUESTION

What is light? How are we affected by light? Is light more than just a source of energy that allows us to see? Explain.

BUILD BACKGROUND

The next reading is a short story called **"A Game of Light and Shade."** It is about a curious man who finds out that things are not always as they appear.

▼ **Piazza del Campo in Siena, Italy**

Learn Literary Words

Imagery is descriptive language that appeals to the senses. Writers create imagery by using sensory details, helping the reader see, hear, touch, smell, or taste what is being described. Here is part of a poem called "Velvet Shoes" by Elinor Wylie. Which of your senses does the language appeal to?

Literary Words

imagery
setting

> Let us walk in the white snow
>   In a soundless space;
> With footsteps quiet and slow,
>   At a tranquil pace,
>   Under veils of white lace.

The words *white snow* and *veils of white lace* appeal to your senses of sight and touch. The words *soundless space* and *footsteps quiet and slow* appeal to your sense of hearing. The poet's use of imagery helps us feel the peacefulness, hear the quietness, and see the beauty of the scene.

The **setting** is the time and place of the action in a literary work. The time might be the year, the season, the day, or the hour. The place might be a city, a forest, a garden, or a kitchen. In "A Game of Light and Shade," the setting is a tower in Siena, Italy, on a sunny winter day.

Practice  Workbook Page 15

Work with a partner to describe your classroom. What do you see as you look around? What sounds do you hear? Does it smell like chalk or sharpened pencils? List sensory details in your notebook. Then use the details to write your description. Share your work with the class.

▲ A snowy scene

33

Learn Academic Words

Study the **red** words and their meanings. You will find these words useful when talking and writing about literature. Write each word and its meaning in your notebook. After you read "A Game of Light and Shade," try to use these words to respond to the text.

approached = moved closer to	➡	I **approached** the scared cat carefully, so it wouldn't run away.
despite = in spite of; regardless of	➡	It is possible to enjoy the sunshine **despite** the cold weather.
equivalent = something that has the same value or importance	➡	How many euros is the **equivalent** of five American dollars?
visual = relating to seeing or sight	➡	Enjoying a beautiful view is an example of a **visual** experience.

Practice  Workbook Page 16

Work with a partner to rewrite the sentences. Use the **red** word in each new sentence. Write the sentences in your notebook.

1. I went over to the police officer to ask him a question. (**approached**)
2. I enjoyed the party in spite of the fact that I knew only one person there. (**despite**)
3. Ten Euros does not have the same value as ten dollars. (**equivalent**)
4. Looking at photos is an activity relating to sight. (**visual**)

▲ A banknote for ten euros. The euro is the unit of money used in the European Union.

34

Word Study: Antonyms

Antonyms are words that have opposite or nearly opposite meanings. Word pairs such as *up/down*, *sunny/shady*, and *light/dark* are examples of antonyms. As you read, you can use antonyms as context clues to help you figure out the meaning of unfamiliar words.

> I was fully expecting my day to be **dull**; instead, to my delight, it turned out to be **fascinating**.

Suppose you knew the word *dull* but not *fascinating*. The word *instead* tells you that what follows is in opposition, so *fascinating* means nearly the opposite of *dull*. Other words that signal opposition include *but*, *yet*, *however*, *in contrast*, and *on the other hand*.

Practice Workbook Page 17

Work with a partner. Write the words *inside*, *empty*, *heavy*, *narrow*, and *strong* in your notebook. Write an antonym for each word. Use a dictionary if necessary. Then write a sentence for each pair of antonyms. Include a signal word or phrase in each sentence.

READING STRATEGY | VISUALIZE

Visualizing helps you understand what the author wants you to see. When you visualize, you make pictures in your mind of what you are reading. To visualize, follow these steps:

- Pay special attention to descriptive words and figurative language.
- Stop from time to time to picture in your mind the characters, places, and events described in the text.
- Think about how the author helped you create mental pictures.

As you read "A Game of Light and Shade," notice the words the author uses to describe the characters, setting, and events. How does visualizing help you understand the story?

Workbook Page 18

Set a purpose for reading Most of the time we perceive light by using our sense of sight. Can we perceive light using other senses?

A Game of Light and Shade

Arturo Vivante

It was a sunny winter day. I had gone up and down the tower, and felt pleased with myself for having taken this initiative, when, outside the little door at the foot, a blind man came toward me. He was a pale, thin man, with sparse black hair and dark glasses that gave him an impenetrable look. He kept close to the inner wall of the courtyard, grazing it with his arm. On reaching the door, he touched the jamb and sharply turned inside. In a moment, he disappeared up the staircase. I stood still, looking at the empty space left by the open door, and at the little plaque that said "To the Tower" nailed to the wall. I felt compelled to follow.

I didn't follow closely. I caught up with him in the ticket office. There I was surprised to see the attendant selling him a ticket as though he were any other visitor. The man fumbled for it, sweeping a little space of desk with his hand until he had it, but the attendant didn't seem to take any notice. Then, with the ticket in one hand and touching the wall with the fingers of the other, he reached the staircase leading to the terrace.

I stood by the desk, watching him until he was out of earshot. "That man is blind," I said to the attendant, and expected him to show some concern, but he just looked at me with his sleepy eyes. He was a heavy man who seemed all one piece with his chair and desk. "He's blind," I repeated.

He looked at me vacantly.

"What would a blind man want to climb up the tower for?" I asked.

He didn't answer.

"Not the view certainly," I said. "Perhaps he wants to jump."

His mouth opened a little. Should he do something? The weight of things was against him. He didn't stir. "Well, let's hope not," he said, and looked down at the crossword puzzle he had begun.

The blind man was now out of sight. I turned toward the staircase.

"The ticket," the attendant said, rising from his chair. It seemed the only thing that could move him.

I handed him a fifty-lira piece, and he detached a ticket from his book. Then I hurried up the staircase.

The man hadn't gone as far as I imagined. Much less time had passed than I thought. A third of the way up the tower, I heard his step. I slowed down and followed him at a little distance. He went up slowly, and stopped from time to time. When he got to the terrace, I was a dozen steps behind. But as I reached it, he wasn't to be seen. I dashed to the first corner of the bell tower, around the next, and saw him.

---

impenetrable, difficult to understand
compelled, forced
fumbled, felt around for something in an awkward way
lira, the form of money used in Italy before the euro

✔ LITERARY CHECK
How does the author establish the setting in the first two sentences?

✔ LITERARY CHECK
What imagery in this paragraph helps you visualize the attendant?

BEFORE YOU GO ON

1 Why does the narrator follow the blind man?

2 What is the narrator afraid that the blind man will do?

On Your Own
Would you like to climb up a tower like the one in this story? Why or why not?

At last, after ten minutes, I approached him. "Excuse me," I said with the greatest courtesy I could summon, "but I am very curious to know why you came up."

"You'd never guess," he said.

"Not the view, I take it, or the fresh air on this winter day."

"No," he said, and he assumed the amused expression of one who poses a puzzle.

"Tell me," I said.

He smiled. "Perhaps, coming up the stairs, you will have noticed—and yet, not being blind, perhaps you won't—how not just light but sun pours into the tower through the narrow, slitlike windows here and there, so that one can feel the change—the cool staircase suddenly becomes quite warm, even in winter—and how up here behind the merlons there is shade, but as soon as one goes opposite a crenel one finds the sun. In all of Siena there is no place so good as this for feeling the contrast between light and shade. It isn't the first time that I've come up."

He stepped into the shade. "I am in the shade," he said. "There is a merlon there." He moved into the sunlight. "Now I am opposite a crenel," he said. We went down the bell tower. "An arch is there," he said.

"You never miss. And the sun isn't even very strong," I said.

"Strong enough," he said, and added, "Now I'm behind a bell."

Coming back down onto the terrace, he went around it. "Light, shade, light, shade," he said, and seemed as pleased as a child who, in a game of hopscotch, jumps from square to square.

We went down the tower together. "A window there," he said, up near the top. "Another window," he said, when we were halfway down.

I left him, gladdened as one can only be by the sunlight.

✔ **LITERARY CHECK**
*In what way is the **setting** critical to this story?*

---

merlons, solid parts of a fortress wall
crenel, cut-out part of a fortress wall

ABOUT THE **AUTHOR**

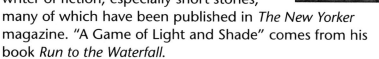

Arturo Vivante was born in Italy in 1923. He earned his medical degree and practiced medicine in Rome for a number of years before he moved to the United States. For over fifty years Vivante has been a full-time writer of fiction, especially short stories, many of which have been published in *The New Yorker* magazine. "A Game of Light and Shade" comes from his book *Run to the Waterfall*.

BEFORE YOU GO ON

1 Why does the blind man think that the narrator may not have noticed the changes in temperature?

2 Do you think the narrator respects the blind man? Why or why not?

On Your Own
Do you associate light more often with happiness or sadness? Give examples.

Review and Practice

READER'S THEATER

Speaking TIP

Use facial expressions and gestures to show the character's feelings and actions.

Act out this scene between the attendant and the blind man.

Attendant: [*looks up from crossword*] Say, do you know a six-letter word for an opening between two merlons?

Blind man: I do! That word is *crenel, c-r-e-n-e-l.* There are some on top of this very tower, if you'd like to see them.

Attendant: Uh, no, thanks. I'll take your word for it.

Blind man: Do go up on a sunny day. There's no better spot for enjoying the contrast between light and shade.

Attendant: Begging your pardon, mister, but aren't you blind?

Blind man: [*smiles*] I don't see it; I *feel* it. The sun shines through the crenels, so that I feel its warmth when I'm opposite one. When I step behind a merlon, I feel the cool shade. Light, shade. Light, shade. You see?

Attendant: [*smiles faintly*] Yeah, I think I do see.

COMPREHENSION

Workbook
Page 19

Right There

1. What is the narrator doing when he first sees the blind man?
2. What is the narrator feeling at the beginning of the story?

Think and Search

3. Why does the blind man climb the tower?
4. How does the blind man feel about being in the tower?

Author and You

5. Why do you think the author uses the word *game* in the title?
6. How is the narrator affected by his talk with the blind man?

On Your Own

7. Have you ever visited a place where you could experience sensations caused by light and shadows? Describe the place.
8. Do you prefer bright days or overcast days? Why?

DISCUSSION

Discuss in pairs or small groups.

1. Discuss the meaning of the last line of the story, "I left him, gladdened as one can only be by the sunlight."

2. How do you think the narrator's conversation with the blind man will affect the narrator's experience the next time he climbs the tower?

Q **What is light?** The blind man was able to "see" the light by feeling the warmth of it on his skin. Do you think that blind people can have experiences that are equivalent to, although different from, the experiences of sighted people? Explain.

RESPONSE TO LITERATURE  Workbook Page 19

Think about an interesting experience you had visiting a particular place. Write a paragraph describing the place and what happened there. Include sensory details so that readers can share your experience. Read your paragraph aloud to the class.

»⑨ Listening TIP

If you don't understand something a speaker says, you can say, "I don't understand. Can you explain, please?" or "Would you repeat that, please?"

▲ Walls with merlons and crenels

Grammar and Writing

Prepositions of Place: *in, at,* and *on*

The prepositions *in, at,* and *on* can be used to indicate place. Look at the chart below.

in	at	on
in Korea	**at** 35 Morton Circle	**on** Walnut Road
in New York City	**at** the restaurant	**on** the ninth floor
in Sarah's room	**at** my house	**on** the shelf
in the top drawer	**at** the back door	**on** the wall

Use *in* for geographical areas such as countries, states, and cities:
   Hideo lives **in** Austin, Texas. He used to live **in** Japan.
Also use *in* for places that surround or enclose people and things:
   Jane is **in** the kitchen. The potatoes are **in** the oven. The bowl is **in** the sink.

Use *at* for complete addresses:
   Janay lives **at** 228 East 34th Street.
Also use *at* to show something that is at a particular point:
   Bob is **at** the bus stop. He studies **at** the library.

Use *on* for the names of streets and other roadways:
   Lisa lives **on** Narcissus Drive. Her school is **on** Patterson Street.
Also use *on* to show something that is on a surface:
   The bread is **on** the table. Pedro is asleep **on** the sofa.

Practice Workbook Page 20

Copy the sentences into your notebook. Complete each sentence with *in, at,* or *on*. Then check your work with a partner. Take turns reading the sentences aloud.

1. My family used to live _____ Italy.

2. There was always a huge pot of pasta _____ the stove.

3. My mother spent most of her time _____ the kitchen.

4. We often played soccer games _____ the field outside my school.

5. My mom wanted to work _____ an Italian restaurant.

WRITING A DESCRIPTIVE PARAGRAPH

Describe a Place

You have learned to use sensory details when writing description. When you describe a place, it is important to present the details in an order that makes sense for the place you are describing. For example, to describe a tower, you might start with the entrance at ground level, continue with the stairway leading up, and then finish with the lookout at the top. To describe your bedroom, you might start with the doorway and allow your eye to move around the room from left to right, describing all the important things you see as you do so. When you describe a place according to the position of the things in it, you are using spatial order.

Here is a paragraph describing a place. Notice that the writer has organized the sensory details using spatial order.

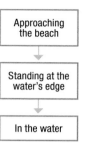

| Approaching the beach |

↓

| Standing at the water's edge |

↓

| In the water |

Ruth Kace

Sun and Sand

The best place to enjoy the sun is at the beach on a hot day. Even approaching the beach from a busy street or burning your feet on the sand on your way to the water is exhilarating. You can't wait to dip your toes in the cold wetness. As your feet dig into the soft folds of sand, you hear nothing but a seagull and the rumble of the surf. You run over to cool the soles of your feet in the wet sand and watch it slowly dry up until the next wave hits. You take a deep breath of salty air. At last, you take a running jump into the water, feeling ecstatic as you plunge in. When you pop up, the sun kisses your cheeks and you feel that you want to stay right where you are for as long as you live.

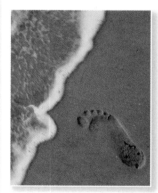

Practice  Workbook Page 21

Write a paragraph describing a favorite place. Examples include a nature preserve, a resort, a park, or a room in your home. Use sensory details to help readers experience what the place is like. Then arrange your details using the type of spatial order that makes sense for your topic. List your details in a graphic organizer like the one above. Be sure to use prepositions of place correctly.

Writing Checklist

WORD CHOICE:
✔ I used sensory details to describe a place.

ORGANIZATION:
✔ I organized my details using spatial order.

43

Prepare to Read

What You Will Learn

Reading
- Vocabulary building: *Context, dictionary skills, word study*
- Reading strategy: *Use visuals*
- Text type: *Informational text (social studies)*

Grammar, Usage, and Mechanics
Identifying and nonidentifying adjective clauses

Writing
Describe an experience

🔍 THE BIG QUESTION

What is light? In this reading, you'll learn that photographs can be used to enlighten people about the need for social reform. Notice that *light* is the base word for *enlighten*. What do you think "to enlighten someone" means?

BUILD BACKGROUND

The excerpt you are about to read from ***The Eye of Conscience*** is a photo-essay. A photo-essay is a group of photographs that tell a story, with or without accompanying text. Lewis W. Hine was a photographer who risked his life to expose poverty and harsh working conditions in America's mills and factories in the early 1900s. Hine traveled all over America taking photographs of children working under horrible conditions. These photographs ultimately helped pass laws protecting children and helped lead to social reform. More than 2,000 of Hine's photographs are preserved at the National Archives and Records Administration in Washington, D.C.

▲ The newsboy selling papers in this photo is seven years old.

Learn Key Words

Read these sentences. Use the context to figure out the meaning of the red words. Use a dictionary to check your answers. Then write each word and its meaning in your notebook.

Key Words

conditions
equipment
immigrants
industrial
inhumanity
miserable

1. The working **conditions** in the warehouse were unhealthy; the lighting was poor, and there were rats everywhere.

2. A camera is a photographer's most important piece of **equipment**.

3. Some **immigrants** left their home countries in search of better jobs.

4. The **industrial** age was a time when more and more industries used machines to help make their products faster.

5. Photographs of poor, ragged children performing adult labor in dirty mills and factories showed the **inhumanity** of child labor.

6. The long hours and the tedious work in the mills made life **miserable** for the children forced to work there.

Practice  **Workbook** Page 22

Write the sentences in your notebook. Choose a red word from the box above to complete each sentence. Then take turns reading the sentences aloud with a partner.

1. Hine's work shows the _____ of forcing children to do hard labor.

2. Many factories were built during the _____ age.

3. Hine used simple _____ —just a camera, a flash, and glass plates.

4. Hine's photos show the _____ childhoods that these children had.

5. _____ who came to America hoped to improve their lives.

6. The working _____ in the mines were dangerous and harsh.

A girl working in a cotton mill, 1909 ▶

Learn Academic Words

Study the **red** words and their meanings. You will find these words useful when talking and writing about informational texts. Write each word and its meaning in your notebook. After you read the excerpt from *The Eye of Conscience*, try to use these words to respond to the text.

Academic Words

dramatic
expose
labor
welfare

dramatic = exciting and impressive	➡	His photographs had a **dramatic** impact on society.
expose = give people information that was previously hidden	➡	They wanted to **expose** the thief by publishing photos of him stealing.
labor = work, especially work using much physical or mental effort	➡	The children had to do ten hours of hard **labor** in the fields each day in order to make enough money for their dinner.
welfare = health, comfort, and happiness	➡	A government should be concerned about the **welfare** of its citizens.

Practice
Workbook
Page 23

Work with a partner to answer these questions. Try to include the **red** word in your answer. Write the sentences in your notebook.

1. What person has made a **dramatic** impact on your life?

2. If you were a journalist or a photographer, what hidden truths would you try to **expose**?

3. What kind of **labor** would you least like to do?

4. What can people do to protect a child's **welfare**?

▲ A five-year-old shrimp picker

46

Word Study: Suffixes

A suffix is a letter or group of letters that, when added to the end of a word, forms a new word. Words ending in *e* + a suffix usually follow certain spelling rules.

To add a suffix to a word ending in *e*, note whether the suffix begins with a consonant or vowel. If it begins with a consonant, usually you do not drop the *e*. If the suffix begins with a vowel, usually you do drop the *e*.

| taste + -ful = tasteful | bereave + -ment = bereavement | sincere + -ly = sincerely |

| nerve + -ous = nervous | prepare + -ation = preparation | devote + -ion = devotion |

There are some exceptions, such as *mileage* and *agreeable*.

| mile + -age = mileage | agree + -able = agreeable |

Practice Workbook Page 24

Add the suffixes to the words below. Write the new words into your notebook.

1. legislate + -ion
2. comfort + -able
3. improve + -ment
4. investigate + -ion
5. enlarge + -ment
6. create + -ion
7. power + -ful
8. measure + -ment
9. close + -ly

READING STRATEGY | **USE VISUALS**

Using visuals helps you understand a text better. Visuals include art, photos, diagrams, charts, and maps. To use visuals, follow these steps:

- Look at each visual. Ask yourself what it shows and how it will help you understand the text.
- Read the titles, headings, labels, and captions carefully.
- If you come across a difficult word or idea, check to see whether it is represented in a visual. This will help your comprehension.

As you read the excerpt from *The Eye of Conscience,* look at the photos. In what ways are the photos as important as the text?

 Workbook Page 25

Set a purpose for reading How did one man's photographs enlighten people about the need to change American laws regarding child labor?

from

The Eye of Conscience

Milton Meltzer and Bernard Cole

It was the year 1909 when Lewis W. Hine smuggled his camera into the southern textile mills. Paul Strand, one of America's great photographers, who studied with Hine in 1908, has underscored the courage it took in those early years to photograph child labor in the South. It was like entering the enemy's armed camp, he said. Hine risked the threats of foremen and factory owners who feared what his camera might expose. They were right to be afraid: the pictures and stories he brought away with him shocked the nation and prepared it to support remedial legislation.

Apparently Hine did not always have to take his pictures secretly, for some of his prints show foremen standing by, sometimes smiling into the camera. Such men may not yet have learned what trouble photographs could make for their employers. Or perhaps they were so flattered to be asked to pose that they forgot to think about the possible consequences. Today, of course, few are so naive.

Although many were made under bad conditions, almost all of Hine's photographs were remarkably powerful. The deep sympathy he felt for the child workers always came through. The pictures and information he gathered became weapons in the hands of the National Child Labor Committee. The photos were seen everywhere—in posters, in books and pamphlets, in newspapers and magazines. They were dramatic proof of the tragedy of child labor to which America had been blind.

---

remedial legislation, laws meant to correct something unjust

pamphlets, small, thin books containing information

▲ Young mill workers, Gastonia, North Carolina, 1908

◄ A boy climbs on the machinery to replace a bobbin in a Georgia cotton mill.

BEFORE YOU GO ON

1. Why did factory owners fear Hine's camera?

2. What was powerful about Hine's photos?

On Your Own
What do you think people found shocking about the photos on this page?

49

▲ Italian immigrants on their way to Ellis Island, 1905

◄ An Italian family arriving at Ellis Island, 1905

The man who made America see the truth started out not as a photographer but as a laborer. Hine was born in Oshkosh, Wisconsin, in 1874. He worked at many unskilled jobs until he decided to get more education. He took courses at night school, and then went to the Oshkosh Normal School, where teachers were trained. The principal, Frank Manny, liked Hine and urged him on.

Encouraged, Hine went to the University of Chicago. The city of Chicago was then the center of a reform movement. The trade unions, the university professors, the welfare workers like Jane Addams, were all talking about and working for a new and better America. They were sickened by the waste and inhumanity created by the swift industrial growth in the years since the Civil War. They wanted an America that put equality and freedom before profits. The welfare of the people should be the concern of the government, they said, not the welfare of corporations.

Hine was excited by the new ideas around him. When his friend and teacher Frank Manny was appointed principal of the Ethical Culture School in New York, Hine, too, left Chicago. He took a job teaching science in Manny's school.

It was there that his life took another turn. Manny began to experiment with photography as a way of making school activities more meaningful. He chose Hine to become school photographer. Knowing nothing about the craft, Hine taught himself simply by using the camera.

It was 1903. Cameras and film had been developed to the point where men with hand cameras were setting the standard. Amateurs were often doing better work than the professionals. They showed more imagination, took more chances, dared to break the rules. Already, one amateur, Jacob Riis, had startled the country with his great photos of slum life in New York.

By 1905 Hine had learned enough camera technique to try a major work. He turned to Ellis Island, the place in New York harbor where every day thousands of immigrants landed from Europe. They came to the promised land looking for decent jobs and the freedom they had not known in the old country.

Ellis Island was packed with lonely people, eager to taste American life, but frightened by the unknown. Hine's camera caught the trust and hope in the immigrants' faces and made a vivid record of the newcomers that is now a national treasure.

The way Hine worked on that first major task became his standard. When he started, he used a 5 x 7 view camera, magnesium powder for open flash, and glass plates. Later he added a 4 x 5 Graflex. His equipment was simple; so was his method. With it he moved directly to the truth.

---

reform movement, people working together to improve something

BEFORE YOU GO ON

1 What was happening in Chicago when Hine attended school there?

2 How did Hine learn his craft?

On Your Own
Why do you think Hine's Ellis Island photos are considered a national treasure?

51

By now he knew photography would be his lifework. In 1908 he published an article about attempts to improve the life of the poor in New York. His pictures showed the filth and disease of the slums. The editor of a magazine devoted to social reform saw the piece and asked Hine to join the staff of *The Survey* as photographer. Hine gave up his teaching job and from that day on used his camera to reform social conditions.

His first assignment was to picture the life of immigrant workers in the Pittsburgh steel district. Then he photographed the workers building the New York State Barge Canal. From that he went to investigating the rapidly growing slums of Chicago and Washington, D.C.

It was while studying the life of the poor that Hine learned how poverty ruined childhood. In the streets and alleys of the slums he saw children robbed of their futures, their bodies stunted and their minds twisted. He learned of children as young as five made to do harsh, cheap labor in the factories.

Already reformers had begun to fight this crime against childhood. The National Child Labor Committee (NCLC) was campaigning for laws to protect children. When the committee head saw Hine's work in *The Survey*, he asked Hine to become staff investigator and photographer.

Hine took the job in 1908 and gave all his heart and strength to it. By that time over 1.7 million children under fifteen years of age were working in fields, factories, mines, and sweatshops. But such figures were just units in a census report. No one could call up in imagination's eye the meaning of that fact—1.7 million child wage earners. Lewis Hine knew how to make the figure flesh and blood. "Photographs of revelation," one editor called them.

Hine was always on the move with his camera; now in a Georgia cotton mill, now in a Pennsylvania coal mine, now in a New York sweatshop. He went into the homes of working children, the slum tenements, and the rural shacks. He asked the children their names, measured their heights against his coat buttons, jotted down their ages. He went from anger to despair as he saw no end to the tasks the industrial age was setting for child labor. "Tasks?" he asked once in bitter irony. "Not so—they are 'opportunities' for the child and the family to enlist in the service of industry and humanity. In unselfish devotion to their homework vocation, they relieve the overburdened manufacturer, help him pay his rent, supply his equipment, take care of his rush and slack seasons, and help him to keep down his wage scale. Of course they must accept with cheery optimism the steady decline in wages that inevitably follows in the wake of homework. Isn't it better for everyone to be working instead of expecting father to do it all?"

His photographs marched thousands of children out of the mines and factories and paraded them before the nation's eyes.

---

slums, poor, overcrowded areas in the city
stunted, not properly developed

sweatshops, places where people are forced to work, usually under horrible conditions
tenements, large buildings divided up into many small apartments
homework, paid work done in the home for an outside employer

▲ New York City's Lower East Side, around 1912

◄ A young boy at work in a glass factory, 1911

1 What were some of the effects poverty had on children?

2 How many children were doing adult labor in 1908?

On Your Own
Do you think you would like to be a photographer? Why or why not?

53

▲ These boys worked as miners for the Pennsylvania Coal Company.

A girl standing between
two mechanical looms in
a cotton mill, 1905 ▶

The comfortable and easy could see what working twelve hours a day or a night at miserable wages did to children. They could see the tired young eyes, the blank faces, the gray skin, the crippled hands, the broken bodies. "The great social peril is darkness and ignorance," Hine said. "Light is required. Light! Light in floods!"

Hine's photographs became the core of pamphlets, bulletins, newspaper and magazine articles, and books, all exposing and attacking child labor. He did not insist on quality of reproduction if he could gain immediacy of effect. At least a score of the NCLC pamphlets were shaped from information he gathered in his reports to the committee. Some he wrote in full or in part, in addition to supplying the photos. Costing a nickel or a dime, the pamphlets were distributed nationally. Hine often spoke at NCLC conferences and showed his photographs through stereopticon enlargements. His biographer, Judith M. Gutman, says he took five thousand photographs for the committee; some five hundred of them have been published.

◀ Lewis Hine and his camera

ABOUT THE **AUTHORS**

Milton Meltzer (pictured) was born in 1915. During his career, he has worked as a professor, a biographer, a historian, and a full-time writer. The focus of his work is often on poverty and discrimination in America. Meltzer's work has won many awards and honors.

Bernard Cole was a photographer and teacher. He traveled throughout the Americas taking photos for international organizations and medical journals. His work has been featured in books and museum exhibits.

BEFORE YOU GO ON

1 What social peril (danger) was Hine fighting to change?

2 In what kind of media did Hine publish his photographs?

On Your Own
Who are "the comfortable and easy," according to the author? Why does the author call them this?

55

Review and Practice

COMPREHENSION

Right There

1. How did Lewis Hine start out his life?
2. What was the subject of Hine's first major work?

Think and Search

3. In what ways did Hine use his photography to help people?
4. How did Hine feel about his work?

Author and You

5. The author says that Hine's photos were "dramatic proof of the tragedy of child labor to which America had been blind." What does the word *blind* mean in this context?
6. What does the author mean when he says that Hine's photos "make the figure flesh and blood"?

On Your Own

7. Have you ever seen photographs that made you feel strong emotions? Explain.
8. Do you think photographs can communicate ideas as well as words can? Why or why not?

IN YOUR OWN WORDS

Imagine you are telling a fellow student or a family member about Hine's photography. How would you describe Hine's images? What interesting details would you share about his life? Explain why you think Hine's work was important. Write your ideas in your notebook and read them aloud to a partner. Then listen to your partner's ideas.

> **Speaking TIP**
>
> Present your ideas clearly; pause for a few seconds between each main point.

DISCUSSION

Discuss in pairs or small groups.

- Do you think photography can still be used for social reform today? Why or why not?

- **Q** **What is light?** What did Hine mean when he said, "Light is required. Light! Light in floods!" Why do you think we associate darkness with ignorance and light with clarity and knowledge?

»⑨ Listening TIP

Do not interrupt your classmates.

READ FOR FLUENCY

When we read aloud to communicate meaning, we group words into phrases, pause or slow down to make important points, and emphasize important words. Pause for a short time when you reach a comma and for a longer time when you reach a period. Pay attention to rising and falling intonation at the end of sentences.

Work with a partner. Choose a paragraph from the reading. Discuss which words seem important for communicating meaning. Practice pronouncing difficult words. Take turns reading the paragraph aloud and give each other feedback.

EXTENSION

Workbook Page 26

Look at the photograph below. Imagine what this boy's life is like. In your notebook, write three or four sentences describing this boy's day in the cotton field. Do you think he works hard? Do you think he has enough food to eat? Do you think he gets enough rest? Explain.

◀ A boy picking cotton

Grammar and Writing

Identifying and Nonidentifying Adjective Clauses

An adjective clause describes a noun, and a relative pronoun begins an adjective clause. The relative pronouns *who, whom* and *that* are used to describe people; *that* and *which* are used to describe things. An adjective clause can be identifying or nonidentifying. Identifying clauses tell us which person, place, or thing the sentence refers to. They are necessary in order to understand the sentence. Do not use commas before and after an identifying clause.

Identifying clauses
The photographer **who / that took the picture** is well known. Do you know the people **who / that posed for this photograph**? The photos **which / that show children working** are among his most famous.

Nonidentifying clauses give extra information, but the meaning of the sentence is clear without it. Use commas with nonidentifying clauses.

Nonidentifying clauses
Oshkosh, **which is his hometown**, is in Wisconsin. Mr. O'Grady, **who has very young children**, owns a lumber mill.

Note that the relative pronoun *that* cannot be used with nonidentifying clauses, only with identifying clauses

Practice  Workbook Page 27

Work with a partner. Copy the sentences into your notebook. Identify the adjective clause in each sentence. Decide whether the clause is identifying or nonidentifying and add the proper punctuation. Then change the relative pronoun to *that* if possible.

1. A photographer is a person who takes photos for a living.
2. The light here is dim which is not good for taking photos.
3. It is the poor, helpless children who are shown in Hine's photos.
4. Lewis Hine who took the photos also wrote the pamphlets.
5. The NCLC which was campaigning for laws to protect children hired Hine to become staff photographer.

WRITING A DESCRIPTIVE PARAGRAPH

Describe an Experience

So far you have described a character, an object, and a place. When you describe an experience, you give the reader a main impression of what occurred instead of telling simple facts. You include sensory details to support or add to the main impression. You can organize your ideas using chronological order (the order in which they happened), spatial order, or order of importance.

Here is a model of a descriptive paragraph about an experience. Before writing, the writer listed his ideas in a graphic organizer like the one here.

Santos Rivera III

My First Day of School

My first day of kindergarten was September 9, 1996. I was expecting torture. The day officially began when I walked into what seemed like a giant classroom. I looked around and got a glimpse of my teacher, who looked like an angel. But I knew better. I was terrified. Suddenly, her second-in-command, the assistant teacher, began moving toward me. I ran away without waiting for her to introduce herself. The torture was becoming real. Somehow I made it through a math lesson and story time, until, finally it was play time. I looked around anxiously, wondering what to do, when a boy named Ralph came over and said hello. We built things out of blocks together and quickly became friends. For the first time that day, I realized that I didn't need to be afraid. I finally saw that school wasn't so bad after all.

Practice

Workbook
Page 28

Write a paragraph describing an important event or experience in your life. Examples might include performing for an audience, learning how to do something new, or helping a friend when you weren't in the mood. Once you have chosen what to write about, list your ideas in a graphic organizer. Include at least one adjective clause, and check to see that you have used it correctly.

Writing Checklist

IDEAS:
☑ I gave the reader a main impression of my experience.

WORD CHOICE:
☑ I chose vivid details to support or add to my main impression.

Link the Readings

Critical Thinking

Look back at the readings in this unit. Think about what they have in common. They all tell about light. Yet they do not all have the same purpose. The purpose of one reading might be to inform, while the purpose of another might be to entertain or persuade. In addition, the content of each reading relates to light differently. Now copy the chart below into your notebook and complete it.

Title of Reading	Purpose	Big Question Link
"Grandmother Spider Brings the Sun"		*Only a wise and clever animal could harness light.*
"Light"	*to inform*	
"A Game of Light and Shade"		
From *The Eye of Conscience*		

Discussion

Discuss in pairs or small groups.

- How does "Grandmother Spider Brings the Sun" relate to "A Game of Light and Shade"? How do they both relate to "Light"?

- **What is light?** Why do you think light represents so many different ideas? How many examples can you think of? Discuss with a partner.

Fluency Check

Work with a partner. Choose a paragraph from one of the readings. Take turns reading it for one minute. Count the total number of words you read. Practice saying the words you had trouble reading. Take turns reading the paragraph three more times. Did you read more words each time? Copy the chart below into your notebook and record your speeds.

	1st Speed	2nd Speed	3rd Speed	4th Speed
Words Per Minute				

Projects

Work in pairs or small groups. Choose one of these projects.

1 Write a myth about a natural feature near your home, such as a river or a lake, or about a weather-related event, such as lightning or a tornado. Explain how this feature or event came about. When you have finished writing, read your myth aloud to the class.

2 Conduct a science experiment using lights and various objects and materials. Find out which objects and materials reflect light regularly. Which objects and materials reflect light diffusely? Do your findings confirm what you have learned in the article "Light"? Explain.

3 Create a photo-essay about a problem in your community. Write captions under the photographs to explain the nature of the problem. Present the photos to your class. If you don't have access to a camera, you can make a collage or draw pictures instead. Ask your classmates questions to make sure you've communicated your ideas clearly.

Further Reading

To find out more about the theme of this unit, choose from these reading suggestions.

The Phantom of the Opera, Gaston Leroux
This Penguin Reader® tells the intriguing tale of someone or something that lurks in the shadows of the Paris Opera House, drawing a young soprano into a world of music and danger.

Light (Experimenting with Science), Antonella Meiani
The experiments in this book offer hands-on experience with the mysteries of light, including reflection, refraction, and colors.

Ansel Adams: America's Photographer, Beverly Gherman
This book describes the famous photographer's rich life and the miracles of nature that shaped his world, revealing the humorous and artistic personality behind his legendary work.

LISTENING & SPEAKING WORKSHOP

Description Guessing Game

You will give an oral description of a person, thing, place, or experience, and let your classmates guess what it is.

1 THINK ABOUT IT Review the readings in this unit, focusing on the descriptions of people, things, places, and experiences. For example, reread the descriptions of the attendant in "A Game of Light and Shade" and of the animal characters in "Grandmother Spider Brings the Sun."

Next, discuss the descriptions in a small group. What made them vivid? Which words helped you visualize what the author was describing? Then work together to develop a list of people, things, places, and experiences you could describe. Write down your ideas. Here are some examples:

- A piece of fruit
- An animal
- A famous person
- An interesting place you have visited
- An experience that you had playing your favorite sport

Choose a topic from your group's list, but don't tell anyone what it is. Your classmates will try to guess your topic after you present your description.

2 GATHER AND ORGANIZE INFORMATION Write down the details you could use in your description. It may help you to close your eyes and visualize the person, place, thing, or experience you are going to describe.

Research Go to the library, look at pictures, or use the Internet to get ideas or find information. Take notes on what you find.

Order Your Notes Choose a logical way to organize your ideas—for example, spatial order. List your ideas in a graphic organizer.

Use Visuals Make a drawing or find a photograph that illustrates what you are describing. You will show the drawing or photograph to the class after someone guesses it correctly. Do not show it to anyone beforehand.

3 PRACTICE AND PRESENT Use your graphic organizer to begin practicing your presentation. Then practice talking to your audience without reading. You may want to look in a mirror as you talk or give your presentation for a friend or family member. See who can guess your topic from your description. Keep practicing until you have to look at your notes only occasionally.

Deliver Your Presentation Look at your audience as you speak. When you're finished, invite students to guess your topic. After someone guesses correctly, or if no one guesses correctly, show your drawing or photo.

4 EVALUATE THE PRESENTATION You will improve your skills as a speaker and as a listener by evaluating each presentation you give and hear. Use this checklist to help you judge your presentation and the presentations of your classmates.

- ☑ Did the description include vivid details?
- ☑ Could you visualize what was being described?
- ☑ Did the speaker go too fast or too slow, talk too loud or too low?
- ☑ Did the speaker seem to enjoy him- or herself?
- ☑ What suggestions do you have for improving the presentation?

Speaking TIPS

Be sure you are speaking slowly and clearly. Ask your listeners for feedback. Can they hear and understand what you are saying? Try to stay relaxed and have fun as you give your description. Remember, this is a game!

Listening TIPS

Listen for clues to the speaker's topic. Try to figure out right away if the topic is a person, place, thing, or experience. Then you can get more specific. Jot down key details as you listen. Pay attention to the speaker's tone of voice and gestures.

WRITING WORKSHOP

Descriptive Essay

In this workshop you will write a descriptive essay. In a descriptive essay, the writer tries to create a vivid picture in the reader's mind of a person, place, thing, or experience. A descriptive essay begins with a paragraph that introduces the topic. The writer develops the topic in three or more body paragraphs and ends with a strong concluding paragraph. Descriptive essays contain sensory details that appeal to a reader's five senses. They also include precise, interesting words.

Your assignment for this workshop is to write a five-paragraph descriptive essay about a special person, place, thing, or experience in your life.

1 PREWRITE Close your eyes briefly and see what images come to mind. Is there an object that you and your family members use and love? Is there an experience that you will never forget? Brainstorm a list of possible topics for your essay in your notebook. Choose someone or something that you can describe vividly and enthusiastically.

List and Organize Ideas and Details Use a graphic organizer such as a sensory-details chart or a word web to organize your ideas. A student named Ruth decided to write a descriptive essay about a beautiful summer day at an amusement park. Here is the sensory-details chart she prepared:

Sight	Sound	Taste	Touch	Smell
serene grass shiny yellow blazing pink and blue	bangs pops	sweet cotton candy	warmth	sunscreen turkey

2 DRAFT Use the model on page 67 and your graphic organizer to help you write a first draft. Remember to include an introductory paragraph, three body paragraphs, and a concluding paragraph.

3 REVISE Read over your draft. As you do so, ask yourself the questions in the writing checklist. Use the questions to help you revise your essay.

SIX TRAITS OF WRITING CHECKLIST

- ☑ **IDEAS:** Do my sensory details create pictures in readers' minds?
- ☑ **ORGANIZATION:** Are my ideas presented in an order that makes sense?
- ☑ **VOICE:** Does my writing convey enthusiasm for my topic?
- ☑ **WORD CHOICE:** Are my words precise and lively enough?
- ☑ **SENTENCE FLUENCY:** Do my sentences flow smoothly?
- ☑ **CONVENTIONS:** Does my writing follow the rules of grammar, usage, and mechanics?

Here are the changes Ruth plans to make when she revises her first draft:

Summer Light

On a beautiful day last July, I went with my friends to visit an amusement park near our homes. We wanted to go on some rides and enjoy ourselves in the summer sunshine. our trip turned out to be a wonderful experience.

Every thing that afternoon seemed to glow in the suns rays. My eye ^golden^ muscels became tired from squinting in the brightness! Each surface and object reflected a different hue. ^A^ man who stood near the ferris wheel held a cluster of blazing pink and blue objects. It took me a while to realize that he was the cotton-candy man. The ferris wheel combined serene grays and shiny yellows. Just looking at the candy, I ^melt^ could feel the airy layers of sweetness in my mouth.

Nearby,

A family was picnicking on the green lush grass. I could smell their

sun screen and their turkey sandwiches. The father and little boy had

turned their faces up toward the sky They clearly liked the warmth of

the sun on their skin.

When the sunlight at last began to fade, I gathered my friends to

start home. Suddenly, I heard bangs and pops and noticed green

sprinkling down the face of my friend Sam

glitter. I turned around to see multicolored fireworks. The colored light

an eruption of

seemed to rain down on the grass and viewers. I started to reach out

to touch the colors, and then I realized that I'd look too foolish! I was

completely at a loss for words.

I left the amusement park that night with a new appreciation

for the things I take for granted. Thinking about every thing I had

felt, seen, heard, tasted, and smelled gave me a sense of clarity and

understanding. Every day I realize all over again that every thing in

the world is beautiful—you just need the light to be able to see it.

4 EDIT AND PROOFREAD

Workbook Page 29

Copy your revised draft onto a clean sheet of paper. Read it again. Correct
any errors in grammar, word usage, mechanics, and spelling. Here are the
additional changes Ruth plans to make when she prepares her final draft.

Ruth Kace

Summer Light

On a beautiful day last July, I went with my friends to visit an amusement park near our homes. We wanted to go on some rides and enjoy ourselves in the summer sunshine. our trip turned out to be a wonderful experience.

Everything that afternoon seemed to glow in the suns golden rays. My eye muscles became tired from squinting in the brightness! Each surface and object reflected a different hue. The ferris wheel combined serene grays and shiny yellows. A man who stood near the ferris wheel held a cluster of blazing pink and blue objects. It took me a while to realize that he was the cotton-candy man. Just looking at the candy, I could feel the airy layers of sweetness melt in my mouth.

Nearby, a family was picnicking on the lush green grass. I could smell their sunscreen and their turkey sandwiches. The father and little boy had turned their faces up toward the sky They clearly liked the warmth of the sun on their skin.

When the sunlight at last began to fade, I gathered my friends to start home. Suddenly, I heard bangs and pops and noticed green glitter sprinkling down the face of my friend Sam. I turned around to see an eruption of multicolored fireworks. The colored light seemed to rain down on the grass and viewers. I was completely at a loss for words. I started to reach out to touch the colors, and then I realized that I'd look too foolish!

I left the amusement park that night with a new appreciation for the things I take for granted. Thinking about everything I had felt, seen heard, tasted, and smelled gave me a sense of clarity and understanding. Every day I realize all over again that everything in the world is beautiful—you just need the light to be able to see it.

5 **PUBLISH** Prepare your final draft. Share your essay with your teacher and classmates.

Learn about *Art* with the
Smithsonian American Art Museum

Capturing the
Power of Contrasts

Sometimes life is easier if we can put things in categories: black or white, light or shadow, good or evil. Such clean dividing lines often help us make decisions. Artists often use strong contrasts in their work to create a mood or make a point. They appeal to the viewer's need for simple, bold storylines.

Edward Hopper, *Ryder's House* (1933)

In *Ryder's House*, Edward Hopper painted outdoors and captured a typical New England house in a natural landscape. Hopper chose to paint a particular view of the two-story structure that emphasized the house's massiveness. The sharp horizontal lines of the rectangular building are repeated in the small hills of grass in the foreground and the sky and clouds above. This contrast gives the viewer the feeling that the house stands firmly in the field.

▲ Edward Hopper, *Ryder's House*, 1933, oil, 36⅛ x 50 in., Smithsonian American Art Museum

The simple, sun-washed, white building projects a feeling of stability that Americans appreciated in the 1930s, when the country was in a terrible economic depression. Hopper's use of light and shadow in *Ryder's House* creates a dramatic effect where many of us might see none.

68

Arthur Dove, *Sun* (1943)

Solar waves of heat roll toward Earth in Arthur Dove's landscape painting *Sun*. The artist used warm yellow-orange colors to capture the sun's heat and light and darker tones to represent our planet's gravitational pull. The circle of the sun is reflected on Earth's surface in the bottom right of the painting. This further emphasizes the connection between the planet and its source of life-giving light. The broad band of colors and the repetition of tones give this painting a joyful energy, as though we can feel the sunny rays coming down on us. Dove himself spent most of his lifetime outdoors. In many of his paintings, he celebrates his love for the natural world.

▲ Arthur Dove, *Sun*, 1943, wax emulsion, 24 x 32 in., Smithsonian American Art Museum

Robert Sperry, *Plate #753* (1986)

In *Plate #753*, artist Robert Sperry plays with light and shadow on a piece of stoneware. First, he painted it with black glaze. Then he used white liquid clay, called slip, to decorate it with spirals and strong brushstrokes down the center. The end result was a huge, 4-foot plate with different surface textures. Because he used only black and white, which are contrasting colors, the artist captured a rhythmic energy.

Robert Sperry, *Plate #753*, ▶
1986, stoneware, 4 x 27⅝ in. diam.,
Smithsonian American Art Museum

Hopper, Dove, and Sperry all understood the power of contrasts: light against dark, sharp lines against soft backgrounds. Their work makes us think more deeply about the energy that radiates from everything, whether it is a house, the sun, or a piece of stoneware.

Apply What You Learned

1 How do these three artists use light and shadow to create contrasts in their artworks?

2 If you were to create an artwork that showed contrast between light and dark, what would it look like?

Q **Big Question**
Why do you think contrasts between objects often create powerful artworks?

Workbook
Pages 31–32

THE BIG QUESTION

How are growth and change related?

This unit is about ways in which people and things grow and change. You'll find out how seeds grow. You'll read about young people growing up and Americans moving. Reading, writing, and talking about these topics will give you practice using academic language and help you become a better student.

READING 1: Science Article, Folktale
- "How Seeds and Plants Grow"
- "Two Brothers and the Pumpkin Seeds" by Barbara Baumgartner

READING 2: Novel Excerpt
- From *Roll of Thunder, Hear My Cry* by Mildred D. Taylor

READING 3: Social Studies Article
- "Migration Patterns"

READING 4: Short Story
- "Abuela Invents the Zero" by Judith Ortiz Cofer

Listening and Speaking

At the end of this unit, you and your classmates will create and perform a **skit**.

Writing

In this unit you'll practice **narrative writing**. Narrative writing tells a story. After each reading, you'll learn a skill that will help you write a narrative paragraph. At the end of the unit, you will use these skills to write a fictional narrative.

QuickWrite

Write *Growing up* in your notebook. Create a word web with words you associate with growing up.

Prepare to Read

What You Will Learn

Reading
- Vocabulary building: *Context, dictionary skills, word study*
- Reading strategy: *Recognize sequence*
- Text type: *Informational text (science)*

Grammar, Usage, and Mechanics
Sequence words

Writing
Write a story with a starter

🔍 THE BIG QUESTION

How are growth and change related? What do you know about the life cycle of plants? How do plants change as they grow? Talk with a partner about changes plants go through, such as a seed sprouting, a flower blooming, or leaves changing color.

BUILD BACKGROUND

"How Seeds and Plants Grow" is a science article that explains what happens inside a seed when it germinates, or first begins to grow. The folktale **"Two Brothers and the Pumpkin Seeds"** is from Korea. It is about two brothers' different experiences planting the same magic pumpkin seeds. Many folktales involve magic seeds or plants. For example, in "Jack and the Beanstalk," Jack plants a magic seed that grows into a giant beanstalk. In "Cinderella," Cinderella's fairy godmother turns a pumpkin into a golden carriage. What stories do you know about magic plants? List the tales in your notebook and discuss them with a partner.

▲ A pumpkin growing on a vine

Learn Key Words

Read these sentences. Use the context to figure out the meaning of the red words. Use a dictionary to check your answers. Then write each word and its meaning in your notebook.

1. Seeds **develop** into plants only when conditions are right and the seeds have all they need in order to grow.
2. The **embryo** is the part of the seed that becomes the plant.
3. **Germination** is the stage at which the embryo inside a seed first begins to grow.
4. When a seed is **inactive**, it does not grow.
5. The **protective** covering on a seed, called the seed coat, keeps the seed from being harmed or drying out.
6. Plant stems **straighten** as they grow toward the sun.

Practice  Workbook Page 33

Write the sentences in your notebook. Choose a red word from the box above to complete each sentence. Then take turns reading the sentences aloud with a partner.

1. The stage at which a seed first begins to grow is called _____.
2. The seed was _____ because we had not planted it or watered it.
3. Most trees _____ as they grow.
4. The hard _____ covering of a seed is called the seed coat.
5. The _____ contains all the basic parts of a plant.
6. Not all seeds _____ into plants.

▲ A germinating sunflower seed

Learn Academic Words

Study the **red** words and their meanings. You will find these words useful when talking and writing about informational texts. Write each word and its meaning in your notebook. After you read "How Seeds and Plants Grow," try to use these words to respond to the text.

environment = the land, water, and air in which plants live	➡	A rain forest is a wet **environment**. A desert is a dry **environment**.
function = the usual purpose of a thing	➡	Each part of a seed has its own **function**. For example, the seed coat protects the plant.
potential = possible	➡	Inside every seed is a **potential** plant.
process = a series of actions, developments, or changes that happen in a sequence	➡	Germination is a **process** that a seed goes through when it first begins to grow.

Practice

Workbook Page 34

Work with a partner to answer these questions. Try to include the **red** word in your answer. Write the sentences in your notebook.

1. What kind of **environment** does a cactus live in?
2. What do you think is the **function** of the embryo?
3. What kind of **potential** plant is inside a pumpkin seed?
4. In what way is writing a **process**?

▲ A cactus in bloom

Word Study: Related Words

Related words are words in the same word family. They share the same base word and have related meanings. Look at similarities and differences among the related words below.

protect (verb) to prevent someone or something from being harmed
protection (noun) the act of protecting or the state of being protected
protective (adjective) used or intended for protection

Once you know the meaning of a base word, you can make a guess about the meanings of other words in that family. Try to memorize the meanings of as many suffixes as possible. This will help when you are trying to understand the meanings of related words.

Practice

Work with a partner. Copy the words in the box below into your notebook. Write the part of speech and the meaning of each word. Then check your work in a dictionary.

action	correction	production
active	corrective	productive

READING STRATEGY RECOGNIZE SEQUENCE

Recognizing sequence will help you understand the order of events in a text. To recognize sequence, follow these steps as you read:

- Look for words that show sequence, such as *first, then, next, finally, last, while, during,* and *after.*
- Look for time expressions, such as *every morning, yesterday, in the spring, next February,* and *on Jan 10, 2010.*
- You may wish to track the events in a sequence-of-events chart.

As you read "How Seeds and Plants Grow" and "Two Brothers and the Pumpkin Seeds," notice the sequence in which things happen.

75

Set a purpose for reading Think about how plants change as they grow. What happens inside a seed as it first begins to grow?

How Seeds and Plants Grow

Parts of a Seed

Most plants produce new plants from seeds. A seed is like a tiny package. It contains the beginning of a very young plant inside a protective covering.

A seed has three important parts—an embryo, stored food, and a seed coat. The embryo contains the basic parts from which a young plant will develop—roots, stems, and leaves. Stored food keeps the young plant alive until it can make its own food through photosynthesis. Seeds contain one or two seed leaves, called cotyledons. In some plants, food is stored in the cotyledons.

The outer protective covering of a seed is called the seed coat. The seed coat is like a plastic wrap; it protects the embryo and stored food from drying out. This protection is necessary because a seed may be inactive—may not begin to grow—for weeks, months, or even years.

Then, when conditions are right, the embryo inside a seed suddenly becomes active and begins to grow. The time when the embryo first begins to grow is called germination.

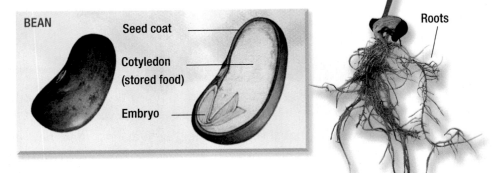

BEAN
Seed coat
Cotyledon (stored food)
Embryo

Leaves

Stem

Roots

▲ A young bean plant

---

photosynthesis, process by which a plant makes food in its leaves

Germination

During germination, the seed absorbs water from the environment. Then the embryo uses its stored food to begin to grow. The seed coat breaks open, and the embryo's roots grow downward. Then its stem and leaves grow upward. As the stem grows longer, it breaks out of the ground. Once it is above the ground, the stem straightens up toward the sunlight, and the first leaves appear on the stem. When the young plant produces its first leaves, it can begin to make its own food by photosynthesis.

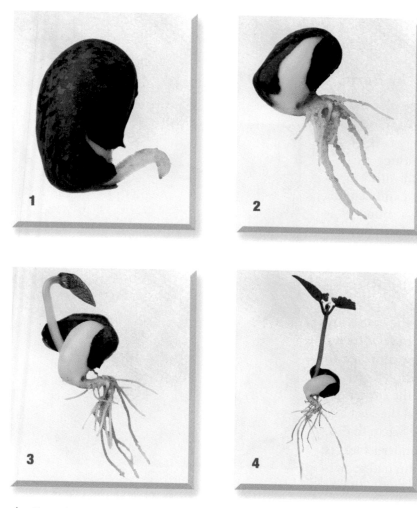

▲ Germination of a runner bean

BEFORE YOU GO ON

1 What are three important parts of a seed?

2 What is the first thing that happens during germination?

On Your Own
Do you enjoy growing plants? Why or why not?

77

Set a purpose for reading Read this folktale about two brothers who each plant a magic seed. Why do they get such different results?

Two Brothers and the Pumpkin Seeds

A Korean folktale retold by Barbara Baumgartner

Long ago in Korea there were two brothers: Chang, who was so stingy he would not share a piece of food with you, and Kim, who was always kind and helpful. One day the two brothers saw a young swallow fall from its nest and break its leg. Kim quickly picked up the bird and bound its leg so that the bone would heal.

Chang shouted, "Foolish! Silly! Wrapping up a bird's leg!"

Kim took the swallow into the house, and when the bird's leg healed, Kim set it free.

A few days later, the swallow returned and dropped a pumpkin seed at Kim's feet. Kim planted the pumpkin seed in the corner of the field. Every day he watered the seed and pulled the weeds. Soon a vine began to grow, with one pumpkin growing under its leaves.

At harvest time the pumpkin had grown so big that Kim thought, *This pumpkin is too heavy to move. I will cut it open and give a piece to each family in the village.*

But when Kim cut the pumpkin open, gold coins tumbled out. So Kim shared the pumpkin and the gold coins with everyone in the village.

---

harvest time, time to gather crops from the fields

78

When Chang saw all that had happened, he decided he would like such good fortune. He found a young swallow, then cruelly broke its leg. He bound the swallow's leg with a bandage and then released the bird. A few days later, the bird returned with a pumpkin seed in its beak. Chang snatched the pumpkin seed and hurried to plant it in the field. Soon a pumpkin vine was growing.

When Chang was ready to harvest his pumpkin, he said to himself, *I will not be foolish like my brother and give away the pumpkin and its gold.*

When he cut into the pumpkin, spiders and snakes began crawling all over him. At the same time, the pumpkin vine began growing up toward the sky. Chang quickly began climbing the pumpkin vine to get away from the spiders and snakes. But when he got into the sky, the vine dried up behind him.

If you ever look at the sky and see a cloud shaped like a boy, you'll know that it is Chang, for he has still not learned the lesson that the swallow tried to teach him.

ABOUT THE **AUTHOR**

Barbara Baumgartner is a librarian, teacher, storyteller, and author, best known for her book *Crocodile! Crocodile! Stories Told Around the World*. When not teaching classes in storytelling or children's literature, Baumgartner visits schools and libraries to share her passion for folklore with people of all ages.

BEFORE YOU GO ON

1. What did Kim do with the pumpkin he grew?

2. What did Chang find inside his pumpkin?

On Your Own
Do you think that kindness can bring a person wealth? Why or why not?

79

COMPREHENSION

Workbook
Page 37

Right There

1. What is the function of the seed coat?
2. What did Kim find inside his pumpkin?

Think and Search

3. What are three basic parts of a plant?
4. How did the swallow trick Chang?

Author and You

5. *Photo* is a Greek root, or word part, meaning "light." Given this information, what conclusion can you draw about photosynthesis?

6. There is a saying, "You reap what you sow." It means that what you harvest reflects what you planted and the energy you put into growing the plants. How does this saying apply to the folktale?

On Your Own

7. Compare seeds with eggs. In what ways are seeds and eggs similar? In what ways are they different?

8. Have you ever been surprised with a reward for doing someone a kindness? Describe your experience.

▲ A white oak seedling

IN YOUR OWN WORDS

Work with a partner. In your own words, explain how a seed germinates and becomes a plant. Include as many new vocabulary words as possible. Ask your partner to listen carefully to your explanation. Are there any key points that you missed? Did you use the vocabulary words correctly?

Speaking TIP

Write important ideas on note cards. Review your notes before you begin speaking.

DISCUSSION

Discuss in pairs or small groups.

1. Which facts from the science article support the ideas presented in the folktale?

2. Do you think Chang deserved what happened to him? Explain.

Q **How are growth and change related?** Have you ever grown a plant from a seed? What did you do? Did the plant grow well, or could you have provided it with a better environment? Explain.

»)⊙ *Listening* TIP

Respect your classmates. Listen politely, even if you disagree with a person's ideas.

READ FOR FLUENCY

It is often easier to read a text if you understand the difficult words and phrases. Work with a partner. Choose a paragraph from the reading. Identify the words and phrases you do not know or have trouble pronouncing. Look up the difficult words in a dictionary.

Take turns pronouncing the words and phrases with your partner. If necessary, ask your teacher to model the correct pronunciation. Then take turns reading the paragraph aloud. Give each other feedback on your reading.

EXTENSION Workbook Page 37

Use the Internet or go to the library to get information about forests that are in danger of disappearing. What causes deforestation? What problems can result from deforestation? What can be done to help solve the problem?

Prepare a short oral report on the topic. Include drawings, posters, or photographs to help your audience understand the information better. Present your report to the class.

▲ Planting a Caribbean pine seedling in the Fiji Islands

Grammar and Writing

Sequence Words

Sequence words help the reader connect events in an informational text or a story. Sequence words and expressions include *first, then, next, after that, afterward, following that, last,* and *finally.*

The events in "Two Brothers and the Pumpkin Seeds" take place in chronological order. You can use sequence words to present the events of the story in the order that they happen. Here are the events in the first half of the story. Notice that a comma follows all sequence words except for *then.*

First, Kim bound the swallow's leg.
Then the swallow's leg healed, and Kim set it free.
Next, the swallow dropped a pumpkin seed at Kim's feet, so Kim planted it.
Afterward, a big pumpkin grew.
Following that, Kim cut the pumpkin open, and gold coins tumbled out.
Finally, Kim shared the pumpkin and the coins with everyone in the village.

Practice
Workbook Page 38

"How Seeds and Plants Grow" is a science article that explains the process of germination. The steps of the process occur in a particular order, or sequence. You can use sequence words to explain the steps of germination in the order they occur.

Copy the chart below into your notebook. Create sentences using the sequence words above to explain the steps of germination.

Sequence Words	Sentences
First,	First, the seed absorbs water from the environment.

82

WRITING A NARRATIVE PARAGRAPH

Write a Story with a Starter

Before you write a narrative, you'll need to learn some skills authors use in narrative writing. A narrative is a story. Most stories include a series of events. The events make up the story's plot. The writer presents the story events in the order that makes the most sense. In "Two Brothers and the Pumpkin Seeds," the events are in chronological order, or time order. The author uses sequence words to make the relationship between events clear.

Here is a model of a story. The writer began his story with this starter: *I had never seen such an amazing plant.* Before writing, he used a sequence-of-events chart to organize his ideas.

First,

↓

Then

↓

Finally,

Nicholas Kasterine

An Amazing Plant

I had never seen such an amazing plant. Its smooth, curling leaves seemed to reach out to me. I wanted badly to touch it. Suddenly, its tentacles shot out and wrapped themselves around me. I tried to break loose, but I was trapped. I started to panic. Then I got an idea. First, I worked my arm free of the tangle. Next, I made an opening in the vegetation near my pants pocket. I pulled out my knife and cut randomly at the leaves and stems. Finally free, I heard a voice. "You, there!" It was a park ranger. "Have you ever seen such an amazing plant?" I shook my head. The ranger smiled and explained that people should never touch this species of plant because it was becoming rare. I turned and looked at the plant. It was in perfect condition, just as it was when I first saw it. Had it all been a daydream?

Practice

Workbook
Page 39

Choose from these story starters or make up your own:

Once, an emperor held a contest to see who would inherit his kingdom.
Once there was a cat that could fly.
Once there was a girl who was so clever she could outsmart anyone.

Then create a story by adding events. List your ideas in a sequence-of-events chart. Be sure to use sequence words correctly.

Writing Checklist

ORGANIZATION:
☑ I presented the story events in order.

WORD CHOICE:
☑ I used sequence words to make the order of events clear.

83

What You Will Learn

Reading

■ Vocabulary building: *Literary terms, context, dictionary skills, word study*

■ Reading strategy: *Compare and contrast*

■ Text type: *Literature (novel)*

Grammar, Usage, and Mechanics
Conditional sentences

Writing
Rewrite a familiar story

THE BIG QUESTION

How are growth and change related? People grow and change both physically and mentally. What kinds of experiences can make people grow and change in terms of their emotions and understanding? Discuss with a partner or in small groups.

BUILD BACKGROUND

This reading is an excerpt from the novel **Roll of Thunder, Hear My Cry**. The novel is historical fiction. The story deals with racism—treating one group of people differently from another because of race.

Before 1954, it was legal for schools and other public places to be segregated, or separated, by race so long as the places were "equal." To determine if schools were "equal," people would look at the school building, furniture, books, and materials. In 1954, the U.S. Supreme Court, the highest court in the United States, ruled that "separate" cannot be "equal." Just the fact that the races were kept segregated made schools and other places unequal.

This passage from *Roll of Thunder, Hear My Cry* takes place in the 1930s, in Mississippi, long before the 1954 Supreme Court ruling. The setting—a segregated school attended by African-American children—is historical. The characters Cassie and her brother, Little Man, are fictional.

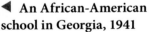
◀ An African-American school in Georgia, 1941

Learn Literary Words

In a narrative, the person telling the story is called the narrator. The narrator tells the story from his or her **point of view**. This means that the reader views things however the narrator describes them. Sometimes the narrator is a character in the story. Then the narrator assumes the first-person point of view, telling the story using the pronouns *I* and *my*. In this excerpt from *Roll of Thunder, Hear My Cry* the main character, Cassie Logan, narrates the story.

Literary Words
point of view
plot
conflict

Because Cassie is the narrator, readers understand the **plot** from her point of view. The plot is the sequence of connected events that make up a story. This reading tells about one event in the novel's plot.

A **conflict** is a struggle between opposing forces. Conflict can be between characters or between a character and him- or herself. Conflict is one of the most important elements of a story because it causes the action and sets the plot in motion. In this reading, the conflict is between Cassie's brother, Little Man, and Miss Crocker, the children's teacher.

Practice

Workbook Page 40

Copy the chart below into your notebook. As you read, complete the chart with details from the story

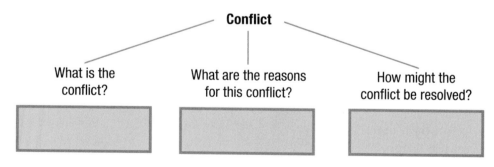

Conflict

What is the conflict?

What are the reasons for this conflict?

How might the conflict be resolved?

Learn Academic Words

Study the red words and their meanings. You will find these words useful when talking and writing about literature. Write each word and its meaning in your notebook. After you read the excerpt from *Roll of Thunder, Hear My Cry*, try using these words to respond to the text.

affect = cause a person to feel strong emotions	⮕	She pretended that the bad news did not **affect** her in order to appear strong.
anticipation = a feeling of excitement because something good or fun is going to happen	⮕	We were filled with **anticipation** as we waited for the show to start.
discrimination = the practice of treating one group of people differently from another in an unfair way	⮕	Laws against **discrimination** help prevent various groups from being treated unfairly.
reaction = something you say or do because of what has happened or been said to you	⮕	His **reaction** to my joke was not what I had hoped. Instead of laughing, he groaned.

Practice

Work with a partner to answer these questions. Try to include the **red** word in your answer.

1. Do you think it is wrong to show how things **affect** you? Explain.

2. In what ways can **anticipation** sometimes lead to disappointment?

3. Which organizations work to help end **discrimination**?

4. What would your **reaction** be if you found out you had won the lottery?

▲ Children in school, 1935

86

Word Study: Homographs

Some words in English are spelled alike but have different meanings. These words are called homographs. There are several ways to figure out the meaning of a homograph. Here are some suggestions:

- Check to see how the word is used. What part of speech is it?
- Look at the other words in the sentence for context clues.
- Use a dictionary to find the correct definition.

The chart below includes some examples of homographs.

Homograph	Part of Speech	Meaning
grave	noun	place in the ground where a dead person is buried
grave	adjective	very serious and worrying
switch	noun	thin stick of wood that bends easily that was used in the past to punish children
switch	verb	exchange one thing for another

Practice

Workbook
Page 42

The following homographs appear in the excerpt from *Roll of Thunder, Hear My Cry: beam, roll, spotted,* and *row*. As you find each word in the reading, copy the context sentence into your notebook. Ask yourself how the word is used in the sentence. What is another meaning of the same word? Use a dictionary to find the meaning used in the context sentence. Record it in your notebook.

READING STRATEGY   COMPARE AND CONTRAST

Comparing and contrasting helps you to understand ideas in a text. When you compare, you see how things are similar. When you contrast, you see how things are different. To compare and contrast, ask yourself the following questions as you read:

- How are the characters and events in this story similar to people and events in my own life?
- How are the characters and events in this story different from the people and events in my own life?
- How are the characters' ideas about the events similar?
- How are the characters' ideas about the events different?

As you read the excerpt from *Roll of Thunder, Hear My Cry*, answer the questions listed above by comparing and contrasting.

Workbook
Page 43

Set a purpose for reading Read this story to find out how Cassie and her brother confront racism. What does Cassie learn from her brother?

from

Roll of Thunder Hear My Cry

Mildred D. Taylor

The narrator is Cassie Logan, the only daughter in a large African-American family struggling against poverty and racism in the Deep South of the 1930s. In this excerpt, Cassie and her little brother learn what it is to be the victim of racial discrimination.

Now Miss Crocker made a startling announcement: This year we would all have books.

Everyone gasped, for most of the students had never handled a book at all besides the family Bible. I admit that even I was somewhat excited. Although Mama had several books, I had never had one of my very own.

"Now we're very fortunate to get these readers," Miss Crocker explained while we eagerly awaited the unveiling. "The county superintendent of schools himself brought these books down here for our use and we must take extra-good care of them." She moved toward her desk. "So let's all promise that we'll take the best care possible of these new books." She stared down, expecting our response. "All right, all together, let's repeat, 'We promise to take good care of our new books.'" She looked sharply at me as she spoke.

"WE PROMISE TO TAKE GOOD CARE OF OUR NEW BOOKS!"

"Fine," Miss Crocker beamed, then proudly threw back the tarpaulin.

Sitting so close to the desk, I could see that the covers of the books, a motley red, were badly worn and that the gray edges of the pages had been marred by pencils, crayons, and ink. My anticipation at having my own book ebbed to a sinking disappointment. But Miss Crocker continued to beam as she called each fourth grader to her desk and, recording a number in her roll book, handed him or her a book.

As I returned from my trip to her desk, I noticed the first graders anxiously watching the disappearing pile. Miss Crocker must have noticed them too, for as I sat down she said, "Don't worry, little ones, there are plenty of readers for you too. See there on Miss Davis's desk." Wide eyes turned to the covered teacher's platform directly in front of them and an audible sigh of relief swelled in the room.

I glanced across at Little Man, his face lit in eager excitement. I knew that he could not see the soiled covers or the marred pages from where he sat, and even though his penchant for cleanliness was often annoying, I did not like to think of his disappointment when he saw the books as they really were. But there was nothing I could do about it, so I opened my book to its center and began browsing through the spotted pages. Girls with blond braids and boys with blue eyes stared up at me. I found a story about a boy and his dog lost in a cave and began reading while Miss Crocker's voice droned on monotonously.

---

unveiling, presentation
tarpaulin, a piece of material used to cover or protect things
marred, ruined
ebbed, grew less; weakened
audible, loud enough to be heard
penchant, liking or fondness
monotonously, boringly; tediously

BEFORE YOU GO ON

1 What announcement does Miss Crocker make to the class?

2 What does the narrator notice about the books on the desk?

On Your Own
Have you ever looked forward to something that turned out to be a disappointment? Explain.

89

Suddenly I grew conscious of a break in that monotonous tone and I looked up. Miss Crocker was sitting at Miss Davis's desk with the first-grade books stacked before her, staring fiercely down at Little Man, who was pushing a book back upon the desk.

"What's that you said, Clayton Chester Logan?" she asked.

The room became gravely silent. Everyone knew that Little Man was in big trouble for no one, but no one, ever called Little Man "Clayton Chester" unless she or he meant serious business.

Little Man knew this too. His lips parted slightly as he took his hands from the book. He quivered, but he did not take his eyes from Miss Crocker. "I—I said may I have another book please, ma'am," he squeaked. "That one's dirty."

"Dirty!" Miss Crocker echoed, appalled by such temerity. She stood up, gazing down upon Little Man like a bony giant, but Little Man raised his head and continued to look into her eyes. "Dirty! And just who do you think you are, Clayton Chester? Here the county is giving us these wonderful books during these hard times and you're going to stand there and tell me that the book's too dirty? Now you take that book or get nothing at all!"

Little Man lowered his eyes and said nothing as he stared at the book. For several moments he stood there, his face barely visible above the desk, then he turned and looked at the few remaining books and, seeming to realize that they were as badly soiled as the one Miss Crocker had given him, he looked across the room at me. I nodded and Little Man, glancing up again at Miss Crocker, slid the book from the edge of the desk, and with his back straight and his head up returned to his seat.

---

appalled, horrified, surprised, and angry
temerity, boldness; lack of respect

Miss Crocker sat down again. "Some people around here seem to be giving themselves airs. I'll tolerate no more of that," she scowled. "Sharon Lake, come get your book."

I watched Little Man as he scooted into his seat beside two other little boys. He sat for a while with a stony face looking out the window; then, evidently accepting the fact that the book in front of him was the best that he could expect, he turned and opened it. But as he stared at the book's inside cover, his face clouded, changing from sulky acceptance to puzzlement. His brows furrowed. Then his eyes grew wide, and suddenly he sucked in his breath and sprang from his chair like a wounded animal, flinging the book onto the floor and stomping madly upon it.

Miss Crocker rushed to Little Man and grabbed him up in powerful hands. She shook him vigorously, then set him on the floor again. "Now, just what's gotten into you, Clayton Chester?"

But Little Man said nothing. He just stood staring down at the open book, shivering with indignant anger.

"Pick it up," she ordered.

"No!" defied Little Man.

"No? I'll give you ten seconds to pick up that book, boy, or I'm going to get my switch."

---

giving themselves airs, acting more important than they are
stony, without expression or feeling; like a stone
vigorously, strongly
switch, a thin stick used at that time to hit a child as punishment

BEFORE YOU GO ON

1. How do the students know that Little Man is in trouble?

2. Why does Little Man object to the book he was given?

On Your Own
Do you think Little Man was wrong to ask for a new book? Why or why not?

91

Little Man bit his lower lip, and I knew that he was not going to pick up the book. Rapidly, I turned to the inside cover of my own book and saw immediately what had made Little Man so furious. Stamped on the inside cover was a chart which read:

PROPERTY OF THE BOARD OF EDUCATION Spokane County, Mississippi September, 1922		
Date of Issuance	Condition of Book	Race of Student
1 September 1922	New	White
2 September 1923	Excellent	White
3 September 1924	Excellent	White
4 September 1925	Very Good	White
5 September 1926	Good	White
6 September 1927	Good	White
7 September 1928	Average	White
8 September 1929	Average	White
9 September 1930	Average	White
10 September 1931	Poor	White
11 September 1932	Poor	White
12 September 1933	Very Poor	nigra
13		
14		
15		
16		
17		
18		
19		
20		

The blank lines continued down to line 20 and I knew that they had all been reserved for black students. A knot of anger swelled in my throat and held there. But as Miss Crocker directed Little Man to bend over the "whipping" chair, I put aside my anger and jumped up.

"Miz Crocker, don't, please!" I cried. Miss Crocker's dark eyes warned me not to say another word. "I know why he done it!"

"You want part of this switch, Cassie?"

---

furious, very angry, enraged

92

"No'm," I said hastily. "I just wanna tell you how come Little Man done what he done."

"Sit down!" she ordered as I hurried toward her with the open book in my hand.

Holding the book up to her, I said, "See Miz Crocker, see what it says. They give us these ole books when they didn't want 'em no more."

She regarded me impatiently, but did not look at the book. "Now how could he know what it says? He can't read."

"Yes'm, he can. He been reading since he was four. He can't read all them big words, but he can read them columns. See what's in the last row. Please look, Miz Crocker."

This time Miss Crocker did look, but her face did not change. Then, holding up her head, she gazed unblinkingly down at me.

"S-see what they called us," I said, afraid she had not seen.

"That's what you are," she said coldly. "Now go sit down."

I shook my head, realizing now that Miss Crocker did not even know what I was talking about. She had looked at the page and had understood nothing.

"I said sit down, Cassie!"

I started slowly toward my desk, but as the hickory stick sliced the tense air, I turned back around. "Miz Crocker," I said, "I don't want my book neither."

The switch landed hard upon Little Man's upturned bottom. Miss Crocker looked questioningly at me as I reached up to her desk and placed the book upon it. Then she swung the switch five more times and, discovering that Little Man had no intention of crying, ordered him up.

"All right, Cassie," she sighed, turning to me, "come on and get yours."

---

hastily, hurriedly; quickly
impatiently, with annoyance or irritation
had no intention of, would refuse to

ABOUT THE **AUTHOR**

Mildred D. Taylor was born in Jackson, Mississippi, in 1943. Many of the ideas found in Taylor's work come from her own life or the lives of her parents, grandparents, and great-grandparents. Two subjects she often writes about are family unity and racism. Taylor has won numerous awards for her work, including a Newbery Medal, Coretta Scott King Awards, and Jane Addams Book Awards.

BEFORE YOU GO ON

1 What makes Little Man so furious?

2 Why does Miss Crocker punish Cassie, too?

On Your Own
How did this story affect you?

Review and Practice

READER'S THEATER

Speaking TIP

Speak slowly and clearly. Adjust your tone of voice to match the emotions the characters are feeling.

In pairs, act out the following scene between Cassie and Little Man.

Little Man: Thanks for sticking up for me today, Cassie.

Cassie: Of course, Little Man. We're family.

Little Man: I got so angry when I saw that chart in the book—and that word in the last row.

Cassie: I know, Little Man.

Little Man: Miss Crocker was angry that we didn't want our books.

Cassie: She didn't understand why we were upset.

Little Man: Where did those books come from, anyway?

Cassie: They're from the white school. They're too old and dirty to be used there, so they gave the books to our school.

Little Man: I wish we got new, clean books instead.

Cassie: Me too. Now we have no books at all.

Little Man: But, Cassie, you don't blame me, do you?

Cassie: No, Little Man; we both did what we had to do.

COMPREHENSION

Workbook
Page 44

Right There

1. What did Cassie see when she opened her book?

2. What was written inside Little Man's book?

Think and Search

3. How old was Little Man's book?

4. What makes Cassie decide not to keep her book?

Author and You

5. In what ways do Cassie and Little Man have more pride and dignity than their own teacher?

6. What do the main characters' experiences show about the ideas of equality at that time in the South?

7. How would you feel if you were forced to use dirty old books? What would you do to change the situation?

8. Do you admire what Cassie and Little Man did? Why or why not?

DISCUSSION

Discuss in pairs or small groups.

1. What do you think Miss Crocker means when she says to Cassie, "That's what you are"?

2. Do you think the condition of your school building, equipment, and materials is related to the quality of your education? Explain.

Q **How are growth and change related?** How do you think the experience affected Cassie? How might it have changed her?

RESPONSE TO LITERATURE

Workbook
Page 44

With a partner, talk about what Cassie and Little Man went through during their day at school. How is their life at school different from yours? How is their life similar to yours? Write a paragraph comparing your day at school with theirs. When you have finished writing, share your work with another pair of students.

Grammar and Writing

GRAMMAR, USAGE, AND MECHANICS

Conditional Sentences

We use conditional sentences to talk about events that may or may not occur, depending on other events or conditions. Each conditional sentence has an *if* clause and a result clause. Here is an example:

> if clause   result clause
>
> If it is dark out, I will take a flashlight with me.

There are different kinds of conditional sentences. Factual conditionals are used to talk about future results of specific events or actions. In factual conditionals, the verb in the result clause is often preceded by *will*.

> If the temperature **drops**, the pond **will freeze**.
> If it **snows** tomorrow, **will** we **go** to school?

Unreal conditionals are used to talk about present unreal conditions and their results. Use the *simple past* in the *if* clause and *could, would,* or *might* + verb in the result clause. If the verb is *be* in the *if* clause, use *were* for all persons.

> If he **were** my father, I **would treat** him with respect.
> If my parents **gave** me such a precious gift, I **would be** grateful.
> If Paul-Edward **moved** to the North, he **might have** an easier life.

Practice

Workbook Page 45

Work with a partner. Copy these sentences into your notebook. For each one, label the *if* clause and the result clause. Say whether it is a factual or an unreal conditional. Check your answers with your teacher.

1. I would be happy if our teacher gave us new books.
2. If you were Little Man's teacher, what would you do?
3. Cassie and Little Man will walk home if it is not too dark outside.
4. If the Logans were wealthy, Cassie and Little Man would go to private school.
5. If you visit Mississippi, you will see some interesting sights.

WRITING A NARRATIVE PARAGRAPH

Rewrite a Familiar Story

When you tell a story, you can tell it from a character's point of view or an outsider's point of view. The story you just read is told from Cassie's point of view. Cassie tells the reader what happened and how she felt about it. But the same event could be narrated from the point of view of another character, such as Little Man. How would his version of the story be different from Cassie's?

Here is a model of the story told from Little Man's point of view. Before the writer began writing, she listed her ideas in a T-chart.

Cassie's point of view	Little Man's point of view

Leah Morales

Roll of Thunder, Hear My Cry

I was excited to be getting a book of my own. But when Miss Crocker handed me that dirty old book, I didn't want it. I asked for a new one, but she said if I didn't take that book, I wouldn't get one at all. I saw that the other books were just as dirty, so I took it. I opened it, and inside the cover was a chart. The chart had a lot of words on it, and I couldn't read them all. But I could read the words in the row for 1933. It said "very poor." And I could tell that the race of the student who got this book was black, but the chart had a different word for it. I jumped up and threw that book on the ground. I stomped on it, thinking that maybe if I stomped hard enough, those words would go away. If we had clean books, without those awful words in them, I would be happy. But nobody could be happy about insults. Suddenly, I felt a pair of strong arms on me. I heard Miss Crocker yelling, but I refused to pick up the book. I wouldn't touch that thing again, even if it did mean the switch.

Practice

Workbook Page 46

Rewrite a familiar story from a new point of view—one that is different from that of the original story. For example, you might rewrite "Two Brothers and the Pumpkin Seeds" using the first-person point of view of either character. It's a good idea to use a story you know well or can refer to. Before you write, list your ideas in a T- chart. Be sure to use conditional sentences correctly.

Writing Checklist

IDEAS:
☑ I changed the details of the story based on a shift in point of view.

CONVENTIONS:
☑ I used conditional sentences correctly.

Prepare to Read

What You Will Learn

Reading
- Vocabulary building: *Context, dictionary skills, word study*
- Reading strategy: *Scan*
- Text type: *Informational text (social studies)*

Grammar, Usage, and Mechanics
Simple past and present perfect

Writing
Write a personal letter

THE BIG QUESTION

How are growth and change related? Have you ever moved? If so, did you move to a new city or state? Why did you move? Was the change difficult for you? Discuss with a partner.

▲ A family moving into a new home

BUILD BACKGROUND

This reading is a social studies article called **"Migration Patterns."** It presents factual information about how often, how far, and why people in the United States move. It also includes statistics, or groups of numbers that represent facts or measurements. The statistics support the author's statements.

This man is taking a census, an official count of all the people in the United States. ▶

98

Learn Key Words

Read these sentences. Use the context to figure out the meaning of the **red** words. Use a dictionary to check your answers. Then write each word and its meaning in your notebook.

1. The number of people moving to the city **declined** this year. Fewer people moved there.
2. The Wilsons bought **property** in the mountains because they want to build a house there.
3. There are few **residents** in that town. Only 300 people live there.
4. My cousins live on a farm in a **rural** area far from a major city.
5. A graph can show a **trend** in behavior. For example, one of the graphs in this reading shows that more people are moving *from* the Northeast than *to* the Northeast.
6. Because the Taylors prefer an **urban** lifestyle, they are moving to one of the big cities in the South.

Practice

Workbook
Page 47

Write the sentences in your notebook. Choose a **red** word from the box above to complete each sentence. Then take turns reading the sentences aloud with a partner.

1. _____ areas often have a low population.
2. The population of a town is the total number of its _____.
3. When fewer people have moved, we say that the moving rate has _____.
4. The city of Austin, Texas, is an _____ area.
5. The building was built on _____ owned by the school.
6. The graph shows this _____ : fewer people are moving to cities than they were ten years ago.

▲ Family members in front of their new home

99

Learn Academic Words

Study the **red** words and their meanings. You will find these words useful when talking and writing about informational texts. Write each word and its meaning in your notebook. After you read "Migration Patterns," try to use these words to respond to the text.

Academic Words

distribution
factors
migration
percent
region

distribution = scattering or spreading of something over an area	➡	The population **distribution** changed when large numbers of people moved from one part of the country to another.
factors = things that influence or cause a situation	➡	To understand why people move, one must consider all the **factors**, including age, marital status and income.
migration = action of a large group of animals, including people, moving from one place to another	➡	There has been a steady **migration** to our state; people from all over the country have moved here because of the nice weather.
percent = equal to a particular amount in every hundred	➡	Half, or 50 **percent**, of the people in our town used to live in a big city.
region = fairly large area of a state or country, usually without exact limits	➡	Boston and New York are in the same **region** of the United States: the Northeast.

Practice

Workbook
Page 48

Work with a partner to answer these questions. Try to include the **red** word in your answer. Write the sentences in your notebook.

1. How does moving affect the population **distribution**?

2. Are **factors** such as niceness and sense of humor important to you when choosing friends? Explain.

3. How might an event like an earthquake or a hurricane cause **migration** of people and other animals?

4. What **percent** of students in your class walk to school? What **percent** of students take a bus?

5. What **region** of the country do you live in?

Word Study: Long *a, i, o* Spelling Patterns

Long vowel sounds can be spelled in different ways. The chart below shows the different spelling patterns for the long vowels *a, i,* and *o*.

Long *a*	Long *i*	Long *o*
a_e: state, same, rate, decade, age, migrate	**i_e**: declined, nine, five	**o_e**: home, opposed
ai, ay: remained, stay, today	**igh**: right, slightly, higher	**ow**: shows, owner, widow, lower

Practice

Work with a partner. Take turns reading the words in the box aloud. After you say a word, identify the long vowel sound and its spelling. Then choose five words and write a sentence for each.

always	flowing	mine	safe	tight
bright	grain	paint	shape	tiles
crow	hides	play	sight	window
drive	late	revive	stone	write

READING STRATEGY　SCAN

Scanning helps you find information you need quickly. When you scan, you read for particular kinds of information, such as names, dates, numbers, and facts. To scan, follow these steps:

- Look at the title, visuals, captions, and labels to see if they contain the information you need.
- Start reading the beginning of the text. Move your eyes quickly over the lines. Don't stop at words you don't know.
- Look for key words related to the information you want to find.
- Stop scanning and begin reading as soon as you find any of the key words you're looking for.

Before you read "Migration Patterns," use the scanning strategy to find three key pieces of information.

Set a purpose for reading As you read this social studies article, consider this question: What factors determine why and where people in the United States move?

Migration Patterns

People in the United States move often. According to the United States Census Bureau, 40.1 million Americans—more than 14 percent of the total population—changed residence between March 2002 and March 2003.

In that year, the people who moved didn't always move a long distance. The pie chart to the right shows that about 59 percent of people who moved stayed within the same county. About 19 percent moved from a different county within the same state. About 19 percent moved from a different state. Only 3 percent moved from another country. Overall, the moving rate has declined slightly over the past decade, but people have tended to move longer distances. In 1998, for example, only 15 percent of people who moved went to another state, as opposed to the 19 percent in 2002–2003. In 1998, almost 65 percent of those who moved stayed within the same county; this number dropped to 59 percent by 2002–2003.

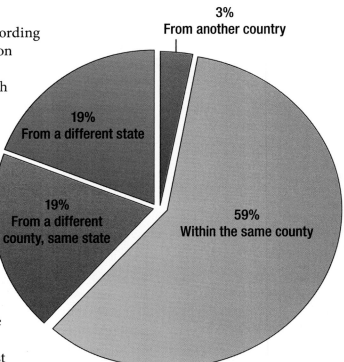

▲ **Percent Distribution of Movers by Type of Move: March 2002 to 2003 (Source: U.S. Census Bureau)**

---

residence, where they live
county, large area of land within a state

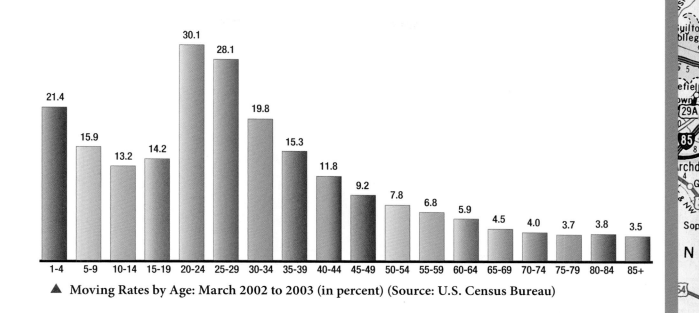

▲ Moving Rates by Age: March 2002 to 2003 (in percent) (Source: U.S. Census Bureau)

Moving rates vary according to such factors as age, marital status, property ownership, and income. The bar graph above shows that in 2002–2003, about 30 percent of twenty- to twenty-nine-year-olds moved, but less than 5 percent of people ages sixty-five to eighty-four moved. Younger people may have moved more often because they got married or because of new jobs. Single people and divorced people moved more often than married people. Widowed people moved least often, possibly because widowed people tend to be older. Over 30 percent of all renters moved in 2002–2003, compared with about 7 percent of homeowners. Finally, lower-income groups were more likely to move than higher-income groups.

---

marital status, state of being married or unmarried

BEFORE YOU GO ON

1 How many Americans changed residence between March 2002 and March 2003?

2 How far did most of them move?

On Your Own
How do you feel about moving? Explain.

103

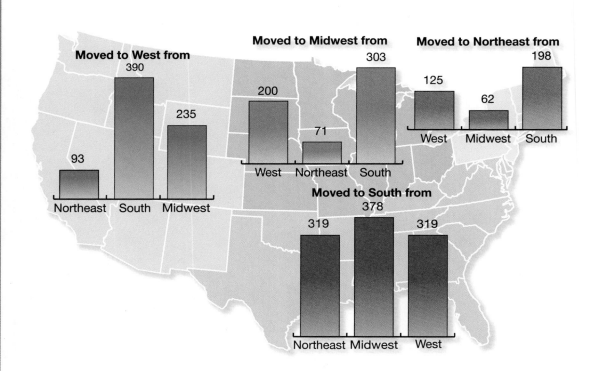

Moved to West from

- Northeast: 93
- South: 390
- Midwest: 235

Moved to Midwest from

- West: 200
- Northeast: 71
- South: 303

Moved to Northeast from

- West: 125
- Midwest: 62
- South: 198

Moved to South from

- Northeast: 319
- Midwest: 378
- West: 319

▲ **Region-to-Region Migration: March 2002 to 2003 (in thousands) (Source: U.S. Census Bureau)**

Moves to different regions in the United States have changed the country's population distribution. Look at the graphs above. As was true throughout the 1990s, more people moved from the Northeast to the South than from the South to the Northeast in 2002–2003. In general, more people moved *from* the Northeast than *to* the Northeast. The number of people moving into and out of urban and rural areas remained about the same.

What will the future population distribution of the United States look like? If today's trends continue, more people may be moving to the South. In addition, the new residents there may be younger than those moving to the South today. The Northeast may become less populated, and more Southerners may migrate to the less densely populated areas of the West and Midwest.

BEFORE YOU GO ON

1 How did the country's population distribution change during 2002–2003?

2 What do these trends suggest for the future?

On Your Own
In what ways has your home city or town changed over the last few years?

August 2, 2009

Dear Tiffany,

I'm sorry it's taken me so long to write, but I've been really busy since the move. Things in Florida are so different from what I'm used to—I have a feeling I'm more of a Pennsylvania person. I'm still adjusting.

How quickly the time has passed! We've been here a whole year. Yet we still have boxes to unpack. Remember when I told you I was worried about moving to Florida? Well, we arrived in the summer, and the weather here reminded me of summer in Japan, which was comforting. However, as time passed, I realized that Florida's weather changes very little. During winter break, I felt strange listening to the radio playing holiday songs and then looking out the window to see people walking in short sleeves and flip-flops. You know how much I love wearing winter clothes. I adore the warm, comfy feeling I get whenever I bundle up to brave the Pennsylvania winter. Even though I knew Florida's winters were much warmer than Pennsylvania's, I still hoped to recapture that feeling I craved so much. I won't need my warm clothes here.

I know you are jealous of how sunny Florida is, but it rarely changes. It is always sunny. I was overwhelmed by the constant sunshine at first. I hoped I would get used to it. I was doing fairly well until I visited Pennsylvania in March. As soon as I arrived, I recognized another important element I was missing: the dead sky. The opaque, slate-gray space edged with thin, wispy clouds is nowhere to be seen in Florida. The sky here is always a beautiful, crisp blue without a cloud in sight. Whenever I look up into the sky, I sigh, wishing for a sight more realistic and less cheery.

I miss you, and I hope to hear from you soon.

Your friend always,

Reina

Review and Practice

COMPREHENSION
Workbook Page 51

Right There

1. Which Americans move the least often?
2. Which Americans move the most often?

Think and Search

3. What factors contribute to single people moving more often?
4. What factor may contribute to widowed people moving less often?

Author and You

5. Who would be more likely to move, a thirty-year-old single person who rents an apartment or an eighty-year-old widow who owns a house? Why?
6. What reasons can you think of to explain why people are moving away from the Northeast?

On Your Own

7. What are some positive points about moving? What are some negative points?
8. If you could move anywhere, would you choose an urban or a rural area? Why?

▲ A census taker interviews a woman.

IN YOUR OWN WORDS

Tell a partner some facts you learned about migration patterns in the United States. Before you begin speaking, you may wish to write sentences using any or all of the words and phrases below.

densely populated	percent	single people
factors	population distribution	trends
homeowners	regions	urban areas
married people	renters	widowed people
moving rate	rural areas	younger people

🔊 *Speaking* TIP

You may wish to use the graphs in this reading to help explain the main ideas presented in the text.

DISCUSSION

Listening TIP

If you have a question, wait until the speaker has finished speaking before asking it.

Discuss in pairs or small groups.

- The world's population continues to grow. How do you think the increase in population will affect the population distribution across the globe?

- **How are growth and change related?** How does moving change a person's life? In what ways does moving force a person to grow?

READ FOR FLUENCY

When we read aloud to communicate meaning, we group words into phrases, pause or slow down to make important points, and emphasize important words. Pause for a short time when you reach a comma and for a longer time when you reach a period. Pay attention to rising and falling intonation at the end of sentences.

Work with a partner. Choose a paragraph from the reading. Discuss which words seem important for communicating meaning. Practice pronouncing difficult words. Give each other feedback.

EXTENSION  Workbook Page 51

Imagine that you and your family have moved. Write a postcard to a friend telling him or her about your new home. How is it different from your old home? What do you like or dislike about it? Share your postcard with a partner.

Grammar and Writing

GRAMMAR, USAGE, AND MECHANICS

Simple Past and Present Perfect

The simple past is used to show that an action began and ended at a definite time in the past. The simple past is usually formed by adding -d or -ed to the base form of the verb. Form the negative with *didn't* + the base form of the verb.

The present perfect is used to show that an action began in the past but ended at an indefinite time. Form the present perfect with *have* or *has* + the past participle. Form the negative with *haven't* or *hasn't*.

Verb	Simple Past	Present Perfect
travel	She **traveled** a long way yesterday.	She **has traveled** all over the world.

The present perfect is also used to show that an action began in the past and continues into the present.

Verb	Simple Past	Present Perfect
work	My father **worked** late last night.	My father **has worked** there for a long time.

Many verbs are irregular in the simple past and the present perfect.

Verb	Simple Past	Present Perfect
come	They **came** from another state.	They **have come** to visit for two weeks.

Practice
Workbook Page 52

Copy the paragraph below into your notebook. Complete the paragraph with the simple past or the present perfect of the verb in parentheses.

I _____ (*move*) from Taiwan in 2002 because my father _____ (*get*) a new job. We _____ (*live*) in San Diego since then. At first it _____ (*be*) difficult, but after I _____ (*get*) acquainted with my new city, it _____ (*become*) easier. Our family _____ (*buy*) a house last year, and I _____ (*transfer*) to a new school. I _____ (*make*) many new friends, but my best friend is Allison. We _____ (*spend*) a lot of time together. Last year I _____ (*go*) on vacation with her family.

108

WRITING A NARRATIVE PARAGRAPH
Write a Personal Letter

Good writers know how to put their personality into their writing, giving their work a distinctive voice. Their work sounds like them. Putting more of yourself into your writing will give it your distinctive voice.

On this page you will write a narrative paragraph in the form of a personal letter. This letter will be to a friend or a family member, so you can be yourself and use informal language. As you write, think about how you speak. This will help give your writing voice.

Here is a model of a personal letter by a student named Adrian Perez. Adrian listed details about himself in a word web.

September 21, 2009

Dear Alex,

How's it going, buddy? Man, everything is so different here. I have no friends and no dog. We had to give him away. I feel so lonely every time I go inside my house. I've been thinking about all those good times we had, playing soccer during lunch, and practicing martial arts in the afternoon. Lunch here is so boring—we just get our food and sit. However, I met a kid named Ricardo who is like you—he likes to play soccer. I've started practicing with him to get in shape for try-outs. I really want to make the team so I can keep busy and stop thinking about all the things I miss. I think Ricardo is going to try out with me. I'll be glad to have someone to partner-up with at practice. Well, enough about me. My parents wanted to know if you'd be able to come for a visit. I hope so.

Take care,
Adrian

Practice

Write a personal letter to a friend or a family member. Tell a story about an experience you had. For example, you might tell about something that happened when you moved to a new home or began attending a new school. List your ideas in a word web like the one above. Be sure to use the simple past and present perfect correctly.

VOICE:
☑ I put my personality into my writing.

CONVENTIONS:
☑ I used the simple past and present perfect correctly.

Prepare to Read

What You Will Learn

Reading

- Vocabulary building: *Literary terms, dictionary terms, word study*

- Reading strategy: *Make inferences*

- Text type: *Literature (short story)*

Grammar, Usage, and Mechanics
Have to + verb

Writing
Write a personal narrative

THE BIG QUESTION

How are growth and change related? Have you ever felt embarrassed by someone you love? What happened? Did you learn from the experience? Did the experience change you in any way? Discuss with a partner.

BUILD BACKGROUND

This reading is a short story called **"Abuela Invents the Zero."** It is about a girl named Connie who is embarrassed by her grandmother. Born in the United States, Connie has lived in New Jersey all her life. Connie's grandmother was born in Puerto Rico and is visiting the United States for the first time. Because her parents insist, Connie takes her grandmother to church and learns an important lesson as a result.

Learn Literary Words

Characterization is the creation and development of a character in a story. Writers sometimes show what a character is like by describing what the character thinks and does.

Literary Words

characterization
dialogue

> Felicia usually called her grandmother every Sunday, but this time she didn't feel like getting up to find her cell phone. Felicia knew that her grandmother would be hurt, but she was too tired to care.

Writers use **dialogue**, or a conversation between two or more characters, to show through their spoken words how the characters feel. In short stories, dialogue usually appears between quotation marks (" ") to indicate a speaker's exact words.

> "Why didn't you call me as soon as you knew you were going to be late?" asked Felicia's grandmother, angrily.
> "I would have, Grandma, but I couldn't find the phone, and then I fell asleep," answered Felicia.
> "Asleep? Why is a girl your age falling asleep in the middle of the day?" retorted Felicia's grandmother.

Practice

Copy the paragraph below into your notebook. With a partner, write a few lines of dialogue to show what the narrator and her cousin are like. Remember to put each speaker's words inside quotation marks.

> I was on a train to Florida to visit my cousin Maria. I was very excited about the trip. I hadn't seen Maria for five years. Maria was beautiful and popular, and she always wore the coolest clothes. When I arrived at the station, I saw her right away. She was standing in the parking lot next to a shiny new convertible.

Learn Academic Words

Study the **red** words and their meanings. You will find these words useful when talking and writing about literature. Write each word and its meaning in your notebook. After you read "Abuela Invents the Zero," try to use these words to respond to the text.

Academic Words

conduct
ignore
instruct
reluctance

conduct = the way someone behaves	➡	The little girl's good **conduct** made her parents feel proud.
ignore = pay no attention to someone or something	➡	They turned their heads away so as to **ignore** the bully's threat.
instruct = officially tell someone what to do or how to do something	➡	A teacher's job is to **instruct** his or her students.
reluctance = unwillingness to do something	➡	His unhappy face showed his **reluctance** to help his mother.

Practice

Workbook
Page 55

Work with a partner to answer these questions. Try to include the **red** word in your answer. Write the sentences in your notebook.

1. Have you ever been ashamed of your own **conduct**?

2. When is it a good idea to **ignore** a person or a situation?

3. Who will **instruct** you about applying for a job?

4. When have you shown **reluctance** to do something?

Word Study: Idioms

An idiom is a group of words with a special meaning that is different from the ordinary meaning of each separate word. Sometimes you can figure out what an idiom means from the context of the sentence. Other times, you may have to look in a dictionary. When you look up an idiom in the dictionary, look under the first noun found in the idiom. If you can't find it there, or if there is no noun, look under the main word in the idiom. For example, you will find the idiom *come down with* under the verb *come*.

Idiom	Meaning
night and day	"all the time"
come down with	"become ill with"
beat somebody to something	"get to or do something before someone"

Practice
Workbook
Page 56

Work with a partner. Look in the reading for each of the idioms in the box below. Try to figure out the meaning of the idiom using the context of the sentence. Then look up the idioms in a dictionary. In your notebook, write the idiom and its meaning. Finally, write a sentence for each idiom.

at the top of her voice	end up	I'm out of here	no way
changes his mind	getting myself into	makes a big deal	she means business

READING STRATEGY   **MAKE INFERENCES**

Making inferences helps you figure out information that the author hasn't given directly. When you make inferences, or infer, you are "reading between the lines." To make inferences, follow these steps as you read:

- Pay close attention to how the author describes the characters, the events, and the setting. What has the author hinted at but not said?

- Think about your own experiences. Do they help you understand the situation that you are reading about?

- Now use the information in the text and your own experiences to make inferences.

As you read "Abuela Invents the Zero," think about what the author is conveying but not saying directly. What inferences can you make?

Workbook
Page 57

113

Set a purpose for reading Read the story to find out how a person can learn an important lesson from someone older and wiser. What lesson does Connie learn?

Abuela Invents the Zero

Judith Ortiz Cofer

"You made me feel like a zero, like a nothing," she says in Spanish, *un cero, nada*. She is trembling, an angry little old woman lost in a heavy winter coat that belongs to my mother. And I end up being sent to my room, like I was a child, to think about my grandmother's idea of math.

It all began with Abuela coming up from the Island for a visit—her first time in the United States. My mother and father paid her way here so that she wouldn't die without seeing snow, though if you asked me, and nobody has, the dirty slush in this city is not worth the price of a ticket. But I guess she deserves some kind of award for having had ten kids and survived to tell about it. My mother is the youngest of the bunch. Right up to the time when we're supposed to pick up the old lady at the airport, my mother is telling me stories about how hard times were for la familia on la isla, and how *la abuela* worked night and day to support them after their father died of a heart attack. I'd die of a heart attack too if I had a troop like that to support. Anyway, I had seen her only three or four times in my entire life, whenever we would go for somebody's funeral. I was born here and I have lived in this building all my life. But when Mami says, "Connie, please be nice to Abuela. She doesn't have too many years left. Do you promise me, Constancia?"—when she uses my full name, I know she means business. So I say, "Sure." Why wouldn't I be nice? I'm not a monster, after all.

So we go to Kennedy to get la abuela and she is the last to come out of the airplane, on the arm of the cabin attendant, all wrapped up in a black shawl. He hands her over to my parents like she was a package sent airmail. It is January, two feet of snow on the ground, and she's wearing a shawl over a thin black dress. That's just the start.

---

slush, partly melted snow
Kennedy, John F. Kennedy International Airport in New York

114

Once home, she refuses to let my mother buy her a coat because it's a waste of money for the two weeks she'll be in *el Polo Norte*, as she calls New Jersey, the North Pole. So since she's only four feet eleven inches tall, she walks around in my mother's big black coat looking ridiculous. I try to walk far behind them in public so that no one will think we're together. I plan to stay very busy the whole time she's with us so that I won't be asked to take her anywhere, but my plan is ruined when my mother comes down with the flu and Abuela absolutely *has* to attend Sunday mass or her soul will be eternally damned. She's more Catholic than the Pope. My father decides that he should stay home with my mother and that I should escort la abuela to church. He tells me this on Saturday night as I'm getting ready to go out to the mall with my friends.

"No way," I say.

---

ridiculous, silly
escort, go with

✔ **LITERARY CHECK**
What examples of **characterization** *can you identify in this paragraph?*

BEFORE YOU GO ON

1 Why does Connie walk far behind her grandmother?

2 What does Connie's father ask her to do?

On Your Own
Did you ever have to spend time with a relative against your will? Explain.

115

I go for the car keys on the kitchen table: he usually leaves them there for me on Friday and Saturday nights. He beats me to them.

"No way," he says, pocketing them and grinning at me.

Needless to say, we come to a compromise very quickly. I do have a responsibility to Sandra and Anita, who don't drive yet. There is a Harley-Davidson fashion show at Brookline Square that we *cannot* miss.

"The mass in Spanish is at ten sharp tomorrow morning, entiendes?" My father is dangling the car keys in front of my nose and pulling them back when I try to reach for them. He's really enjoying himself.

"I understand. Ten o'clock. I'm out of here." I pry his fingers off the key ring. He knows that I'm late, so he makes it just a little difficult. Then he laughs. I run out of our apartment before he changes his mind. I have no idea what I'm getting myself into.

Sunday morning I have to walk two blocks on dirty snow to retrieve the car. I warm it up for Abuela as instructed by my parents, and drive it to the front of our building. My father walks her by the hand in baby steps on the slippery snow. The sight of her little head with a bun on top of it sticking out of that huge coat makes me want to run back into my room and get under the covers. I just hope that nobody I know sees us together. I'm dreaming, of course. The mass is packed with people from our block. It's a holy day of obligation and everyone I ever met is there.

I have to help her climb the steps, and she stops to take a deep breath after each one, then I lead her down the aisle so that everybody can see me with my bizarre grandmother. If I were a good Catholic, I'm sure I'd get some purgatory time taken off for my sacrifice. She is walking as slow as Captain Cousteau exploring the bottom of the sea, looking around, taking her sweet time. Finally she chooses a pew, but she wants to sit in the *other* end. It's like she had a spot picked out for some unknown reason, and although it's the most inconvenient seat in the house, that's where she has to sit. So we squeeze by all the people already sitting there, saying, "Excuse me, please, *con permiso*, pardon me," getting annoyed looks the whole way. By the time we settle in, I'm drenched in sweat. I keep my head down like I'm praying so as not to see or be seen. She is praying loud, in Spanish, and singing hymns at the top of her creaky voice.

I ignore her when she gets up with a hundred other people to go take communion. I'm actually praying hard now—that this will all be over soon.

✔ LITERARY CHECK

*How does the author use **dialogue** to help develop Connie's character?*

---

retrieve, pick up

holy day of obligation, day when Catholics are obliged to, or must, go to church

bizarre, very strange

purgatory, according to the Catholic faith, a place where the souls of dead people go before entering heaven

communion, part of the mass in which people go up to the altar to eat a small piece of bread that is a sign of Jesus Christ's body

But the next time I look up, I see a black coat dragging around and around the church, stopping here and there so a little gray head can peek out like a periscope on a submarine. There are giggles in the church, and even the priest has frozen in the middle of a blessing, his hands above his head like he is about to lead the congregation in a set of jumping jacks.

I realize to my horror that my grandmother is lost. She can't find her way back to the pew. I am so embarrassed that even though the woman next to me is shooting daggers at me with her eyes, I just can't move to go get her. I put my hands over my face like I'm praying, but it's really to hide my burning cheeks. I would like for her to disappear. I just know that on Monday my friends, and my enemies, in the barrio will have a lot of senile-grandmother jokes to tell in front of me. I am frozen to my seat. So the same woman who wants me dead on the spot does it for me. She makes a big deal out of getting up and hurrying to get Abuela.

---

periscope, tube with mirrors inside it, used to look over the top of something
shooting daggers, shooting fierce looks
barrio, part of an American city where Spanish-speaking people live
senile, mentally confused or behaving strangely because of old age

BEFORE YOU GO ON

1 What happens to Abuela in church?

2 Why doesn't Connie get up to help her grandmother?

On Your Own
Do you feel sympathetic to Connie? Why or why not?

117

The rest of the mass is a blur. All I know is that my grandmother kneels the whole time with her hands over *her* face. She doesn't speak to me on the way home, and she doesn't let me help her walk, even though she almost falls a couple of times.

When we get to the apartment, my parents are at the kitchen table, where my mother is trying to eat some soup. They can see right away that something is wrong. Then Abuela points her finger at me like a judge passing a sentence on a criminal. She says in Spanish, "You made me feel like a zero, like a nothing." Then she goes to her room.

I try to explain what happened. "I don't understand why she's so upset. She just got lost and wandered around for a while," I tell them. But it sounds lame, even to my own ears. My mother gives me a look that makes me cringe and goes in to Abuela's room to get her version of the story. She comes out with tears in her eyes.

"Your grandmother says to tell you that of all the hurtful things you can do to a person, the worst is to make them feel as if they are worth nothing."

I can feel myself shrinking right there in front of her. But I can't bring myself to tell my mother that I think I understand how I made Abuela feel. I might be sent into the old lady's room to apologize, and it's not easy to admit you've been a jerk—at least, not right away with everybody watching. So I just sit there not saying anything.

My mother looks at me for a long time, like she feels sorry for me. Then she says, "You should know, Constancia, that if it wasn't for this old woman whose existence you don't seem to value, you and I would not be here."

That's when *I'm* sent to *my* room to consider a number I hadn't thought much about—until today.

---

cringe, move back or away from something because it pains you
jerk, person who does things that annoy or hurt other people
existence, state of being alive

ABOUT THE **AUTHOR**

Judith Ortiz Cofer is an accomplished author of poetry, short stories, and novels for young adults. Born in Puerto Rico in 1952, she and her family moved to New Jersey when she was a girl. Cofer's work has won many awards. *An Island Like You* was named Best Book of the Year by the American Library Association in 1995. *The Meaning of Consuelo* won the America's Award for Children's and Young Adult Literature in 2003. In addition to writing, Cofer teaches English and Creative Writing at the University of Georgia.

BEFORE YOU GO ON

1 Why is Abuela hurt and angry?

2 How does Connie feel about what she did?

On Your Own
Did you ever learn a painful lesson growing up? Explain.

119

READER'S THEATER

Act out the following scene between Connie and her father.

Connie: May I have the keys, Dad? I'm going out.

Father: Not so fast! [*holds the keys above his head*] I'll let you go under one condition.

Connie: [*sighs*] Hurry, Dad, *please*. My friends are waiting for me.

Father: You can go with your friends now, but you must take your grandmother to mass tomorrow. No excuses. Mass begins at 10:00 A.M. sharp.

Connie: But Dad!

Father: No "buts," Connie. You will do this for your family.

Connie: Okay, fine. I'll do it. Now please give me the keys. I don't want to miss the fashion show!

COMPREHENSION Workbook Page 58

Right There

1. How many times had Connie seen Abuela before this visit?

2. What makes Abuela look ridiculous to Connie?

Think and Search

3. What is Connie afraid will happen on Monday?

4. Why doesn't Abuela speak to Connie on the way home from church?

Author and You

5. How do you think the author feels about Connie's conduct?

6. The barrio is a small community. What effect does that have on Connie?

On Your Own

7. Do you worry about what your neighbors will say about you and your family? Why or why not?

8. Has anyone ever made you feel like a zero? Explain.

DISCUSSION

Discuss in pairs or small groups.

1. Do you think Connie and Abuela do not understand each other because of a difference in age and culture? Explain.

2. What could Connie have done to make Abuela feel welcome?

3. What lesson did Abuela teach Connie?

Q How are growth and change related? Do you identify with Connie's embarrassment or do you think she was being selfish? How do you think she will change as a result of her experience with Abuela?

RESPONSE to LITERATURE

Workbook
Page 58

How are senior citizens treated in your home culture? How are they treated in other cultures? Do research at the library or on the Internet to find information about how a culture other than your own treats elderly people. Write a paragraph summarizing your findings. You may wish to work with your classmates to publish your paragraphs in a class book.

Grammar and Writing

Have to + Verb

Use the phrase *have to* plus the base form of a verb to express necessity or lack of necessity. The present of *have to* is *have to/has to*. The past of *have to* is *had to*. To form the negative of *have to*, use *don't/doesn't have to* in the present and *didn't have to* in the past. Notice that the verb *have* does not change in the negative.

Sentence	Meaning
I **have to be** polite to my grandmother.	It is necessary that I be polite to my grandmother.
She **has to go** to church on Sunday.	It is necessary that she go to church on Sunday.
I **don't have to help** her put on her coat.	It is not necessary that I help her put on her coat.
She **had to go** to her room.	It was necessary that she go to her room.
She **did not have to stay**.	It was not necessary that she stay.

Practice

Workbook Page 59

Copy the chart below into your notebook. Complete the chart with things you have to do and things you don't have to do. A sample sentence has been filled in for you. Compare your chart with a partner's. Then put each sentence in the past using *had to*.

Positive or Negative	Sentence
negative	Example: *On Saturdays, I don't have to get up early.*
positive	Every morning,
negative	On weekends,
positive	After dinner,
negative	During the summer,
positive	At night,

122

WRITING A NARRATIVE PARAGRAPH

Write a Personal Narrative

A personal narrative is a story in which you are the narrator and main character. In a personal narrative, you tell about an event or an experience that was meaningful to you. The event or experience you tell about usually involves one or more other characters. In the story you just read, the characters Connie and Abuela seemed real because the author described them skillfully. The author also included dialogue, letting us know what the characters say to each other. Dialogue is important in a story because it helps develop the characters as it moves along the plot.

Who was there	What happened	What was said

Here is a model of a personal narrative that includes dialogue. Before writing, the writer listed her ideas in a three-column chart.

Andrea Vargas

Rainy River Day

We'd had everything ready since Friday, but when we woke up on Saturday, it was raining. My relatives were supposed to meet us at Grandpa's, and from there we'd go to the river together. When we got to Grandpa's, everyone was asleep. My parents woke up my relatives by announcing, "We are not going to let an aguasero ruin our trip!" While everyone was getting ready, the sun came out. We walked down a big mountain to get to the river. We swam, played ball, and slept on the gigantic rocks. For lunch, we made Sancocho de Pollo in a huge pot. We cooked it over a campfire. After we ate and swam some more, we were about to head home when it started raining again. It was a huge aguasero. On the way out we had to climb up the mountain. But this time there was a lot of mud, and it was very slippery. My dad held onto my arm, and I had to walk on the edge of the river. It was a great day.

Practice

Workbook Page 60

Write a personal narrative. You might write a paragraph about a memorable experience you had with a family member or an adventure you had with a friend. List your ideas in a three-column chart like the one above. Be sure to use *have to* + verb correctly.

Writing Checklist

IDEAS:
☑ I included dialogue.

VOICE:
☑ I tried to sound like myself.

123

Link the Readings

Critical Thinking

Look back at the readings in this unit. Think about what they have in common. They all tell about growth and change. Yet they do not all have the same purpose. The purpose of one reading might be to inform, while the purpose of another might be to entertain or persuade. In addition, the content of each reading relates to growth and change differently. Now copy the chart below into your notebook and complete it.

Title of Reading	Purpose	Big Question Link
"How Seeds and Plants Grow" "Two Brothers and the Pumpkin Seeds"		
From *Roll of Thunder, Hear My Cry*		
"Migration Patterns"	*to inform*	
"Abuela Invents the Zero"		*Connie learns a lesson.*

Discussion

Discuss in pairs or small groups.

- Compare the story "Abuela Invents the Zero" with the excerpt from *Roll of Thunder, Hear My Cry*. How are the lessons Connie and Cassie learn similar? How are they different?

- **How are growth and change related?** Think about the meanings of the words *change* and *grow*. How are these meanings expressed in each of the readings?

Fluency Check

Work with a partner. Choose a paragraph from one of the readings. Take turns reading it for one minute. Count the total number of words you read. Practice saying the words you had trouble reading. Take turns reading the paragraph three more times. Did you read more words each time? Copy the chart below into your notebook and record your speeds.

	1st Speed	2nd Speed	3rd Speed	4th Speed
Words Per Minute				

Projects

Work in pairs or small groups. Choose one of these projects.

1 What plants grow in your city or town? Choose a plant that is commonly found where you live and write a story about it. Read your story aloud to the class.

2 Do research to learn about migration patterns in your city or town. Make a bar graph or a pie chart with the information you find. Display your graph or chart and explain your findings to your classmates.

3 What do you think will happen when Cassie and Little Man get home from school? Write a short dialogue that occurs when they tell their mother what happened with Miss Crocker.

4 Do research at the library or on the Internet to learn how to grow a plant. Buy a packet of seeds and follow the instructions on the packet. As the plant grows, create a photo-essay of the different stages. Display your work for the class.

Further Reading

To find out more about the theme of this unit, choose from these reading suggestions.

Martin Luther King, Coleen Degnan-Veness
This Penguin Reader® tells the amazing story of Dr. King's nonviolent struggle for racial equality and its powerful impact.

Her Life in Pictures (Helen Keller), George Sullivan
Helen Keller's journey from being sight- and hearing-impaired to becoming a college-educated woman and social activist is an inspiring example of growth, change, and determination.

Where the Red Fern Grows, Wilson Rawls
Billy and his coonhound pups win the coveted gold cup in the annual coon-hunt contest. But when triumph turns to tragedy, Billy learns the beautiful Native American legend of the sacred red fern.

Put It All Together

LISTENING & SPEAKING WORKSHOP

Skit

You will write and perform a skit that tells a story.

1 **THINK ABOUT IT** Work in small groups. Review the elements of a story by listing the people, places, and events described in "Abuela Invents the Zero." Who are the characters? What is the setting? What events make up the plot?

Think of a story that your group could present as a skit, or short play. You may create your own story, choose one from this book, or use a familiar fairy tale or fable.

2 **GATHER AND ORGANIZE INFORMATION** Discuss your story. Make a list of the characters, and write down key details about the characters, setting, and plot.

Order Your Notes Make a story map to help you organize your ideas.

Characters Who?	Setting Where and when?
Problem What conflict does the plot grow out of?	Solution How does the conflict get resolved?

Prepare a Script Decide who will play each character. Then use your notes and story map to write a script. The dialogue should look like this:

Chang: What are you doing with that bird?
Kim: I'm wrapping up its leg so that it will heal correctly.
Chang: Silly fool! That won't get you anywhere.

Include important details about the setting, props, and action:

Kim carefully binds swallow's leg and carries the bird into the house. Time passes as the bird's leg heals. Then Kim sets the bird free.

Use Visuals Make or find the costumes and props you need for your skit.

3 **PRACTICE AND PRESENT** As a group, practice your skit until you can perform it without looking at the script. If possible, ask a friend or family member to serve as *prompter* while you practice. (A prompter watches the skit and follows along in the script. If someone forgets what to say or do, the prompter quietly reminds him or her.) Practice using your props and wearing your costumes.

Perform Your Skit Face the audience and speak loudly and clearly, even when your body is pointing in another direction. Pay attention to the other actors, and be ready when it's your turn to speak or move!

4 **EVALUATE THE PRESENTATION**
A good way to improve your speaking and listening skills is to evaluate each presentation you give and hear. When you evaluate yourself, think about what you did well and what you can do better. Use this checklist to help you judge your group's skit and the skits of your classmates.

☑ Could you understand the story?

☑ Did the actors know their parts well?

☑ Were the costumes and props helpful and appropriate?

☑ Could you hear and understand the actors' words?

☑ What suggestions do you have for improving the skit?

WRITING WORKSHOP

Fictional Narrative

A fictional narrative is a story invented by the writer. Both novels and short stories are fictional narratives. The events that make up the plot of a fictional narrative are usually told in sequence and focus on a conflict or problem. In the beginning of the story, the problem is introduced. The problem is developed in the middle of the story and is resolved by the end. Fictional narratives also occur in a specific time and place, called the setting. Another characteristic of fictional narratives is dialogue, or the words characters say to one another. Dialogue helps bring the characters to life.

Your assignment for this workshop is to write a fictional narrative that includes two or more characters, a plot, a setting, and dialogue.

1 **PREWRITE** Think about stories you have read and liked. What did you most enjoy? Were the characters amusing? Was the plot mysterious? Was the setting vivid? Then brainstorm a list of characters for your story in your notebook. Also, think about the point of view from which your narrative will be told. From whose perspective will readers see events?

List and Organize Ideas and Details Use a story chart to organize ideas for your fictional narrative. A student named Micah decided to write a story about a musical squirrel named Sammy. Here is his story chart:

Characters Who? Sammy Squirrel Robins and forest friends	Setting Where and when? Forest
Problem What conflict does the plot grow out of? Nobody will let Sammy sing!	Solution How does the conflict get resolved? Sammy finds a new way to make music.

2 **DRAFT** Use the model on page 131 and your story chart to help you write a first draft. Remember to tell events in chronological order. Include dialogue to help reveal what your characters are thinking and feeling.

3 **REVISE** Read over your draft. As you do so, ask yourself the questions in the writing checklist. Use the questions to help you revise your fictional narrative.

SIX TRAITS OF WRITING CHECKLIST

☑ **IDEAS:** Is my plot original and interesting?

☑ **ORGANIZATION:** Are events presented in sequence?

☑ **VOICE:** Does my writing express my personality?

☑ **WORD CHOICE:** Does the dialogue suit my characters?

☑ **SENTENCE FLUENCY:** Do my sentences vary in length and type?

☑ **CONVENTIONS:** Does my writing follow the rules of grammar, usage, and mechanics?

Here are the changes Micah plans to make when he revises his first draft:

The Squeaky Squirrel Sings

Hi there! The name's Sammy—
~~My name is~~ Sammy Squirrel. I live in the forest, and there's always

plenty to do here. My favorit*e* activity use*d* to be listening to the Robins

sing. Whenever they sang, every body gathered around to listen.

One day, I decided to to sing along. Unfortunately, I have a *squeaky* voice

that isn't so pleasing to the ear. As I sang along, the crowd turned

toward me in disgust.

You have to stop!
"Hey!" shouted one of the Robins. "This concert is for animals with

fine singing voices, not squeaky screeches!"

wiped away a tear and
The crowd began to laugh. I quickly ran away. For a while I

wondered around the forest alone. [a] Finally, I met some new friends—Wilson Woodpecker, Tommy Turtle, and Ricky Rattler. Wilson's large beak prevents him from singing; Tommy is too slow and lazy to sing; and Ricky can only hiss. ~~They can't sing either.~~

One afternoon, as I was climbing down a tree, I accidentally dropped an acorn ~~and~~ that hit Tommy's shell. Shocked by the impact, Tommy ~~shouted.~~ yelped. Shocked by Tommy's ~~shout,~~ yelp, Ricky rattled his tail, while Wilson tapped his beak against a branch.

"Hold on! I shouted, "Did you here what we just did?"

"What? All we did was drop acorns, rattle tails, and peck trees," said Wilson.

"Exactly!" I declared. "If we come up with the right arrangement, these thumps and pecks will turn into a fabulous rhythm!" Excited about this new discovery, we began to work. We created a great beat! Before long, All the animals of the forest began to stop by to listen to us. Soon, the Robins invited us to join them in a concert. Combined with the Robin's singing, our strong beat has led to a new kind of music that ~~could~~ involves the whole forest, whether good singers or not. And that's how this squeaky squirrel helped bring music into ~~the~~ our forest world!

4 EDIT AND PROOFREAD 📖 Workbook Page 61

Copy your revised draft onto a clean sheet of paper. Read it again. Correct any errors in grammar, word usage, mechanics, and spelling. Here are the additional changes Micah plans to make when he prepares his final draft.

Micah Cowher

The Squeaky Squirrel Sings

Hi, there! The name's Sammy—Sammy Squirrel. I live in the forest, and there's always plenty to do here. My favorite activity used to be listening to the Robins sing. Whenever they sang, every body gathered around to listen. One day, I decided to sing along. Unfortunately, I have a squeaky voice that isn't so pleasing to the ear. As I sang along, the crowd turned toward me in disgust.

"Hey! You have to stop!" shouted one of the Robins. "This concert is for animals with fine singing voices, not squeaky screeches!"

The crowd began to laugh. I wiped away a tear and quickly ran away. For a while, I wandered around the forest alone. Finally, I met some new friends—Wilson Woodpecker, Tommy Turtle, and Ricky Rattler. They can't sing either. Wilson's large beak prevents him from singing; Tommy is too slow and lazy to sing; and Ricky can only hiss.

One afternoon, as I was climbing down a tree, I accidentally dropped an acorn that hit Tommy's shell. Shocked by the impact, Tommy yelped. Shocked by Tommy's yelp, Ricky rattled his tail, while Wilson tapped his beak against a branch.

"Hold on!" I shouted, "Did you here what we just did?"

"What? All we did was drop acorns, rattle tails, and peck trees," said Wilson.

"Exactly!" I declared. "If we come up with the right arrangement, these thumps and pecks will turn into a fabulous rhythm!" Excited about this new discovery, we began to work. We created a great beat!

Before long, all the animals of the forest began to stop by to listen to us. Soon, the Robins invited us to join them in a concert. Combined with the Robin's singing, our strong beat has led to a new kind of music that involves the whole forest, whether good singers or not. And that's how this squeaky squirrel helped bring music into our forest world!

5 PUBLISH Prepare your final draft. Share your fictional narrative with your teacher and classmates.

Cycles of Nature

*A*rtists regularly explore our place in the natural world and the life cycles that we all experience before we die. No one goes through life without facing change and undergoing personal and physical growth on some level.

Thomas Hart Benton, *Wheat* (1967)

In Thomas Hart Benton's painting *Wheat*, neat rows of wheat fill the canvas. Ripe stalks of grain crowd the top part of the painting. The first two rows have been cut, but the artist paints green shoots on the bottom to show that the next crop is already on its way.

Benton often dealt with political issues in his work. He may have felt that the neat rows of grain symbolized the democratic masses of America. He chose an angle and a close-up view that brings the viewer in among the rows or "masses." The painting celebrates the natural cycle of crops and the bounty of the harvest in a very fertile land, the United States.

One broken stalk strays across the center of the painting. Benton managed to capture all three vital stages of life in one frame: infancy, mature adulthood, and death.

Thomas Hart Benton, ▶
Wheat, 1967, oil, 20 x 21 in.,
Smithsonian American Art Museum

Mary Vaux Walcott, *Untitled (Mixed Flowers)* (1876)

Mary Vaux Walcott, who specialized in painting wildflowers, spent as much time as possible outdoors. She often hiked deep into the wilderness so she could capture the fleeting beauty of various blossoms. She understood that flowers "withered quickly." She wanted to represent what they really looked like rather than paint them as fancier or more colorful than they really were. The Smithsonian American Art Museum has almost 800 of her detailed watercolors in its collection. Her art forms a permanent record of passing beauty.

▲ Mary Vaux Walcott, *Untitled (Mixed Flowers),* 1876, watercolor, 5⅛ x 2⅜ in., **Smithsonian American Art Museum**

Heikki Seppä, *Lupin Wedding Crown* (1982)

In *Lupin Wedding Crown*, Heikki Seppä uses a very different medium—silver and gold—to celebrate the natural world. The gold tip of the crown represents a sprig of lupine (alternate spelling), a plant that has tiny honeycomb-like flowers that symbolize abundance and fertility.

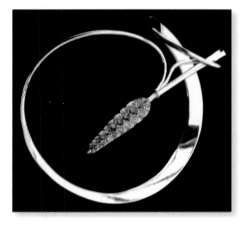

◄ Heikki Seppä, *Lupin Wedding Crown,* 1982, gold, silver, and diamond, 4 x 8 x 8 in., **Smithsonian American Art Museum**

The shape and name of the crown reflect Seppä's own roots in Finland, where he was born. There they have a wedding tradition called the Dance of Crowns. Unmarried bridesmaids circle the blindfolded bride, who then tries to place a gold crown on one of their heads. Whoever gets the crown is supposed to be the next one to marry.

All three artists tapped into natural imagery to capture or celebrate a stage of life. Every living thing on Earth is born, grows, and dies. In between these cycles lies many other layers of growth and change. Some are good and some are difficult. It's all part of the natural world.

Apply What You Learned

1 Which of these artworks do you think best captures the cycles of nature? Explain your answer.

2 If you were to create an artwork that shows the cycles of nature, what would it look like?

Big Question
In what way does each of these artworks reflect a different aspect of cycles in nature? Explain your answer.

Workbook Pages 63–64

How can we tell what's right?

THE BIG QUESTION

This unit is about right and wrong. You'll read about lessons that teach right from wrong. You'll learn why it is wrong to call Pluto a planet. You'll also learn how one woman fought for social rights by singing. Reading, writing, and talking about these topics will give you practice using academic language and help you become a better student.

READING 1: Fable
- "The Golden Serpent" by Walter Dean Myers

READING 2: Editorial
- "I ♥ Pluto" by Tim Kreider

READING 3: Novel Excerpt
- From *A Single Shard* by Linda Sue Park

READING 4: Social Studies Article
- "Marian Anderson: A Voice for Change"

Listening and Speaking

At the end of this unit, you will create and perform a **radio commercial**.

Writing

In this unit, you'll practice **persuasive writing**. Persuasive writing tries to persuade the reader. After each reading, you'll learn a skill to help you write a persuasive paragraph. At the end of the unit, you'll use the skills you've learned to write a speech.

QuickWrite

Write the words *Right* and *Wrong* at the top of a sheet of paper. List ideas and actions you believe to be right or wrong under the appropriate word.

Prepare to Read

THE BIG QUESTION

How can we tell what's right? Every culture has stories that teach you a lesson. Sometimes that lesson teaches how to tell right from wrong. For example, you may know this story, "The Fox and the Crow":

> A fox once saw a crow fly off with a piece of cheese in its beak and settle on the branch of a tree. "That's for me," said the fox, and walked up to the foot of the tree. "Good day, Mistress Crow," he cried. "How well you are looking today. How glossy your feathers are. If your voice is half as beautiful as those feathers, it would please my ears to hear you sing!" The crow lifted up her head and began to caw her best. But the moment she opened her mouth the piece of cheese fell to the ground, only to be snapped up by the fox. "That was all I wanted," said he. "In exchange for your cheese, I will give you this piece of advice: Do not trust flatterers."

Which stories from your own culture teach a lesson? In small groups, discuss the stories and the lessons they teach. Compare stories from your own culture with those from other cultures. In what ways are the lessons similar?

BUILD BACKGROUND

"The Golden Serpent" is a fable, or a brief story that teaches a lesson. From India, it is about a wise man who solves problems for the people in his village. Fables have been told in India for thousands of years. The oldest Indian fables have been gathered in a collection called *Panchatantra*.

▲ An illustration of the fable "The Fox and the Crow"

Learn Literary Words

A **moral** is a lesson taught in a literary work, especially a fable. It is a practical lesson about right and wrong ways to behave. Many fables have a stated moral that comes at the end of the story. In "The Fox and the Crow," the moral is the last sentence: *Do not trust flatterers.*

Motivation is the reason for a character's actions. Motivation results from a combination of the character's personality and the situation in which the character finds him- or herself. For example, in "The Fox and the Crow," the fox is motivated by hunger. The crow is motivated by her need for compliments.

Literary Words
moral
motivation

Practice
Workbook Page 65

Work with a partner. Read the fable below. What is the crow's motivation? What is the moral of the fable? Is the moral stated directly or left for the reader to figure out? Explain your answer.

A crow, near dead with thirst, came upon a pitcher of water. But when the crow tried to drink from the pitcher, he found that there was only a little bit of water in it. He could not reach his head down into the pitcher to get to the water, however hard he tried. At last the poor crow gave up in despair. Then suddenly he had an idea. He dropped a pebble into the pitcher. Then he dropped another pebble into the pitcher. Again and again he dropped pebble after pebble into the pitcher. At long last he saw the water mount up near him, and with a few more pebbles he was able to quench his thirst and save his life. And so the crow learned a valuable lesson: Little by little does the trick.

▲ *Aesop's Fable*, a painting by Lizzie Riches

Learn Academic Words

Study the **red** words and their meanings. You will find these words useful when talking and writing about literature. Write each word and its meaning in your notebook. After you read "The Golden Serpent," try to use these words to respond to the text.

consult = ask for advice from someone who might have the answer	➡	People from the village **consult** Pundabi, the wise man, when they have a problem and want his advice.
contrast = a large difference between people or things that are compared	➡	Visitors to the village can see the sharp **contrast** between how the rich and the poor people live.
creative = original and inventive	➡	Pundabi, the wise man, thinks of **creative** ways to solve problems.
reveal = make something known that was previously hidden or unseen	➡	Pundabi tries to **reveal** to the king how poor most people in his kingdom are.

The Indian philosopher Madhva ▶

Practice

Work with a partner to answer these questions. Try to include the **red** word in your answer. Write the sentences in your notebook.

1. Whom do you **consult** when you have a problem?
2. What **contrast** can you think of between city life and country life?
3. Do you think it's important for a person who solves problems to be **creative**? Why or why not?
4. Is it always wise to **reveal** the truth? Why or why not?

Word Study: Irregular Plurals

Most nouns in English can be made plural by adding *-s* or *-es*. There are also nouns that are irregular in the plural form. Nouns with irregular plural spellings must be memorized. Study the rules below:

Add *-es* to nouns that end with *-s, -z, -x, -sh,* and *-ch*. Add *-es* to some nouns that end with *-o.*

> The king filled his **glass** and several other **glasses** with punch.
> The villagers consider Pundabi a **hero**. Many stories are about **heroes**.

For nouns that end with a consonant + *-y*, change *-y* to *-i* and add *-es.*

> A **spy** was sent to look for clues. The king had many **spies**.

For nouns that end in *-f*, or *-fe*, change *-f* to *-v* and add *-es.*

> The king's **wife** lives in a castle, but the poor men's **wives** do not.

Some nouns don't change in the plural form: *deer, series,* and *sheep.*

Practice  Workbook Page 67

In your notebook, write the plural forms of these nouns: *search, mystery, loaf, potato,* and *cry.* Then write a sentence with each word.

READING STRATEGY | IDENTIFY PROBLEMS AND SOLUTIONS

Identifying problems and solutions helps you understand a text better. To identify problems and solutions, ask yourself these questions:

- What problem does the main character have?
- What would you do about the problem?
- There may be more than one solution to the problem. What do you think the main character will do?
- How does the main character solve his or her problem? Would you have done the same thing? Explain.

As you read "The Golden Serpent," ask yourself what problem Pundabi has. What does Pundabi do to solve his problem?

Workbook Page 68

Set a purpose for reading Read the fable to find out how Pundabi cleverly turns the king's mystery into a life lesson. What does Pundabi think is right?

The Golden Serpent

An Indian fable retold by Walter Dean Myers

There was once a very wise man. He lived on a high mountain and was called Pundabi. With him lived a young boy. The boy's name was Ali.

Each morning Ali would come down the mountain. He would sit in the shade of a fig tree. Many people would come to him. They brought him loaves of bread. In the bread were pieces of fine linen. There would be questions on the linen for the wise Pundabi to answer. They would be questions of life and death, or about the search for happiness.

Each evening Ali would climb the mountain and give the loaves of bread to Pundabi. Pundabi would answer all the questions. Then they would eat the bread.

Ali would take the answers down the mountain. He would give them to the waiting people. Pundabi and Ali lived well this way, and the people loved them dearly.

One day a tall shadow fell across Ali. It was the shadow of the king himself.

"Are you Ali?" the king asked.

"I am he," Ali answered.

"And you live with the wise man Pundabi?"

"That is so," Ali replied.

"And it is true that he is very wise?"

"Yes, it is true," said Ali.

"Then you must bring him to me," the king said.

So Ali went up the mountain. He told Pundabi of the king's request. Pundabi and Ali came down the mountain. They set out for the palace. They went past the river and through the marketplace. They went through the village. Finally they reached another high mountain.

On top of this mountain was the palace.

"I want you to solve a mystery for me." The king spoke from his high throne. "But first we must have lunch." He clapped his hands twice.

Five men brought in five trays of food. There was a tray for Pundabi. There was a tray for Ali. And three trays for the king.

"I am very rich," the king said. "I have much gold and many rubies. And you, Pundabi, are very wise. I can pay you very well."

"What is the mystery?" asked Pundabi.

"I do not know," said the king. "That is for you to discover!"

"But how can Pundabi solve a mystery"—Ali wrung his hands—"if there is none to solve?"

"If you are truly wise, Pundabi, it will be done. If you do not solve it, then you are a fraud. I will put you in jail where you belong."

---

wrung, rubbed or pressed together nervously

BEFORE YOU GO ON

1 What does the king want Pundabi to do?

2 Why is Ali afraid?

On Your Own
What question would you like to ask a wise man like Pundabi?

141

Ali was very afraid. He began to shake.

But Pundabi said, "Let us take a walk. Perhaps our eyes will speak to us."

So they began to walk. They walked by the river. They walked through the village. They stopped by the home of an old woman. They walked around the marketplace. Pundabi's eyes spoke to him.

Then Pundabi began to walk up the mountain toward the palace.

"We will surely go to jail," Ali said. "We cannot solve the mystery. We do not know what it is."

"But we do know what the mystery is." Pundabi spoke, a smile upon his face. "And perhaps we can solve it. Let us go and see the king."

"Have you solved the mystery yet?" the king asked.

"No," said Pundabi. "But we know what the mystery is! It is the mystery of the Golden Serpent."

"The Golden Serpent?" said the king.

"Yes," Pundabi said. "Where is your Golden Serpent?"

"I didn't know I had one," the king said.

"The thief must be very clever," Pundabi said.

"You must find it for me," said the king.

"Let us see," Pundabi said. "Someone must have taken it to sell. Let us go to the market."

So the king called his guards. And off they went to the market.

✔ **LITERARY CHECK**
*What is Pundabi's **motivation**? How is it different from the king's **motivation**?*

142

In the market they came upon a young boy. The boy was turning wood.

"Perhaps he has stolen the Golden Serpent." The king seized the boy by the arm.

"I have no Golden Serpent," the boy said. "I could not run away with it. My leg is bent from turning."

But the guards searched him well. They searched his blouse and the hay upon which he slept. They even looked at his bent leg.

"It is true," the guards said. "He has nothing. He can hardly walk."

Next they went to the village. They stopped at the house of a widow.

"We are searching for the Golden Serpent," said Pundabi, "which was stolen from the king."

"I do not have it," said the widow. "I have only this small cup of grain."

But the king did not trust her. So the guards searched her hut. They looked in the corners. They looked in the cupboard.

"It is true," said the guards. "She has nothing but this cup of grain."

"Let us go from this dismal place," the king said.

Outside they heard a strange cry. Three men walked together. They sang a sad song. The first had a stick. He swung it before him as he walked. The second walked behind the first. The third walked behind the second. Each had a hand on the other's shoulder.

"Perhaps," said Pundabi, "these are your thieves."

"These?" said the king. "Why, they cannot see!"

"How clever of them," said Pundabi.

So they stopped the three blind men and asked of the king's Golden Serpent.

"No," said the first. "I have only this stick for comfort."

"No," said the second. "I have only the few coins I am given."

"No," said the third. "I have but these two friends."

---

turning wood, spinning wood against a tool in order to shape it or carve designs in it

dismal, making you feel unhappy and hopeless

BEFORE YOU GO ON

1 Why do the king's guards search the young boy?

2 Why does the king want to leave the widow's hut?

On Your Own
What do you think the mystery of the Golden Serpent is?

143

But the king did not trust them. So the guards searched the three blind men.

"They have nothing," said the guards, "except a worm-eaten stick and a few coins. Nothing more."

"Let us return to the palace," the king said.

"But we have not found the Golden Serpent," Pundabi said.

"I no longer want it," the king said bitterly. "I will pay you and you can leave."

At the palace, the king had his counters pay Pundabi in gold coins.

"And what about your people?" Pundabi asked.

"My people?" asked the king.

"Yes. The crippled boy, the poor widow, and the blind beggars," said Ali.

"What about them, indeed!" said the king. "They did not find my Golden Serpent."

"Ah," said Pundabi, "I see. But I have solved your mystery. I know where the Golden Serpent is."

"You do?" said the king. "How splendid!"

"You must close your eyes and count slowly until you reach a hundred. But make sure you are alone so that no one can steal the Golden Serpent again. Then open your eyes. The Golden Serpent will be in your room."

144

The king closed his eyes and began to count slowly as Pundabi picked up his bag of gold and left the palace.

He went down the steep hill.

He gave some of the gold to the crippled boy.

He gave some to the widow.

He gave some to the blind beggars.

"Pundabi," said Ali. "You are both wise and generous. But there is still one problem."

"And what is that?" asked Pundabi.

"When the king opens his eyes," said Ali, "he will still not find the Golden Serpent."

"No," said Pundabi. "Some people never do. But that is another mystery."

✔ **LITERARY CHECK**
*What do you think the **moral** of the story is?*

ABOUT THE **AUTHOR**

Walter Dean Myers is the author of more than fifty young adult novels and picture books. Born in West Virginia, he grew up in Harlem after moving there at a young age. Myers held a variety of jobs before he won a picture-book writing contest and decided to become a full-time author. Two of his books, *Scorpions* and *Somewhere in the Darkness* are Newbery Honor books. Myers, an avid basketball fan, now lives in New Jersey with his family.

BEFORE YOU GO ON

1 The king doesn't find the Golden Serpent, but he pays Pundabi anyway. Why?

2 What does Pundabi do with the gold?

On Your Own
Do you think Pundabi was truly wise? Why or why not?

145

Review and Practice

READER'S THEATER

Speaking TIP

Practice your lines a few times before acting out the scene.

Act out the following scene.

King: I want you to solve a mystery for me.

Pundabi: Very well. What is the mystery?

King: I do not know. That is for you to figure out!

Ali: [*wrings his hands*] How can Pundabi solve a mystery if there is no mystery to solve?

King: [*to Pundabi*] If you are really a wise man, Pundabi, it will be done. If you do not solve it, then you are a fraud. I will put you in jail where you belong.

Pundabi: [*calmly, to Ali*] Let us take a walk. Perhaps our eyes will tell us the mystery.

              [*later*]

King: [*to Pundabi*] Have you solved the mystery yet?

Pundabi: No, but we know what the mystery is! It is the mystery of the Golden Serpent.

King: The Golden Serpent?

Pundabi: Yes, your Golden Serpent is missing.

King: I didn't know I had a Golden Serpent.

Pundabi: The thief must be very clever.

COMPREHENSION

Workbook
Page 69

Right There

1. How do the villagers get their questions to Pundabi? What does Pundabi do with the questions?

2. What does the king think happened to his Golden Serpent?

Think and Search

3. How did Pundabi's eyes speak to him when he and Ali walked through the village and around the marketplace?

4. Why doesn't the king trust the blind men?

Author and You

5. What makes the king decide he no longer wants to find the Golden Serpent?

6. Does the king learn anything from Pundabi's lesson? Explain.

On Your Own

7. Has anyone ever taught you a lesson by tricking you? Explain.

8. Is it okay to trick a person in order to teach a lesson? Explain.

DISCUSSION

Discuss in pairs or small groups.

- What is the other mystery that Pundabi refers to at the end of the fable? What do you think Pundabi means?

- **How can we tell what's right?** Why was the king so unaware of the wrongs suffered by the people in his own kingdom?

»)ᗡ *Listening* TIP

To make sure you have understood a speaker, restate what you think he or she has said. Were you right? If not, why not?

RESPONSE TO LITERATURE

Workbook
Page 69

Write a fable in comic strip form. You may rewrite an existing fable or write an original one. First, decide which scenes from the story you wish to illustrate. Then draw a picture to illustrate each scene. You can use speech bubbles to show dialogue and captions to show narration. Below is an example.

The Lion and the Mouse

Moral: Little friends may prove to be great friends.

Grammar and Writing

The Modal *must*

Use the modal *must* to express necessity and obligation, or to talk about something you have to do. Use *must* + the base form of the verb.

> Then you **must bring** him to me. But first we **must have** lunch.

Also use the modal *must* to speculate, or make guesses. Use *must* + the base form of the verb to speculate about the present.

> Pundabi **must know** who stole the Golden Serpent.

Use *must have* + past participle to speculate about the past.

> Someone **must have taken** it to sell.

Practice

Copy the sentences below into your notebook. Work with a partner. For each sentence, decide if *must* is used for necessity and obligation, speculation about the present, or speculation about the past. Next to each sentence, write *necessity and obligation*, *speculation about the present*, or *speculation about the past*, as appropriate.

1. "We must find the thief," said Ali.
2. Ali must have been afraid for his friend.
3. Fables must have a moral at the end.
4. The people in the village must have been very poor.
5. The king's subjects must do as he wishes.
6. "You must solve the mystery!" said the king.
7. "The thief must be very clever," said Pundabi.
8. The king must know very little about his subjects.

148

Write a Review

At the end of this unit, you will write a speech. In order to do this, you'll need to learn some of the skills writers use in persuasive writing. One kind of persuasive writing is a review. When you write a review, you state your opinion of the work you are reviewing. You also give a reason for your opinion and support it with examples from the work.

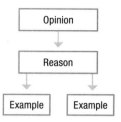

For example, suppose you liked a story because it was funny. You would support this opinion with examples of funny parts of the story. These could be quotations or descriptions of funny moments.

The model below is a review of the story you just read. The writer states his opinion and supports it with examples. Before he began writing, he listed his ideas in a graphic organizer like the one above.

Dylan Bishop

Review of "The Golden Serpent"

"The Golden Serpent" is a clever story. It is about a wise man named Pundabi who helps people in the village. I liked the fact that Pundabi outsmarts the king. The king orders Pundabi to solve a mystery that doesn't exist. So Pundabi makes up a mystery, telling the king that someone must have stolen his Golden Serpent. Although he has never had a Golden Serpent, the king is greedy and foolish enough to believe that someone has taken his. He tells Pundabi to find it. Pundabi takes the king to the poorest people in the kingdom: a widow, a boy with a lame leg, and three beggars. Although these people have nothing, they are searched. But the Golden Serpent is not found. Unhappy, the king says he no longer wants the Golden Serpent and pays Pundabi for his services. Pundabi passes the money on to the widow, the boy, and the three men. I thought it was smart of Pundabi to trick the king into sharing his money. I liked the fact that the reader understands more than the king does.

Writing Checklist

IDEAS:
- ✔ I supported my opinion with examples from the work.

CONVENTIONS:
- ✔ I used the modal *must* correctly.

Practice

Workbook Page 71

Write a review of a story, book, movie, or television show. Once you have selected the work you'd like to review, fill in a graphic organizer like the one above. Be sure to use the modal *must* correctly.

149

What You Will Learn

Reading

- Vocabulary building: *Context, dictionary skills, word study*

- Reading strategy: *Distinguish fact from opinion*

- Text type: *Informational text (science)*

Grammar, Usage, and Mechanics
Some and indefinite pronouns

Writing
Write a letter to the editor

THE BIG QUESTION

How can we tell what's right? Work with a partner. Discuss what you know about the former planet Pluto. How is it like the eight planets that make up our solar system? How is it different from them? Why do you think scientists decided that they were wrong about Pluto's being a planet?

BUILD BACKGROUND

"**I ♥ Pluto**" is an editorial. An editorial is a persuasive article that expresses the opinion of the writer. The writer of this editorial talks about his fondness for Pluto and his frustration with the scientific community for challenging Pluto's status as a planet. For reasons that are explained in the article and the text on page 157, Pluto is now considered a dwarf planet.

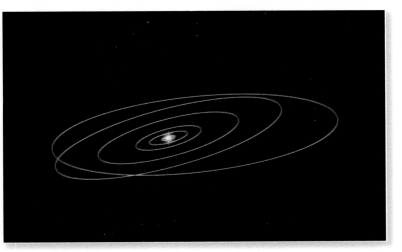

▲ This illustration shows how Pluto's orbit (outermost) overlaps Neptune's orbit, making Neptune farther from the sun at times.

VOCABULARY

Learn Key Words

Read these sentences. Use the context to figure out the meaning of the **red** words. Use a dictionary to check your answers. Then write each word and its meaning in your notebook.

Key Words
astronomy
celestial
eccentric
proposed
revolution
terrestrial

1. My brother decided to study **astronomy** because he enjoys learning about stars and planets.

2. Stars, planets, moons, and other objects in the sky are often called **celestial** bodies.

3. All the planets have orbits that are **eccentric**, like squashed circles, but Pluto's orbit is more **eccentric** than their orbits.

4. Some scientists **proposed**, or suggested, that we expand the number of planets from nine to twelve.

5. Earth takes one year, or 365 days, to make a complete **revolution** around the sun.

6. Mercury, Venus, and Mars are **terrestrial** planets because, like Earth, they are made mostly of rock.

Practice

Workbook
Page 72

Write the sentences in your notebook. Choose a **red** word from the box above to complete each sentence. Then take turns reading the sentences aloud with a partner.

1. Pluto's orbit is more _____ than the orbits of the planets in our solar system.

2. The _____ planets are made mostly of rock.

3. Some astronomers _____ reclassifying Pluto as an ice dwarf.

4. To become an astronomer, you must study _____ and take courses in math and science.

5. Earth and its moon are two examples of _____ objects.

6. The moon completes one _____ around Earth in about twenty-nine days.

Earth and its moon ▶

151

Learn Academic Words

Study the **red** words and their meanings. You will find these words useful when talking and writing about informational texts. Write each word and its meaning in your notebook. After you read "I ♥ Pluto," try to use these words to respond to the text.

biased = unfair because of a preference or dislike of something		As an astronomer who had studied Pluto for years, the woman was **biased** about Pluto's importance.
debate = formal discussion of a subject in which people express differing opinions		When I take part in a **debate**, I always make sure I am prepared to argue my point.
define = clearly show what something is or means		Astronomers worked together to **define** what a planet is.
objectively = in a way that is not influenced by a person's feelings, beliefs, or ideas		She had a strong opinion about the decision, so it was not easy for her to listen to both sides **objectively**.

Practice

Workbook
Page 73

Work with a partner to answer these questions. Try to include the **red** word in your answer. Write the answers in your notebook.

1. Are you **biased** about any particular topic? Explain.
2. Do you or would you enjoy being in a **debate**? Why or why not?
3. How would you **define** what makes a good friend?
4. Is it difficult to listen to your friends' opinions **objectively**? Explain.

▲ High school students from different countries take part in a debate.

152

Word Study: Prefixes

A **prefix** is a group of letters added to the beginning of a word. When you add a prefix to a word, you change its meaning and make a new word. Look at the examples below.

Prefix	Meaning	Examples
inter-	between or among a group of things or people	**inter**national, **Inter**net
un-	shows an opposite action; shows an opposite state or negative	**un**learn, **un**qualified
re-	again in a new and better way	**re**classified, **re**write

Practice

Work with a partner. Copy the sentences below into your notebook. Complete the sentences by adding the prefix *inter-*, *un-*, or *re-* to the word in parentheses. Use a dictionary if necessary.

1. Scientists are trying to _____ (lock) the mysteries of the solar system.

2. Astronomers had to _____ (consider) their definition of a planet.

3. Some people are _____ (happy) that Pluto is no longer a planet.

4. The author _____ (viewed) several experts before writing the article.

5. The conference was _____ (continental), with astronomers from all over the world attending.

▲ This Hubble photograph shows Pluto, its moon Charon, and two smaller moons.

READING STRATEGY DISTINGUISH FACT FROM OPINION

Distinguishing facts from opinions will help you form your own ideas about what you read. A fact is something that can be proven, or is true. An opinion is what someone believes or thinks. It's not necessarily true. To distinguish between facts and opinions, follow these steps:

- Ask yourself whether what you are reading can be proven.
- Look for phrases the author uses to give opinions, for example, *I think, I believe, I suppose, personally.*
- Make a note of the facts and opinions you are reading about. Ask yourself how you know which are facts and which are opinions.

As you read "I ♥ Pluto" and the text on page 157, look for facts and opinions. How can you tell the difference between them?

Set a purpose for reading Read this humorous editorial about one person's fondness for Pluto. Why is it hard for some of us to believe that what we learned in science class can be wrong?

I ♥ Pluto

Tim Kreider

August 23, 2006
Charlestown, MD

My love for our picked-on ninth planet is deeply, perhaps embarrassingly, personal.

I took my first public stand on Pluto's fate when I addressed the Forum on Outer Planetary Exploration in 2001. I informed the scientists that, first of all, no way was I or anyone else about to unlearn anything we'd been forced to learn in school. More important, I felt sure that, as former children, we all respected the principle: no takebacks.

Planets, like Supreme Court justices, are appointed for life, and you can't oust them no matter how unqualified they may prove to be. If they could kick out Pluto, I warned, they could do it to anything, or anyone.

I admit: it's a highly emotional issue and maybe I got carried away in the heat of debate.

Even I was a little abashed last week when the International Astronomical Union proposed an absurdly broad

---

oust, force out of a position of power
abashed, embarrassed or ashamed

definition of planethood that included moons and asteroids. Any half-formed hunk of frozen crud that could pull itself together into a ball long enough to get photographed by the Hubble would be considered a planet.

For longtime Pluto fans, there was something almost punitive about this proposal: happy now?

I guess I always knew in my heart that Pluto didn't belong. Pluto is what my old astronomy textbook rather judgmentally called a "deviant," and I've always felt a little defensive on its behalf. Neither a terrestrial planet nor a gas giant, Pluto is mostly ice. It's smaller than our own Moon. It has an orbit so eccentric that it spends 20 years of each revolution inside Neptune's orbit. Its orbital plane is tilted at a crazy 17-degree angle relative to the rest of the solar system. Its satellite Charon is so large in proportion to it that it's been called a double planet.

Lately I've thought of Saturn's moon Titan as the Homecoming Queen of the solar system, courted and fawned over. Pluto is more like the girl in black who never talked to anybody and wrote poems about dead birds. I just can't stand by and watch as the solar system's oddball gets pushed farther down into the substrata of social ostracism.

All I really wanted was a little velvet-rope treatment for Pluto. I didn't expect them to throw open the doors to all this Kuiper Belt riffraff.

Hubble, powerful orbiting telescope that takes photos of the celestial bodies in outer space
deviant, one who is different, in a bad way

ostracism, state of being excluded
Kuiper Belt, orbiting objects in the outer regions of our solar system

◀ One of the reasons for reclassifying Pluto was that it is smaller than the dwarf planet Xena (now called Eris).

BEFORE YOU GO ON

1 How is Pluto different from the eight planets in our solar system?

2 How does the writer feel about Pluto?

On Your Own
How do you feel about Pluto?

155

It's like that point at a party when you look around and ask: Who are these people? Sedna? Xena? Ceres? Ceres is an *asteroid*. Why not just make Greenland a planet? And I have nothing but respect for Charon, but come on: it's obviously Pluto's moon.

The solar system is a mess.

The astronomical union is to vote on Pluto tomorrow. For the record, I would accept a separate (but equal!) class of planetoids, including Sedna and Xena. After all, the childhood mnemonic is easily fixed: My Very Energetic Mother Just Served Us Nine Pizzas, Sans Xenophobia.

If we do create a category for "ice dwarves," I hope they'll at least all be named after dwarves: Gimli, Sneezy, Rumpelstiltskin.

But what I really wish is that we'd just grandfather Pluto in and then close all the loopholes. Let's do it, not for scientific reasons, but for sentimental ones.

---

mnemonic, device that helps you remember things—in this case, the order of the planets
grandfather Pluto in, allow Pluto to remain a planet in spite of the facts

As a friend of mine at NASA said, "It would prove our humanity to let Pluto stay in." It would be like that moment of grace when the doorman is about to escort you out of a private party where you don't belong, but then someone who knows you taps him on the shoulder and says, "Wait a minute, I know this guy. He's O.K."

ABOUT THE AUTHOR

Tim Kreider is a writer and cartoonist whose cartoon, *The Pain—When Will It End?* can be seen in the Baltimore *City Paper* and has run in the Jackson *Planet Weekly, The New York Press, The Stranger,* and *Philadelphia Weekly.* His essays have appeared in *The New York Times, Film Quarterly, The Comics Journal, Jump Cut,* and *Lip.*

Why Pluto Is Not a Planet

The International Astronomical Union has come up with three defining characteristics of a planet. A celestial body must have all three characteristics to be considered a planet.

1. It must orbit the sun.

Earth takes 365 days to orbit the sun. Pluto takes 248 years! This is because Pluto is billions of miles away from the sun. But according to this first characteristic, Pluto is a planet. Even though it is so far away from the sun, there is no other object comparable to the sun close enough to Pluto to pull it out of orbit.

2. Its gravity must be strong enough for it to maintain a round shape.

Every object has its own gravity. Huge objects, like planets, have so much gravity that they actually pull on themselves until they become round in shape. And since Pluto has enough gravity to stay round, it is a planet according to this second characteristic.

3. It must be able to clear the neighborhood around its orbit.

To do this, a planet must be large enough that the force of its gravity affects surrounding objects. The objects collide with the planet, making it grow. As the planet gets bigger, the number of objects around it gets smaller. A planet's gravity can also change other objects' orbits, making future collisions unlikely. Hundreds of objects orbit in the Kuiper Belt with Pluto. Pluto is not large enough to remove them. One of these, Eris (formerly known as Xena), is larger than Pluto. So Pluto is not a planet according to this third characteristic. On August 24, 2006, Pluto was reclassified as a "dwarf planet."

BEFORE YOU GO ON

1 What are the three defining characteristics of a planet?

2 What was Pluto reclassified as?

On Your Own
How can scientific facts and opinions become confused?

157

COMPREHENSION

Workbook
Page 76

Right There

1. What happened on August 24, 2006?

2. The International Astronomical Union proposed a broader definition of planethood. Which celestial objects were included in this group?

Think and Search

3. Which defining characteristic of a planet does Pluto *not* have?

4. Why does Pluto's orbit overlap Neptune's path?

Author and You

5. Would the author of "I ♥ Pluto" agree with this statement: "Ceres should be a planet"? Why or why not?

6. How would you describe the author's voice in "I ♥ Pluto"? Is it different from the author's voice in the text on page 157?

On Your Own

7. Do you think Pluto should still be considered a planet? Why or why not?

8. Do you think there are undiscovered planets in our solar system? Why or why not?

IN YOUR OWN WORDS

Review "I ♥ Pluto" and the text on page 157. Then write the most important facts you learned from these articles in your notebook. Finally, use your own words to tell a partner why scientists no longer consider Pluto a planet.

> **Speaking TIP**
>
> Draw a large picture showing the orbits of the planets in our solar system. Include Pluto's orbit. Use the visual to help classmates understand why Pluto doesn't qualify as a planet.

DISCUSSION

Discuss in pairs or small groups.

- Can you think of other examples of scientific "facts" that turned out to be wrong? Explain.
- **How can we tell what's right?** Do you think the scientists' decision to change Pluto's status as a planet was right or wrong? Why?

READ FOR FLUENCY

It is often easier to read a text if you understand the difficult words and phrases. Work with a partner. Choose a paragraph from the reading. Identify the words and phrases you do not know or have trouble pronouncing. Look up the difficult words in a dictionary.

Take turns pronouncing the words and phrases with your partner. If necessary, ask your teacher to model the correct pronunciation. Then take turns reading the paragraph aloud. Give each other feedback on your reading.

EXTENSION 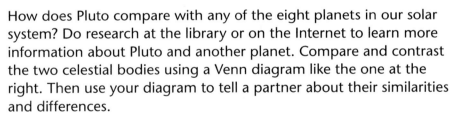 Workbook Page 76

How does Pluto compare with any of the eight planets in our solar system? Do research at the library or on the Internet to learn more information about Pluto and another planet. Compare and contrast the two celestial bodies using a Venn diagram like the one at the right. Then use your diagram to tell a partner about their similarities and differences.

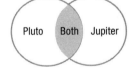

Pluto Both Jupiter

Grammar and Writing

Some and Indefinite Pronouns

Some and indefinite pronouns are used in generalizations. *Some* is used to express an indefinite quantity. It is always plural and can be used as an adjective with a noun or as a pronoun if the noun is understood.

> **Some** (scientists) proposed expanding the number of planets to 12.

Indefinite pronouns are always singular. Indefinite pronouns that begin with *every-* mean all persons or things. Those that begin with *some-* mean a particular person or thing; use them for affirmative statements. Those that begin with *any-* mean the opposite of *some-*, or not a particular person or thing; use them for negative statements and questions. Those that begin with *no-* mean the opposite of *every-*, or none.

everyone	someone	anyone	no one
everybody	somebody	anybody	nobody
everything	something	anything	nothing

Example Sentences
Everybody agrees that the issue of Pluto is emotional.
For Pluto fans, there was **something** almost punitive about the proposal.
No way was I or **anyone** else about to let Pluto go without a fight.
I have **nothing** but respect for Charon, but come on: it's obviously Pluto's moon.

Practice

Workbook Page 77

Write the following sentences in your notebook. Choose the correct word to complete each sentence.

1. (Nothing / Someone) from the IAU should defend Pluto.
2. (Anyone / No one) thinks that asteroids are planets.
3. Has (anything / everything) been discovered recently?
4. (Anybody / Some) proposed making Ceres a dwarf planet.
5. The scientists took (everything / anything) into consideration.

WRITING A PERSUASIVE PARAGRAPH

Write a Letter to the Editor

Another kind of persuasive writing is a letter to the editor of a publication. When you write a letter to the editor, you must think about your audience. Who will be reading your letter? What approach would persuade this particular audience to agree with you? What voice should you use? A letter to a student newspaper, for example, would be a lot less formal than a letter to a scientific journal.

Here is a model of a letter to the editor of a school newspaper. Before the writer began writing, she listed her ideas in a word web.

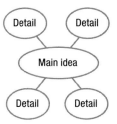

Light Pollution

To the Editor,

Light pollution is a serious problem. You may know that it prevents people in urban areas from seeing stars at night. But you may not know that it harms people and animals. Lights can shine into people's eyes as they are driving, preventing them from seeing where they are going. Streetlights can harm nocturnal animals such as bats and owls. These animals are active in the dark, and the constant light makes them visible to predators. Light pollution has already endangered sea turtles. Newly hatched sea turtles head toward brightness—the brightest spot on a dark beach would normally be the light from the night sky reflected in the water. That's how they find the sea. Artificial lights attract the babies, leading them in the wrong direction. But we can reduce light pollution. Simple things we can do include turning off lights when they aren't needed and switching to environmentally friendly lighting methods. I strongly urge everyone to take part in fighting this problem.

Ruth Kace
April 23, 2009

Practice

Workbook
Page 78

Write a persuasive letter to the editor of a newspaper, magazine, or some other publication. You might write about a problem in your community or school. Use a word web to organize your ideas. Be sure to use *some* and indefinite pronouns correctly.

Writing Checklist

IDEAS:
- ✔ I supported my main idea with details.

VOICE:
- ✔ I used a voice that would appeal to my audience.

Prepare to Read

What You Will Learn

Reading

- Vocabulary building: *Literary terms, word study*

- Reading strategy: *Identify author's purpose*

- Text type: *Literature (novel excerpt)*

Grammar, Usage, and Mechanics
The uses of *would*

Writing
Write a persuasive paragraph

THE BIG QUESTION

How can we tell what's right? Whom do you go to when you have a question about right and wrong? Why do you respect this person's opinion? Discuss with a partner.

BUILD BACKGROUND

This reading is an excerpt from ***A Single Shard***, a novel by Linda Sue Park. The story takes place in twelfth-century Korea. It is about a poor, hungry boy named Tree-ear.

Until as recently as the twentieth century, Korea's economy was based on farming. Rice was and still is the most important crop and a staple food.

▼ A Korean farmer carrying rice plants on his back

Learn Literary Words

As you may recall, a conflict is a struggle between opposing forces. It is the main problem in a story. It is also one of the most important story elements because it sets the story's plot in motion. An **internal conflict** is a conflict within a character. One example of an internal conflict is when a character has to choose between two courses of action. In Tree-ear's case, his hunger tells him to do one thing, but his conscience tells him to do another. You will find out what Tree-ear chooses to do when you read the excerpt.

The **theme** of a work of fiction is its central idea, or message. A theme can usually be expressed as a general statement about people or about life. The theme is not just a summary of the plot. It is the writer's main point. For example, the theme of "The Golden Serpent" (pages 140–145) might be expressed in these words: Some people will never see what they need to see in order to become better.

Literary Words

internal conflict
theme

Practice

Workbook Page 79

Work with a partner. Have you ever had to make a decision that caused you to have an internal conflict? Talk about this internal conflict with your partner. Then write a few lines of dialogue presenting your internal conflict as a conversation with yourself.

▲ A Korean farmer plowing a rice paddy

163

Learn Academic Words

Study the **red** words and their meanings. You will find these words useful when talking and writing about literature. Write each word and its meaning in your notebook. After you read the excerpt from *A Single Shard*, try to use these words to respond to the text.

analyze = examine or think about something carefully in order to understand it	➡	The man had to **analyze** the ingredients listed on the package to make sure he could eat the bread.
ethical = having to do with right and wrong	➡	Whether or not to keep something that you found is an **ethical** question.
justify = give a reasonable or acceptable explanation for something	➡	He was able to **justify** his absence from school by explaining that he had been ill.
principle = a moral or set of ideas that makes you behave in a certain way	➡	One **principle** that most people live by is that stealing is wrong.

Practice  **Workbook** Page 80

Write the sentences in your notebook. Choose a **red** word from the box above to complete each sentence. Then take turns reading the sentences aloud with a partner.

1. My father taught me one _____ I have always lived by.

2. Sarah tried to _____ her behavior even though she knew what she had done was wrong.

3. We have to _____ the situation before we can make a decision.

4. Deciding whether someone did the right thing is an _____ issue.

Steamed rice ▶

Word Study: Long and Short Vowels

Some vowel patterns stand for different sounds. Learning about these vowel patterns and their different pronunciations will help you read and understand new words. The letters *ea* often stand for long *e* as in *season*. Sometimes these letters stand for long *a* as in *great* or short *e* as in *head*.

Long *e*	Long *a*	Short *e*
leak	great	bread
steal	break	heavy

Practice

Work with a partner. Read aloud the words in the box below. All of the words contain the letters *ea*, but the vowel sound that these letters stand for is not always the same. In your notebook, make a chart like the one above. Sort the words and write them in your chart under the appropriate headings. Then choose five words and write a sentence using each.

ahead	dead	heaps	reach	stream
beans	eaten	meadow	steak	wealth

▲ A Korean badge showing a crane in flight

READING STRATEGY | **IDENTIFY AUTHOR'S PURPOSE**

Identifying an author's purpose can help you analyze a text better. Three of the most common reasons authors write are to inform, entertain, or persuade. To identify an author's purpose, ask yourself these questions:

- Is the text entertaining? Am I enjoying reading it?
- Am I learning new information from what I'm reading?
- Is the author trying to persuade me about something or change my opinion?
- Did the author have more than one reason for writing the text? If so, what are the reasons?

As you read the excerpt from *A Single Shard*, try to identify the author's purpose (or purposes) for writing.

165

Set a purpose for reading Read this novel excerpt to find out how Tree-ear struggles with his conscience after he gets himself and his friend a free meal. Was what Tree-ear did right or wrong?

from

A Single Shard *Linda Sue Park*

The two main characters in the story, Tree-ear and Crane-man, live in a small village. They are dirt poor—living off the scraps of food they find day to day. Crane-man is older and wiser than his young companion, who often asks his advice. In this excerpt, the two friends have a discussion about how Tree-ear came to have a bag of rice.

"Eh, Tree-ear! Have you hungered well today?" Crane-man called out as Tree-ear drew near the bridge.

The well-fed of the village greeted each other politely by saying, "Have you eaten well today?" Tree-ear and his friend turned the greeting inside out for their own little joke.

Tree-ear squeezed the bulging pouch that he wore at his waist. He had meant to hold back the good news, but the excitement spilled out of him. "Crane-man! A good thing that you greeted me so just now, for later today we will have to use the proper words!" He held the bag high. Tree-ear was delighted when Crane-man's eyes widened in surprise. He knew that Crane-man would guess at once—only one thing could give a bag that kind of smooth fullness. Not carrot-tops or chicken bones, which protruded in odd lumps. No, the bag was filled with *rice*.

Crane-man raised his walking crutch in a salute. "Come, my young friend! Tell me how you came by such a fortune—a tale worth hearing, no doubt!"

Tree-ear had been trotting along the road on his early-morning perusal of the village rubbish heaps. Ahead of him a man carried a heavy load on a *jiggeh*, an open-framed backpack made of branches. On the *jiggeh* was a large woven-straw container, the kind commonly used to carry rice.

Tree-ear knew that the rice must be from last year's crop; in the fields surrounding the village this season's rice had only just begun to grow. It

---

protruded, stuck out
perusal, checking or inspection

would be many months before the rice was harvested and the poor allowed to glean the fallen grain from the bare fields. Only then would they taste the pure flavor of rice and feel its solid goodness in their bellies. Just looking at the straw box made water rush into Tree-ear's mouth.

The man had paused in the road and hoisted the wooden *jiggeh* higher on his back, shifting the cumbersome weight. As Tree-ear stared, rice began to trickle out of a hole in the straw box. The trickle thickened and became a stream. Oblivious, the man continued on his way.

For a few short moments Tree-ear's thoughts wrestled with one another. *Tell him—quickly! Before he loses too much rice!*

No! Don't say anything—you will be able to pick up the fallen rice after he rounds the bend. . . .

Tree-ear made his decision. He waited until the man had reached the bend in the road, then ran to catch him.

"Honorable sir," Tree-ear said, panting and bowing. "As I walked behind you, I noticed that you are marking your path with rice!"

The farmer turned and saw the trail of rice. A well-built man with a broad suntanned face, he pushed his straw hat back, scratched his head, and laughed ruefully.

---

glean, gather
oblivious, unaware of what is around you

1 What is Tree-ear's good news?

2 What does Tree-ear decide to do about telling the man about his rice?

On Your Own
Would you have done what Tree-ear did? Why or why not?

167

"Impatience," said the farmer. "I should have had this container woven with a double wall. But it would have taken more time. Now I pay for not waiting a bit longer." He struggled out of the *jiggeh's* straps and inspected the container. He prodded the straw to close the gap but to no avail, so he threw his arms up in mock despair. Tree-ear grinned. He liked the farmer's easygoing nature.

"Fetch me a few leaves, boy," said the farmer. Tree-ear complied, and the man stuffed them into the container as a temporary patch.

The farmer squatted to don the *jiggeh*. As he started walking, he called over his shoulder. "Good deserves good, urchin. The rice on the ground is yours if you can be troubled to gather it."

"Many thanks, kind sir!" Tree-ear bowed, very pleased with himself. He had made a lucky guess, and his waist pouch would soon be filled with rice.

Tree-ear had learned from Crane-man's example. Foraging in the woods and rubbish heaps, gathering fallen grain-heads in the autumn—these were honorable ways to garner a meal, requiring time and work. But stealing and begging, Crane-man said, made a man no better than a dog.

"Work gives a man dignity, stealing takes it away," he often said.

Following Crane-man's advice was not always easy for Tree-ear. Today, for example. Was it stealing, to wait as Tree-ear had for more rice to fall before alerting the man that his rice bag was leaking? Did a good deed balance a bad one? Tree-ear often pondered these kinds of questions, alone or in discussion with Crane-man.

"Such questions serve in two ways," Crane-man had explained. "They keep a man's mind sharp—and his thoughts off his empty stomach."

Now, as always, he seemed to know Tree-ear's thoughts without hearing them spoken. "Tell me about this farmer," he said. "What kind of man was he?"

Tree-ear considered the question for several moments, stirring his memory. At last, he answered, "One who lacks patience—he said it himself. He had not wanted to wait for a sturdier container to be built. And he could not be bothered to pick up the fallen rice." Tree-ear paused. "But he laughed easily, even at himself."

---

foraging, searching for food
garner, gather; collect
dignity, worth; self-respect

168

"If he were here now, and heard you tell of waiting a little longer before speaking, what do you think he would say or do?"

"He would laugh," Tree-ear said, surprising himself with the speed of his response. Then, more slowly, "I think . . . he would not have minded."

Crane-man nodded, satisfied. And Tree-ear thought of something his friend often said: *Scholars read the great words of the world. But you and I must learn to read the world itself.*

✔ LITERARY CHECK
*What do you think the **theme** of the story is?*

ABOUT THE **AUTHOR**

Linda Sue Park was born and raised in Illinois. As a child, she loved to read and has been writing poems and stories ever since. Her novel *A Single Shard* won the Newbery Medal in 2002. Park currently lives in upstate New York with her husband and two children.

BEFORE YOU GO ON

1. How do Crane-man and Tree-ear usually get food?

2. Why is Crane-man satisfied with Tree-ear's actions?

On Your Own
Do you think a good deed can balance a bad one? Explain.

Review and Practice

Act out the following scene between Tree-ear and the farmer.

Tree-ear: [*to himself*] That farmer is carrying rice! I bet it is from last year's crop. Oh, no! There is a hole in the container! Should I tell him now or wait until there is more on the ground for me to take? [*waits a moment*] Honorable sir!

Farmer: What is it, young man?

Tree-ear: As I walked behind you, I saw that you were losing rice from your container.

Farmer: [*laughs*] I am so impatient! I did not weave my container well enough. Now I have lost some of my rice. Fetch me some leaves to patch the hole. You can have the rice that is on the ground, if you can be troubled to gather it.

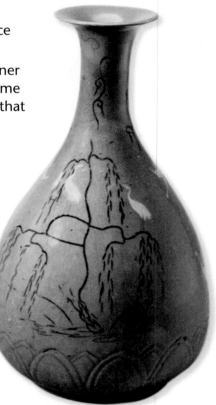

▲ A Korean pear-form bottle

Speaking TIP

Use tone of voice, facial expressions, and gestures to convey your character's feelings.

COMPREHENSION

Workbook Page 83

Right There

1. How do Tree-ear and Crane-man greet each other?
2. What does Crane-man think about begging?

Think and Search

3. Why does Tree-ear wait before telling the farmer about the rice?
4. What kind of man is the farmer?

Author and You

5. What does Crane-man and Tree-ear's joke about hunger tell you about their personalities?
6. Do you think the author considers Crane-man and Tree-ear to be good "readers of the world"? Why or why not?

On Your Own

7. Do you enjoy pondering questions of right and wrong? Explain.
8. Do you agree that work gives people dignity? Why or why not?

Discuss in pairs or small groups.

- How does Tree-ear justify his behavior at the end of the excerpt? Do you think what Tree-ear did was ethical? Why or why not?

- **Q How can we tell what's right?** Have you ever been in a situation where you did something that you shouldn't have? How did you justify it?

RESPONSE TO LITERATURE

Workbook
Page 83

Work with a partner. Using the words in the box below, discuss the excerpt from *A Single Shard*. What is the theme of the story? What makes you think this? Can various readers interpret the theme differently? Share your opinion with the class.

| analyze | ethical | internal conflict | justify | principle | theme |

▲ A Korean painting in Seoul National Museum

Grammar and Writing

The Uses of *would*

We usually use *will* to express the future. The excerpt from *A Single Shard* is a narrative told in the past. In a narrative, an author uses *would* + the base form of a verb to express the future in the past. *Would* is the past form of *will*.

> He knows that Crane-man **will guess** at once. (future)
> He knew that Crane-man **would guess** at once. (future in the past)

Would can also be used in implied conditions. In an implied condition, the *if* clause is omitted. Use *would have* + participle to express a condition in the past.

> I think he **would not have minded**. (Implied condition: If he had been here, he would not have minded.)

Use *would rather* to state a preference. Use *would rather* or the contraction *'d rather* + the base form of the verb.

> Tree-ear **would rather have** rice than carrot tops.
> I**'d rather not gather** the fallen rice.

Practice
Workbook Page 84

Work with a partner. Read the sentences below. Decide if each sentence is *would* as past of *will*, *would* or *would have* in an implied condition, or *would* in *would rather*.

1. I would never have taken the rice.
2. Tree-ear waited. He knew he would get some rice.
3. I'd rather take rice from a rich farmer than starve.
4. Tree-ear and Crane-man would have gone hungry.
5. Crane-man would never guess how Tree-ear got the rice.

172

WRITING A PERSUASIVE PARAGRAPH

Write a Persuasive Paragraph

When you write a persuasive paragraph, be sure to take a stand, or state your opinion. Support your opinion with examples, facts, and details. Explain the pros and cons of the issue. If you write about why your school should spend money on a new sports arena, the pros might be: *Sporting events would bring in money; the money could pay for computers and art supplies; the arena would be paid off in one year with donations from the community.* The cons might be: *The arena would take several years to complete; students would need to have many fundraisers.* Explain why the pros would outweigh the cons.

Here is a model of a persuasive paragraph. Before the writer began writing, she listed her ideas in a T-chart like the one above.

Pros	Cons

Jessica Reider

Tree-ear's Actions

Tree-ear notices that a farmer is trailing rice behind him as he walks. What should Tree-ear do? He is very hungry, but he is also honest. If Tree-ear waits to tell the farmer, he might end up with enough rice for a meal or two. But would that be dishonest? If Tree-ear tells the farmer right away, then he'd feel good about his conscience, but his stomach would be empty. And isn't the farmer responsible for his problem? Didn't the farmer get himself into this situation? And wouldn't he be grateful to Tree-ear for telling him about the rice he is losing? Some people may think that Tree-ear's waiting to tell the farmer about his rice was like stealing. But I don't think Tree-ear did anything wrong. He guessed that the farmer would be good-natured about his having waited, and he was right. The farmer didn't have to give Tree-ear the rice that had already fallen, but he did so to reward Tree-ear.

Practice  Workbook Page 85

Write a persuasive paragraph on a topic or question you feel strongly about. You might state your opinion of reality shows or explain the benifits of playing competitive sports. List your ideas in a T-chart. Be sure to use *would* correctly.

Writing Checklist

IDEAS:
☑ I took a stand.

CONVENTIONS:
☑ I used *would* correctly.

What You Will Learn

Reading
- Vocabulary building: *Context, dictionary skills, word study*
- Reading strategy: *Summarize*
- Text type: *Informational text (social studies)*

Grammar, Usage, and Mechanics
Superlative adjectives

Writing
Write an advertisement

THE BIG QUESTION

How can we tell what's right? Sometimes we have to fight for what we believe in. Have you ever had to fight for the right to do something that was important to you? What did you do? How did you feel about your struggle? In pairs, discuss your experiences.

BUILD BACKGROUND

"Marian Anderson: A Voice for Change" is about an African-American singer who lived during a time when black people did not have equal rights. In many places during the early 20th century, black people had to go to separate schools, restaurants, and churches. They often could not live where they chose or do what they were qualified to do for a living.

For Anderson, living during this time meant fighting for the right to pursue her goals. Despite her talent, she was rejected from the music school of her choice because of her skin color. Anderson struggled against such injustice her entire life.

In time, however, Anderson was recognizied for her talent and courage. She was chosen to sing at John F. Kennedy's inauguration in 1961. In 1963 she was awarded the Presidential Medal of Freedom. And in 1991 she won a Grammy Award for Lifetime Achievement.

◄ President Lyndon Johnson presents the Presidential Medal of Freedom to Marian Anderson in 1963.

VOCABULARY

Learn Key Words

Read these sentences. Use the context to figure out the meaning of the red words. Use a dictionary to check your answers. Then write each word and its meaning in your notebook.

1. The new **auditorium** was large enough for all the students in the school to watch the play at one time.
2. Alex is going to a **concert** to see her friend play the violin.
3. The church has a small **congregation**; only about seventy-five people come to pray together every Sunday.
4. Marian Anderson had **determination**; she never gave up on her dream of becoming a singer in spite of the difficulties she faced.
5. Refusing women the right to vote was a great **injustice**. Thankfully this unfair practice ended in 1920.
6. African-American slaves created and sang songs called **spirituals** to help them endure the horrors of living in bondage.

Practice  Workbook Page 86

Write the sentences in your notebook. Choose a red word from the box above to complete each sentence. Then take turns reading the sentences aloud with a partner.

1. Our math teacher, Mr. Beckmann, surprised us by getting up on stage and playing the clarinet during the _____.
2. Hard work and _____ help a person succeed in life.
3. Marian Anderson sang popular American songs, classical songs, and _____.
4. The _____ of St. Edward's held a bake sale to raise money for a new organ.
5. Treating one group of people differently from another because of their religion is an example of social _____.
6. We gathered in the _____ for an all-school meeting.

Key Words

auditorium
concert
congregation
determination
injustice
spirituals

175

Learn Academic Words

Study the **red** words and their meanings. You will find these words useful when talking and writing about informational texts. Write each word and its meaning in your notebook. After you read "Marian Anderson: A Voice for Change," try to use these words to respond to the text.

Academic Words

achievement
individual
issue
pursue

achievement = something important you succeed in doing as a result of your actions	➡	Graduating from high school is a memorable **achievement** in a person's life.
individual = person considered separately from other people in the same group	➡	Each **individual** must make his or her own choices and decisions.
issue = a subject, problem, or question that people discuss	➡	Giving women the right to vote was an **issue** that people debated for many years.
pursue = continue doing an activity or trying to achieve something over a long time	➡	She decided to **pursue** her studies during the day while working as a waitress at night.

Practice

Workbook Page 87

Work with a partner to answer these questions. Try to include the **red** word in your answer. Write the answers in your notebook.

1. What has been the greatest **achievement** in your life so far?

2. What **individual** has made an impact on your life?

3. What is an important social **issue** in your class at school?

4. If you won a prize and suddenly had millions of dollars, would you still **pursue** your education? Why or why not?

▲ Anderson performs on stage, accompanied by pianist Franz Rupp.

Word Study: Synonyms

Synonyms are words that have the same or nearly the same meaning. For example, *cheerful* is a synonym for *happy*, and *simple* is a synonym for *plain*. As you read, you can use synonyms as context clues to help you figure out the meaning of unfamiliar words.

> Marian Anderson's main **ambition** was to be a professional singer, and toward this **goal** she worked long and hard.

Suppose you knew the word *goal* but not *ambition*. The context of the sentence lets you know that *ambition* is similar in meaning to *goal*.

Practice
Workbook
Page 88

Work with a partner. Write the words *excellent*, *unusual*, *barriers*, and *difficult* in your notebook. Write a synonym for each word, using a dictionary if necessary. Then write a sentence for each synonym pair.

READING STRATEGY   SUMMARIZE

Summarizing helps you check your understanding of a text. When you summarize, you identify the main ideas in a text and rewrite them in a few short sentences. To summarize, follow these steps:

- Read the text. Then reread each paragraph or section. What is the author writing about?
- Identify the main idea in each paragraph or section. Make notes.
- Leave out details. Just focus on the most important points.
- Write a few sentences that convey the main ideas in the text. Use your own words.

As you read "*Marian Anderson: A Voice for Change*," make notes of the main ideas. Summarize the text in two or three sentences.

Workbook
Page 89

177

Set a purpose for reading Read this article to find out how one woman changed the course of history. What did Marian Anderson do to bring about change?

MARIAN ANDERSON
A Voice for Change

▲ Marian Anderson at age 21

Gifted with a magnificent singing voice, Marian Anderson didn't set out to change America. She set out only to sing. From childhood on, her ambition was to become a professional singer. She hoped to study at top music schools and train with the best teachers. She wished to perform in well-established concert halls, ones with excellent acoustics to allow listeners to hear the music in all its glory.

---

acoustics, the qualities of a room, such as its shape and size, which affect the way sound is heard in it

178

But because Anderson was African American, these goals were not easy to achieve. During her lifetime, many schools, churches, and theaters in the United States were segregated. It was not unusual for music schools and concert halls to welcome only white students, audiences, and performers. Anderson didn't let these obstacles stop her. In struggling to realize her dream, she overcame racial barriers in her own life and advanced the cause of racial equality in the United States.

▲ Anderson at 31

The Baby Contralto

Marian Anderson was born in 1897 and grew up in Philadelphia. She went to church every Sunday, and it was there that she first sang in public. At age six, Anderson joined her church's junior choir. Her natural singing voice was low and rich—a contralto—but she had an amazing three-octave range. Anderson thrilled listeners with the way she sang the spirituals that were part of the service.

Nicknamed "the baby contralto," Anderson was chosen to join a choir of singers from many different African-American congregations. By the time she was ten, she was invited to give solo concerts at benefits and other events. When she was twelve, her father died as a result of an accident. Anderson, her mother, and two sisters moved in with her grandparents, and Mrs. Anderson went to work as a cleaning woman to support her daughters. Throughout Marian Anderson's life, her mother's strength and determination helped sustain her.

Turning Points

When Anderson graduated from eighth grade, she had reached a turning point. If she wanted to sing professionally, she needed training. Her church raised money for her to attend music school, but Anderson was rejected solely on the basis of her race. It was a blow she never forgot.

Anderson studied with teachers, both black and white, who taught black students. They helped her expand her repertoire of spirituals and popular songs to include arias from operas and other classical songs. Now in demand as a concert artist, she organized her own tours, choosing venues that welcomed black musicians. On tour in the South, she sang mostly in African-American churches and colleges. Travel through the South was difficult. "Colored only" train cars were dirty, and many hotels served only white people.

---

segregated, meant to be used or attended by members of one race or religion
contralto, lowest female singing voice
octave, the range of notes between the first note of a musical scale and the last

BEFORE YOU GO ON

1 What was Marian Anderson's singing voice like?

2 How did Anderson begin her musical training?

On Your Own
What is your favorite kind of music? Why?

179

In 1925, Anderson won the chance to sing as a soloist with the great New York Philharmonic Orchestra in a large stadium in New York City. An audience of more than 7,000 people attended. Her concert was a triumph, and success followed success over the next few years.

Despite mostly enthusiastic reviews, Anderson wasn't yet satisfied with the quality of her own work. Since operas were usually written in Italian or German, she decided to go to Europe to perfect her skills in these languages. She appeared in dozens of concerts there from 1930 to 1935, enchanting European audiences.

A more accomplished and self-confident Anderson returned to the American stage. In 1936, she performed at the White House for President Franklin D. Roosevelt and First Lady Eleanor Roosevelt. Marian Anderson had become an international singing sensation.

A Historic Concert

In 1938, Howard University invited Anderson to appear in the nation's capital, Washington, D.C., where she had often performed. Officials at Howard tried to rent the largest and best theater in the area, Constitution Hall, for her concert. The concert hall owners rejected the request.

An organization called the Daughters of the American Revolution, known as the DAR, owned Constitution Hall. Although black patrons could sit in a small section at the back of the hall, the DAR had instituted a "white artists only" policy in 1932.

When the DAR denied Marian Anderson the right to appear there, her fans of all races and nationalities were outraged. One of them was Eleanor Roosevelt, who was a member of the DAR. To show her disapproval, she resigned her membership.

Concert organizers also turned to the local school board for help, requesting use of the largest school auditorium in the area. Since it was located in an all-white school, the board agreed that Anderson could appear there, but insisted that no other African-American artists be allowed to do so. The concert organizers rejected the offer.

With the help of the National Association for the Advancement of Colored People, or the NAACP, a location for Anderson's concert was finally found. The NAACP invited her to sing from the steps of the Lincoln Memorial, the monument created to honor the Great Emancipator, Abraham Lincoln.

▲ Singing at the Lincoln Memorial on April 9, 1939

On April 9, 1939, Marian Anderson appeared in a groundbreaking open-air concert before an audience of 75,000 people. Her concert at the Lincoln Memorial became a lasting symbol of the senseless injustice of racial prejudice and of the need to guarantee equal rights for all.

From that point on in her career, Anderson insisted on "vertical" seating in segregated cities. Vertical seating meant that an imaginary line was drawn down the center of a theater—from front to back—with black patrons on one side and white on the other, for separate but equal seating. By the 1950s, however, Anderson would no longer perform where audiences were segregated in any way.

A Busy Life

Anderson's career continued in the years after her historic concert, although her personal and professional life changed. In 1943, she married the architect Orpheus Fisher, whom she had known since high school. In 1958 Anderson served as a delegate to the United Nations. She sang again on the steps of the Lincoln Memorial in 1963, when Martin Luther King Jr. delivered his "I Have a Dream" speech. She received the Presidential Medal of Freedom in 1963. Although she retired only a few years later, she continued to travel and to speak at public events.

Marian Anderson died in 1993 at the age of ninety-six. Today, listeners can still hear recordings of some of her performances and witness the voice whose power moved audiences to tears and helped to inspire change in America.

▲ First Lady Eleanor Roosevelt presents the NAACP's Spingarn Medal to Marian Anderson.

Marian Anderson sings on April 9, 1939, at the Lincoln Memorial to an audience of 75,000 people. ▼

BEFORE YOU GO ON

1 How did Eleanor Roosevelt help Marian Anderson?

2 Where did Anderson end up singing on April 9, 1939?

On Your Own
Did you ever do something brave or heroic without really meaning to? Explain.

COMPREHENSION  Workbook Page 90

Right There

1. Where did Marian Anderson first sing?

2. What is vertical seating?

Think and Search

3. What were some of Marian Anderson's early goals?

4. How did Anderson's congregation help her train as a singer?

Author and You

5. What does the author consider Anderson's most important performance to be? Explain.

6. Do you think the author shows bias in this text? Why or why not?

On Your Own

7. Do you think artists should try to help improve the world? Why or why not?

8. Can you think of any other artists who have helped to correct a social injustice?

IN YOUR OWN WORDS

Review the steps for summarizing on page 177. Then copy the chart below into your notebook. Use the chart to summarize the important events in Marian Anderson's life. Be sure to include specific dates. When you have finished, compare charts with a partner.

The Life of Marian Anderson	
The Early Years	
The Middle Years	
The Later Years	

DISCUSSION

Discuss in pairs or small groups.

Listening TIP

As you listen to your classmates' ideas, think about how they are similar to or different from your own.

1. In what ways did Marian Anderson's individual struggle help African Americans in general?

2. What professional choices do people have today that Marian Anderson didn't have in her lifetime? Why?

Q How can we tell what's right? What is one injustice that you feel strongly about? What would you do to fight against this injustice?

READ FOR FLUENCY

Reading with feeling helps make what you read more interesting. Work with a partner. Choose a paragraph from the reading. Read the paragraph. Ask each other how you felt after reading the paragraph. Did you feel happy or sad?

Take turns reading the paragraph aloud to each other with a tone of voice that represents how you felt when you read it the first time. Give each other feedback.

EXTENSION

Workbook
Page 90

Spirituals were very common in Marian Anderson's time and are still popular today. Do research at the library or on the Internet to find out the history of spirituals in American culture. What role have spirituals played? To whom are spirituals important? Why are they popular? What impact do spirituals have on an audience? Find a spiritual that you think is interesting. Share your findings with the class.

Grammar and Writing

Superlative Adjectives

In the reading about Marian Anderson, the author uses superlative adjectives to compare three or more things. A superlative adjective usually precedes the noun it modifies.

Rule	Adjective	Superlative
For most one-syllable superlative adjectives, add -*est* (or -*st* if the adjective ends in an *e*).	old wise large	the oldest (woman) the wisest the largest
For two-syllable superlative adjectives that end in *y*, change the *y* to an *i* and add -*est*.	busy funny crazy	the busiest (evening) the funniest the craziest
For most other two-syllable superlative adjectives, use *most*.	famous popular	the most famous (singer) the most popular
For superlative adjectives with three syllables or more, use *most*.	important fascinating	the most important (concert) the most fascinating
Some adjectives have irregular superlative forms.	good bad	the best (performance) the worst

Practice
Workbook Page 91

In your notebook, rewrite the sentences below so that the words are in the correct order. You will need to add words to make the sentences complete.

1. singer / the / The / contralto / best
2. the / She / voice / group / had / loudest
3. worker / She / hardest / of all / the
4. was / Eleanor Roosevelt / supporter / most famous
5. was / She / finest / African-American singer / her time

184

WRITING A PERSUASIVE PARAGRAPH

Write an Advertisement

At the end of this unit, you will write a speech. To do this, you'll need to learn some of the skills writers use in persuasive writing. When you write a print advertisement, include facts, information, and descriptive details that will appeal to your target audience. For example, to create a print ad about a sports drink, first think about who will buy the product. Words such as *delicious*, *refreshing*, and *thirst-quenching* are descriptive details about the drink that would appeal to readers. Facts about how the drink works make the drink sound effective. Finally, a picture of the sports drink shows readers what to look for.

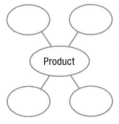

Here is a model of a print ad. Before writing, the writer listed her ideas in a word web like the one above.

Jessica Reider

Surround Yourself with Sound

Hey, music lovers! Are you looking for an audio system that will treat your ears to the richest, most accurate sound? Do you want to hear your favorite songs or symphonies at their best? Then check out the finest audio system money can buy—the 3600XL. The system includes exciting state-of-the-art features such as full-range high-definition sound, a digital equalizer, and a bass-reflex speaker system. The 3600XL has all the components of other systems on the market, but the elegance of its design enables it to fit easily on a bookshelf or a bedside table. Drop batteries into its sleek compartment and you can take it anywhere—on a picnic, to the beach, or to a barbeque. With a handy remote and a choice of three colors—black, white, or silver—the 3600XL is the perfect gift for friends and family members. So stop by your local electronics store and pick up one today! It's never been easier to surround yourself with beautiful sound.

Practice

Workbook
Page 92

Create a print ad. Choose a product or an event you enjoy or a singer or an artist whom you admire. List your ideas in a word web. Be sure to use superlatives that appeal to the target audience.

Writing Checklist

IDEAS:
☑ I included facts and details that will appeal to my target audience.

CONVENTIONS:
☑ I used superlatives correctly.

185

Link the Readings

Critical Thinking

Look back at the readings in this unit. Think about what they have in common. They all tell about right and wrong. Yet they do not all have the same purpose. The purpose of one reading might be to inform, while the purpose of another might be to entertain or persuade. In addition, the content of each reading relates to right and wrong differently. Now copy the chart below into your notebook and complete it.

Title of Reading	Purpose	Big Question Link
"The Golden Serpent"		
"I ♥ Pluto"		
From *A Single Shard*		*Was what Tree-ear did right?*
"Marian Anderson: A Voice for Change"	*to inform*	

Discussion

Discuss in pairs or small groups.

- Look at the chart above. Compare and contrast the readings' purposes and themes.
- **Q How can we tell what's right?** What conclusions can you draw about the ways right and wrong are discussed in each reading? How are they similar? How are they different?

Fluency Check

Work with a partner. Choose a paragraph from one of the readings. Take turns reading it for one minute. Count the total number of words you read. Practice saying the words you had trouble reading. Take turns reading the paragraph three more times. Did you read more words each time? Copy the chart below into your notebook and record your speeds.

	1st Speed	2nd Speed	3rd Speed	4th Speed
Words Per Minute				

Projects

Work in pairs or small groups. Choose one of these projects.

1 Do research to learn about a musician who has struggled to have his or her music heard. Gather information about his or her life and summarize it in a brief essay. Present the essay to the class. Provide a sample of one of the musician's songs.

2 Create a model of our solar system. Include Pluto and other dwarf planets. Display your model for the class and give important details about each celestial body. Explain why Pluto is no longer considered a planet.

3 Do research to learn about rice farming in different countries. Create a flow chart showing the steps of the farming process. Share your work with the class.

4 Find a fable that is important in your home culture. Read the fable aloud to the class. Have the class guess the moral.

Further Reading

To find out more about the theme of this unit, choose from these reading suggestions.

The Interpreter, Charles Randolph
In this Penguin Reader® adaptation, Silva, an interpreter at the United Nations, overhears a dangerous plot. Can the plot be stopped in time?

The House on Mango Street, Sandra Cisneros
Esperanza Cordero's neighborhood is full of harsh realities and harsh beauty. She is all too aware of the low expectations people have of her. So she must invent for herself what she will become.

Walk Two Moons, Sharon Creech
On a car trip from Ohio to Idaho with her grandparents, Salamanca Tree Hiddle traces her missing mother's steps. Drawing strength from her Native American ancestry, Salamanca is able to face the truth about her mother.

Put It All Together

LISTENING & SPEAKING WORKSHOP
Radio Commercial

You and a partner will create and present a radio commerical.

1 **THINK ABOUT IT** Think about the author's opinion of Pluto in "I ♥ Pluto." What words does the author use to make a case for keeping Pluto's status as a planet? How do these words make you feel?

In pairs, discuss how persuasive words can cause you to believe something or change your mind. Think about persuasive words you have heard used in TV and radio commercials. Make a list of these words.

Work together to list ideas for a radio commercial. Write down your ideas. Here are some examples:

- To generate support for the high-school fundraiser
- To advertise a new product that cleans everything
- To advertise a class that teaches you how to take tests
- To advertise a concert featuring your favorite singer

2 **GATHER AND ORGANIZE INFORMATION** With your partner, choose a topic from your list. Then write down the information you want to include in your radio commercial. What words will you use to persuade a listener to buy your product or support your cause? You might want to brainstorm for ideas.

Research Go to the library or search on the Internet to get information about your product or event. Use a dictionary or thesaurus to find persuasive language for your commercial. Take notes on what you find.

Order Your Notes Make a list of arguments, examples, and supporting details you will use to persuade your listener. Then organize your ideas in an outline or another graphic organizer.

3 **PRACTICE AND PRESENT** Use your outline or other graphic organizer to prepare your presentation. With your partner, choose which parts you will each present. Practice presenting the commercial together. Develop oral, visual, or written cues to help you know when it is your turn to speak. Since your radio audience can't see you, work to convey your message with your words and tone of voice.

Deliver Your Radio Commerical Give your presentation from the back of the room so that your classmates can hear but not see you—as if you were radio announcers. Emphasize certain words by changing the volume or tone of your voice. Slow down when you come to the most important points. At the end of the presentation, ask listeners if your radio commercial was effective. Give audience members a chance to "call in" and tell whether they plan to try your product or event.

4 **EVALUATE THE PRESENTATION**
You will improve your skills as a speaker and a listener by evaluating each presentation you give and hear. Use this checklist to help you judge your commercial and the commericals of the other pairs.

☑ Was the radio commercial persuasive? Why or why not?

☑ Was the purpose of the radio commercial clear?

☑ Did the speakers give important details in a way that was easy to understand and remember?

☑ Did the pair speak clearly and loudly?

☑ What suggestions do you have for improving the radio commerical?

Speaking TIPS

Be sure to speak clearly and to repeat important details so that your listeners will understand and remember them.

Use sound effects and your voice to catch the listener's attention. Work with your partner to improve your timing when you speak.

Listening TIPS

What is the radio commercial trying to persuade you to do? If you don't understand, ask questions at the end of the presentation.

Listen for the information you would need to buy the product or attend the event. Try to remember the important details.

WRITING WORKSHOP

Speech

In persuasive writing, the writer tries to persuade readers to change their ideas, beliefs, or behavior. An effective speech begins with a paragraph that clearly states the writer's opinion. It gives reasons, facts, and examples that support the writer's position. Skilled speechwriters also present both sides of an argument in order to anticipate and counter opposing opinions. A speech concludes with a paragraph that restates the writer's opinion in a new way.

You will write a five-paragraph speech that expresses your opinion about something that you feel needs to be changed in your school or community.

1 PREWRITE Brainstorm a list of possible topics for your speech in your notebook. What do you think needs to change in your school or community? How can you persuade others to agree with your opinion? Select one item on your list to write about.

List and Organize Ideas and Details After you choose a topic, make a T-chart. In the Pros column, give arguments that support your opinion. In the Cons column, give arguments that oppose your opinion so that you can counter these in your speech. A student named Leah decided to write a speech in favor of wearing school uniforms. Here is the T-chart she prepared.

Pros	Cons
Uniforms promote equality. They would reduce economic tension. It would be easier to get dressed in the morning.	Uniforms suppress individuality. Uniforms cost money.

2 DRAFT Use the model on page 193 and your T-chart to help you write a first draft. Make sure that the tone of your speech suits your audience. Include reasons, facts, and examples to support your opinion.

3 **REVISE** Read over your draft. As you do so, ask yourself the questions in the writing checklist. Use the questions to help you revise your speech.

SIX TRAITS OF WRITING CHECKLIST

☑ **IDEAS:** Is my opinion clear?

☑ **ORGANIZATION:** Are my ideas presented in an order that makes sense?

☑ **VOICE:** Does my tone suit my audience?

☑ **WORD CHOICE:** Do I use persuasive words that will appeal to listeners?

☑ **SENTENCE FLUENCY:** Do my sentences flow well when read aloud?

☑ **CONVENTIONS:** Does my writing follow the rules of grammar, usage, and mechanics?

Here are the changes Leah plans to make when she revises her draft:

School Uniforms—A Very Good Idea!

In public schools, students do not wear school uniforms. Though [most ^] there is a dress code, students [are generally allowed to ^] wear whatever they want. If ~~people~~ [anyone] asked a student at my school, "Would you like school uniforms?" I can guarantee that the majority would say <u>no</u>. But if we really ~~take a moment to~~ think about the advantages of uniforms, the idea seems a lot more appealing.

The most important reason that school uniforms would be a good idea is that they would reduce tension between students There would be less focus on who's wearing ~~nicer~~ [the nicest] clothes and how much money someone's clothes cost. As a result, student would be able to focus more on learning and making friends, which is what school is really about.

191

School uniforms would also make life a lot easier for other reasons, too. There would be less stress every morning about clothes. Students come to school late, complaining that they've had a bad morning because they didn't know what to wear or couldn't find a certain shirt. They would have more time *for* to get a better night's sleep and be less likely to come to school late.

Shouldn't we, as students, try to express ourselves, not through clothes, but through actions? Whether or not we are wearing uniforms, we can still do what makes us happy. A frequent argument against school uniforms is that they suppress individuality. A musician can still play an instrument. An athlete can still play a sport. What makes each of us an individual should be shown through what we do, not what we wear.

When we assess the pros and cons of school uniforms, school uniforms don't seem bad. They would teach students that clothes aren't everything and that school shouldn't feel like a contest. I believe that uniforms can help *simplify our lives* reduce the barriers between students, while enhancing our focus on learning.

4 EDIT AND PROOFREAD  Workbook Page 93

Copy your revised draft onto a clean sheet of paper. Read it again. Correct any errors in grammar, word usage, mechanics, and spelling. Here are the additional changes Leah plans to make when she prepares her final draft.

Leah Morales

School Uniforms—A Very Good Idea!

In most public schools, students do not wear school uniforms. Though there is a dress code, students are generally allowed to wear whatever they want. If anyone asked a student at my school, "Would you like school uniforms?" I can guarantee that the majority would say <u>no</u>. But if we really think about the advantages of uniforms, the idea seems a lot more appealing.

The most important reason that school uniforms would be a good idea is that they would reduce tension between students. There would be less focus on who's wearing the nicest clothes and how much money someone's clothes cost. As a result, students would be able to focus more on learning and making friends, which is what school is really about.

School uniforms would make life a lot easier for other reasons, too. There would be less stress every morning about clothes. Some Students come to school late, complaining that they've had a bad morning because they didn't know what to wear. They would have more time for sleep and be less likely to come to school late.

A frequent argument against school uniforms is that they suppress individuality. Shouldn't we, as students, try to express ourselves, not through clothes, but through actions? Whether or not we are wearing uniforms, we can still do what makes us happy. A musician can still play an instrument. An athlete can still play a sport. What makes each of us an individual should be shown through what we do, not what we wear.

When we assess the pros and cons of school uniforms, school uniforms don't seem bad. They would teach students that clothes aren't everything and that school shouldn't feel like a contest. I believe that uniforms can help simplify our lives, while enhancing our allowing us to focus on learning.

5 **PUBLISH** Prepare your final draft. Share your speech with your teacher and classmates.

193

Learn about *Art* with the
Smithsonian American Art Museum

That's Art?

*F*or centuries when people looked at art, they expected to see traditional paintings or sculptures of recognizable subjects, such as the human body. But over time, artists began to ask the question, "What is art?" Their answers have pushed the definition way beyond framed paintings on a wall.

Deborah Butterfield, *Monekana* (2001)

In *Monekana*, Deborah Butterfield finds a way to create a full-sized image of a horse from what appears to be random pieces of wood. In fact, it's a bronze sculpture based on pieces of Hawaiian Okea wood. The artist brought the wood together into a horse shape and then cast the work in bronze. The special patina, or coating, on the bronze gives it the color of driftwood. *Monekana* is the Hawaiian word for Montana, the state where Butterfield lives and teaches at a university.

◄ Deborah Butterfield, *Monekana*, 2001, bronze, 96 x 129½ x 63½ in., Smithsonian American Art Museum

Sam Gilliam, *Swing* (1969)

In *Swing*, Sam Gilliam cuts his painting loose from any kind of frame. He lets it hang by a few strands of rawhide. Gilliam may have been the first painter to introduce the idea of an unsupported canvas. Traditionally, artists would always stretch a canvas and attach it to a wooden frame before painting it. Inspired in part by the sight of laundry hanging on a clothesline, Gilliam folded and squeezed a huge piece of paint-stained wet canvas and then hung it up before it dried. Even the title of the final work, *Swing*, suggests a movement not normally associated with a finished painting. Gilliam believed that good artists "just work and let things go."

▲ Sam Gilliam, *Swing*, 1969, acrylic and aluminum, 119⅝ x 283½ in., Smithsonian American Art Museum

Man Ray, *Cadeau (Serie II)* (1970)

Man Ray's iron has sharp tacks glued to its bottom. It hardly seems like a *cadeau*, which means "gift" in French. Man Ray once said he took the "greatest pleasure" in changing

actual objects. He would remove them from their everyday locations, sometimes alter them, and then exhibit them as art. In the early 1920s, Man Ray was a leader among American and European artists who pushed to redefine what could be officially considered "art." He was one of the first to say that art is just about anything that serves an artist's creative purposes.

▲ Man Ray, *Cadeau (Serie II)*, 1970, iron, 6⅛ x 4 x 3½ in., Smithsonian American Art Museum

All three of these artists had to think about what it means to be an artist and what materials they felt they could use and still call their work "art." In each case, the viewer understands that the object they are looking at is not simply wood, canvas, or an iron, but part of some bigger story shaped by the artist's hand.

Apply What You Learned

1 How do the three artists use everyday objects in their artworks?

2 In what way does each artist push the boundaries as to what can be considered art?

Big Question

Do you think all of these objects could be considered art, or would you look at one or more of them and exclaim, *That's art?!* Explain your answer.

Workbook
Pages 95–96

195

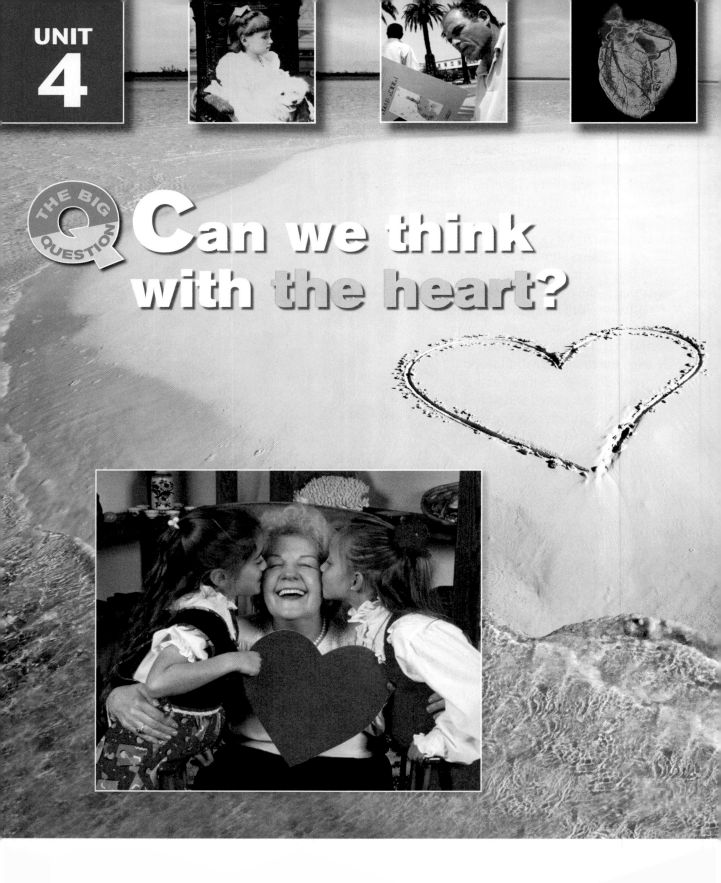

UNIT 4

THE BIG QUESTION

Can we think with the heart?

This unit is about love, friendship, and the human heart. You will read about different kinds of love. You will also read about the heart and the circulatory system. Reading, writing, and talking about these topics will give you practice using academic language and help you become a better student.

READING 1: Autobiography
- From *The Story of My Life* by Helen Keller

READING 2: Play Excerpt
- From *The Little Prince: The Play* by Rick Cummins and John Scoullar, adapted from the novel by Antoine de Saint-Exupéry

READING 3: Science Article
- "The Heart: Our Circulatory System" by Seymour Simon
- Heart-Healthy Recipe

READING 4: Short Story
- "Ginger for the Heart" by Paul Yee

Listening and Speaking

At the end of this unit, you will prepare and give a **demonstration**.

Writing

In this unit, you will practice **expository writing**. Expository writing gives information about a topic. After each reading, you will learn a skill that will help you write an expository paragraph. At the end of the unit, you will use the skills you've learned to write an expository essay.

QuickWrite
Talk with a partner about things you associate with hearts. List your ideas on a sheet of paper.

What You Will Learn

Reading
- Vocabulary building: *Context, dictionary skills, word study*
- Reading strategy: *Identify main idea and details*
- Text type: *Informational text (social studies)*

Grammar, Usage, and Mechanics
Possessive adjectives

Writing
Write a critique

THE BIG QUESTION

Can we think with the heart? What emotional difficulties do you think a person who could not see or hear would have? What kind of emotional help might he or she need? Discuss with a partner.

BUILD BACKGROUND

You are about to read excerpts from **The Story of My Life**, Helen Keller's autobiography. An autobiography is a story that a person writes about his or her own life.

Helen Keller was born on June 27, 1880, a perfectly healthy baby. When she was just nineteen months old, she became gravely ill. Although she recovered, her illness left her hearing impaired (unable to hear) and sight impaired (unable to see). When Helen was almost seven years old, a teacher named Anne Sullivan came to live with her and her family. These excerpts tell what happened when Anne Sullivan first came into Helen's life.

▲ Helen Keller standing in her study, reading a Braille book

Learn Key Words

Read these sentences. Use the context to figure out the meaning of the **red** words. Use a dictionary to check your answers. Then write each word and its meaning in your notebook.

Key Words

bitterness
defects
eventful
imitate
sensation
tangible

1. Before Helen Keller met Anne Sullivan, she was filled with an intense anger, or **bitterness**.

2. The diamond was a perfect gem; it had no flaws or **defects**.

3. That day in 1887 was **eventful** for Helen because it was when Anne Sullivan entered her life and changed it forever.

4. Some birds, such as parrots, can **imitate** people by repeating words they hear people say.

5. She had the **sensation**, or feeling, that something interesting was about to happen.

6   Helen was surrounded by a darkness so **tangible**, she could almost feel it.

Practice

Write the sentences in your notebook. Choose a **red** word from the box above to complete each sentence. Then take turns reading the sentences aloud with a partner.

1. In dance class, you need to watch the teacher closely and _____ his moves.

2. The day my mother came home with my baby sister was an _____ day for my family.

3. Helen paused for a moment, enjoying the _____ of sun and a gentle breeze on her face.

4. Before she understood the concept of language, Helen got her information from _____ things that she could touch.

5. Because she was filled with _____ and frustration, Helen often misbehaved.

6. Before you buy something, you should examine it to make sure it has no _____.

199

Learn Academic Words

Study the **red** words and their meanings. You will find these words useful when talking and writing about informational texts. Write each word and its meaning in your notebook. After you read the excerpts from *The Story of My Life,* try to use these words to respond to the text.

Academic Words

communicate
concept
manual
persistence

communicate = express your thoughts and feelings so that other people understand them	→	People **communicate** by using language, facial expressions, and physical gestures, or movements.
concept = idea	→	Anne Sullivan had to teach Helen the **concept** of language as well as the language itself.
manual = having to do with the hand or hands	→	Miss Sullivan taught Helen how to spell words using the **manual** alphabet.
persistence = the act of continuing firmly in some state, purpose, or course of action	→	Helen's **persistence** and determination helped her achieve her goals.

Practice  **Workbook** Page 98

Work with a partner to answer these questions. Try to include the **red** word in your answer. Write the sentences in your notebook.

1. What are some ways we **communicate** without using words?

2. In what ways is the **concept** of language both simple and complex at the same time?

3. What reasons might some people have for preferring **manual** labor to other kinds of work?

4. Do you think **persistence** is a good quality or a bad quality? Why?

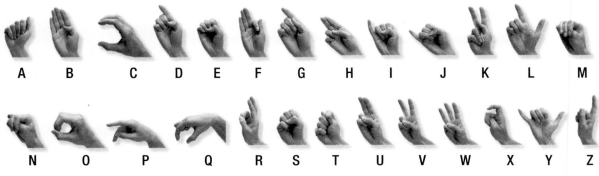

A   B   C   D   E   F   G   H   I   J   K   L   M

N   O   P   Q   R   S   T   U   V   W   X   Y   Z

▲ Hands demonstrating the letters of the manual alphabet

Word Study: The Suffix *-ful*

A suffix is a group of letters added to the end of a word to form a new word. Adding a suffix often changes the word's meaning and its part of speech. The suffix *-ful* means "full of." Adding the suffix *-ful* to a noun changes it to an adjective. When adding *-ful* to a word that has two or more syllables and ends in *y*, such as the word *beauty*, change the *y* to an *i* before adding the suffix *-ful*.

---

color + **-ful** = color**ful** (meaning "full of color")
beauty + **-ful** = beaut**iful** (meaning "full of beauty")

Practice

Work with a partner. Copy the chart below into your notebook. Complete the chart by adding *-ful* to each word. Then write a sentence with each new word and read the sentences aloud to your partner. If you need help understanding the meaning of a word, use a dictionary.

Base word	+ -ful	Meaning
event		
bounty		
care		
pity		
wonder		

READING STRATEGY | IDENTIFY MAIN IDEA AND DETAILS

Identifying the main ideas and details in a reading helps you see the key points the author is making. Main ideas are the most important ideas in a text. The details are pieces of information that support the main ideas. To identify the main ideas and details, follow these steps:

- Read the first paragraph. What do you think is the most important idea in it? What facts, examples, or other pieces of information tell more about the main idea? These are the details.
- Read the whole text. Look for main ideas and supporting details.
- Remember that the main ideas can be anywhere in a text.

As you read the excerpt from *The Story of My Life*, identify the main ideas. Then find details that support each main idea.

Set a purpose for reading Read this excerpt from Helen Keller's autobiography to find out how meeting Anne Sullivan changed Helen's life. How did Miss Sullivan affect Helen emotionally?

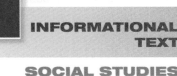

This photograph was taken when Helen Keller was seven years old. ▶

from

The Story of My Life

Helen Keller

Chapter 1

One brief spring, musical with the song of robin and mockingbird, one summer rich in fruit and roses, one autumn of gold and crimson sped by and left their gifts at the feet of an eager, delighted child. Then, in the dreary month of February, came the illness which closed my eyes and ears and plunged me into the **unconsciousness** of a newborn baby. They called it acute congestion of the stomach and brain. The doctor thought I could not live. Early one morning, however, the fever left me as suddenly and mysteriously as it had come. There was great **rejoicing** in the family that morning, but no one, not even the doctor, knew that I should never see or hear again.

---

unconsciousness, lack of awareness

rejoicing, celebrating

✳ ✳ ✳

Gradually I got used to the silence and darkness that surrounded me and forgot that it had ever been different, until she came—my teacher—who was to set my spirit free. But during the first nineteen months of my life I had caught glimpses of broad, green fields, a luminous sky, trees, and flowers which the darkness that followed could not wholly blot out. If we have once seen, "the day is ours, and what the day has shown."

---

blot out, wipe out completely

◀ Anne Sullivan at around age fifteen

✳ ✳ ✳

Chapter 3

My aunt made me a big doll out of towels. It was the most comical, shapeless thing, this improvised doll, with no nose, mouth, ears or eyes—nothing that even the imagination of a child could convert into a face. Curiously enough, the absence of eyes struck me more than all the other defects put together. I pointed this out to everybody with provoking persistency, but no one seemed equal to the task of providing the doll with eyes. A bright idea, however, shot into my mind, and the problem was solved. I tumbled off the seat and searched under it until I found my aunt's cape, which was trimmed with large beads. I pulled two beads off and indicated to her that I wanted her to sew them on my doll. She raised my hand to her eyes in a questioning way, and I nodded energetically. The beads were sewed in the right place and I could not contain myself for joy. . . .

---

improvised, made without preparation, using materials at hand
provoking, making others angry or annoyed

BEFORE YOU GO ON

1 What happened when Helen was nineteen months old?

2 What bothered Helen about her doll? How did she solve the problem?

On Your Own
In what ways was young Helen just like any other girl?

203

▲ Anne spelling words into Helen's hand in 1893

* * *

Chapter 4

The most important day I remember in all my life is the one on which my teacher, Anne Mansfield Sullivan, came to me. I am filled with wonder when I consider the immeasurable contrasts between the two lives which it connects. It was the third of March, 1887, three months before I was seven years old.

On the afternoon of that eventful day, I stood on the porch, dumb, expectant. I guessed vaguely from my mother's signs and from the hurrying to and fro in the house that something unusual was about to happen, so I went to the door and waited on the steps. The afternoon sun penetrated the mass of honeysuckle that covered the porch and fell on my upturned face. My fingers lingered almost unconsciously on the familiar leaves and blossoms which had just come forth to greet the sweet southern spring. I did not know what the future held of marvel or surprise for me. Anger and bitterness had preyed upon me continually for weeks and a deep languor had succeeded this passionate struggle.

---

immeasurable, enormous

languor, feeling of tiredness
passionate, involving intense feelings

Have you ever been at sea in a dense fog, when it seemed as if a tangible white darkness shut you in, and the great ship, tense and anxious, groped her way toward the shore with plummet and sounding-line, and you waited with beating heart for something to happen? I was like that ship before my education began, only I was without compass or sounding-line and had no way of knowing how near the harbor was. "Light! Give me light!" was the wordless cry of my soul, and the light of love shone on me in that very hour.

I felt approaching footsteps. I stretched out my hand as I supposed to my mother. Someone took it, and I was caught up and held close in the arms of her who had come to reveal all things to me, and, more than all things else, to love me.

---

groped, felt around for something to hold onto

◀ Helen sitting with her dog and reading a book in 1904

The morning after my teacher came she led me into her room and gave me a doll. The little blind children at the Perkins Institution had sent it and Laura Bridgman had dressed it; but I didn't know this until afterward. When I had played with it a little while, Miss Sullivan slowly spelled into my hand the word "d-o-l-l." I was at once interested in this finger play and tried to imitate it. When I finally succeeded in making the letters correctly I was flushed with childish pleasure and pride. Running downstairs to my mother, I held up my hand and made the letters for doll. I did not know that I was spelling a word or even that words existed; I was simply making my fingers go in monkey-like imitation. In the days that followed, I learned to spell in this uncomprehending way a great many words, among them *pin, hat, cup,* and a few verbs like *sit, stand,* and *walk*. But my teacher had been with me several weeks before I understood that everything has a name.

Perkins Institution, school for sight-impaired students founded in 1832
Laura Bridgman, hearing- and sight-impaired woman who had learned to read and write at the Perkins Institution in the 1830s

BEFORE YOU GO ON

1 What does Helen say she was like before Anne Sullivan came?

2 Why does Helen call spelling "finger play"?

On Your Own
Have you ever felt like a ship lost at sea in a fog? Explain.

One day, while I was playing with my new doll, Miss Sullivan put my big rag doll into my lap also, spelled "d-o-l-l" and tried to make me understand that "d-o-l-l" applied to both. Earlier in the day we had had a tussle over the words "m-u-g" and "w-a-t-e-r." Miss Sullivan had tried to impress it upon me that "m-u-g" is *mug* and that "w-a-t-e-r" is *water*, but I persisted in confounding the two. In despair, she had dropped the subject for the time, only to renew it at the first opportunity. I became impatient at her repeated attempts and, seizing the new doll, I dashed it upon the floor. I was keenly delighted when I felt the fragments of the broken doll at my feet. Neither sorrow nor regret followed my passionate outburst. I had not loved the doll. In the still, dark world in which I lived there was no strong sentiment of tenderness. I felt my teacher sweep the fragments to one side of the hearth, and I had a sense of satisfaction that the cause of my discomfort was removed. She brought me my hat, and I knew I was going out into the warm sunshine. This thought, if a wordless sensation may be called a thought, made me hop and skip with pleasure.

We walked down the path to the well-house, attracted by the fragrance of the honeysuckle with which it was covered. Someone was drawing water and my teacher placed my hand under the spout. As the cool stream gushed over one hand she spelled into the other the word *water*, first slowly, then rapidly. I stood

---

sentiment, feeling or emotion
drawing water, pumping water from a well

▼ The water pump at Helen's home in Tuscumbia, Alabama

◀ Helen, age 31, working at her desk

still, my whole attention fixed upon the motions of her fingers. Suddenly I felt a misty consciousness as of something forgotten—a thrill of returning thought; and somehow the mystery of language was revealed to me. I knew then that "w-a-t-e-r" meant the wonderful cool something that was flowing over my hand. That living word awakened my soul, gave it light, hope, joy, set it free! There were barriers still, it is true, but barriers that could in time be swept away.

I left the well-house eager to learn. Everything had a name, and each name gave birth to a new thought. As we returned to the house every object which I touched seemed to quiver with life. That was because I saw everything with the

strange, new sight that had come to me. On entering the door I remembered the doll I had broken. I felt my way to the hearth and picked up the pieces. I tried vainly to put them together. Then my eyes filled with tears; for I realized what I had done, and for the first time I felt repentance and sorrow.

I learned a great many new words that day. I do not remember what they all were; but I do know that *mother*, *father*, *sister*, and *teacher* were among them—words that were to make the world blossom for me, "like Aaron's rod, with flowers." It would have been difficult to find a happier child than I was as I lay in my crib at the close of that eventful day and lived over the joys it had brought me, and for the first time longed for a new day to come.

---

vainly, without success
repentance, regret; remorse
Aaron's rod, the staff carried by Moses's brother Aaron, believed to have miraculous power

BEFORE YOU GO ON

1 What was the first word that Helen understood?

2 How did learning one word change Helen's attitude about life?

💡**On Your Own**
Have you ever learned something important from someone who loved you? Explain.

COMPREHENSION

Workbook
Page 101

Right There

1. For how much of her life did Helen have the abilities to see and hear?

2. How did Helen feel when she first smashed her doll?

Think and Search

3. Why does Helen describe the time before and after Anne Sullivan came into her life as two lives of "immeasurable contrasts"?

4. What "mystery of language" did Helen finally understand when she felt the water coming out of the pump?

Author and You

5. Why do you think Helen was suddenly able to feel repentance?

6. Do you think the fact that Helen could once see and hear helped her understand that words are names for things? Explain.

On Your Own

7. Did you ever have a breakthrough of understanding after working hard at something? Explain.

8. What would your life be like if you suddenly had no means of communicating with people?

IN YOUR OWN WORDS

Reread the excerpts and list all the main ideas and details you can identify. You can complete a graphic organizer like the one below for each main idea. When you have finished, review your work with a partner. Revise your graphic organizers to include any new ideas. Then use your revised work to tell a friend or a family member about the reading.

> **Speaking TIP**
>
> Refer to your notes when you need to, but keep your eyes on your listeners as much as possible.

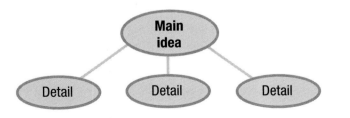

DISCUSSION

Discuss in pairs or small groups.

1. How did Anne Sullivan change Helen Keller's life?

2. Why was it so important for Helen Keller to understand that the letters she was making with her fingers spelled words and that words were names for things?

Q **Can we think with the heart?** What does Helen Keller's experience say about the power of love?

))) **Listening TIP**

Be a patient listener. Give each speaker a chance to express his or her ideas.

READ FOR FLUENCY

Reading with feeling helps make what you read more interesting. Work with a partner. Choose a paragraph from the reading. Read the paragraph. Ask each other how you felt after reading the paragraph. Did you feel happy or sad?

Take turns reading the paragraph aloud to each other with a tone of voice that represents how you felt when you read it the first time. Give each other feedback.

EXTENSION

Workbook
Page 101

The story is written from Helen Keller's point of view. What would the story be like if Anne Sullivan told it instead of Helen? Imagine that you are Anne Sullivan and write a journal entry in your notebook. Tell what happened when you were working with Helen and how you felt about it. When you are finished, read your journal entry to a partner.

▲ Helen Keller and Anne Sullivan play chess in 1900.

Grammar and Writing

Possessive Adjectives

A possessive adjective shows possession, or ownership. It is always followed by a noun. A possessive adjective agrees with the noun or pronoun that reflects who the owner is—*not* with the noun it modifies.

	Possessive Adjective	Modifies a Singular Noun	Modifies a Plural Noun
1st Person Singular	**my**	**my** teacher	**my** teachers
2nd Person Singular	**your**	**your** key	**your** keys
3rd Person Singular	**her** (Helen's) **his** (the father's) **its** (the doll's)	**her** hand **his** hat **its** eye	**her** hands **his** hats **its** eyes
1st Person Plural	**our**	**our** dog	**our** dogs
2nd Person Plural	**your**	**your** book	**your** books
3rd Person Plural	**their** (Helen's and Anne's)	**their** story	**their** stories

Practice

Copy the sentences into your notebook. Work with a partner. Choose the correct possessive adjective to replace the words in parentheses.

1. I pulled two beads off _____ cape. (Aunt Jane's)

2. The seasons sped by and left _____ gifts at my feet. (the seasons')

3. Mr. Keller hired Anne Sullivan to teach _____ daughter. (Mr. Keller's)

4. I held the doll and stroked _____ hair. (the doll's)

5. Anne Sullivan said, "She's _____ pupil!" (Anne Sullivan's)

WRITING AN EXPOSITORY PARAGRAPH

Write a Critique

To write an expository essay at the end of this unit, you'll need to learn some of the skills used in expository writing. One type of expository writing is a critique. When you write a critique, you judge a work based on standards. You tell what the standards are and then explain why the work did or didn't meet them. For example, suppose you enjoy films that make you laugh but also make you think. Then you would judge films based on these two standards: Was it funny? Was it thought-provoking?

Standards met	Standards not met

This model is a critique of the film about Helen Keller and Anne Sullivan called *The Miracle Worker*. Before the writer began writing, he listed his ideas in a T-chart like the one above.

Santos Rivera III

The Miracle Worker

Recently I saw a movie called <u>The Miracle Worker</u>—now, it is my favorite film. It has every quality that I look for in a movie: It is exciting, inspiring, and based on a true story. It realistically portrays the difficulties Helen Keller experienced growing up. It shows how Anne Sullivan helped Helen understand what language is by using her fingers to spell words into Helen's hand. My favorite scene in the movie is also the most exciting one. Sullivan puts one of Helen's hands under running water and spells the word <u>water</u> into the other hand. Helen suddenly understands that "w-a-t-e-r" means the liquid gushing over her hand. Anne Sullivan was an amazing teacher, truly deserving of the title "miracle worker." The film definitely lived up to my expectations. It was uplifting and inspirational. It teaches a valuable lesson—that no matter how great certain obstacles may seem, anything is possible.

Practice

Workbook Page 103

Write a critique of a story, book, movie, or play. List your ideas in a T-chart like the one above. Be sure to use possessive adjectives correctly.

Writing Checklist

IDEAS:
☑ I identified the standards on which I based my judgment.

SENTENCE FLUENCY:
☑ I varied my sentence length.

211

Prepare to Read

What You Will Learn

Reading
- Vocabulary building: *Literary terms, word study*
- Reading strategy: *Analyze text structure*
- Text type: *Literature (play)*

Grammar, Usage, and Mechanics
Present and past progressive

Writing
Write a summary

THE BIG QUESTION

Can we think with the heart? Have you ever made a new friend when you weren't expecting to? What can we learn from unexpected friendships? Discuss with a partner.

BUILD BACKGROUND

This excerpt is from a play based on the novel ***The Little Prince***, written by Antoine de Saint-Exupéry in 1943. Originally written in French, *The Little Prince* has been translated into many different languages and is still widely read all over the world.

The novel is about the adventures of the Little Prince, who lives by himself on an asteroid. On the asteroid there is a special rose that the Little Prince takes care of every day. One day he leaves his asteroid to find out what the rest of the universe is like. In this excerpt the Little Prince is visiting Earth, where he meets the Fox. During his time with the Fox, he makes a new friend and learns a valuable lesson.

▲ Lahbib Fouad translated *The Little Prince* into Amazigh, the language of the ethnic Berbers living in many of Morocco's rural areas.

Learn Literary Words

A **fantasy** is an imaginative story that usually includes characters, settings, or events not found in real life. Fantasies often involve supernatural elements or imaginary creatures and places. What elements of fantasy can you find in the play excerpt below?

Ben:	Hello? Is someone there?
Speck:	[*comes out from bushes*] Ben! [*sniffs ground*] It's me! Your dog!
Ben:	Speck? I—uh—I don't understand. . . . Did you *say* something?
Speck:	Yep, I sure did. Funny thing is, I don't know why I'm talking—it's mighty queer. [*sniffs air*] But now that I can talk, I can't stop. [*sniffs the grass*] You know, the smell of grass reminds me of a time . . .
Ben:	[*groans and puts his head in his hands*] Oh, no . . .

Plays are written to be performed on a stage. **Stage directions** are instructions that tell the actors what they should do and how they should do it. Stage directions also describe sets, lighting, and sound effects. They are in italic type, set off by brackets or parentheses, and are not spoken. It is important to read the stage directions when you read a play because they help you visualize the action. Reread the example above. What do the stage directions tell you?

Practice  **Workbook Page 104**

Work with a partner. Read the play excerpt below. As you read, answer these questions: How can you tell it is a play? Who are the characters? What are the stage directions? Which lines are spoken?

Ben:	Speck, nothing personal, but I liked you better before. Maybe if you go back into the bushes, you'll be yourself again.
Speck:	[*pauses*] But then you'd miss your big chance.
Ben:	My big chance?
Speck:	To be famous! How many talking-dog owners do you know? You'd be on the news, on talk shows, in a movie! Can't you see it?
Ben:	I'm not interested. I just want my dog back. I miss Speck. [***Speck** goes into bushes and trots back out, barking. **Ben** tosses ball offstage. **Speck** exits left. **Ben** exits left. Lights fade to black.*]

Learn Academic Words

Study the **red** words and their meanings. You will find these words useful when talking and writing about literature. Write each word and its meaning in your notebook. After you read the excerpt from *The Little Prince: The Play*, try to use these words to respond to the text.

Academic Words

establish
source
unique
version

establish = begin or set in motion	➡	The boy wanted to **establish** a friendship with his classmate so he could have someone to study with.
source = the cause of something or the place where it starts	➡	The **source** of the bad smell was an old piece of fruit that had fallen under the stove.
unique = being the one and only of its kind	➡	I decided to buy the shirt because it was **unique**; I had never seen anything like it.
version = a reworking of an existing work	➡	This play is a new **version** of the novel that was written years ago.

Practice  **Workbook** Page 105

Work with a partner to answer these questions. Try to include the **red** word in your answer. Write the sentences in your notebook.

1. What actions do you take to **establish** a friendship?

2. What is one **source** of happiness in your life? What is one **source** of annoyance or frustration?

3. What are some of the traits that make you **unique**?

4. Do you usually prefer the book or movie **version** of a story? Explain.

▲ This wreath was set afloat in the Mediterranean Sea on July 31, 2004, to mark the day—sixty years earlier—when Antoine de Saint-Exupéry disappeared during a wartime flying mission.

214

Word Study: Contractions

A contraction is a word that comes from two words that have been joined. An apostrophe (') indicates where letters have been deleted. Contractions are used with pronouns in speaking and informal writing. Below are some examples of commonly used contractions.

Rules	Examples
pronoun + **will**	**We'll** sit down together.
pronoun + **have** + past participle	**I've had** lots of practice.
pronoun + **be**	**I'm** beginning to understand.
pronoun + **would**	**I'd** like to, really.
pronoun + **had better**	**You'd better** watch out.
could + **have** + past participle	I **could've** stayed for days.
Let + **us**	**Let's** play hide and seek.
negative	I **don't** have much time.

Practice  Workbook Page 106

Copy the sentences below into your notebook. Change the bold words to contractions. Then read the sentences aloud with a partner.

1. "**(I will)** _____ be your friend," said the Little Prince.
2. "**(We would)** _____ have fun together," said the Fox.
3. "We **(could have)** _____ spent yesterday together," said the Fox.
4. "**(We have)** _____ wasted a day," said the Little Prince.
5. "**(Does not)** _____ it look nice?" asked the Fox.

READING STRATEGY | **ANALYZE TEXT STRUCTURE**

Analyzing text structure tells you what kind of text you're reading. There are many different kinds. Read these descriptions:

- Stories are written in paragraphs. Dialogue is enclosed within quotation marks.
- Poems are usually written in lines and groups of lines. Punctuation doesn't always follow standard rules.
- Plays are mainly written in dialogue. The dialogue has the speakers' names, followed by colons, and then the words the speaker says. Stage directions are usually in parentheses or brackets.

Review the text structure of the excerpt from *The Little Prince: The Play.*

 Workbook Page 107

215

Set a purpose for reading Read this play excerpt to find out about an interesting and unusual pair. What do the Little Prince and the Fox learn about friendship?

from

The Little Prince: The Play

Rick Cummins and John Scoullar

FOX: Good morning.

LITTLE PRINCE: [*stops crying, looks around*] Good morning.

FOX: [*scampers across to a tree*] I'm right here under the apple tree.

LITTLE PRINCE: Who are you? You're very pretty to look at. [*Little Prince starts to approach Fox. Fox scampers away nervously. . . .*]

FOX: I'm a fox.

LITTLE PRINCE: Will you come play with me? I'm so unhappy. [. . . *Little Prince moves toward him. Fox growls.*]

FOX: Play with you—I can't play with you!

LITTLE PRINCE: Why not?

FOX: Because—because—I'm not tamed—and you're a— one of them.

LITTLE PRINCE: Them? [. . . *Fox scampers away again.*]

FOX: The ones . . . with the guns. The hunters. [*Fox scampers nervously.*] Yeah, you're one of those hunters . . . oh, sure, you don't look dangerous cause you're little. But how can I be sure it's not a trap. Very clever. No, no, as things are, I'd better just—[*Fox begins to scamper off. Little Prince stops Fox from leaving. . . .*]

LITTLE PRINCE: But I don't have a gun! [*Fox stops and looks as Little Prince opens his arms wide to display no concealed weapon.*] See.

---

scampers, runs with short, quick steps

216

Fox: [*looking around*] Then you'd better watch out for them, too. [*He keeps his distance throughout the scene.*]

Little Prince: What does that mean "tamed"?

Fox: You don't live around here, do you?

Little Prince: What does that mean "tamed"?

Fox: What are you looking for?

Little Prince: I was looking for men.

Fox: Men—Brrr! Grr. They have guns and they hunt. It's very disturbing!

Little Prince: Oh.

Fox: They also raise chickens. Guns and chickens. These are their only interests.

Little Prince: Ah.

Fox: Are you looking for chickens?

Little Prince: What?

Fox: Chickens.

Little Prince: No. I was looking for men.

Fox: Oh, that's right.

Little Prince: What does that mean "tamed"?

Fox: [*sighs*] Boy, you don't let go of a question, do you? It's an act too often neglected. It means . . . to establish ties.

Little Prince: To establish ties?

---

neglected, disregarded; ignored

BEFORE YOU GO ON

1 Why won't the Fox play with the Little Prince?

2 What does "tamed" mean to the Fox?

On Your Own Would you want to tame the Fox? Why or why not?

217

Fox: Yeah . . . see, to me you're just another little boy just like a hundred thousand other little boys and I have no need of you. And you—well, have no need of me. To you, I'm nothing more than a fox like a hundred thousand other foxes.

LITTLE PRINCE: Oh, I see.

Fox: But if you tamed me—to me you'd be unique in all the world. And to you, I'd be unique in all the world. Then—we'd need each other.

LITTLE PRINCE: I'm beginning to understand. There was a flower— a rose.

Fox: Like the ones on that wall down the road?

LITTLE PRINCE: [*nods sadly*] I think she tried to tame me.

Fox: It's possible. On Earth one sees all sorts of things.

LITTLE PRINCE: Oh, but this wasn't on Earth.

Fox: Wasn't on Earth?

LITTLE PRINCE: No.

Fox: Some other planet, maybe?

LITTLE PRINCE: Yes.

Fox: Right—are there hunters on that planet?

LITTLE PRINCE: No.

Fox: Hmm . . . Are there chickens?

LITTLE PRINCE: No.

Fox: Well, nothing's perfect.

LITTLE PRINCE: No.

Fox: No. [*Pause.*] My life, you know . . . it's well, it's . . . I hunt chickens. Men hunt me. All the chickens are alike. All the men are alike. It's—very monotonous.

LITTLE PRINCE: What?

Fox: Well see, I search me out a chicken —hey, a fella's got to eat. But then, the hunters, they chase me through the woods and down the hills until I have to dive into a hole to hide from them until they give up. Every day it's pretty much the same old thing. [*Yawn.*] Search, run, hide. Sometimes I sit down in that hole for hours just thinking.

---

monotonous, boring because it's always the same
search me out a chicken, try to find a chicken for myself

✔ **LITERARY CHECK**
How do you know this play is a fantasy?

LITTLE PRINCE: About what?

FOX: About—what it might be like if it was—different. If someday, someone came along—someone without a gun. Someone whose footsteps would make me excited instead of sending me scurrying away. Someone who would—[*He looks at **Little Prince**.*] . . . tame me.

LITTLE PRINCE: I'd like to, really, but I don't have much time. I have so many things to understand.

FOX: You only understand the things you tame. Men have no time to understand anything, so they have no friends. If you want to understand—if you want a friend—you've got to tame me.

LITTLE PRINCE: What must I do to tame you?

FOX: You must be very patient. I'm still a wild animal, after all. First, we'll sit down together in the grass. [***Fox** indicates **Little Prince** to sit further and further away until they are quite far apart.*] Then I'll look at you out of the corner of my eye and you will say nothing. Words are the source of misunderstanding. But every day we will sit a little closer. Day after day.

LITTLE PRINCE: Shall we begin?

FOX: Tomorrow. Meet me right here.

LITTLE PRINCE: Tomorrow?

FOX: Tomorrow.

[***Little Prince** exits. Lights change. **Little Prince** reenters.*]

LITTLE PRINCE: Good morning! [***Little Prince** catches **Fox** asleep and is much too close. **Fox** reflexively growls ferociously and snaps, catching **Little Prince**'s hand in his mouth. After a moment he slowly extracts it, battling with his own nature. **Little Prince** rubs his hand. **Fox** puts distance between them.*]

FOX: Say—uh—Don't do that!

LITTLE PRINCE: What is it that—

FOX: Like I said, my experience with people has not been all that good. You okay there?

LITTLE PRINCE: I think so.

FOX: You know, maybe this just isn't such a good idea, maybe—

LITTLE PRINCE: No, no really, I'm fine. But—what is it that I did?

FOX: WELL! You can't just stroll up for a visit anytime at all. If you're gonna tame me, you've got to come at the same time every day. Didn't I mention that? [***Little Prince** shakes his head.*] It's got to be a ritual. If you come at the same time every day, then every day about an hour before you're due, I'll start getting excited. Rituals are very important. Especially in taming.

BEFORE YOU GO ON

1 Why does Fox want the Little Prince to tame him?

2 What does the Little Prince have to do to tame the Fox?

On Your Own
Would you like to be tamed? Why or why not?

219

LITTLE PRINCE: I think I understand.

FOX: Do you think? You see those grain fields down yonder. Well, wheat is of no use to me. I mean, the wheatfields have nothing to say to me and that is sad. But you have hair that is the color of gold. Now if you tamed me, the wheat, which is also golden, will bring me back the thought of you and I shall love to listen to the wind in the wheat.

LITTLE PRINCE: I understand now. Shall we begin?

FOX: Ready when you are.

BOTH: One, two, three, go!

[. . . *They proceed to perform a ritual representing the taming process. . . . They circle around . . . and then back . . . passing the point where they started. They come to rest at a distance from each other. . . . **Little Prince** and **Fox** face the audience, occasionally looking at each other out of the corner of their eyes, awkwardly trying to maintain a silence.*]

LITTLE PRINCE: I was thinking, did you ever—

FOX: Shh. Not a word! [*Disappointed at their failure, they repeat circle action, saluting as they go, with lighting changes, arriving a little closer to one another. Again they stand facing the audience in awkward silence.*] Nice scarf.

LITERARY CHECK
How do the stage directions help to tell the story?

---

wheatfields have nothing to say to me, I don't care about wheatfields
saluting, waving "hello" or "good-bye"

LITTLE PRINCE: Nice tail.

FOX: It was a gift from my mother. [*Repeat same actions, saluting again, circling more hopefully. Their movements accelerate. . . . They extend their pattern to make a figure-eight past each other. Then they do-si-do around each other. **Little Prince** and **Fox** finally arrive face-to-face.*]

LITTLE PRINCE: Are you tame now?

FOX: I don't know. Let's find out. [*Slowly, **Little Prince** reaches to touch him. **Fox** tries to fight off urge to growl and finally **Little Prince** pets him. **Fox** doesn't growl. In fact, much to his surprise, he nuzzles **Little Prince**.*] YES! I'm tame! I'm finally tame. [*They sit. **Fox** nuzzles like a puppy dog as lights fade.*]

[*. . . After a brief pause, lights come up again. **Little Prince** is sitting, absorbed in his own thoughts as **Fox** is moving around playfully.*]

FOX: Let's see. Yesterday we explored the hills, and the day before, the forest. Shall we dance today, or shall we chase each other through the wheatfields?

LITTLE PRINCE: No, I don't think so. [***Little Prince** sits down in the grass.*]

FOX: I know. Let's play hide and seek. I'll hide. I've had lots of practice.

LITTLE PRINCE: Not today.

FOX: [*nestles down next to him. After a moment:*] You are thinking about your rose again. Listen to me. Go now and take another look at the wall full of roses and you'll understand.

LITTLE PRINCE: Understand what?

---

do-si-do, walk around each other with
 their backs to each other
nuzzles, rubs with the nose

BEFORE YOU GO ON

1 Why does the Fox want the Little Prince to come at the same time every day?

2 How can the Little Prince tell that the Fox is tame?

On Your Own
Do you agree that rituals are important? Why or why not?

221

Fox: You'll see. Then come back to say goodbye to me.

Little Prince: Goodbye? What do you mean?

Fox: Just go. And when you come back I will tell you a secret.

[As ***Little Prince*** *returns to the wall of roses, they are giggling. He sees them . . . and sighs.*]

Little Prince: You are not at all like my rose. As yet you are nothing. No one has tamed you and you have tamed no one. You are beautiful, but you are empty. One could not die for you. You are like my fox when I first met him—like a hundred thousand other foxes. But now I have tamed him, and made him my friend and now he is unique in all the world. An ordinary passerby would think that my rose looked just like you—the rose that belongs to me. But she is more important than all the hundreds of you other . . . roses because it is she that I have watered; because it is she that I have sheltered behind the screen; because it is for her that I have killed the caterpillars except the two or three we saved to become butterflies, because it is she that I have listened to when she asked questions, or grumbled, or even sometimes when she said nothing, because she is my rose.

[. . . ***Little Prince*** *returns to Fox.*]

Little Prince: The time has come for me to go.

Fox: Ah . . . I shall cry.

Little Prince: But I never wished you harm—you wanted me to tame you.

Fox: Yes, that is so.

Little Prince: Then it has done you no good at all.

Fox: It has done me good—because of the wheatfields. I will always remember you when I see them because they are the color of your hair. One runs the risk of weeping a little, when one allows himself to be tamed.

Little Prince: Goodbye.

Fox: Goodbye. And now here is my secret. A very simple secret. Repeat after me so you will always remember it. It is only with the heart that one can see rightly. [*Fox lays his hand on Little Prince's heart.*]

Little Prince: It is only with the heart that one can see rightly. [*Little Prince lays his hand on Fox's heart.*]

Fox: What is essential is invisible to the eye. [*Fox touches Little Prince's eye.*]

Little Prince: What is essential is invisible to the eye.

ABOUT THE **AUTHORS**

Antoine de Saint-Exupéry (1900–1944) was a French writer and aviator. His work—both fiction and nonfiction—was heavily influenced by his experiences flying. His most famous novel is *The Little Prince*, written in 1943. In 1944 de Saint-Exupéry disappeared over the Mediterranean Sea while flying on a mission during World War II.

Rick Cummins composes music for plays and musicals, including many off-Broadway productions and well-known works by playwrights such as Shakespeare, Arthur Miller, and Tennessee Williams.

John Scoullar is a performer and writer who has worked in theater and television for years. His writing includes plays, musicals, lyrics for cabaret performers and children's songs, and rock videos.

BEFORE YOU GO ON

1. What is risky about being tamed?

2. What is the Fox's secret?

On Your Own
Should we let our hearts guide our thinking? Why or why not?

223

READER'S THEATER

🔊 *Speaking* TIP

Rehearse your lines with your partner a few times before performing in front of an audience.

Act out this scene with a partner and follow the stage directions.

Little Prince: [*looks confused*] How am I going to tame you?

Fox: Be patient! Let's sit on the grass. I'll watch you, and you do not talk to me. Sometimes when we talk, it confuses things. So we'll just sit together for a while.

[**Fox** *sits down and closes one eye. He looks at* **Little Prince** *out of the corner of his open eye.*]

Little Prince: [*sits*] What happens now?

Fox: I watch, and you say nothing. Can you remember that?

Little Prince: I'll try.

[*the next day*]

Little Prince: [*claps hand on* **Fox**'s *back*] Hello friend!

Fox: [*scampers away*] What are you doing? Do not come near me!

Little Prince: Why?

Fox: I don't trust people. Not yet.

Little Prince: [*sits down, looks confused again*] Wow. This is not easy.

COMPREHENSION

Workbook
Page 108

Right There

1. What does the Little Prince tell the Fox he is looking for?
2. What does the Fox tell the Little Prince about the wheatfields?

Think and Search

3. How does the Fox say taming relates to understanding?
4. How does the Fox teach the Little Prince an important lesson?

Author and You

5. How are words the source of misunderstanding?
6. Do you think it is significant that a wild animal is teaching a prince a lesson? Why or why not?

7. Have you ever been "tamed"? Explain what happened.

8. Do you think getting hurt from time to time is a necessary part of friendship? Why or why not?

DISCUSSION

Discuss in pairs or small groups.

- What is the difference between the roses on the wall and the Little Prince's rose?

- **Q** **Can we think with the heart?** What do you think the Fox means when he says, "It is only with the heart that one can see rightly"? Do you agree?

*))) Listening TIP

Wait until each speaker is finished before making a comment or asking a question.

RESPONSE TO LITERATURE

Workbook
Page 108

The Fox teaches the Little Prince an important lesson. His words are in the first column of the chart. Think about the meaning of the Fox's words. Explain them in your own words, and tell why you agree or disagree. Then copy the chart into your notebook and complete it.

What the Fox Says	In My Own Words	Why I Agree or Disagree
"What is essential is invisible to the eye."		
"One runs the risk of weeping a little, when one allows himself to be tamed."		

GRAMMAR, USAGE, AND MECHANICS

Present and Past Progressive

Use the present progressive to describe an ongoing action that is happening now. Use *be + -ing* verb to form the present progressive.

> What **are** you **looking** for?
> I'**m beginning** to understand.
> You **are thinking** about your rose again.

The present progressive is used with *always* to express a repeated action. This usually expresses a negative reaction to a situation.

> The hunters **are** always **trying** to get the Fox.

Use the past progressive to describe an ongoing action that was in progress during a period of time in the past. Use *was* or *were + -ing* verb.

> I **was looking** for men.
> The Fox and the Little Prince **were talking** to each other.

Non-action verbs are usually not used in the progressive. Non-action verbs describe emotions (*love, hate*), mental functions (*remember, understand*), wants (*need, want*), senses (*hear, see*), appearance (*look, seem*), and possession (*have, own*).

Practice **Workbook** Page 109

Complete the sentences below using the present or the past progressive and the verbs in parentheses.

1. The Little Prince said that he _____ (begin) to understand.
2. _____ you _____ (look) for chickens right now?
3. The Fox _____ always _____ (run) from the hunters.
4. When the Fox first saw the Little Prince, the boy _____ (cry).
5. As the Little Prince tries to tame the Fox, the Fox _____ (battle) with his own nature.

WRITING an EXPOSITORY PARAGRAPH

Write a Summary

To write an expository essay at the end of this unit, you'll need to learn some of the skills we use in expository writing. On this page you will learn how to write a summary.

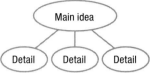

When you write a summary, you must include the main ideas and a few of the most important details. For example, if you write about an action movie with a superhero, explain what is driving the plot. Then give several details about the superhero.

Here is a summary of the play excerpt you just read. Before writing, the writer listed his ideas in a main-idea-and-details web.

Adrian Perez

The Little Prince

<u>The Little Prince</u> is a play about a young prince and a wild fox who become friends. The Little Prince is unhappy because he is lonely. Then one day, he notices the Fox. The Fox is sitting under an apple tree, and the Little Prince asks him if he wants to play. But the Fox is a wild animal and is scared of humans because hunters always chase him and try to kill him. The Little Prince shows the Fox that he isn't a hunter and just wants a friend. The Fox tells the Little Prince that a wild animal cannot be friends with a human unless it is tamed first. So every day, at the same time, the Little Prince meets the Fox at the apple tree. Each day they move closer and closer to each other, until finally the Fox becomes used to having the Little Prince around, and allows the boy to pet him. The two become great friends and spend time with each other from that day on. The Fox teaches the Little Prince that "it is only with the heart that one can see rightly." In other words, sometimes the emotional mind is more reliable than the intellectual mind.

Practice

Workbook
Page 110

Write a paragraph summarizing a story, play, book, movie, or television show. You can write your paragraph about one that you really enjoyed or one that you did not like. List your ideas in a main-idea-and-details web. Be sure to use the present and past progressive correctly.

Writing Checklist

IDEAS:
✔ I included only the most important ideas.

ORGANIZATION:
✔ I supported the main ideas with details.

Prepare to Read

What You Will Learn

Reading

- Vocabulary building: *Context, dictionary skills, word study*

- Reading strategy: *Monitor comprehension*

- Text type: *Informational text (science)*

Grammar, Usage, and Mechanics
Imperatives

Writing
Write instructions

THE BIG QUESTION

Can we think with the heart? Every time your heart beats, it pumps blood throughout your body. The blood brings food and oxygen to each cell. Have you ever noticed the beating of your heart? How does it beat when you are feeling emotional? Discuss with a partner.

BUILD BACKGROUND

"The Heart: Our Circulatory System" is a science article that explains what the heart and the circulatory system do. The human body functions using twelve systems: circulatory, digestive, endocrine, excretory, immune, integumentary, lymphatic, muscular, nervous, reproductive, respiratory, and skeletal. These systems work together to keep us alive and healthy. The circulatory, or cardiovascular, system is one of the most important in the body because it delivers blood to every cell in the body.

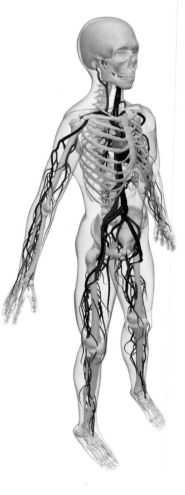

The human circulatory system ▶

Learn Key Words

Read these sentences. Use the context to figure out the meaning of the **red** words. Use a dictionary to check your answers. Then write each word and its meaning in your notebook.

Key Words

arteries
blood vessels
capillaries
circulatory
pulmonary
veins

1. The femoral **arteries**, or large blood vessels, in your thighs carry blood away from your heart.

2. **Blood vessels** transport blood all over the body. Arteries and veins are types of blood vessels that have different functions.

3. In the cold weather, the **capillaries** brought blood to her cheeks and turned them red.

4. His **circulatory** system was not working well, so his blood wasn't moving well throughout his body.

5. The young woman stopped smoking because she wanted to avoid **pulmonary** problems.

6. All **veins** work by carrying blood to the heart.

Practice  **Workbook Page 111**

Write the sentences in your notebook. Choose a **red** word from the box above to complete each sentence. Then take turns reading the sentences aloud with a partner.

1. _____ carry blood toward the heart.

2. _____ carry blood away from the heart.

3. The circulatory system is a network of different types of _____.

4. _____ are so tiny that they are very difficult to see.

5. The lungs are part of the _____ system.

6. It is important to eat right and exercise to keep your _____ system working properly.

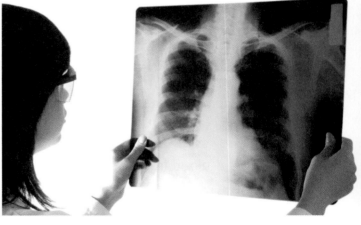

▲ An X ray of healthy lungs

Learn Academic Words

Study the **red** words and their meanings. You will find these words useful when talking and writing about informational texts. Write each word and its meaning in your notebook. After you read "The Heart: Our Circulatory System," try to use these words to respond to the text.

Academic Words

constantly
contract
network
regulate
transport

constantly = always or regularly	➡ The human body is **constantly** working—twenty-four hours a day!
contract = become smaller or tighter	➡ A lack of oxygen to the brain caused the man's arteries to **contract**, cutting off the blood supply.
network = a system of lines or tubes that cross one another and are connected to one another	➡ The human body is made up of a **network** of systems that all work together.
regulate = adjust things within a system to keep the system operating well	➡ Our brains **regulate** the systems in our bodies. Without the brain, the body would not function.
transport = move or carry from one place to another	➡ His circulatory system was weak and could no longer **transport** blood to his limbs.

Practice  **Workbook** Page 112

Write the sentences in your notebook. Choose a **red** word from the box above to complete each sentence. Then take turns reading the sentences aloud with a partner.

1. When blood vessels _____, less blood can travel through them.
2. Veins _____ blood from the tips of your fingers and toes back to your heart.
3. The heart is _____ pumping blood through the body.
4. The circulatory system helps _____ your body's temperature.
5. Veins, arteries, and capillaries are part of a _____.

Word Study: Related Words

Related words are words that belong to the same word family. They share the same base word and have related meanings. Look at similarities and differences among the related words below:

> **circulate** (*verb*) to move around within a system, or to make something do this
> **circulation** (*noun*) the movement of blood around your body
> **circulatory** (*adjective*) relating to the movement of blood through the body

Once you know the meaning of a base word, you can make a guess about the meaning of other words in that word family. Try to memorize the meanings of as many suffixes as possible. This will help when you are trying to understand the meanings of related words.

Practice  **Workbook** Page 113

Work with a partner. Copy the words below into your notebook. Write the part of speech and the meaning of each word. Check your work in a dictionary. Finally, use each word in a sentence.

constant	power	prevent	regulate	regulatory
constantly	powerful	prevention	regulation	

READING STRATEGY | MONITOR COMPREHENSION

Monitoring comprehension helps you to understand difficult texts. To monitor comprehension, follow these steps:

- Read the text. Stop from time to time and ask yourself how much of it you have understood.
- Reread the text. Make a list of words or ideas that are difficult. Try to figure out their meanings from the context. If you can't, look them up in a dictionary.
- Try to put the information you read into your own words.

As you read "The Heart: Our Circulatory System," stop from time to time. Ask yourself whether you understand what you are reading.

 **Workbook** Page 114

Set a purpose for reading Read this science article to find out how the heart works. Why does it beat faster when you are feeling emotional?

The Heart
Our Circulatory System

Seymour Simon

Make a fist. This is about the size of your heart. Sixty to one hundred times every minute your heart muscles squeeze together and push blood around your body through tubes called blood vessels.

Try squeezing a rubber ball with your hand. Squeeze it hard once a second. Your hand will get tired in a minute or two. Yet your heart beats every second of every day. In one year your heart beats more than thirty million times. In an average lifetime a heart will beat over 2,000,000,000 (two thousand million) times.

The heart works hard when we relax or sleep and even harder when we work or exercise. It never stops for rest or repair. The heart is a most incredible pump.

Every minute, the heart pushes a pulsing stream of blood through a network of blood vessels to every cell in your body. The constantly moving blood brings food and oxygen to each cell, carries away such wastes as carbon dioxide, and serves as an important component in the body's immune system. The heart, blood, and web of blood vessels make up your circulatory system.

Your heart is in the middle of your chest, tilted slightly to the left. It weighs only about ten ounces, about as much as one of your sneakers. It is divided into two halves by a thick wall of muscle called the septum, and each side has two hollow chambers, one above the other. Blood enters the heart in the atria, which then pump it down to the lower chambers. Each atrium has a one-way valve that opens when the blood is pushed to the ventricles and then closes so the blood can't flow backward.

The ventricles, the lower chambers of the heart, are heavier and stronger than the atria. The muscular right ventricle pumps blood into the lungs. The even more muscular left ventricle pumps blood to every cell in the body, from the head to the toes. Each ventricle also has a one-way valve to prevent blood from going backward.

---

immune system, system that protects the body against illnesses

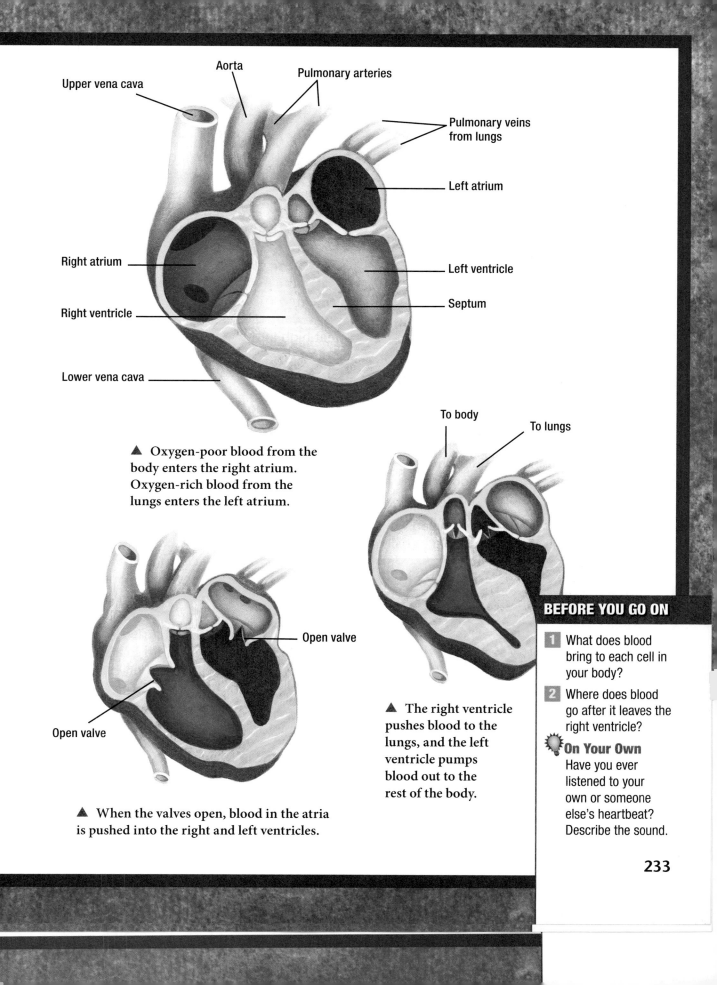

Upper vena cava

Aorta

Pulmonary arteries

Pulmonary veins from lungs

Left atrium

Right atrium

Left ventricle

Right ventricle

Septum

Lower vena cava

▲ Oxygen-poor blood from the body enters the right atrium. Oxygen-rich blood from the lungs enters the left atrium.

To body

To lungs

Open valve

Open valve

▲ The right ventricle pushes blood to the lungs, and the left ventricle pumps blood out to the rest of the body.

▲ When the valves open, blood in the atria is pushed into the right and left ventricles.

BEFORE YOU GO ON

1 What does blood bring to each cell in your body?

2 Where does blood go after it leaves the right ventricle?

On Your Own
Have you ever listened to your own or someone else's heartbeat? Describe the sound.

233

Blood is made up of red cells, white cells, and platelets, all floating in the clear pale gold fluid called plasma that makes up a little more than half of our blood. Plasma is mostly water but also contains many proteins, minerals, and sugars used by the body to build and repair cells. Going all around the body, the plasma carries nutrients from the food that has been digested in the stomach and small intestine to the cells for use as fuel.

Because plasma is a liquid, it can pass through the walls of small blood vessels right into the cells. Blood plasma also helps to regulate the body's temperature, moving heat from deep within the body to the skin, head, arms, and legs.

Red blood cells are the most common cells in the human body. We each have about twenty-five trillion red blood cells, hundreds of times more blood cells than there are stars in the Milky Way galaxy. Shaped something like a doughnut without a hole, each red blood cell is too tiny to see without a microscope. Yet stacked one upon another in a single column, the red blood cells in our bodies would tower thirty thousand miles high!

Red blood cells contain a chemical called hemoglobin, which combines with oxygen in the lungs and gives these blood cells their bright red color. The hemoglobin is the part of the blood that carries oxygen from the lungs to the body's cells and then transports such wastes as carbon dioxide from the cells back to the lungs.

Some one hundred thousand times a day, the muscles of the heart squeeze together. The contraction of the heart is so powerful it could send a jet of water six feet high into the air. As the blood pushes out of the left ventricle of the heart, it smashes with great force into the aorta, the largest blood vessel in the body. This is the beginning of a double journey that will take the blood from the heart to every cell in your body, back to the heart, out to the lungs, and back again to the heart.

The aorta is an artery, a type of blood vessel that carries blood away from the heart. The walls of an artery have three layers: a slippery, waterproof inner lining;

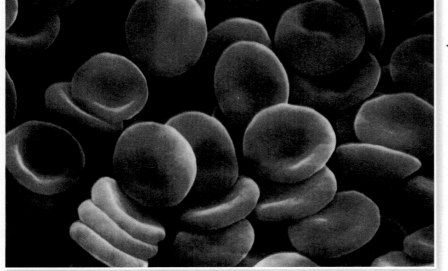

◀ Red blood cells

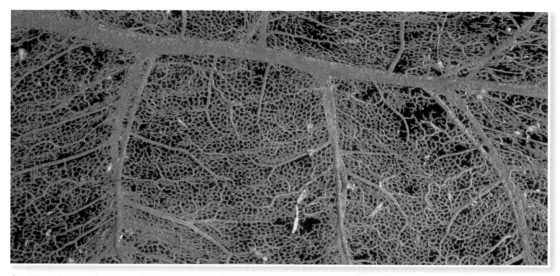

▲ Blood vessels branching into smaller and smaller vessels (capillaries)

a middle layer of elastic tissue and muscle; and an outer casing. The main arteries are as thick as your thumb. They bulge out with each jet of blood from the heart, then squeeze back to their normal width, pushing the blood forward. As they get farther from the heart, the arteries branch into smaller and smaller vessels called arterioles. Compared to the walls of the larger arteries, those of the arterioles are made mostly of muscle and are less elastic. The arterioles squeeze and relax regularly, forcing blood into the billions of tiny capillaries that fan out all over the body.

Blood doesn't flow at the same speed in all parts of the body. It spurts from the heart very quickly, but by the time it reaches the capillaries, it has slowed down to a gentle stream. One at a time, red blood cells squeeze through the narrow channels of the capillaries.

In most parts of the body, each cell is only a millionth of an inch from a capillary.

---

elastic, able to stretch and return to its original shape

Oxygen in the blood passes through the thin walls of the capillaries into the cells. These walls are only one cell thick, thinner than a human hair. Nutrients from food also pass into the cells. At the same time, carbon dioxide and other wastes move out of the cells and into the blood in the capillaries.

After being pushed through the capillaries, blood passes into small blood vessels called venules, which join to form larger blood vessels called veins. The largest veins are about as thick as a pencil. The bluish-looking blood vessels you see beneath your skin are veins.

Veins, which carry blood toward the heart, have muscular walls like arteries, but the walls are much thinner. Whenever we move, the muscles of our body press against the veins, helping the blood to circulate. The larger veins contain one-way

BEFORE YOU GO ON

1 What is the function of hemoglobin?

2 Where does blood go from the capillaries?

On Your Own
How do you think drinking water helps your circulatory system?

235

valves that are like little parachutes. They flap open and then close to trap the blood and keep it from flowing backward.

Like the water in streams that joins rivers that return to the sea, blood flows slowly at first after it leaves the capillaries, but then, as veins link together, blood speeds up and comes back to the heart in a steady current. Two large veins feed blood into the heart. The upper vena cava carries blood returning from the brain and the chest, and the lower vena cava carries blood from the stomach and the lower body.

The right atrium receives blood that has just traveled through the body. This blood is dark red, because it has little oxygen. As soon as the blood enters the heart, the muscles of the right atrium squeeze together and push the blood through a one-way valve into the right ventricle. In the next instant, the muscles of the right ventricle squeeze even more powerfully and send a surge of blood into the pulmonary arteries, which lead to the lungs. From there the blood goes into pulmonary arterioles and finally into pulmonary capillaries.

The lungs are spongy, filled with hundreds of millions of tiny air-filled sacs called alveoli. Each air sac is surrounded by capillaries. Oxygen that has been breathed into the lungs passes through the walls of the sacs and into the capillaries, where it binds to the hemoglobin in the blood. Carbon dioxide escapes from the blood into the alveoli and is exhaled. The blood returns to the left atrium by way of the pulmonary veins.

* * *

The heart pushes over three million quarts of blood a year through sixty thousand miles of blood vessels in the human body. Our bodies have a double circulation, one to the lungs, called the pulmonary circulation, the other to the rest of the body, called the systemic circulation. Each red blood cell makes the trip out to the body and back to the lungs over one thousand times a day.

Within each of us flows a river unlike any river on planet Earth. This river of blood flows past every part of the body on an incredible sixty-thousand-mile voyage, enough to travel two and a half times around the world. It is a journey as strange and wonderful as any journey to the stars.

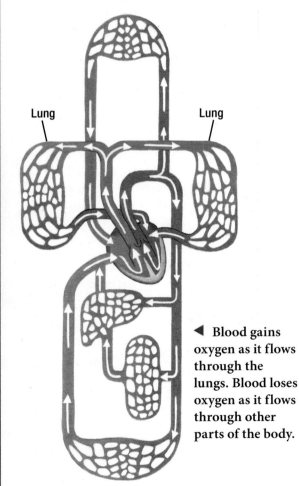

◀ Blood gains oxygen as it flows through the lungs. Blood loses oxygen as it flows through other parts of the body.

Heart-Healthy Recipe

Guacamole

Guacamole is good for your heart. Avocados, the main ingredient, contain a kind of fat that may help lower cholesterol, a substance that can clog your arteries.

This recipe makes about 2 cups.
Ingredients:

2 large ripe avocados
¼ medium onion
¼ teaspoon salt
Optional: 1 jalapeño pepper

1. Finely chop onion and set aside.
2. Carefully cut each avocado in half. Remove the pits.
3. With a spoon, scoop out the avocado and place in a bowl.
4. Using a fork, mash the avocado with onion and salt.
5. If you like it spicy, add finely chopped jalapeño pepper.

ABOUT THE **AUTHOR**

Seymour Simon has written more than 200 highly acclaimed books for young people, covering a wide range of topics in the sciences. He has received many awards, including the New York State Knickerbocker Award for Juvenile Literature and the Eva L. Gordon Award, presented by the American Nature Society. Also known for his fiction, he is the creator of the Einstein Anderson series.

BEFORE YOU GO ON

1. Why is the blood received by the right atrium dark red?

2. What happens to blood inside the pulmonary capillaries?

On Your Own
Why do you think the heart is associated with love?

Review and Practice

COMPREHENSION

Workbook
Page 115

Right There

1. What makes up the circulatory system?
2. What is blood made up of?

Think and Search

3. What two jobs does plasma do?
4. How are veins different from arteries?

Author and You

5. Why would the ventricles need to be stronger than the atria?
6. Would a person with poor circulation have warm or cold hands and feet? Why?

On Your Own

7. Why is it important to understand how your body works?
8. Do you think your emotional state can affect your health? Explain.

IN YOUR OWN WORDS

Work with a partner. Review "The Heart: Our Circulatory System" and write down the most important ideas. You may wish to make a chart tracking the flow of blood through the body. Then take turns explaining to your partner how the heart works, using the words in the box below.

arteries	capillaries	circulatory	pulmonary	transport
blood vessels	chemical	constantly	regulate	veins

Speaking TIP

Use the diagrams in this reading to help you explain how the heart works.

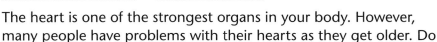

DISCUSSION

Discuss in pairs or small groups.

1. Discuss how the heart and the lungs work together.
2. Why is it important for all networks in the body to work together?

Q **Can we think with the heart?** What can people do to take care of their hearts? What kinds of foods make up a healthy diet? What are the best kinds of exercise?

»)) Listening TIP

Concentrate on what the speaker is saying. Do not be distracted by his or her manner of speaking.

READ FOR FLUENCY

It is often easier to read a text if you understand the difficult words and phrases. Work with a partner. Choose a paragraph from the reading. Identify the words and phrases you do not know or have trouble pronouncing. Look up the difficult words in a dictionary.

Take turns pronouncing the words and phrases with your partner. If necessary, ask your teacher to model the correct pronunciation. Then take turns reading the paragraph aloud. Give each other feedback on your reading.

EXTENSION
Workbook Page 115

The heart is one of the strongest organs in your body. However, many people have problems with their hearts as they get older. Do research at the library or on the Internet to find information about what happens to our hearts as we age. What are some of the problems? How can we prevent heart problems? What can doctors do to solve heart problems? Share your findings.

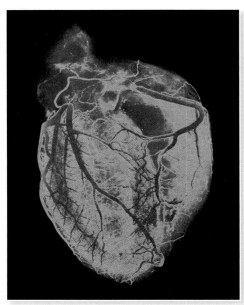

An X ray of a healthy heart ▶

239

Grammar and Writing

Imperatives

Use an imperative to give directions, orders, advice, or warnings. The implied subject of an imperative statement is always *you*. In imperatives, do not say or write *you*.

Directions	**Take** one pill every day with food.
Orders	**Don't eat** fried food.
Advice	**Go** to the doctor once a year.
Warnings	**Slow** down!

Imperatives are also used to make requests and make informal invitations. Use *please* along with the imperative.

Requests	**Come** with me, **please**.
Informal Invitations	**Please join** us, Dr. Stevens.

Practice

Work with a partner. Copy the following sentences into your notebook. Complete the sentences with the words in the box. Use each word only once.

come	forget	look	remember	stop	tell	wait	walk

1. _____ talking!
2. _____ where you are going!
3. _____ to unplug the fan before you leave the house.
4. _____ two blocks and turn left.
5. Please _____ for dinner tomorrow night.
6. _____ James that story about the heartbeat.
7. Don't _____ to preheat the oven.
8. _____ for me by the front door.

▲ Many signs use imperatives.

WRITING AN EXPOSITORY PARAGRAPH

Write Instructions

To write an expository essay at the end of this unit, you'll need to learn skills for expository writing. One type of expository writing is writing instructions. When you write step-by-step instructions explaining how to do something, use a clear sequence of steps. This will make the instructions easy to follow. For example, if you explain how to make bran muffins, start by telling which ingredients are needed. Tell the reader how to mix the ingredients together. Have the reader bake the muffins for the proper amount of time.

Here is a model of a paragraph with step-by-step instructions. Before writing, the writer listed his ideas in a graphic organizer.

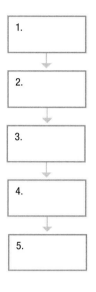

Evan Arbogast

How to Make a Fruit Smoothie

With all of the tasty, yet unhealthy food that exists in the world today, it is easy to eat too much of it! This is why it is important to have a healthy, balanced diet. However, just because something is healthy doesn't mean it has to taste bad! Fruit smoothies are delicious, healthy drinks that keep you energized. Here are some simple steps to making this healthy treat. First, get a blender and plug it into an outlet. Next, decide which types of fruits you are going to have in your smoothie. If you are using fruits that have a peel, like a banana, take the peel off before adding it to the blender. Keep in mind that more types of fruit means a more unique flavor. You may want to add some fruit juice as well. Next, mix all of the fruits in the blender. The last step? Drink and enjoy!

Practice

Write an expository paragraph giving step-by-step instructions that explain how to do something. For example, you might explain how to take your pulse or how to change your diet to be healthier. List your ideas in a graphic organizer. Be sure to use imperatives correctly.

Writing Checklist

WORD CHOICE:
☑ My instructions are easy to follow.

CONVENTIONS:
☑ I double-checked my work for errors.

4

What You Will Learn

Reading
- Vocabulary building: *Literary terms, word study*
- Reading strategy: *Analyze cultural context*
- Text type: *Literature (short story)*

Grammar, Usage, and Mechanics
Compound and complex sentences

Writing
Write a critical analysis

THE BIG QUESTION

Can we think with the heart? At one time or another, most of us have had to go somewhere and leave behind a person or a place we cared deeply about. Did this ever happen to you? What did you do to make yourself feel better? Discuss with a partner.

BUILD BACKGROUND

The next reading is a short story from the book *Tales from Gold Mountain: Stories of the Chinese in the New World*. This book tells about the struggles that some of the first Chinese Americans faced. **"Ginger for the Heart"** takes place during the gold rush in North America, during the nineteenth century. Many people moved to northwestern North America during this time to try to find gold and become rich. Hundreds of thousands of Chinese immigrants took part in the gold rush.

This story is about a young Chinese-American woman named Yenna. In this story Yenna has to make a choice between her family and her true love.

▲ Chinese immigrants panning for gold in California

242

VOCABULARY

Learn Literary Words

A **symbol** is anything that stands for or represents something else. Authors use symbols to create an added level of meaning. Read the poem below.

The Eagle

He clasps the crag with crooked hands;
Close to the sun in lonely lands,
Ringed with the azure world, he stands.

The wrinkled sea beneath him crawls;
He watches from his mountain walls,
And like a thunderbolt he falls.

—*Alfred, Lord Tennyson*

In the poem above, the eagle is more than an ordinary eagle. It is a symbol of power and physical strength. This eagle is master of the azure sky, living close to the sun and watching the sea crawl beneath him.

Many things can be symbols: animals, objects, people, or images. In "Ginger for the Heart," the author uses objects and images as symbols for ideas and feelings.

Practice

Work with a partner. Copy the chart below into your notebook. What would you choose as a symbol to represent each idea? Why?

Idea	Symbol
love	
evil	
balance	
luck	
peace	

Learn Academic Words

Study the **red** words and their meanings. You will find these words useful when talking and writing about literature. Write each word and its meaning in your notebook. After you read "Ginger for the Heart," try to use these words to respond to the text.

abstract = existing only as an idea or quality rather than as something concrete you can see and touch	→	The dove is a symbol for the **abstract** ideas of peace and love.
devoted = giving someone or something a lot of love, concern, or attention	→	The woman was very **devoted** to her parents and spent a lot of time taking care of them.
mutual = felt by two or more people toward one another	→	The two men had a **mutual** respect for each other.
significance = importance or meaning of something	→	We could not understand the **significance** of our father's watch until he told us the story of how he got it.

Practice

Workbook Page 119

Work with a partner to answer these questions. Try to include the **red** word in your answer. Write the sentences in your notebook.

1. What **abstract** ideas is the heart a symbol of?

2. Who are you most **devoted** to?

3. Do you have a relationship of **mutual** respect with your friends?

4. What things do you own that have a lot of **significance** to you?

244

Word Study: The /z/ Sound

The /z/ sound is found in words that have the letters *z*, *x*, or *s*. The /z/ sound may be at the beginning or end of syllables.

The letter *s* often stands for the /z/ sound. The letter *s* is often pronounced /z/ when it is after a voiced consonant. The third-person singular (*-s*) and plurals (*-s*, *-es*) are usually pronounced with the /z/ sound.

Beginning of a Syllable	End of a Syllable
mu**s**ic	other**s**
vi**s**ible	storie**s**
zoo	ja**zz**
ha**z**y	ama**z**ement

Practice

Workbook Page 120

With a partner, write a sentence for each word in the box below. Practice saying the /z/ sound by reading your sentences aloud to your partner. Use a dictionary to find the definition of any new words.

balconies	crazy	miners	refuses
because	invisible	railings	wiser

READING STRATEGY ANALYZE CULTURAL CONTEXT

Analyzing the cultural context of a story helps you understand it better. Cultural context includes the beliefs, art, ideas, and values of a particular group. Follow these steps:

- Think about the characters' native culture. In what ways is it important to the story?
- Pay attention to ideas and beliefs the characters have.
- Think about what you already know about the culture. How does this help you understand the story?

As you read "Ginger for the Heart," think about what Chinese immigrants who came to North America in the 1800s experienced.

Workbook Page 121

Set a purpose for reading Read this story to find out how a gift of ginger helps keep a couple's love alive. What do you think the ginger represents?

Ginger for the Heart

Paul Yee

The buildings of Chinatown are stoutly constructed of brick, and while some are broad and others thin, they rise no higher than four solid storeys. Many contain stained-glass windows decorated with flower and diamond patterns, and others boast balconies with fancy wrought-iron railings.

Only one building stands above the rest. Its turret-like tower is visible even from the harbor, because the cone-shaped roof is made of copper.

In the early days, Chang the merchant tailor owned this building. He used the main floor for his store and rented out the others. But he kept the tower room for his own use, for the sun filled it with light. This was the room where his wife and daughter worked.

His daughter's name was Yenna, and her beauty was beyond compare. She had ivory skin, sparkling eyes, and her hair hung long and silken, shining like polished ebony. All day long she and her mother sat by the tower window and sewed with silver needles and silken threads. They sang songs while they worked, and their voices rose in wondrous harmonies.

---

ebony, hard black wood

In all Chinatown, the craftsmanship of Yenna and her mother was considered the finest. Search as they might, customers could not discern where holes had once pierced their shirts. Buttonholes never stretched out of shape, and seams were all but invisible.

One day, a young man came into the store laden with garments for mending. His shoulders were broad and strong, yet his eyes were soft and caring. Many times he came and many times he saw Yenna. For hours he would sit and watch her work. They fell deeply in love, though few words were spoken between them.

Spring came and boats bound for the northern gold fields began to sail again. It was time for the young man to go. He had borrowed money to pay his way over to the New World, and now he had to repay his debts. Onto his back he threw his blankets and tools, food and warm jackets. Then he set off with miners from around the world, clutching gold pans and shovels.

Yenna had little to give him in farewell. All she found in the kitchen was a ginger root as large as her hand. As she stroked its brown knobs and bumpy eyes, she whispered to him, "This will warm you in the cold weather. I will wait for you, but, like this piece of ginger, I, too, will age and grow dry." Then she pressed her lips to the ginger, and turned away.

"I will come back," the young man said. "The fire burning for you in my heart can never be extinguished."

Thereafter, Yenna lit a lamp at every nightfall and set it in the tower window. Rains lashed against the glass, snow piled low along the ledge, and ocean winds rattled the frame. But the flame did not waver, even though the young man never sent letters. Yenna did not weep uselessly, but continued to sew and sing with her mother.

There were few unmarried women in Chinatown, and many men came to seek Yenna's hand in marriage. Rich gold miners and sons of successful merchants bowed before her, but she always looked away. They gave her grand gifts, but still she shook her head, until the men grew weary and called her crazy. In China, parents arranged all marriages, and daughters became the property of their husbands. But Chang the merchant tailor treasured his daughter's happiness and let her be.

One winter, an epidemic ravaged the city. When it was over, Chang had lost his wife and his eyesight. Yenna led him up to the tower where he could feel the sun and drifting clouds move across his face. She began to sew again, and while she sewed, she sang for her father. The lamp continued to burn steadily at the tower window as she worked.

---

discern, see
New World, America
extinguished, put out
epidemic, a large number of cases of a particular infectious disease happening at the same time

✔ **LITERARY CHECK**
What is the fire a symbol of here?

BEFORE YOU GO ON

1 Where does the young man go?

2 What does Yenna give the young man as a farewell present?

💡**On Your Own**
Did you ever want to give someone a gift but had nothing to give? Explain.

247

With twice the amount of work to do, she labored long after dusk. She fed the flame more oil and sent her needle skimming through the heavy fabrics. Nimbly her fingers braided shiny cords and coiled them into butterfly buttons. And when the wick sputtered into light each evening, Yenna's heart soared momentarily into her love's memories. Nights passed into weeks, months turned into years, and four years quickly flew by.

One day a dusty traveler came into the store and flung a bundle of ragged clothes onto the counter. Yenna shook out the first shirt, and out rolled a ginger root. Taking it into her hand, she saw that pieces had been nibbled off, but the core of the root was still firm and fragrant.

She looked up. There stood the man she had promised to wait for. His eyes appeared older and wiser.

"Your gift saved my life several times," he said. "The fire of the ginger is powerful indeed."

"Why is the ginger root still firm and heavy?" she wondered. "Should it not have dried and withered?"

"I kept it close to my heart and my sweat coated it. In lonely moments, my tears soaked it." His calloused hands reached out for her. "Your face has not changed."

"Nor has my heart," she replied. "I have kept a lamp burning all these years."

"So I have heard," he smiled. "Will you come away with me now? It has taken many years to gather enough gold to buy a farm. I have built you a house on my land."

---

nimbly, quickly; skillfully
calloused, covered in thick, hard skin

For the first time since his departure, tears cascaded down Yenna's face. She shook her head. "I cannot leave. My father needs me."

"Please come with me," the young man pleaded. "You will be very happy, I promise."

Yenna swept the wetness from her cheeks. "Stay with me and work this store instead," she implored.

The young man stiffened and stated proudly, "A man does not live in his wife's house." And the eyes that she remembered so well gleamed with determination.

"But this is a new land," she cried. "Must we forever follow the old ways?"

She reached out for him, but he brushed her away. With a curse he hurled the ginger root into the fireplace. As the flames leapt up, Yenna's eyes blurred. The young man clenched and unclenched his fists in anger. They stood like stone.

At last the man turned to leave, but suddenly he knelt at the fireplace. Yenna saw him reach in with the tongs and pull something out of the flames.

"Look!" he whispered in amazement. "The ginger refuses to be burnt! The flames cannot touch it!"

Yenna looked and saw black burn marks charring the root, but when she took it in her hand, she found it still firm and moist. She held it to her nose, and found the fragrant sharpness still there.

The couple embraced and swore to stay together. They were married at a lavish banquet attended by all of Chinatown. There, the father passed his fingers over his son-in-law's face and nodded in satisfaction.

Shortly after, the merchant Chang died, and the young couple moved away. Yenna sold the business and locked up the tower room. But on nights when boats pull in from far away, they say a flicker of light can still be seen in that high window. And Chinese women are reminded that ginger is one of their best friends.

> ✔ **LITERARY CHECK**
> *What is the ginger root a **symbol** of?*

ABOUT THE **AUTHOR**

Paul Yee grew up in Vancouver's Chinatown. Many of his stories are about Chinese people growing up and living in America, feeling torn between two very different cultures. His list of award-winning books includes *Roses Sing on New Snow* and *Ghost Train*, which won the Governor General's Literary Award and the Amelia Frances Howard-Gibbon Award.

BEFORE YOU GO ON

1. Why does the young man throw the ginger into the fireplace?

2. What happens to the ginger root in the fire?

On Your Own
Do you think "a fire burning in your heart" is a good description of love? Why or why not?

249

READER'S THEATER

Speaking TIP

Use realistic voices and facial expressions.

Act out the following scene between Yenna and her father.

Chang: Why do you hang a lamp in the window every night?

Yenna: If the flame goes out, I know the man I love will not come home to me

Chang: But Yenna, he has been gone for four years. And he has not written you one letter in all that time.

Yenna: Yes, that is true.

Chang: Daughter, you know I treasure your happiness. I am afraid for you. What if he does not come back?

Yenna: I gave him my promise. I will wait for him.

Chang: You are sure of him?

Yenna: I am sure of my own heart. My heart is as steady as that lamp burning in the window.

COMPREHENSION

Workbook
Page 122

Right There

1. Why does the young man go to the gold fields?

2. What causes Chang to lose his wife and his eyesight?

Think and Search

3. Why doesn't Yenna leave with the young man when he first asks her to marry him?

4. Why doesn't the ginger root burn in the fire?

Author and You

5. How did the ginger root save the young man's life?

6. What is "fire of the ginger"?

On Your Own

7. Have you ever eaten or drunk anything flavored with ginger? Describe your experience.

8. Have you ever had to wait a long time for something you wanted? Explain.

DISCUSSION

Discuss in pairs or small groups.

1. Chang was a loving father, and Yenna was a devoted daughter. Do you think Yenna did the right thing by not leaving her father? Why or why not?

2. What is the significance of the fact that the ginger didn't burn? Do you think it would have burned if it had dried up? Explain.

Q Can we think with the heart? Do you think that Yenna and her true love thought with their hearts? Explain.

Listening TIP

Listen for facts and examples to support the speaker's ideas.

RESPONSE TO LITERATURE

Workbook Page 122

During the gold rush in the 1800s, many people, including Chinese immigrants, went to northwestern North America to find gold and get rich. Write a letter from Yenna's young man telling about his experiences. Do research at the library or on the Internet to learn more about this period of time.

▲ Chinese workers panning for gold in California

Grammar and Writing

Compound and Complex Sentences

A compound sentence contains two independent clauses. They are usually connected with a coordinating conjunction, such as *and, but, or,* or *so.* Use a comma before the conjunction. A comma is not necessary if the independent clauses are short.

> independent clause   independent clause
> His daughter's name was Yenna, **and** her beauty was beyond compare.

A complex sentence contains an independent clause and one or more dependent clauses. The two clauses are connected with a subordinating conjunction, such as *while, though, because,* or *until.* If the dependent clause begins the sentence, use a comma.

> dependent clause   independent clause
> **While** some are broad and others are thin, the buildings rise no higher than four solid storeys.
>
> independent clause   dependent clause
> They sang songs **while** they worked.

Practice  Workbook Page 123

Write the sentences in your notebook. Identify each sentence as compound or complex. Then rewrite the complex sentences, switching the order of the clauses. Remember to use correct punctuation.

1. The building's tower is visible from the harbor because the cone-shaped roof is made of copper.
2. Many buildings have stained-glass windows, but Chang's building does not.
3. Yenna had sparkling eyes, and her hair hung long and silken.
4. Until the wind lashed against the glass, the flame did not waver.
5. While Yenna sewed, she sang for her father.

WRITING AN EXPOSITORY PARAGRAPH

Write a Critical Analysis

A critical analysis is a type of expository writing in which you analyze and explain some aspect of a literary work. To write a critical analysis, begin with a personal response. Did you enjoy the story? Did you care about the characters? What interested you most about the story?

Whatever interested you most would make a good topic for your critical analysis. Suppose "Ginger for the Heart" left you wondering about the significance of the ginger root. You could reread the story, analyzing the author's treatment of the ginger root. What language does he use to describe the ginger? What ideas does he associate with it? Then you could explain what you think the ginger means in the story, supporting your ideas with details from the text.

Here is a model of a critical analysis of "Ginger for the Heart." Before writing, the writer listed her ideas in a T-chart.

Ideas	Textual evidence

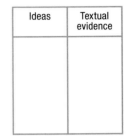

Andrea Vargas

Ginger for the Heart

"Ginger for the Heart" is a story about a woman named Yenna who meets a young miner during the gold rush. They are Chinese immigrants who have moved to North America. The man has to leave Yenna to go to the gold fields. Before he goes, Yenna gives him a ginger root to remember her by. Four years later the man returns. Yenna is surprised to see that the ginger root is still "firm and fragrant." When she asks why the ginger hasn't dried out, the man says his sweat and tears kept it moist. The man asks Yenna to come away with him, but Yenna can't leave her father. Angry, the man throws the ginger root into the fire, but it doesn't burn. Taking this as a sign, the two vow to stay together forever. The ginger root symbolizes the couple's love. The ginger stayed firm and moist, just as their love stayed strong. It didn't burn because their love could not be destroyed.

Practice

Write a critical analysis of a story or another piece of literature. Explain the meaning of some aspect of the work, supporting your ideas with textual evidence. Organize your ideas in a T-chart. Be sure to use compound and complex sentences correctly.

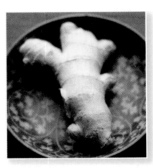

Writing Checklist

IDEAS:
- ✔ I supported my ideas with details from the text.

SENTENCE FLUENCY:
- ✔ I varied my sentences to achieve fluency.

Link the Readings

Critical Thinking

Look back at the readings in this unit. Think about what they have in common. They all tell about matters of the heart. Yet they do not all have the same purpose. The purpose of one reading might be to inform, while the purpose of another might be to entertain or persuade. In addition, the content of each reading relates to matters of the heart differently. Now copy the chart below into your notebook and complete it.

Title of Reading	Purpose	Big Question Link
From *The Story of My Life*		*Anne Sullivan's love changed Helen Keller's life.*
From *The Little Prince: The Play*		
"The Heart: Our Circulatory System"		
"Ginger for the Heart"	*to entertain*	

Discussion

Discuss in pairs or small groups.

- The excerpts from *The Story of My Life* and *The Little Prince: The Play* and the story "Ginger for the Heart" are about love of one form or another. Compare the different kinds of love in the three readings.

- **Q** **Can we think with the heart?** Why is the heart used as a symbol of love? What other things symbolize love?

Fluency Check

Work with a partner. Choose a paragraph from one of the readings. Take turns reading it for one minute. Count the total number of words you read. Practice saying the words you had trouble reading. Take turns reading the paragraph three more times. Did you read more words each time? Copy the chart below into your notebook and record your speeds.

	1st Speed	2nd Speed	3rd Speed	4th Speed
Words Per Minute				

Projects

Work in pairs or small groups. Choose one of these projects.

1 Create a poster of the human circulatory system. Use arrows to demonstrate how blood moves inside the heart and through the body. Present your poster to the class and, in your own words, explain what happens to the blood as it travels through the body.

2 Write a short story about love, friendship, or another matter of the heart. Have one character give a gift to another as a symbol of his or her affection. When you are finished writing, read your story aloud to the class.

3 *The Little Prince: The Play* is based on the novel *The Little Prince*. Read *The Little Prince* and write a poem about one of the themes or characters that you find interesting.

4 Read the rest of Helen Keller's autobiography, *The Story of My Life*. Tell the class what new information you learned about Helen Keller's life. What were her accomplishments?

Further Reading

To find out more about the theme of this unit, choose from these reading suggestions.

The Hunchback of Notre-Dame, Victor Hugo
This Penguin Reader® tells the classic story of the deformed Quasimodo and his love for the beautiful, doomed Esmeralda.

Our Town, Thornton Wilder
This Pulitzer Prize-winning drama perfectly describes the relationships between the people living in the small village of Grover's Corners.

Bird, Angela Johnson
Determined to find her stepfather, Cecil, and bring him home, Bird runs away from her Cleveland home to Alabama. Along the way, she helps two lonely boys and comes to understand what family really means.

Put It All Together

LISTENING & SPEAKING WORKSHOP

How-To Demonstration

You will tell and show the class how to do something.

1 THINK ABOUT IT Have you ever shown a friend or family member how to do something? Think about something that you know how to do well. How would you show someone else how to do it?

In pairs, make a list of words you might use during a demonstration. Review how to use the imperative to give simple commands and instructions.

Work together to make a list of ideas for a how-to demonstration. Think of activities you could demonstrate in class. Here are some examples:

- How to bake heart-healthy cookies
- How to check your heart rate
- How to play the guitar
- How to make a puppet

2 GATHER AND ORGANIZE INFORMATION Choose a topic from your list. Write down what you already know about how to do the activity. Try to write step-by-step instructions. Consider what supplies or tools you will need for your demonstration. Which imperative words will you use in each step?

Research Go to the library, talk to an adult or a professional, or search on the Internet to get information. Take notes on what you find.

Order Your Notes Make a list of the steps needed to do your activity. Check to be sure that your steps are in logical order.

Use Visuals Find or make props you can use as you demonstrate the steps of your activity. You may wish to create posters, pictures, or other visuals to make your presentation more interesting and effective.

3 **PRACTICE AND PRESENT** Use your list when you begin practicing your demonstration. Then try talking to your audience without looking at your notes. You may want to give your presentation in front of a mirror or to a friend or family member. Keep practicing until you are relaxed and confident.

Deliver Your How-To Presentation Look at your audience as you speak. Be clear as you present your steps. Slow down when you come to the most important points. At the end of the presentation, ask listeners if they have any questions about your demonstration.

4 **EVALUATE THE PRESENTATION**
You will improve your skills as a speaker and a listener by evaluating each presentation you give and hear. Use this checklist to help you judge the demonstrations of your classmates.

- ☑ Did the speaker present the how-to demonstration in logical steps?
- ☑ Did the demonstration give you enough information to do the activity on your own?
- ☑ Did the speaker use props and pictures or other visuals effectively?
- ☑ Did the speaker answer your questions to your satisfaction?
- ☑ What suggestions do you have for improving the demonstration?

Speaking TIPS

Be sure to speak clearly and ask your listeners for feedback. Can they hear and understand what you are saying?

Use your props and visuals effectively. Show each one at the right time and make sure everyone can see it. Do not fidget or look away from the audience while speaking.

Listening TIPS

Watch and listen carefully. Give the speaker your full attention.

Think about what you are hearing. Does it make sense? Would you be able to explain the steps to someone else? Write down questions and ask them at the end of the demonstration.

WRITING WORKSHOP

Expository Essay

In this workshop you will write an expository essay. An expository essay provides information about a topic. A good expository essay begins with a paragraph that introduces the writer's main idea. The essay includes several body paragraphs that support and explain the main idea by presenting details and examples. This information is presented in a logical order. A concluding paragraph summarizes the main idea and the most important details in a lively and interesting way.

Your writing assignment for this workshop is to expand one of the paragraphs you wrote for this unit into a five-paragraph essay.

1 **PREWRITE** Choose the paragraph you want to expand. Then think about your readers. What do they already know about your topic? What questions do you think they will have? List these questions in your notebook. Try to answer them in your essay. Also think about interesting details you want to add when you expand your paragraph into an essay.

List and Organize Ideas and Details List your main ideas and the most important supporting details in a graphic organizer. A student named Santos decided to expand the paragraph he wrote summarizing his favorite movie. Here is the graphic organizer he prepared.

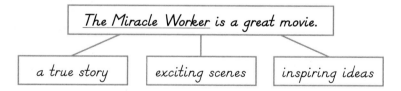

The Miracle Worker is a great movie.

a true story | exciting scenes | inspiring ideas

2 **DRAFT** Use the model on page 261 and your main idea chart to help you write a first draft. Remember to include an introductory paragraph, three body paragraphs, and a concluding paragraph.

3 **REVISE** Read over your draft. As you do so, ask yourself the questions in the writing checklist. Use the questions to help you revise your essay.

SIX TRAITS OF WRITING CHECKLIST

☑ **IDEAS:** Is my main idea clear?

☑ **ORGANIZATION:** Do I present supporting details in a logical order?

☑ **VOICE:** Does my writing show my interest in the topic?

☑ **WORD CHOICE:** Do I use sequence words to tell when events happen?

☑ **SENTENCE FLUENCY:** Do my sentences vary in length and type?

☑ **CONVENTIONS:** Does my writing follow the rules of grammar, usage, and mechanics?

Here are the changes Santos plans to make when he revises his first draft.

The Miracle Worker

Recently, I ~~thought~~ was thinking that a ~~movie called~~ The Miracle Worker is my favorite film. It tells the true story of a remarkabel woman named Helen Keller. When she is only nineteen months old, an illness destroys her sight and hearing. Although she faces huge obstacles, Helen goes on to become the first sight- and hearing-impaired woman to earn a college degree.

As a young child who can neither see nor hear, Helen is unable to learn basic aspects of everyday life. She does not know what things are, what people want, or how to behave. Helen needs a teacher who specializes in helping children with disabilities.

When Helen is seven, her family finds a skilled tutor named Anne
(the "miracle worker" of the film's title)
Sullivan. At first, the teacher makes little progress in helping Helen.

s
She uses her fingers to spell words into Helen's hand. Still, Helen

represent
doesn't understand that the finger movements are words. At one point,

Sullivan becomes frustrated because Helen is unable to distinguish

between the words water and mug.

Then
Sullivan has a brilliant idea. She takes Helen to the water pump.

the
This is most exciting scene in the movie! Sullivan puts one of Helen's

and
hands into the running water. Sullivan finger-spells the word water

into Helen's other hand. Helen suddenly understands that "w-a-t-e-r"

s
meant the liquid gushing over her hand. Learning this one word is a

break through for Helen. Once she knows that everything has a name,

she is eager to learn as many new words as she can.

Although The Miracle Worker is both uplifting and sad at the same

time, there is a larger idea symbolized by Helen's break through.

No matter how great the obstacles may seem, no matter what the

setbacks, anything is possible. You should take my advice and watch

this movie.

---

4 EDIT AND PROOFREAD

Workbook
Page 125

Copy your revised draft onto a clean sheet of paper. Read it again. Correct
any errors in grammar, word usage, mechanics, and spelling. Here are the
additional changes Santos plans to make when he prepares his final draft.

Santos Rivera III

The Miracle Worker

Recently, I was thinking that <u>The Miracle Worker</u> is my favorite film. It tells the true story of a remarkabel woman named Helen Keller. When she is only nineteen months old, an illness destroys her sight and hearing. Although she faces huge obstacles, Helen goes on to become the first sight- and hearing-impaired woman to earn a college degree.

As a young child who can neither see nor hear, Helen is unable to learn basic aspects of everyday life. She does not know what things are, what people want, or how to behave. Helen needs a teacher who specializes in helping children with disabilities.

When Helen is seven, her family finds a skilled tutor named Anne Sullivan (the "miracle worker" of the film's title). At first, ~~the teacher~~ Sullivan makes little progress in helping Helen. She uses her fingers to spell words into Helen's hand. Still, Helen doesn't understand that the finger movements represent words. At one point, Sullivan becomes frustrated because Helen is unable to distinguish between the words <u>water</u> and <u>mug</u>.

Then Sullivan has a brilliant idea. She takes Helen to the water pump. This is the most exciting scene in the movie! Sullivan puts one of Helen's hands into the running water and finger-spells the word <u>water</u> into Helen's other hand. Helen suddenly understands that "w-a-t-e-r" means the liquid gushing over her hand. Learning this one word is a break through for Helen. Once she knows that everything has a name, she is eager to learn as many new words as she can.

Although <u>The Miracle Worker</u> is both uplifting and sad, there is a larger idea symbolized by Helen's break through. No matter how great the obstacles may seem, no matter what the setbacks, anything is possible. Take my advice and watch this movie!

5 **PUBLISH** Prepare your final draft. Share your essay with your teacher and classmates.

Workbook
Page 126

261

Learn about Art with the
Smithsonian American Art Museum

Bonding or Breaking?

*A*rtists love drama, and matters that involve human emotions often provide plenty of it. The portrayal of friendship, lovers, or family ties in paintings, sculpture, and other media has served as the storyline of some amazing American art.

William T. Wiley, *Love Poem— Poem by Michael Hannon* (1997)

For almost thirty years, painter William T. Wiley created works of art inspired by the poems of Michael Hannon. In *Love Poem*, Wiley uses the following poem by Hannon, which appears at the bottom center of the painting's border:

> Fear of death—a kind of desire,
> and fear of desire—a kind of death.
>
> Clouds like ships—ships like clouds.
>
> I love you, even if this world
> is just a dream—even if it isn't.

Wiley obviously captured the ship, clouds, and water imagery in his watercolor, but he added something of his own to the "poem." Notice the musical clefs which look like fancy *f*s throughout the watercolor. There is one on each side

William T. Wiley, *Love Poem—Poem by Michael Hannon,* **1997, watercolor, 41 × 27 in., Smithsonian American Art Museum** ▶

262

of the larger heart floating in the center of the wave, and then two more in the white center of the heart. Wiley loved to work with repeating shapes. He also played music, in particular the fiddle and the mandolin—both instruments have this clef shape on their wooden fronts. The heart is a symbol of love, but some unsettling things are happening in this watercolor. The water swirls, and the ship is so close to the edge of a wave it looks as if it might topple over. But, of course, Hannon's poem is also a bit edgy since it uses words that contrast sharply: fear and desire, love and death.

▲ Washington Allston, *Hermia and Helena*, before 1818, oil, 30⅜ x 25¼ in., Smithsonian American Art Museum

Washington Allston, *Hermia and Helena* (before 1818)

The two friends pictured in this painting sit so close together that they look like one figure. Each has a hand on the book they share. Washington Allston borrowed the storyline for this cozy scene from the British playwright William Shakespeare's play, *A Midsummer Night's Dream*. The comedy centers on two friends who fall in love with the same man. Can their friendship survive as they compete for his affections? In the play, Shakespeare has Helena (the figure on the right in the painting) describe what her bond with Hermia has felt like as they grew up together.

> So we grew together,
> Like a double cherry . . .
> Two lovely berries moulded on one stem.

In his painting, Allston shows the two women as a "double cherry" sitting on a rock in a splendid landscape. The setting suggests the enchanted wood where most of the comedy's action takes place.

Love is the greatest emotion, but also perhaps the most difficult. Both of these artists make it clear that when it comes to matters of the heart, things can be complicated.

Apply What You Learned

1 What does each artwork add to the literature it was based on?

2 If you were to create an artwork based on a piece of literature, what would you choose and how would you illustrate it?

Big Question
How does each of these artworks show the concepts of bonding or breaking?

Workbook
Pages 127–128

THE BIG QUESTION

What can we learn from times of war?

This unit is about war. You'll read about World War I—often called the "Great War." You'll also read about ordinary heroes of World War II. Reading, writing, and talking about this topic will give you practice using academic language and help you become a better student.

READING 1: Social Studies Article

■ "World War I"

READING 2: Poems, Song, and Letter

■ "In Flanders Fields" by John McCrae
■ "Anthem for Doomed Youth" by Wilfred Owen
■ "Three Wonderful Letters from Home" by Goodwin, MacDonald, and Hanley
■ "Letter Home" by Frank Earley

READING 3: News Article

■ "In the Name of His Father" by Fred Tasker

READING 4: Autobiography

■ From *Farewell to Manzanar* by J. W. Houston and J. D. Houston

Listening and Speaking

You'll give an **oral report** at the unit's end.

Writing

In this unit, you'll practice **expository writing**. Expository writing gives factual information. After each reading, you'll learn a skill that will help you write an expository paragraph. At the end of the unit, you'll expand one of your paragraphs into an expository essay.

QuickWrite

Write *war* in your notebook. List things you associate with war under the word.

Visit LongmanKeystone.com

265

What You Will Learn

Reading

■ Vocabulary building: *Context, dictionary skills, word study*

■ Reading strategy: *Identify cause and effect*

■ Text type: *Informational text (social studies)*

Grammar, Usage, and Mechanics
Appositives

Writing
Write a cause-and-effect paragraph

THE BIG QUESTION

What can we learn from times of war? War causes great pain and suffering, but it can also teach us important lessons. We study history to learn these lessons. How does war change people's lives? How does it affect history?

BUILD BACKGROUND

"World War I" is an article that tells what caused World War I and what made it different from all previous wars. The map below shows Europe in 1914, at the beginning of the war. The timeline shows four important events that occurred during the war.

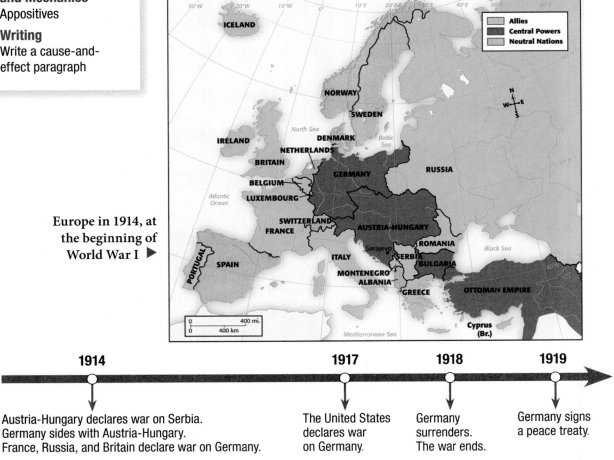

Europe in 1914, at the beginning of World War I ▶

1914
Austria-Hungary declares war on Serbia.
Germany sides with Austria-Hungary.
France, Russia, and Britain declare war on Germany.

1917
The United States declares war on Germany.

1918
Germany surrenders.
The war ends.

1919
Germany signs a peace treaty.

266

Learn Key Words

Read these sentences. Use the context to figure out the meaning of the red words. Use a dictionary to check your answers. Then write each word and its meaning in your notebook.

1. The United States banded together with other countries, forming an **alliance** to fight Austria-Hungary and Germany.

2. In 1918 Germany signed an **armistice**, an agreement to stop fighting immediately.

3. In 1914 a man killed Archduke Franz Ferdinand, nephew to the emperor of Austria-Hungary. As a result of the archduke's **assassination**, Austria-Hungary declared war on Serbia.

4. Unfortunately, during a war many **civilians**—citizens who are not members of the military forces—are hurt or killed.

5. The Germans **surrendered** because they realized that they could not win the war.

6. The soldiers spent most of their time in deep holes called **trenches**, where they were protected from enemy fire.

Key Words
alliance
armistice
assassination
civilians
surrendered
trenches

Practice

Write the sentences in your notebook. Choose a red word from the box above to complete each sentence. Then take turns reading the sentences aloud with a partner.

1. The man was arrested for planning an _____ of the president.

2. The soldiers dug _____ that were 6 to 8 feet deep.

3. It is not easy to reach an _____ when groups of people are at war.

4. The two countries formed an _____ to work together for one cause.

5. Many _____ —while waiting at home, worrying about their loved ones—were injured when a bomb accidentally went off in their neighborhood.

6. The enemy _____ after recognizing that the war could not be won.

▲ An American war photographer sets up a camera in a waterlogged trench.

Learn Academic Words

Study the **red** words and their meanings. You will find these words useful when talking and writing about informational texts. Write each word and its meaning in your notebook. After you read "World War I," try to use these words to respond to the text.

Academic Words

neutral
resources
technology
tension
vehicles

neutral = not supporting either side in an argument, competition, or war	➡	Sweden did not wish to get involved in the war, so it remained **neutral**.
resources = all the money, property, and other goods that are available for use	➡	Germany's desire for land and other **resources** helped to bring about the war.
technology = the combination of all the latest knowledge, equipment, and methods used in scientific or industrial work	➡	The invention of computers and other advances in **technology** have changed how people fight wars.
tension = the emotionally charged relationship between people or groups of people	➡	The mounting **tension** between the two groups suddenly erupted in an act of violence that started a war.
vehicles = machines such as cars, buses, or trucks used for carrying people or things from one place to another		During wartime, various **vehicles**, including planes, trains, submarines, tanks, and ships, are used to transport people.

Practice  Workbook Page 130

Write the sentences in your notebook. Choose a **red** word from the box above to complete each sentence. Then take turns reading the sentences aloud with a partner.

1. There was so much _____ between the two countries that people expected fighting to break out soon.

2. Advances in _____ enabled many countries to build deadlier weapons.

3. During the war, _____ transported weapons from one place to another.

4. The two groups hoped that by sharing their _____, they could find a solution faster.

5. Switzerland is a _____ country; it will not support either side in a war.

▲ WWI soldiers wearing gas masks operate a machine gun.

268

Word Study: Roots

Many English words come from Greek or Latin and still retain parts of the words from which they came. These word parts are called roots. The chart below shows some roots, their meanings, their origins, and some English words that contain them.

Root	Meaning	Origin	English Word
capit	head	Latin	capital
cent	one hundred	Latin	century
civ	citizen	Latin	civilian
fac	do, make	Latin	factories
mar	sea	Latin	submarine
photo	light	Greek	photograph
port	carry	Latin	support, transport
scope	see, watch	Greek	periscope
techn	art, skill	Greek	technology
tens	stretch, strain	Latin	tension

Practice

With a partner, look through "World War I" to find each of the English words in the chart above. In your notebook, copy the sentences in which you find the words. Then talk about what each word means. Write a definition under each sentence.

READING STRATEGY   IDENTIFY CAUSE AND EFFECT

Identifying cause and effect can help you understand relationships between events. A cause is something that makes something else happen. An effect is what happens. To identify causes and effects, follow these steps:

- As you read, look for important events. The reasons for events are causes. The events themselves may be causes or effects.
- Look for words and phrases that signal causes and effects. Examples include *because, the reason for this, caused by, since,* and *as a result.*

As you read "World War I," look for causes and effects. Make sure you understand the relationship between the different events.

269

Set a purpose for reading Read this article to find out the major causes and effects of World War I. How did the war change the world for ever?

World War I

Background to the Conflict

At the beginning of the twentieth century, there was tension among countries in Europe. One reason for this tension was the shifting balance of power. Each country worked hard to ensure that no other country had more power than it did. Britain, France, and Germany were competing against one another for overseas trade. The British were alarmed that the Germans were building larger, more modern factories. The Germans were anxious that France was gaining power and wealth in the form of colonies. Germany wanted more land and resources and greater military strength. In addition, Russia and Austria-Hungary were struggling for power in the Balkan states in southeastern Europe. Because of these tensions, six countries formed two powerful alliances:

- Britain, France, Russia
- Germany, Austria-Hungary, Italy

By the middle of 1914, Europe was close to war.

▲ A German factory in 1914

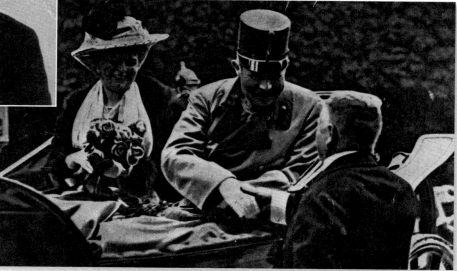

◀ Gavrilo Princip, the man who assassinated Archduke Franz Ferdinand and his wife

▲ Archduke Franz Ferdinand and his wife, Sophie, before the assassination

The Assassination

In 1914, Austria-Hungary ruled Bosnia and Herzegovina, a province in the Balkans in southeastern Europe. Bosnia and Herzegovina and Serbia, a country in the same area, were at one time both part of the Ottoman Empire. Serbia won its independence, but Bosnia and Herzegovina was made part of Austria-Hungary. Because many Serbs lived in Bosnia and Herzegovina, Serbia wanted control over the province. This rivalry caused tension between Serbia and Austria-Hungary.

Archduke Franz Ferdinand, the nephew of the emperor of Austria-Hungary and heir to the throne, visited Sarajevo, the capital of Bosnia and Herzegovina. The Serbs living in the province were angered by the archduke's visit. On June 28, 1914, a Bosnian student, supported by a group of Serbian terrorists, assassinated him. Austria-Hungary declared war on Serbia on July 28. The war quickly spread as other countries defended their allies. By mid-August 1914, most of Europe was at war.

Ottoman Empire, empire based in Turkey, which included large parts of Eastern Europe, Asia, and North Africa. It began about 1300 and ended in 1922.
terrorists, people who use violence against ordinary people to obtain political demands

BEFORE YOU GO ON

1 Who ruled Bosnia and Herzegovina in 1914? Why did this cause tension?

2 What happened as a result of Archduke Franz Ferdinand's assassination?

On Your Own
What other assassinations do you know about?

Within a year, many countries had joined in the war. This chart shows how the countries were divided.

Allied Nations ("The Allies")		Central Powers (Fighting against the Allies)
Britain	Australia	Germany
France	New Zealand	Austria-Hungary
Russia	Canada	Bulgaria
Belgium	South Africa	Ottoman Empire (Turkey, etc.)
Portugal	Italy (having changed	
Greece	sides joined the	
Serbia	Allies in 1915)	
Montenegro	Soldiers from French	
Romania	and British colonies	

The First Modern War

World War I is often called the first modern war because new technology made the weapons deadlier than ever. In addition, factories could produce larger quantities of weapons. Here are some of the modern weapons used during the war:

Machine guns These guns, invented by an American, shot many bullets very quickly.

Submarines These underwater ships shot torpedoes—bombs that are fired underwater.

Poison gas and gas masks Poison gas caused choking, blindness, blisters, and sometimes death. Gas masks protected soldiers from poison gas.

Tanks These combat vehicles carried two machine guns apiece and had metal belts over their wheels to help them climb over obstacles five feet high. They were covered with heavy armor, so they were difficult to destroy.

Periscope rifles Two mirrors were attached to a rifle so that when lifted over the top of the trenches, the soldier could see the enemy.

Fighter airplanes These small planes were armed with machine guns.

---

blisters, bumps on the skin containing clear liquid, often caused by a burn
obstacles, objects that block a person's way
armor, a strong metal layer or shell that protects

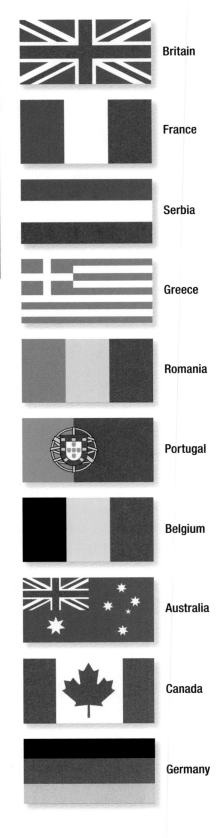

Britain
France
Serbia
Greece
Romania
Portugal
Belgium
Australia
Canada
Germany

A submarine ▶

◀ A gas mask

SUBMERGED.
(A FORE AND AFT SECTION.)

PERISCOPE PERISCOPE

▲ A fighter airplane

◀ A tank

T 9171

BEFORE YOU GO ON

1 Why is World War I often called the first modern war?

2 What were tanks able to do? Why were they difficult to destroy?

On Your Own
Do you think World War I was more or less civilized than preceding wars? Explain.

273

◀ **American troops in the trenches near Verdun, France**

The trenches stretched almost 650 kilometers (400 mi.). ▼

BELGIUM

GERMANY

LUXEMBOURG

FRANCE

Trenches ----

Life in the Trenches

Soldiers dug trenches for protection from the enemy. The trenches were muddy after it rained, so soldiers put wooden boards—called duckboards—on the ground to help keep their feet dry. The trenches were stifling in the summer and bitterly cold in the winter. Rats and lice spread diseases such as a brand-new illness called trench fever.

Soldiers spent about a week at a time in the trenches. Then they went to a rest area where they could wash and change clothes before returning to their underground posts. Most of the fighting was at night, so soldiers often slept during the day. They wrote letters home or kept diaries. Many soldiers were homesick. They had a hard life in the trenches.

The United States Enters the War

From the beginning of the war, President Woodrow Wilson wanted the United States to stay neutral. People in the United States were divided about the war. Many U.S. citizens were from European countries, so there was support for both sides. In 1915, Germany announced it would attack all neutral ships headed to Britain. In 1917, Germany announced unrestricted submarine warfare.

---

stifling, very hot and difficult to breathe in
unrestricted, not limited by anyone or anything

This meant that Germany's submarines would attack all foreign cargo ships to stop supplies from getting to Britain. When Germany sank some U.S. ships, President Wilson declared war on Germany and joined the Allies.

Germany Surrenders

By 1918, the Allies had stopped supplies from going to Germany, where people were starving because there was so little food. By October, the Allies had defeated Bulgaria and Turkey. In November, Germany asked the Allies for an armistice. They signed an armistice on November 11, 1918. After more than four years, the war finally ended. Germany surrendered and a peace treaty was signed on June 28, 1919.

After the War

With the end of World War I, the map of Europe changed. Some countries, such as Germany, had to give up land. Other countries, such as Greece, gained land. Austria-Hungary and the Ottoman Empire were broken up into separate countries.

More than 65 million soldiers fought in the war, of whom more than half were killed or injured—8 million killed, 2 million dead of illness and diseases, 21 million wounded, and nearly 8 million taken prisoner or missing. More than 6 million civilians died, too. People hoped it would be the "war to end all wars," but it wasn't. World War II followed only twenty-one years later.

▲ U.S. president Woodrow Wilson

Country	Soldiers Killed
Germany	1,773,700
Russia	1,700,000
France	1,357,800
Austria-Hungary	1,200,000
British Empire	908,371
United States	116,516
Serbia	45,000

BEFORE YOU GO ON

1 What was hard about life in the trenches?

2 Why did the United States decide to enter the war?

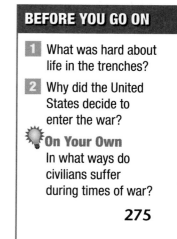
On Your Own
In what ways do civilians suffer during times of war?

Review and Practice

COMPREHENSION

Workbook
Page 133

Right There

1. Why did Serbia want control over Bosnia and Herzegovina in 1914?

2. Why did Austria-Hungary declare war on Serbia?

Think and Search

3. What events led to Germany's surrender?

4. How did the map of Europe change as a result of World War I?

Author and You

5. Why do you think the war ended so quickly after the United States joined the Allies?

6. The reading states that life in the trenches was very difficult. How was trench warfare different from warfare today?

On Your Own

7. In some parts of the world, young men and women are required to serve in the armed forces for a certain period of time. Do you think this is fair? Why or why not?

8. Do you think warfare should be subject to rules or codes of behavior? Why or why not?

IN YOUR OWN WORDS

Work with a partner. Use cause-and-effect charts like the one below to discuss the key events of World War I. Complete the first box with facts about the death of the archduke. You may wish to use the following vocabulary in your discussion: *alliance, armistice, assassination, civilians, neutral, resources, surrendered, technology, tension, trenches,* and *vehicles.*

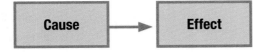

> ### 🔊 Speaking TIP
>
> Read your charts several times before you begin speaking so that you don't have to refer to them often.

DISCUSSION

Discuss in pairs or small groups.

- Do you think war might have been declared even if Archduke Franz Ferdinand had not been assassinated? Explain.

- **What can we learn from times of war?** World War II was declared just twenty-one years after World War I ended. Why do you think this was so? Why do you think the countries involved did not learn from the mistakes they made in the First World War?

»))9 Listening TIP

If you don't understand a classmate's comment, ask him or her to clarify it for you.

READ FOR FLUENCY

It is often easier to read a text if you understand the difficult words and phrases. Work with a partner. Choose a paragraph from the reading. Identify the words and phrases you do not know or have trouble pronouncing. Look up the difficult words in a dictionary.

Take turns pronouncing the words and phrases with your partner. If necessary, ask your teacher to model the correct pronunciation. Then take turns reading the paragraph aloud. Give each other feedback.

EXTENSION

Workbook Page 133

Work in small groups. Compare the map with the map on page 266. Which countries gained land as a result of World War I? Which countries lost land? Which countries are new?

Europe in 1919, after World War I ▶

Grammar and Writing

Appositives

An appositive is a noun or noun phrase that further defines or identifies another noun. An appositive immediately follows the noun it defines.

> In 1914, Austria-Hungary ruled Bosnia and Herzegovina, **a province in the Balkans**.
> [appositive defines *Bosnia and Herzegovina*]
> Serbia, **a country in the same area,** was at one time part of the Ottoman Empire.
> [appositive defines *Serbia*]
> Archduke Franz Ferdinand, **the nephew of the emperor of Austria-Hungary and heir to the throne,** visited Sarajevo, **the capital of Bosnia and Herzegovina**.
> [appositives define *Archduke Franz Ferdinand* and *Sarajevo*]

An appositive can be restrictive or nonrestrictive. A restrictive appositive is essential to the noun it identifies; a nonrestrictive appositive is not essential information and when omitted, can be understood.

Restrictive—do not use commas	The country **Serbia** was with the Allies. [There is more than one country. The information, *Serbia*, is essential.]
Nonrestrictive— use comma(s)	Ferdinand died in the capital of Bosnia and Herzegovina, **Sarajevo**. [There is only one capital of Bosnia and Herzegovina. The information, *Sarajevo*, is not essential.]

Practice

Workbook Page 134

Copy the sentences into your notebook. Work with a partner. Circle the appositive in each sentence and underline the noun it defines. Discuss whether each appositive is restrictive or nonrestrictive.

1. World War I, the first modern war, began with the assassination of Archduke Franz Ferdinand.
2. The archduke and his wife, Sophie, were visiting Sarajevo.
3. Bosnian student Gavrilo Princip shot the archduke at close range.
4. Soldiers put pieces of wood, called duckboards, on the ground to help keep their feet dry.
5. Machine guns, an American invention, shot many bullets quickly.

WRITING AN EXPOSITORY PARAGRAPH

Write a Cause-and-Effect Paragraph

At the end of this unit, you will write an expository essay. To do this, you'll need to learn some of the skills writers use in expository writing.

There are many ways to organize ideas in an expository paragraph. One of these is by cause and effect. In a cause-and-effect paragraph, you explain the causes and effects of an event, or you discuss a topic in terms of cause and effect. For example, a cause-and-effect paragraph about World War I might list the events that led up to the war. It might also discuss the situations that came about as a result of the war. You must show clearly how the causes and effects are related.

Here is a model of a cause-and-effect paragraph. Before writing, the writer listed her ideas in a graphic organizer.

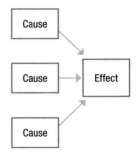

Andrea Vargas

World War I

World War I had many causes. First, there was great tension among European countries in the nineteenth century. Each country wanted more power than its neighbor. Countries with similar interests formed alliances. Britain, France, and Russia formed the Allied Powers, while Germany, Austria-Hungary, and Italy formed the Central Powers. This added to the tension. The war finally started after the assassination on June 28, 1914, of Archduke Franz Ferdinand, the nephew of the emperor of Austria-Hungary. The United States was neutral until 1917, when Germany attacked U.S. cargo ships heading to Britain. Then the United States was forced to fight. The war lasted until 1918. About 10 million soldiers and 6 million civilians died. It was more destructive than previous wars because factories could produce deadlier weapons more quickly than ever. The war's effect on Europe was devastating.

Practice

Workbook
Page 135

Write a cause-and-effect paragraph. You might write about a problem in your community (such as pollution or illegal dumping), a conflict between social groups at your school, or a problem you learned about in social studies. List your ideas in a graphic organizer. Be sure to use appositives correctly.

Writing Checklist

IDEAS:
☑ I showed how the causes and effects were related.

VOICE:
☑ I used the formal language of a social studies textbook.

279

What You Will Learn

Reading
- Vocabulary building: *Literary terms, dictionary skills, word study*
- Reading strategy: *Analyze historical context*
- Text type: *Literature (poetry, song, prose)*

Grammar, Usage, and Mechanics
Contrast and opposition

Writing
Write to compare and contrast

THE BIG QUESTION

What can we learn from times of war? The works you are about to read were written during World War I. Times of war are always highly emotional. People have to cope with feelings of anger, sadness, and loss. During wartime, writers and other artists can be especially productive. Talk with a partner about the kinds of feelings that wars bring out in people. Why might times of war also be times of great artistic achievement?

BUILD BACKGROUND

This reading includes two poems, part of a song, and a personal letter. The poems are both about the deaths of World War I soldiers. **"In Flanders Fields"** was written by Lieutenant Colonel John McCrae, a Canadian doctor who worked as a surgeon on the battlefield. He wrote the poem for a friend who died in battle. McCrae himself died of pneumonia while on active duty in 1918.

The English poet Wilfred Owen wrote the second poem, **"Anthem for Doomed Youth."** Owen was one of the most famous World War I poets. He died one week before the war ended. Three Americans wrote the song **"Three Wonderful Letters from Home"** in 1918. **"Letter Home"** was written by a young British journalist, Frank Earley, from the front.

▲ American soldiers writing letters in 1918

VOCABULARY

Learn Literary Words

Figurative language adds layers of meaning to the literal meanings of words. While *literal* language means exactly what it says, *figurative* language goes beyond the literal level. Figurative language usually asks the reader to compare two unlike things in order to create fresh associations, to express a complex idea, or to produce a sensory effect.

Personification is a type of figurative language. It is the lending of human qualities to nonhuman things. This example of personification is taken from a Wilfred Owen poem called "Arms and the Boy."

> Let the boy try along this bayonet-blade
> How cold steel is, and keen with hunger of blood;

Steel is a metal—not something that has feelings. Yet the poem says that it is "keen with hunger of blood," meaning that it is angry and hungry for blood. Here is another example from the same poem:

> Lend him to stroke these blind, blunt bullet-leads,
> Which long to nuzzle in the hearts of lads,

Calling the bullet-leads "blind" suggests that they could at one time see. The second line suggests that they want to kill young men.

Practice

Workbook Page 136

Work with a partner. Copy this poem by Emily Dickinson into your notebook. Circle the examples of figurative language. Of these examples, which ones are also examples of personification? Explain.

> The morns are meeker than they were,
>   The nuts are getting brown;
> The berry's cheek is plumper,
>   The rose is out of town.
>
> The maple wears a gayer scarf,
>   The field a scarlet gown.
> Lest I be old-fashioned,
>   I'll put a trinket on.

Learn Academic Words

Study the **red** words and their meanings. You will find these words useful when talking and writing about literature. Write each word and its meaning in your notebook. After you read the poems, song, and letter, try to use these words to respond to the texts.

context = situation and conditions which surround something		The reader must know the **context** of these poems—World War I—in order to appreciate them fully.
create = make		Sometimes wars **create** new job opportunities for people.
impact = the effect that an event or situation has on someone or something		A war in the Middle East may have an **impact** on gas prices around the world.
similar = almost the same		The two poems express **similar** ideas—they both discuss the terrible experiences soldiers have during war.

Practice  Workbook Page 137

Write the sentences in your notebook. Choose a **red** word from the box above to complete each sentence. Then take turns reading the sentences aloud with a partner.

1. The two countries became allies because they had _____ beliefs and ideas.

2. Writers and other artists sometimes _____ works of art as a way of dealing with pain and loss.

3. After we read about the war, we began to understand the war in terms of the _____ of the time.

4. The change in leadership in the small country had an _____ felt throughout the world.

▲ A newspaper headline announces the United States' entering World War I in 1917.

282

Word Study: Homophones

A homophone is a word that sounds exactly like another word but has a different spelling and meaning. Look at the pairs of homophones and their definitions below.

Word	Part of speech	Meaning
real	adjective	actually existing and not just imagined
reel	noun	a round object onto which things such as film or special string for fishing can be wound

Practice
Workbook
Page 138

Work with a partner. Find at least one word from each pair of homophones below in the poems, song, or letter. Try to figure out the meaning of the words through context. Then use a dictionary to check the meaning and to find the meaning of the other words. Write sentences using the other words.

break/brake	their/they're/there	weight/wait
here/hear	through/threw	write/right

READING STRATEGY | ANALYZE HISTORICAL CONTEXT

Analyzing the historical context of a work of literature can make it more meaningful and easier to understand. Historical context includes the political and cultural changes that were happening at a particular time. To analyze historical context, follow these steps as you read:

- Pay attention to the events described in the work. Where and when did they take place? What was happening in the world at the time?

- Think about what you already know about the context of the work. How did the events during that time affect literature in general?

- Notice how the subject matter is determined by the events of the time.

As you read the poems, the song, and the letter, think about the effect of World War I. How did the war influence literary and personal writing?

Workbook
Page 139

Set a purpose for reading Read these works written during World War I. How did people respond differently to the horrors of the war?

In Flanders Fields

In Flanders fields the poppies blow
Between the crosses row on row,
    That mark our place; and in the sky
    The larks, still bravely singing, fly
Scarce heard amid the guns below.

We are the Dead. Short days ago
We lived, felt dawn, saw sunset glow,
    Loved and were loved, and now we lie
      In Flanders fields.

Take up our quarrel with the foe:
To you from failing hands we throw
    The torch; be yours to hold it high.
    If ye break faith with us who die
We shall not sleep, though poppies grow
      In Flanders fields.

—John McCrae, MD (1872–1918)
Lieutenant Colonel
in the Canadian Army

✔ **LITERARY CHECK**
What is the **figurative** *meaning of "we throw the torch"?*

---

poppies, bright red flowers
quarrel, complaint
foe, enemy

ABOUT THE POET

John McCrae was born in Canada in 1872. He wrote "In Flanders Fields," perhaps the most famous World War I poem ever written, in 1915 while working as a medical officer in Belgium. Shortly after, he was transferred to France to run a hospital. There he died of pneumonia in 1918.

Letter Home

Sunday afternoon, 1st September, 1918

My dear Father,

It is a strange feeling to me but a very real one, that every letter now that I write home to you or to the little sisters may be the last that I shall write or you read. I do not want you to think that I am depressed; indeed on the contrary, I am very cheerful. But out here, in odd moments the realization comes to me of how close death is to us. A week ago I was talking with a man . . . who had been out here for nearly four years, untouched. He was looking forward with certainty to going on leave soon. And now he is dead—killed in a moment during our last advance. Well, it was God's will.

I say this to you because I hope that you will realize, as I do, the possibility of the like happening to myself. I feel very glad myself that I can look the fact in the face without fear or misgiving. Much as I hope to live through it all for your sakes and my little sisters'! I am quite prepared to give my life as so many have done before me. All I can do is put myself in God's hands for him to decide, and you and the little ones pray for me to the Sacred Heart and Our Lady. . . .

Well, I have not much time left and I must end. With my dear love.
Pray for me.

Your son,
Frank

THERE'S ROOM FOR YOU

ENLIST TO-DAY

---

depressed, sad
going on leave, taking time off from active duty
misgiving, doubt or negative feeling about the future

ABOUT THE AUTHOR

Frank Earley was a British journalist. His letters home were usually full of cheer. It is only in this last letter that he sounds thoughtful. The day after Earley wrote this letter, he suffered a wound to the chest and died. He was nineteen years old.

BEFORE YOU GO ON

1 How did the letters make the soldier in the song feel?

2 How did Frank Earley feel about the possibility of dying in battle?

On Your Own
Why are times of war times of heightened artistic expression?

287

Review and Practice

DRAMATIC READING

Work in groups to reread, discuss, and interpret "In Flanders Fields" and "Anthem for Doomed Youth." Read each poem line by line and talk about the images that come to mind. Identify figurative language and sensory words. Discuss how each poem makes you feel. Try to figure out difficult words or phrasing from context. Consult a dictionary or your teacher for help if necessary.

After you analyze the poems, choose one to memorize. Have each student learn a few lines. Then recite the poem within your group. Comment on one another's reading and make suggestions for improvements. You may wish to hold a contest with the class in which each group competes for the best oral reading.

🔊 *Speaking* TIP

Let the punctuation in the poem guide you as you read aloud. A period, dash, semicolon, or comma is a signal to pause.

COMPREHENSION

Workbook
Page 140

Right There

1. What are the "passing-bells" that the dying soldiers hear in Owen's poem?

2. What is the strange feeling Frank Earley talks about in his letter?

Think and Search

3. What do the rows of crosses in Flanders Fields mark?

4. An anthem is a song. What kind of song does the choir in Owen's poem sing?

"If ye break faith — we shall not sleep"

BUY VICTORY BONDS

▲ This poster advertising Victory Bonds includes a quote from "In Flanders Fields."

Author and You

5. Which poem expresses a bleaker attitude? Explain.

6. What purpose might the songwriters have had for writing "Three Wonderful Letters from Home"?

On Your Own

7. Why do you think soldiers wrote letters and poems while at war?

8. Why might a song be an effective way to comfort soldiers?

DISCUSSION

Discuss in pairs or small groups.

1. Why do you think flowers are mentioned in both poems?

2. Of the three genres included in this reading, the song is the only one that does not focus on death. Why do you think this is so?

Q **What can we learn from times of war?** What do the poems, the song lyrics, and the letter tell you about this period in history? What do you think each of the authors wanted to convey about World War I?

Workbook
Page 140

RESPONSE TO LITERATURE

During World War I, young men from different countries fought side-by-side in trenches under horrible conditions. Imagine that you have been asked to write a letter for an American soldier who has been wounded in France. He wants you to reassure his family that he is getting good care and that he will recover soon. Include details that will help to calm his family during this difficult time. When you have finished, read your letter aloud to the class.

▼ American troops using French tanks during World War I

Grammar and Writing

GRAMMAR, USAGE, AND MECHANICS

Contrast and Opposition

In the reading selections, the authors use words and expressions like *but*, *on the contrary*, and *much as* to show contrast and opposition.

But is a coordinating conjunction and is used to connect two clauses or a clause and a phrase. Usually, a comma is used only when *but* connects two clauses or when a phrase with *but* begins the sentence. However, in poetry, the rule is not strict. Look at the examples below.

> It is a strange feeling to me **but** a very real one.
> **But** out here, in odd moments the realization comes to me of how close death is . . .
> Not in the hands of boys, **but** in their eyes . . .

On the contrary is a transition. A transition connects two independent clauses using a semicolon (;), or it can come at the beginning of a sentence.

> I do not want you to think I am depressed**; on the contrary**, I am very cheerful.

Much as is an adverbial expression and begins an adverb clause. Usually a comma is used after an adverb clause. However, when writing an informal letter, this rule is not strict.

> **Much as** I hope to live, I'm prepared to die as others have done before me.

Practice

 **Workbook** Page 141

Read the sentence starters. Work with a partner to complete the sentences using facts from the unit. Write the completed sentences in your notebook.

1. The Allies feared they would lose the war; on the contrary . . .
2. The United States wanted to stay neutral, but . . .
3. Serbia was made an independent country, but Bosnia and Herzegovina . . .
4. Well, much as I enjoy writing, I must . . .

290

WRITING AN EXPOSITORY PARAGRAPH

Write to Compare and Contrast

At the end of this unit, you will write an expository essay. To do this, you'll need to learn how writers organize expository writing. When you compare and contrast, you organize your ideas accordingly. One way to organize ideas in compare-and-contrast writing is to compare in one part and contrast in another. For a two-paragraph piece of writing, you would tell how the things are similar in the first paragraph and how they are different in the second paragraph.

This model compares and contrasts the song and the letter you've just read. Before writing, the writer listed her ideas in a Venn diagram.

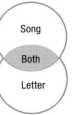

Song

Both

Letter

Jessica Reider

Letters to and from Home

"Three Wonderful Letters from Home" and "Letter Home" are both similar and different. They are similar in that they both have to do with the loneliness a soldier experiences during war and his longing to return home. The song and the letter are both written during the same time period—World War I. They also are similar in purpose: The song was written to cheer up soldiers, and the letter was written to cheer up loved ones at home.

The two pieces of writing also have many differences. "Three Wonderful Letters from Home" is a song, whereas "Letter Home" is a personal letter. The point of view is different in the two pieces. "Three Wonderful Letters from Home" is written in the third person about an imaginary soldier, while "Letter Home" is written in the first person, by an actual soldier to his family members. The two pieces also have very different tones. The song is sentimental and hopeful, but the letter has a thoughtful, somber tone.

Practice
Workbook Page 142

Write two paragraphs that compare and contrast two things that are important to you. You can write about books, movies, sports, or foods. Remember that your details will support how the things are alike and how they are different. Use a Venn diagram to organize your ideas. Be sure to use contrast and opposition words correctly.

Writing Checklist

IDEAS:

☑ I showed how the things are alike and how they are different.

CONVENTIONS:

☑ I used contrast and opposition words correctly.

291

What You Will Learn

Reading

■ Vocabulary building: *Context, dictionary skills, word study*

■ Reading strategy: *Draw conclusions*

■ Text type: *Informational text (social studies)*

Grammar, Usage, and Mechanics
Passive voice in the present perfect

Writing
Write a news article

THE BIG QUESTION

What can we learn from times of war? Think about heroes you have read about. What did they do that was heroic? What risks did they take? How does war bring out the worst and the best in people? Discuss with a partner.

BUILD BACKGROUND

"In the Name of His Father" is a news article about a man named Chiune (chee-YOO-nay) Sugihara. During World War II, Sugihara lived in Lithuania and worked as a diplomat for Japan. At that time, the German dictator, Adolf Hitler, directed a major effort to kill the Jewish people of Europe. Hitler's soldiers forced Jews to live in places called concentration camps, where they were treated cruelly and, in many cases, killed.

▲ German poster of Adolf Hitler, 1930s

Sugihara knew what was happening. He found a way to help Jewish refugees and, in doing so, risked his own life. Sugihara saved the lives of thousands of people and has come to be considered a hero. Hitler was eventually defeated and World War II ended in 1945, but not before more than 6 million innocent Jewish people died.

VOCABULARY

Learn Key Words

Read these sentences. Use the context to figure out the meaning of the **red** words. Use a dictionary to check your answers. Then write each word and its meaning in your notebook.

1. Some of the American government workers who represent the United States in Italy work at the **consulate** in Milan.

2. The American **diplomat** represented the views of his country at the meeting with other countries in Germany.

3. The soldiers showed great **heroism** when they rescued the children in the village.

4. They **honor** people for brave deeds by awarding them a medal.

5. During the **lecture**, the professor told his class about great heroes of World War II.

6. The people who live in a country at war often lose their homes and become **refugees** who must move to a new place.

Practice  **Workbook** Page 143

Write the sentences in your notebook. Choose a **red** word from the box above to complete each sentence. Then take turns reading the sentences aloud with a partner.

1. My family helped the _____ who arrived here after escaping from the war in their home country.

2. My father is going to work for the government at the _____ in Lyon, France.

3. The speaker gave a very interesting _____ about his experiences as a soldier.

4. The Russian _____ spoke on behalf of his country at the conference.

5. They are going to _____ a soldier who fought in the Gulf War by naming a park after him.

6. The woman showed true _____ when she helped her elderly neighbors escape the fire.

United States Marines raise the American flag in Iwo Jima after capturing the island from the Japanese in 1945. ▶

293

Learn Academic Words

Study the **red** words and their meanings. You will find these words useful when talking and writing about informational texts. Write each word and its meaning in your notebook. After you read "In the Name of His Father," try to use these words to respond to the text.

document = a piece of paper that has official information written on it	→	Your birth certificate is an official **document** that you can use to get a passport.
estimate = guess the value, size, number, etc., of something	→	They **estimate** that there will be thousands of refugees after the war.
exploits = brave and exciting actions	→	My grandfather told us all about his **exploits** and adventures as a soldier during the war.
integrity = the quality of being honest and having high moral principles	→	She demonstrated her **integrity** by being a witness and telling the truth during the trial.
sympathetic = showing that you understand how sad, hurt, lonely, etc., someone feels	→	We were **sympathetic** to the struggle of the refugees and wanted to help them in any way we could.

Practice

Work with a partner to answer these questions. Try to include the **red** word in your answer. Write the sentences in your notebook.

1. What official **document** shows that a person is the citizen of a country?

2. What do you **estimate** your score will be on the history test?

3. Name a hero or heroine you read about. What were his or her **exploits**?

4. Do you know someone who has a lot of **integrity**? Describe him or her.

5. When have you felt **sympathetic** toward a friend or family member?

▲ An American passport stamped with visa stamps from different countries

Word Study: The Suffix *-ness*

A suffix is a letter or group of letters added to the end of a word. When you add a suffix to the end of a word, you often change the meaning and part of speech of the word. The suffix *-ness* can be added to an adjective to make a noun. Generally, adding the suffix *-ness* will not change the spelling of a word. However, if the word has two or more syllables and ends in *y*, such as *happy*, change the *y* to an *i* before adding *-ness*.

Adjective	+ *ness* = Noun
awkward	awkwardness
conscious	consciousness
happy	happiness
silly	silliness

Practice  Workbook Page 145

Work with a partner. List the words in the box below in your notebook. Add *-ness* to the end of each word to make a new word. Then write a sentence with each new word, and read it aloud to your partner.

empty	kind	lonely	strange	thick

READING STRATEGY | DRAW CONCLUSIONS

Drawing conclusions helps you understand a text. Good readers are like detectives. They find "clues" in the text, put the clues together, and then draw a conclusion. To draw a conclusion, follow these steps:

- As you read, look for facts or ideas that might be clues.
- Think about what you already know about the topic.
- Add up the clues, and apply these new ideas to what you already know.
- Draw your conclusion from the ideas you have added up.

As you read "In the Name of His Father," look for facts and ideas that may help you draw conclusions about the exploits of Chiune Sugihara.

Workbook Page 146

Set a purpose for reading As you read this article, think about what kind of person Chiune Sugihara was. Why did he risk his life to save thousands of people he didn't know?

In the Name of His Father

Fred Tasker

The Miami Herald
January 24, 2000

It's with a certain awkwardness that Hiroki Sugihara, 63, travels the world to lecture about the heroic acts of his late father during World War II. It violates a cultural sense of modesty. "For a Japanese, it sounds like you are showing off," he says.

Yet he must. Too few in the world are aware of that heroism, he believes. Too few know what his father, Chiune Sugihara, "the Japanese Schindler," did in 1940 when, as a mid-ranking diplomat in Lithuania, against the orders of his own government, he wrote 6,000 exit visas to get desperate Polish Jews out of the way of the approaching Nazi Holocaust.

"Thanks to him, I'm alive," says George Borenstein, then a 36-year-old Polish Army soldier, now 86, retired in Delray Beach, Florida. Borenstein had fled to Lithuania after the Germans defeated the Polish Army. And he knew the German Army

▲ Chiune Sugihara

was killing Jews and the Soviet Army was sending such refugees to Siberia. "They were starving in Siberia. I lost a brother there. But [Sugihara] got me a visa. I got out."

Ousted from the foreign ministry after the war, Sugihara lived in obscurity for decades, selling light bulbs, then importing oil, until an Israeli diplomat in Tokyo, another of the refugees he saved, sought him out and set about making things right.

Schindler, German man who saved the lives of 1,200 Jews during World War II
retired, no longer working

obscurity, the state of not being known

Now he has been honored by the Israeli government as one of "the righteous among nations"—non-Jews who helped save Jews during the Holocaust. It's the same honor given German businessman Oskar Schindler and Swedish diplomat Raoul Wallenberg, whose efforts to save Jews from death at the hands of the Nazis are far better known.

Sugihara has been the subject of an Oscar-winning documentary, and on Feb. 6, his family will be given a heroism award from The Immortal Chaplains' Foundation.

Finally his story is being told.

Hiroki Sugihara remembers it well, even though he was not quite 4 when it happened. It was 1940. German troops invading Poland had expelled that country's Jews, and hundreds were huddled in the square in Kaunas, Lithuania, where his father's consulate stood, seeking permission to flee to any safe country that would take them. And the United States and Great Britain were balking at accepting new refugees.

"I asked my father why I couldn't go outside to play as usual," Sugihara says. "He told me it might be dangerous. The refugees were very agitated. I asked him what would happen to them, and he said they might be killed. I was concerned for the children, because some of them were my age. So I said, 'Why can't you help them?' And he said, 'I might.'"

---

balking at, refusing to
agitated, very nervous and upset

BEFORE YOU GO ON

1 Where did Sugihara live and work in 1940?

2 What did Sugihara do in 1940 to help Polish Jews?

On Your Own
In what ways can times of war inspire people to act bravely and selflessly?

297

▲ **Yukiko Sugihara**

For seven fevered weeks that July and August, the elder Sugihara worked 20 hours a day, writing an estimated 6,000 to 10,000 exit visas for the refugees. Three times he wired his government for permission to write more; three times he was told to stop. He kept writing.

Even as he and his family boarded the train to leave Lithuania for Berlin on his government's orders, Sugihara kept writing visas, throwing them out the window to refugees running alongside. "We will never forget you," one of them called, according to one book on Sugihara's exploits.

With documentation, the refugees were able to travel across Russia, take the Siberian Express railway to Vladivostok and eventually reach Japan or other countries. There they were treated well during the war. Despite its alliance with Nazi Germany, [Japan] had little history of anti-Semitism.

---

anti-Semitism, hatred of Jewish people

"When there were shortages, the [Japanese] people even shared their food with them," says Anne Akabori, the Sacramento librarian who, in 1996, translated into English the book *Visas for 6,000 Lives*, written by Sugihara's wife, Yukiko.

As the war ended, Sugihara, then posted in Romania, was captured by the Soviets and sent to a concentration camp with his wife and son for 18 months. Arriving back in Japan in 1947, he approached the country's postwar foreign ministry, hoping for a sympathetic reception and perhaps even a new assignment. Instead, they demanded his resignation.

The world knew little of [Sugihara] until 1968, when Joshua Nisri, economic attaché to the Israeli Embassy in Tokyo, sought him out. Nisri was a Polish teen in 1940, one of the refugees Sugihara saved. Since then, Sugihara's story has been slowly seeping into the world consciousness.

In 1985, just a year before Sugihara died, the Israeli government honored him as "A Man of Justice of the Peoples of the World."

His story spread further after the fall of communism freed Lithuania and other Eastern European countries to express their true feelings. It was only in 1991, during a celebration of Lithuanian independence, that a monument was erected and a street named after Sugihara in Kaunas.

---

resignation, leaving his job permanently
seeping into the world consciousness, becoming known to the world
monument, large structure built to remind people of an important event or to honor a famous person

In 1996, Boston University religion Professor Hillel Levine published a book, *In Search of Sugihara* (The Free Press, $25), calling Sugihara's exploits braver even than those of Wallenberg and Schindler, both of whom also rescued thousands of Jews during the war.

Wallenberg was sent to Hungary by the Swedish government with its specific backing, Levine argued; Schindler had at least a partial economic motive, using the Jews he saved to work in his factories. Sugihara acted purely on principle, Levine said. Sugihara's story became better known in the United States after 1994, when the movie *Schindler's List* raised the world's interest in those who had helped Jewish refugees during the war. In 1997, a documentary about Sugihara, *Visas and Virtue*, by Chris Tashima and Chris Donahue, won an Oscar in the Live Action Short Category.

More recently, Sugihara was honored by the Holocaust Oral History Project and the Wiesenthal Museum of Tolerance in Los Angeles at a ceremony attended by *Schindler's List* filmmaker Stephen Spielberg.

One of the first questions the younger Sugihara is asked during his lectures is why an obedient Japanese diplomat would take such a risk to himself and his family to help strangers.

Levine's book says survivors remember him as "the angel," a kind man who "treated them with respect, smiled at them and offered a cup of tea."

Says Akabori, the Sacramento librarian: "I believe it was deeply rooted in the Japanese spirit called 'bushido,' which means reaching the highest level of physical, mental, and spiritual attainment. When you think something is right you do it, without worrying about yourself." After all, she says, Sugihara's family is descended from Samurai, the ancient warrior caste to whom honor came before money or personal safety.

The younger Sugihara credits that explanation: "When he was growing up, he was taught that code. You have to sacrifice yourself to help somebody else."

The elder Sugihara, in a speech in 1985, a year before he died, put it more simply: "It is the kind of sentiment anyone would have when he actually sees the refugees face to face, begging with tears in their eyes.

"He just cannot help but sympathize with them."

Oscar, film awards granted by the Academy of Motion Picture Arts and Sciences

---

obedient, rule-following
attainment, something you have succeeded in getting
caste, group of people who have a particular position in society

BEFORE YOU GO ON

1 What happened to Sugihara when he returned to Japan?

2 What is "bushido"?

On Your Own
If you were Hiroki Sugihara, how would you feel about what your father did in 1940? Explain.

Review and Practice

Right There

1. What did Sugihara do after he was ousted from the foreign ministry after the war?
2. What is the estimated number of Jewish refugees that Sugihara wrote exit visas for?

Think and Search

3. How was Sugihara finally honored?
4. Why is Hiroki Sugihara hesitant about describing his father's heroic acts in his lectures?

Author and You

5. How did Chiune Sugihara view what he did in 1940?
6. Do you think the author of this article agrees with Sugihara's opinion of his own acts? Why or why not?

On Your Own

7. What might make a person want to help people he or she doesn't even know?
8. What other people do you consider heroic?

IN YOUR OWN WORDS

The people whose lives Sugihara saved considered him a hero. Many, many years later, others recognized his heroism. Draw conclusions about Sugihara's life and personality based on what you have read. Copy and complete the word web below to help you tell a partner about what Sugihara did and why you think he deserves to be honored.

> **Speaking TIP**
>
> Be sure to convey interest in your topic. Your enthusiasm will help to keep your audience engaged.

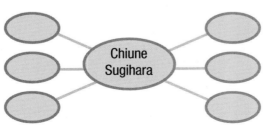

Chiune Sugihara

DISCUSSION

Discuss in pairs or small groups.

- Do you agree with Akabori, the librarian, that Sugihara was influenced by *bushido*? Why or why not?

- **What can we learn from times of war?** Sugihara's acts of heroism were on a grand scale and affected many people. What defines an act of heroism? Can people commit "small" acts of heroism? Explain.

Listening TIP

Be sure to let a speaker know when he or she makes an interesting point.

READ FOR FLUENCY

Reading with feeling helps make what you read more interesting. Work with a partner. Choose a paragraph from the reading. Read the paragraph. Ask each other how you felt after reading the paragraph. Did you feel happy or sad?

Take turns reading the paragraph aloud to each other with a tone of voice that represents how you felt when you read it the first time. Give each other feedback.

EXTENSION

Workbook
Page 147

Sugihara was a man of courage and integrity. What do the words *courage* and *integrity* mean to you? Do you know someone who has these qualities? Write a paragraph about a person whom you admire for his or her courage and integrity. Tell your readers about this person's actions and personality. Share your writing with the class.

▲ Refugees from across Central Europe line up for food at an Allied Forces refugee camp in Germany.

Grammar and Writing

Passive Voice in the Present Perfect

Writers use the active voice when the focus is on the performer of the action—who or what does the action. They use the passive voice when the focus is on the receiver of the action. A *by* phrase identifies the performer.

The passive voice can be used with different tenses. Use the simple past when the action happened at a definite time in the past. Form the passive voice in the simple past with *was/were* + the past participle.

Use the present perfect when the action happened at an indefinite time in the past or the action is still important now. Form the passive voice in the present perfect with *has/have been* + the past participle.

Active Voice / Simple Past	Passive Voice / Simple Past
The Soviets **captured** Sugihara at the end of the war.	Sugihara **was captured** by the Soviets at the end of the war.
Active Voice / Present Perfect	**Passive Voice / Present Perfect**
The Holocaust Oral History Project **has honored** Sugihara.	Sugihara **has been honored** by the Holocaust Oral History Project.

The *by* phrase may be omitted if the performer is unknown or not as important as the receiver.

> Sugihara **was ousted** from the foreign ministry after the war.
> A street **was named** after Sugihara in Kaunas.

Practice
Workbook Page 148

Work with a partner. Rewrite the sentences below in your notebook, changing the active voice to the passive voice. Use either the simple past or the present perfect.

1. The government of Israel has honored Sugihara.

2. The police treated the refugees very badly.

3. Film critics have praised the documentary about Sugihara.

4. The Immortal Chaplains' Foundation gave Sugihara's family an award on February 6, 2000.

5. Anne Akabori has translated the book *Visas for 6,000 Lives* into English.

WRITING AN EXPOSITORY PARAGRAPH

Write a News Article

At the end of this unit, you will write an expository essay. To do this, you'll need to learn skills writers use in expository writing. One kind of expository writing is a news article.

A good news article gives the reader information in a quick and interesting way. Your first paragraph should answer as many of the 5Ws as possible. The 5Ws are the questions *Who? What? When? Where?* and *Why?* Try to grab the reader's attention with an interesting opening and include details to give your news story life.

This news article is about a trip to Washington, D.C. The writer began by listing his ideas in a 5Ws chart.

Who	
What	
When	
Where	
Why	

Students Visit D.C.

Nicholas Kasterine

April 13, 2009

 While most of us finished an uneventful week, Mrs. Bell's social studies class spent last Thursday and Friday sightseeing in Washington, D.C. By all reports, the trip's highlight was a visit to the Vietnam Veterans Memorial, built to honor the soldiers who died or went missing during the Vietnam conflict. The history of the memorial is noteworthy. In 1980, five years after the war ended, a contest was held for the memorial's design. Maya Ying Lin, only 20 years old, won with a simple idea—two huge black walls jutting out of the ground, forming a V-shape. The names of the dead or missing men and women have been carved into the walls. The design sparked controversy at first because it was abstract and didn't include statues or other traditional features. But, according to Mrs. Bell's students, the monument is very moving. It honors each soldier individually, yet seeing all the names together makes you think about the total human cost of the war.

Practice

Workbook Page 149

Write a short news article about a class trip, a visit to a museum, or an issue that affects you at home or in school. Before you begin writing, list your ideas in a 5Ws chart. Use the passive voice correctly.

Writing Checklist

IDEAS:
- [x] I answered as many of the 5Ws as I could.

ORGANIZATION:
- [x] I tried to grab my reader's attention in the opening.

What You Will Learn

Reading

- Vocabulary building: *Literary terms, dictionary skills, word study*

- Reading strategy: *Ask questions*

- Text type: *Literature (autobiography)*

Grammar, Usage, and Mechanics
Using infinitives

Writing
Write a problem-and-solution paragraph

THE BIG QUESTION

What can we learn from times of war? Sometimes people are forced to leave their homes during wartime. Leaving home when your country is at war is difficult and painful. Refugees of war may find comfort in having family members near.

Have you ever traveled somewhere with your family? How did you feel about being away from home? Did being with your family help you feel more comfortable? Discuss with a partner.

BUILD BACKGROUND

World War II began in 1939 when Germany invaded Poland. On December 7, 1941, Japanese fighters bombed Pearl Harbor, a United States military base on the island of Oahu, Hawaii. It was then that the United States entered the war. The attack caused many Americans to fear and resent Japanese Americans.

In 1942, President Roosevelt signed an order to place 120,000 Japanese Americans into internment, or confinement, camps. Even Japanese Americans who were born in the United States were forced to go. Many of those who were sent to the camps lost everything—homes, jobs, and even family members.

This reading is an excerpt from ***Farewell to Manzanar***, the autobiography of a girl whose family was sent to Manzanar War Relocation Center. The camp was in California at the foot of the Sierra Nevada. All of the camps were eventually closed by 1945. Today, people realize that forcing Japanese Americans into internment camps was a terrible mistake.

◀ Manzanar War Relocation Center

Learn Literary Words

Diction is an author's choice of words. A writer's diction can be formal or informal. These lines from *Farewell to Manzanar* are an example of informal diction:

> "Hey, brother Ray, Kiyo," he said. "You see these tin can lids?"
> "Yeah, yeah," the boys said drowsily, as if going back to sleep. They were both young versions of Woody.
> "You see all them knotholes in the floor and in the walls?"
> They looked around. You could see about a dozen.
> Woody said, "You get these covered up before breakfast time. Any more sand comes in here through one of them knotholes, you have to eat it off the floor with ketchup."

The **tone** of a literary work is the writer's attitude toward his or her subject and audience. A tone can often be formal or informal, serious or playful, positive or negative. What is the tone of this passage?

> Woody stood up very straight, which in itself was funny, since he was only about five-foot-six.
> "Don't worry about the cracks," he said. "Different kind of sand comes in through the cracks."
> He put his hands on his hips and gave Kiyo a sternly comic look, squinting at him through one eye the way Papa would when he was asserting his authority. Woody mimicked Papa's voice: "And I can tell the difference. So be careful."

Practice

Workbook Page 150

Work with a partner. Refer to the passages above as you answer the following questions. If you have trouble understanding a word or expression, look in a dictionary or ask your teacher for help.

1. Why do the boys say "Yeah, yeah" when Woody is talking to them?
2. Is Woody serious when he says, "Any more sand comes in here . . . you have to eat it off the floor with ketchup"? How do you know?
3. How did the author tell you Woody was asserting his authority?
4. Why do you think the author refers to Woody as "sternly comic"?
5. What do you think the author's attitude toward Woody is?

Learn Academic Words

Study the **red** words and their meanings. You will find these words useful when talking and writing about literature. Write each word and its meaning in your notebook. After you read the excerpt from *Farewell to Manzanar*, try to use these words to respond to the text.

Academic Words

isolated
relocate
survival
temporary

isolated = far away from other things	➡	We were **isolated** from our family during the conflict. We lived in one city and our family lived in another city.
relocate = move to a new place	➡	They had to **relocate** to a new place during the war because the enemies were setting off bombs close to their homes.
survival = the state of continuing to live, especially after a difficult time or a dangerous situation	➡	The refugees ate any food they could find as a means of **survival**.
temporary = existing or happening only for a limited period of time	➡	We had to live in a **temporary** home for a while after the war until our home could be repaired.

Practice

Workbook
Page 151

Work with a partner to answer these questions. Try to include the **red** word in your answer. Write the sentences in your notebook.

1. Was there ever a time when you were **isolated** from friends or family?

2. Have you ever had to **relocate** from one place or city to another? Why?

3. What are some of the basic things people need for **survival**?

4. What is an example of something that was **temporary** in your life?

▲ The first group of Japanese Americans arrive at Manzanar War Relocation Center.

Word Study: Borrowed Words

The English language borrows many words from other languages.
This can sometimes explain why certain words are spelled the way
they are. Notice that some words change their spelling, but some
do not.

Borrowed Word	Original Word	Borrowed From
authority	autorité	French
karate	karate	Japanese
mattress	matrah	Arabic

Practice

Work with a partner. Find the words in the box below in the reading.
Try to figure out the meaning of each word using the context of the
sentence. Then look up the words in a dictionary. In your notebook,
write the word, its meaning, and the language it was borrowed from.
Finally, write a sentence for each word.

dessert	ketchup	kimono	soy	syrup

READING STRATEGY   ASK QUESTIONS

Asking questions as you read helps you get more information from a
text. Ask yourself these questions: *Who? What? When? Where? Why?*
These are sometimes called the 5Ws. They focus on people, events, time,
places, and reasons. To ask questions, follow these steps:

- Read a paragraph. Stop and ask yourself one of the five questions.
- Now try to answer the question from what you've learned in
  the text.
- Read on and see if your answer is correct. Then ask more questions.
- Be sure to look at visuals that may help answer your questions.

  As you read the excerpt from *Farewell to Manzanar*, ask yourself the five
questions. Take notes as you read to answer each question.

Set a purpose for reading As you read, ask yourself this question: What events in the story show how the human spirit can triumph over adversity?

from

Farewell to Manzanar

Jeanne Wakatsuki Houston and James D. Houston

Farewell to Manzanar *is the true story of one Japanese-American family's experience living in an internment camp during World War II. This excerpt describes what happens immediately after they first arrive at Manzanar War Relocation Center.*

We had pulled up just in time for dinner. The mess halls weren't completed yet. An outdoor chow line snaked around a half-finished building that broke a good part of the wind. They issued us army mess kits, the round metal kind that fold over, and plopped in scoops of canned Vienna sausage, canned string beans, steamed rice that had been cooked too long, and on top of the rice a serving of canned apricots. The Caucasian servers were thinking that the fruit poured over rice would make a good dessert. Among the Japanese, of course, rice is never eaten with sweet

---

chow, food
mess kits, small sets of cooking and eating utensils for soldiers

foods, only with salty or savory foods. Few of us could eat such a mixture. But at this point no one dared protest. It would have been impolite. I was horrified when I saw the apricot syrup seeping through my little mound of rice. I opened my mouth to complain. My mother jabbed me in the back to keep quiet. We moved on through the line and joined the others squatting in the lee of half-raised walls, dabbing courteously at what was, for almost everyone there, an inedible concoction.

After dinner we were taken to Block 16, a cluster of fifteen barracks that had just been finished a day or so earlier—although finished was hardly the word for it. The shacks were built of one thickness of pine planking covered with tarpaper. They sat on concrete footings, with about two feet of open space between the floorboards and the ground. Gaps showed between the planks, and as the weeks passed and the green wood dried out, the gaps widened. Knotholes gaped in the uncovered floor.

Each barracks was divided into six units, sixteen by twenty feet, about the size of a living room, with one bare bulb hanging from the ceiling and an oil stove for heat. We were assigned two of these for the twelve people in our family group; and our official family "number" was enlarged by three digits—16 plus the number of this barracks. We were issued steel army cots, two brown army blankets each, and some mattress covers, which my brothers stuffed with straw.

The first task was to divide up what space we had for sleeping. Bill and Woody contributed a blanket each and partitioned off the first room: one side for Bill and Tomi, one side for Woody and Chizu and their baby girl. Woody also got the stove, for heating formulas.

---

savory, having a taste that is not sweet, especially a salty or spicy taste
inedible concoction, a mixture that isn't eatable
barracks, groups of buildings where soldiers live

BEFORE YOU GO ON

1 Why didn't the narrator want to eat her rice?

2 How many people had to live in each sixteen-by-twenty-foot unit?

On Your Own
If you were the narrator, would you have complained about the food? Why or why not?

309

The people who had it hardest during the first few months were young couples like these, many of whom had married just before the evacuation began, in order not to be separated and sent to different camps. Our two rooms were crowded, but at least it was all in the family. My oldest sister and her husband were shoved into one of those sixteen-by-twenty-foot compartments with six people they had never seen before—two other couples, one recently married like themselves, the other with two teenage boys. Partitioning off a room like that wasn't easy. It was bitter cold when we arrived, and the wind did not abate. All they had to use for room dividers were those army blankets, two of which were barely enough to keep one person warm. They argued over whose blanket should be sacrificed and later argued about noise at night—the parents wanted their boys asleep by 9:00 p.m.—and they continued arguing over matters like that for six months, until my sister and husband left to harvest sugar beets in Idaho. It was grueling work up there, and wages were pitiful, but when the call came through camp for workers to alleviate the wartime labor shortage, it sounded better than their life at Manzanar. They knew they'd have, if nothing else, a room, perhaps a cabin of their own.

That first night in Block 16, the rest of us squeezed into the second room—Granny, Lillian, age fourteen, Ray, thirteen, May, eleven, Kiyo, ten, Mama, and me. I didn't mind this at all at the time. Being youngest meant I got to sleep with Mama. And before we went to bed I had a great time jumping up and down on the mattress. The boys had stuffed so much straw into hers, we had to flatten it some so we wouldn't slide off. I slept with her every night after that until Papa came back.

We woke early, shivering and coated with dust that had blown up through the knotholes and in through the slits around the doorway. During the night Mama had unpacked all our clothes and heaped them on our beds for warmth. Now our cubicle looked as if a great laundry bag had exploded and then been sprayed with fine dust. A skin of sand covered the floor. I looked over Mama's shoulder at Kiyo, on top of his fat mattress, buried under jeans and overcoats and sweaters. His eyebrows were gray, and he was starting to giggle. He was looking at me, at my gray eyebrows and coated hair, and pretty soon we were both giggling. I looked at Mama's face to see if she thought Kiyo was funny. She lay very still next to me on our mattress, her eyes scanning everything—bare rafters, walls, dusty kids—scanning slowly, and I think the mask of her face would have cracked had not Woody's voice just then come at us through the wall. He was rapping on the planks as if testing to see if they were hollow.

---

evacuation, act of leaving your home, usually very suddenly
abate, decrease, weaken
alleviate, relieve, lessen
cubicle, small, partially enclosed part of a room

"Hey!" he yelled. "You guys fall into the same flour barrel as us?"

"No," Kiyo yelled back. "Ours is full of Japs."

All of us laughed at this.

"Well, tell 'em it's time to get up," Woody said. "If we're gonna live in this place, we better get to work."

He gave us ten minutes to dress, then he came in carrying a broom, a hammer, and a sack full of tin can lids he had scrounged somewhere. Woody would be our leader for a while now, short, stocky, grinning behind his mustache. He had just turned twenty-four. In later years he would tour the country with Mr. Moto, the Japanese tag-team wrestler, as his sinister assistant Suki—karate chops through the ropes from outside the ring, a chunky leg reaching from under his kimono to trip up Mr. Moto's foe. In the ring Woody's smile looked sly and crafty; he hammed it up. Offstage it was whimsical, as if some joke were bursting to be told.

"Hey, brother Ray, Kiyo," he said. "You see these tin can lids?"

"Yeah, yeah," the boys said drowsily, as if going back to sleep. They were both young versions of Woody.

Japs, offensive term for people of Japanese descent
scrounged, found after searching through things
sinister, bad, evil
whimsical, amusing

✔ **LITERARY CHECK**
*How does the **diction** in this dialogue help the characters seem natural and real?*

BEFORE YOU GO ON

1 Why were they covered with dust on their first morning?

2 What do you think Mama was thinking as her eyes scanned the room?

💡**On Your Own**
Would you have laughed at the situation if you were the narrator? Why or why not?

"You see all them knotholes in the floor and in the walls?"

They looked around. You could see about a dozen.

Woody said, "You get these covered up before breakfast time. Any more sand comes in here through one of them knotholes, you have to eat it off the floor with ketchup."

"What about sand that comes in through the cracks?" Kiyo said.

Woody stood up very straight, which in itself was funny, since he was only about five-foot-six.

"Don't worry about the cracks," he said. "Different kind of sand comes in through the cracks."

He put his hands on his hips and gave Kiyo a sternly comic look, squinting at him through one eye the way Papa would when he was asserting his authority. Woody mimicked Papa's voice: "And I can tell the difference. So be careful."

The boys laughed and went to work nailing down lids. May started sweeping out the sand. I was helping Mama fold the clothes we'd used for cover, when Woody came over and put his arm around her shoulder. He was short; she was even shorter, under five feet.

He said softly, "You okay, Mama?"

She didn't look at him, she just kept folding clothes and said, "Can we get the cracks covered too, Woody?"

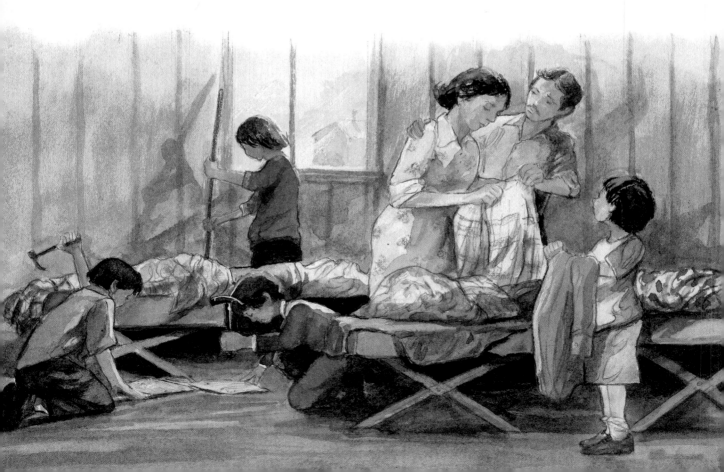

Outside the sky was clear, but icy gusts of wind were buffeting our barracks every few minutes, sending fresh dust puffs up through the floorboards. May's broom could barely keep up with it, and our oil heater could scarcely hold its own against the drafts.

"We'll get this whole place as tight as a barrel, Mama. I already met a guy who told me where they pile all the scrap lumber."

"Scrap?"

"That's all they got. I mean, they're still building the camp, you know. Sixteen blocks left to go. After that, they say maybe we'll get some stuff to fix the insides a little bit."

Her eyes blazed then, her voice quietly furious. "Woody, we can't live like this. Animals live like this."

It was hard to get Woody down. He'd keep smiling when everybody else was ready to explode. Grief flickered in his eyes. He blinked it away and hugged her tighter. "We'll make it better, Mama. You watch."

We could hear voices in other cubicles now. Beyond the wall Woody's baby girl started to cry.

"I have to go over to the kitchen," he said, "see if those guys got a pot for heating bottles. That oil stove takes too long—something wrong with the fuel line. I'll find out what they're giving us for breakfast."

"Probably hotcakes with soy sauce," Kiyo said, on his hands and knees between the bunks.

"No." Woody grinned, heading out the door. "Rice. With maple syrup and melted butter."

✔ **LITERARY CHECK**
*What is the author's **tone** in this paragraph?*

---

buffeting, hitting with great force
scrap, extra; leftovers not being used

ABOUT THE **AUTHORS**

Jeanne Wakatsuki Houston was born in Inglewood, California. She studied journalism and sociology at San Jose State College, where she met her husband, James Houston. After they married, they joined the Unites States Air Force and lived in Europe for a while, but eventually moved back to the United States.

James D. Houston was born in San Francisco. The author of three novels, a collection of short stories, and two works of nonfiction, he won the Joseph Henry Jackson Award for Fiction. He and Jeanne now live in Santa Cruz.

BEFORE YOU GO ON

1 What makes Mama so furious?

2 What kind of person is Woody?

💡 **On Your Own**
Why do you think the United States now considers the internment camps a mistake?

313

READER'S THEATER

Speaking TIP

Face toward the audience and your fellow actor as you say your lines.

Act out the following scene between Woody and Mama.

Mama: I am worried, Woody. It's so cold. The food is inedible. And the dust is everywhere!

Woody: I know Mama, but we'll fix it. You see how Ray and Kiyo are covering the knotholes? You see how the tin can lids keep out the dust?

Mama: [*softly*] Can we get the cracks covered, too?

Woody: We'll seal every last crack. Wait till you see! This place will be tight as a barrel. I already met a guy who told me where they pile all the leftover lumber.

Mama: Leftover lumber?

Woody: Well, I can only get the leftovers. They are still building the barracks. After they finish, maybe we'll get some stuff to fix this place up.

Mama: We are not animals! We cannot live like this!

Woody: [*gently*] Don't worry Mama, we'll make it better. Just you wait and see.

COMPREHENSION

Workbook Page 154

Right There

1. Why didn't anyone complain about the food?
2. Why did the narrator's sister and her husband leave the camp?

Think and Search

3. What did Mama do to help keep her family members warm?
4. What were the living conditions in the camp like?

Author and You

5. Why do you think Mama is more upset than other family members?
6. Why does Woody make the joke about rice, maple syrup, and butter?

7. Why is having courage important in times of war?

8. Do you think using humor can be a good way to deal with a difficult situation? Explain why or why not.

DISCUSSION

Listening TIP

If you can't hear your classmate, say, "Excuse me, could you speak louder, please?"

Discuss in pairs or small groups.

1. In what ways did the people who built the barracks and served the food fail to understand Japanese-American culture?

2. What basic needs did the family have to have for survival?

Q **What can we learn from times of war?** How do you think you would feel if you were forced to relocate against your will because your country was at war? How would you feel about your country?

RESPONSE TO LITERATURE

Workbook
Page 154

Imagine that Woody and his brothers and sisters create a play to cheer up their mother and grandmother. Do some research at the library or on the Internet to find a short Japanese fable or folktale.

In a small group, rewrite the story as a play. You may wish to divide the tasks so that two people write the dialogue and stage directions, while two others focus on costumes, props, and set design. Other tasks include music, lighting, and sound effects. Keep things simple (don't forget you are in Manzanar without many supplies) and have fun.

▲ Internees sing around the piano.

Grammar and Writing

Using Infinitives

Look at some of the ways infinitives can be used. Infinitives can be subjects, subject complements, or objects.

> It was hard **to get** Woody down. [subject of sentence]
> The first task was **to divide up** what space we had for sleeping.
>   [subject complement of *the first task*]
> He was starting **to giggle**. [object of verb *was starting*]

Infinitives can express a purpose. They answer the question *Why?*

> I opened my mouth **to complain**. [Why did I open my mouth? To complain.]
> My sister and her husband left **to harvest** sugar beets.
>   [Why did they leave? To harvest (sugar beets).]

Infinitives can follow certain adjectives. Here are a couple of them:

> Mama was **sorry to leave** home.
> Woody was **determined to make** the best of the situation.

Infinitives can be used with *too* and *enough*. Too + adjective + infinitive implies something negative; adjective + *enough* + infinitive implies something positive.

> That stove takes **too long to heat** the baby's bottle. [It won't heat the bottle.]
> Two blankets were **thick enough to keep** us warm. [They kept us warm.]

Practice

Workbook
Page 155

Copy the sentences into your notebook. Work with a partner. Circle the infinitives. Discuss the way in which each infinitive is used.

1. The rice was too sweet to eat.

2. Mama jabbed me in the back to keep me quiet.

3. We were not ready to live in the barracks.

4. I got to sleep with Mama.

5. I looked at Mama's face to see if she thought Kiyo was funny.

316

WRITING AN EXPOSITORY PARAGRAPH

Write a Problem-and-Solution Paragraph

At the end of this unit, you will write an expository essay. To do this, you'll need to learn some skills writers use in expository writing. One way to organize your ideas is by problem and solution.

To write a problem-and-solution paragraph, first introduce the problem. Then include specific examples to show how to solve the problem. Finally, show clearly how your solution worked. Imagine that you had a problem understanding a math assignment. Possible solutions include hiring a tutor, asking your teacher for help after class, or joining a math study group. Choose the solution that you think will work best.

Here is a model of a problem-and-solution paragraph. Before writing, the writer listed his ideas in a problem-and-solution chart.

Problem
↓
Solution

Dylan Bishop

Making Life More Livable at Manzanar

The narrator of <u>Farewell to Manzanar</u> describes many of the challenges faced by the internees forced to live at Manzanar War Relocation Center. One problem was that the living areas were small and cramped. Many internees were made to share tiny rooms with people they didn't know. In order to give themselves a feeling of privacy, internees used blankets as room dividers. Another problem was that the barracks were not well built. There were knotholes in the wooden planks, which allowed the wind and dust to blow into the barracks constantly. To solve this problem, some internees covered the knotholes with tin can lids. At night, it was too cold to sleep, especially for those who had used their blankets as room dividers. The narrator's mother's solution to this problem was to pile all the clothes her family members had brought on top of their beds at night.

Practice

Workbook
Page 156

Write a problem-and-solution paragraph about a difficult situation that you or others solved. List your ideas in a problem-and-solution chart. Be sure to use infinitives correctly.

Writing Checklist

ORGANIZATION:
☑ I clearly stated problems and included solutions.

CONVENTIONS:
☑ I used infinitives correctly.

317

Link the Readings

Critical Thinking

Look back at the readings in this unit. Think about what they have in common. They all tell about times of war. Yet they do not all have the same purpose. The purpose of one reading might be to inform, while the purpose of another might be to entertain or persuade. In addition, the content of each reading relates to times of war differently. Now copy the chart below into your notebook and complete it.

Title of Reading	Purpose	Big Question Link
"World War I"		*explains the history of World War I*
"In Flanders Fields" "Anthem for Doomed Youth" "Three Wonderful Letters from Home" "Letter Home"		
"In the Name of His Father"	*to inform*	
From *Farewell to Manzanar*		

Discussion

Discuss in pairs or small groups.

- "In the Name of His Father" and the excerpt from *Farewell to Manzanar* are both about Japanese or Japanese-American people. Compare and contrast the roles these people played in their different situations.

- **Q What can we learn from times of war?** What lessons do you think we should have learned from World War I and World War II?

Fluency Check

Work with a partner. Choose a paragraph from one of the readings. Take turns reading it for one minute. Count the total number of words you read. Practice saying the words you had trouble reading. Take turns reading the paragraph three more times. Did you read more words each time? Copy the chart below into your notebook and record your speeds.

	1st Speed	2nd Speed	3rd Speed	4th Speed
Words Per Minute				

Projects

Work in pairs or small groups. Choose one of these projects.

1 Do research at the library or on the Internet to find poetry that was written during other wars. What is the tone of the poems? Choose a poem and memorize it. Then recite the poem for the class.

2 Wars have inspired artists to create great works of art. Do research at the library or on the Internet to find out more information about artists who worked during times of war. Study their artwork. Then create a collage, sculpture, painting, or other work of art that expresses your feelings about war.

3 Photographers and photojournalists document images of displaced persons and refugees during wartime. Do research at the library or on the Internet to find photos of war refugees. Make prints or photocopies of the photos and display them for the class. Explain what and whom the photos show and why you chose to share them with your classmates.

Further Reading

To find out more about the theme of this unit, choose from these reading suggestions.

A Time to Kill, John Grisham
This Penguin Reader® adaptation tells the story of a murder that divides a town already beset by anger and violence.

The Big Lie, Isabella Leitner
When the Nazis took over Europe during World War II, Isabella and her family were taken from their home in Hungary and sent to concentration camps. Isabella's story is one of pain, loss, survival, and hope.

Thura's Diary: My Life in Wartime Iraq, Thura Al-Windawi
In a diary written during the first year of the Iraq war, Thura, the oldest daughter of a Shia family living in Baghdad, shares her experiences and feelings.

Put It All Together

LISTENING & SPEAKING WORKSHOP

Oral Report

You will give an oral report about any topic related to the subject of war.

1 THINK ABOUT IT In small groups, discuss the texts you have read in this unit. Which ones were most interesting to you? What new information did you learn about times of war? What questions do you still have?

Work together to develop a list of war-related topics for an oral report. Write down your ideas. Here are some examples:

- Civilian life during a war
- The manufacturing of weapons
- The causes of World War I or World War II
- The role of women in World War I or World War II

2 GATHER AND ORGANIZE INFORMATION Choose a topic from your group's list. Write down what you already know about the topic. Look at an encyclopedia or a website to find out more about it. Decide what the focus of your oral report will be.

Research Go to the library, talk to an adult, or use the Internet to find more information about your topic. Look for facts, examples, and details to support your main ideas. Take notes as you read. Be sure to write down the sources of the information you wish to include.

Order Your Notes Make an outline that lists your main ideas and the facts, examples, and details to support them. Be prepared to tell where you got your information. Think of an interesting way to begin your oral report—perhaps with a question, a quotation, or an anecdote. Plan a conclusion that summarizes your findings. You may wish to copy your outline onto numbered note cards.

Use Visuals To make your report more interesting and effective, find or create pictures, maps, posters, or other visuals that can help convey your ideas. Indicate in your outline or note cards when you will use each visual.

3 **PRACTICE AND PRESENT** Practice giving your oral report, referring to your outline or note cards to make sure you include all the important ideas and facts. Keep practicing until you can speak smoothly and confidently, glancing occasionally at your notes. Practice in front of a mirror or give your speech to a friend or family member. Make sure you are facing your listeners.

Deliver Your Oral Report Although a report is a formal presentation, you should appear relaxed and comfortable as you deliver it. Pause at the beginning and in between the different parts of your report. Speak in a clear but natural voice and hold up or display your visuals so everyone can see them. Emphasize important points by slowing down and changing the tone of your voice. At the end of your report, ask the audience members if they have any questions.

4 **EVALUATE THE PRESENTATION** You will improve your skills as a speaker and as a listener by evaluating each presentation you give and hear. Use this checklist to help you judge your oral report and the reports of your classmates.

- ☑ Were the speaker's main ideas clear and related to the subject of war?
- ☑ Did the speaker support his or her ideas with facts, examples, and details?
- ☑ Could you hear and understand the speaker easily?
- ☑ Did the speaker answer your questions?
- ☑ What suggestions do you have for improving the oral report?

Speaking TIPS

Connect with your audience by making eye contact with as many people as possible.

Pronounce names and numbers correctly. Label your visuals clearly. Write in large enough letters for your audience to read easily.

Listening TIPS

Focus on the speaker's main ideas. If you have a question, write it down so you can ask it later. Don't let it distract you as you listen.

Listen for the speaker's sources. Do you think his or her information is reliable? Why or why not?

WRITING WORKSHOP
Expository Essay

In this workshop, you will write an expository essay. As you have learned, an expository essay provides information about a topic. One type of expository writing is a news article. A news article reports on an event or issue of current interest to readers. The first paragraph of a news article introduces the topic and answers the 5Ws: **Who** participated? **What** happened? **When** did it happen? **Where** did it happen? **Why** did it happen? Two or more body paragraphs develop this information with additional details, facts, and examples. A concluding paragraph sums up the information in a way that readers will remember.

Your assignment for this workshop is to write a five-paragraph news article reporting on an event or issue of current interest in your school, neighborhood, community, state, or another place that concerns you.

1 **PREWRITE** Brainstorm a list of topics in your notebook. Before you choose one, think about your readers. Are you planning to write your article for the school newspaper, a family newsletter, or a local newspaper? Once you have decided on your target audience, review your list of topics. Choose one that your readers will want to know about.

List and Organize Ideas and Details Use a 5Ws chart to organize your ideas. A student named Nicholas decided to write an article for his school newspaper about a class trip to Washington, D. C. Here is his chart:

Who?	*Mrs. Bell's social studies class*
What?	*Class trip*
When?	*Last Thursday and Friday*
Where?	*Washington, D.C.*
Why?	*Sightseeing*

2 **DRAFT** Use the model on page 325 and your 5Ws chart to help you write a first draft. Include an introductory paragraph, three body paragraphs, and a concluding paragraph. Be sure to answer the 5Ws in your first paragraph and to develop the information in your body paragraphs.

3 **REVISE** Read over your draft. As you do so, ask yourself the questions in the writing checklist. Use the questions to help you revise your essay.

SIX TRAITS OF WRITING CHECKLIST

- ✔ **IDEAS:** Does my first paragraph introduce my topic in a interesting way?
- ✔ **ORGANIZATION:** Do I present the events in a logical order?
- ✔ **VOICE:** Does my tone fit my topic and audience?
- ✔ **WORD CHOICE:** Do I use words appropriately?
- ✔ **SENTENCE FLUENCY:** Do my sentences vary in length and rhythm?
- ✔ **CONVENTIONS:** Does my writing follow the rules of grammar, usage, and mechanics?

Here are the changes Nicholas plans to make when he revises his first draft:

Students Visit D.C.

While most of us finished an uneventful week, Mrs. Bell's social studies class spent last Thursday and Friday sightseeing in Washington, D.C. By all reports, the trip's highlight was a visit to the Vietnam Veterans Memorial, built ~~for honoring~~ to honor the soldiers who died or went missing during the Vietnam war. The memorial covers two achres and consist of 4 four parts: the Wall of Names, the Three Servicemen Statue, the Vietnam Women's Memorial, and the In Memory Plaque. The memorial attracts over three million people every year yet it was once the subject of controversy.

According to tour guide Bill Walsh, in 1980 congress created a
national contest ~~for selecting~~ to select the design of the memorial. The jury
choose the winner on May 6, 1981, a young woman named Maya Ying
Lin, who had designed the memorial as a project for Yale University.

Lin's design was ~~very~~ controversial, in part because it was original
and didn't include many of the things that traditional memorials do,
such as statues. The memorial has ~~now~~ since been enlarged to include the
other components. Lin proposed just a simple, plain wall with the
names of the ~~deceesed~~ deceased and missing listed on it. Some people did not like
this and wanted a different kind of monument.

Much as students were impresed by all parts of the memorial, some
found the wall especially moving. The black granite on which the
names are engrave d is reflective, so visitors can see their own faces as
they walk along. This symbolizes the linking of past and present.

The Vietnam veterans Memorial is visited by many people each year.
Some, like Mrs. Bell's students, come on school trips; others travel long
distances to see the name of a loved one on the wall. The memorial is powerful. Several students said that it made
them feel closer to the men and women who served our country in the
Vietnam conflict.

4 EDIT AND PROOFREAD   Workbook Page 157

Copy your revised draft onto a clean sheet of paper. Read it again. Correct
any errors in grammar, word usage, mechanics, and spelling. Here are the
additional changes Nicholas plans to make when he prepares his final draft.

Nicholas Kasterine

Students Visit D.C.

April 13, 2009

While most of us finished an uneventful week, Mrs. Bell's social studies class spent last Thursday and Friday sightseeing in Washington, D.C. By all reports, the trip's highlight was a visit to the Vietnam Veterans Memorial, built to honor the soldiers who died or went missing during the Vietnam War. The memorial covers two acres and consists of four parts: the Wall of Names, the Three Servicemen Statue, the Vietnam Women's Memorial, and the In Memory Plaque. The memorial attracts over three million people every year, yet it was once the subject of controversy.

According to tour guide Bill Walsh, in 1980 congress created a national contest to select the design of the memorial. The jury choose the winner on May 6, 1981, a young woman named Maya Ying Lin, who had designed the memorial as a project for Yale University.

Lin's design was controversial, in part because it was original and didn't include many of the things that traditional memorials do, such as statues. Lin proposed just a simple, plain wall with the names of the deceased and missing listed on it. Some people did not like this and wanted a different kind of monument. The memorial has since been enlarged to include the other components.

Much as students were impresed by all parts of the memorial, some found the wall especially moving. The black granite on which the names are engraved is reflective, so visitors can see their own faces as they walk along. This symbolizes the linking of past and present.

The Vietnam veterans Memorial is visited by many people each year. Some, like Mrs. Bell's students, come on school trips; others travel long distances to see the name of a loved one on the wall. The memorial is powerful. Several students said that it made them feel closer to the men and women who served our country in the Vietnam conflict.

5 **PUBLISH** Prepare your final draft. Share your essay with your teacher and classmates.

Workbook
Page 158

Citizens on the Home Front

*A*lmost every country in the world has experienced times of war. War *involves deep emotions and harsh consequences. Artists often use their work to try to make sense of it all.*

Norman Rockwell, *Save Freedom of Speech* (1943)

In *Save Freedom of Speech*, Norman Rockwell celebrates the right of the common man to speak his mind. The speaker, shown with rough hands, is wearing an old jacket. Most of the other people are turning to look at him, so that everything focuses on the speaker. The other men in suits and ties look like successful businessmen, but the speaker stands straight, looks firmly ahead, and speaks his mind without fear.

Save Freedom of Speech was one of four paintings that Rockwell created after the United States entered World War II in 1941. President Franklin Delano Roosevelt believed that the country had to do whatever it took to protect what he called the four freedoms: freedom of speech, freedom of worship, freedom from want, and freedom from fear. Rockwell's paintings were eventually made into posters that the U.S. government used to help sell bonds to raise money to support the war.

▲ Norman Rockwell, *Save Freedom of Speech*, 1943, lithograph, 56 x 48 in., Smithsonian American Art Museum

326

Roger Shimomura, *Diary: December 12, 1941* (1980)

In *Diary: December 12, 1941*, Roger Shimomura shows a young Japanese woman wearing a kimono. She is sitting in a traditional Japanese-style room. In contrast, the shadow of Superman, an American comic book character, appears on one of the screens. Normally, this comic image projects strength and security, but the fact that it's a shadow makes it a little scary.

Shimomura captures the mixed feelings many Japanese Americans felt after the Japanese bombed a U.S. naval station in Hawaii called Pearl Harbor in 1941. The U.S. government became suspicious of anyone with Japanese ancestry, even if they were U.S. citizens and their family had lived in this country for generations. Many Japanese Americans were forced from their homes and put into goverment detention camps where they could be watched for any signs of betrayal. Shimomura's grandmother was one of the Japanese Americans put into a camp in Idaho. She kept a daily journal of her experiences, which Shimomura later found and read when he was an adult. He decided to do a series of twenty-five paintings, uniform in size and style, based on parts of her diary. He blended comic art with a style found in more traditional Japanese printmaking to compose his complex scene.

▲ Roger Shimomura, *Diary: December 12, 1941*, 1980, acrylic, 50¼ x 60 in., Smithsonian American Art Museum

Apply What You Learned

1 Compare and contrast the two artworks. How are their points of view about war both similar and different?

2 Why do you think Roger Shimomura included the comic book character Superman in his painting, and what does this figure stand for?

Big Question

How did each artist use the subject of citizens on the home front to help them try to make sense of the war?

Workbook
Pages 159–160

THE BIG
Q
QUESTION

What makes animals so amazing?

This unit is about animals. You'll read science articles, poems, and a story about different animals. Reading, writing, and talking about this topic will give you practice using academic language and help you become a better student.

READING 1: Short Story
- "The Parrot Who Wouldn't Say 'Cataño'" by Pura Belpré

READING 2: Science Article
- "Getting to Know Real Bats" by Laurence Pringle

READING 3: Poems
- "The Bat" by Theodore Roethke
- "A Narrow Fellow in the Grass" by Emily Dickinson
- "Daybreak" by Galway Kinnell
- "Birdfoot's Grandpa" by Joseph Bruchac

READING 4: Science Article
- From *The Chimpanzees I Love* by Jane Goodall

Listening and Speaking

At the end of this unit, you'll prepare and present a **TV documentary**.

Writing

In this unit, you'll write a **research report**. You'll present information you've learned by doing research. After each reading, you'll learn a skill that will help you write a research report. At the unit's end, you will choose one of your paragraphs and develop it into a research report.

QuickWrite
Make a T-chart labeled *Animals* and *Abilities*. List animals and their abilities.

What You Will Learn

Reading

- Vocabulary building: *Literary terms, dictionary skills, word study*

- Reading strategy: *Connect ideas*

- Text type: *Literature (short story)*

Grammar, Usage, and Mechanics
Reduction of adjective clauses to adjective phrases

Writing
Write an introductory paragraph

THE BIG QUESTION

What makes animals so amazing? Have you or has someone you know ever tried to teach a pet to do something? If so, then you know that it takes patience and understanding to train an animal. In a small group, talk about the skills that a pet owner or an animal trainer might need to teach an animal a new skill.

BUILD BACKGROUND

"The Parrot Who Wouldn't Say 'Cataño'" is a folktale about a retired sailor from Cataño, Puerto Rico. Puerto Rico is an island in the Caribbean Sea, south of the eastern United States. Cataño is a town located across the bay from San Juan, the capital of Puerto Rico.

▼ San Juan Harbor, Puerto Rico

Learn Literary Words

An **archetype** is a type of character or situation that appears in literature often enough to be considered universal. Many of the best known characters in literature are based on archetypes. In the classic Charles Dickens novel *A Christmas Carol*, the main character, Ebenezer Scrooge, is an example of an archetype: the mean, miserly, rich man who cares only for money. Scrooge's clerk, Bob Cratchit, is an example of another archetype: the poor man with a heart of gold.

You might say that Scrooge is all money and no heart, while Cratchit is all heart and no money. Such "opposite" character types are called foils. A **foil** is a character who, by contrast, highlights the qualities of another character. Scrooge's cold manner and stinginess are set in relief by Cratchit's warm generosity in spite of his poverty.

Literary Words

archetype
foil

Practice  **Workbook Page 161**

Work with a partner. For each of the archetypes in the numbered list below, choose a character from the word box that would serve as a foil. Then choose two pairs and write a sentence about each pair.

fool	nagging housewife
helpless victim	villain in black
humble underdog	

1. wise man
2. hen-pecked husband
3. loud-mouthed braggart
4. white knight
5. bully

▲ **Ebenezer Scrooge and Bob Cratchit**

Learn Academic Words

Study the **red** words and their meanings. You will find these words useful when talking and writing about literature. Write each word and its meaning in your notebook. After you read "The Parrot Who Wouldn't Say 'Cataño,'" try to use these words to respond to the text.

Academic Words

attached
challenge
consequence
response

attached = strongly connected to someone or something	➡	The young child was **attached** to his mother and never wanted to leave her.
challenge = something new, exciting, or difficult that needs a lot of skill and effort to do	➡	It was a **challenge** to get the stubborn animal to cooperate.
consequence = something that happens as a result of a particular action	➡	One **consequence** of the storm was that many people did not have electricity.
response = something that is said, written, or done as a reply to something else	➡	I received a **response** to my e-mail a few minutes after I sent it.

Practice

Work with a partner to answer these questions. Try to include the **red** word in your answer. Write the sentences in your notebook.

1. What person are you **attached** to? What object are you **attached** to?
2. What is your biggest **challenge** at school?
3. What is a **consequence** of not studying for a test?
4. What do you do when you get no **response** to an important e-mail, telephone message, or letter?

▲ Monk parakeets

Word Study: Suffixes

A suffix is a letter or groups of letters added to the end of a word. Suffixes show the part of speech of a word—adjective, adverb, noun, or verb. When you add a suffix to a word, you change the meaning of the word. Study the chart of suffixes below, and discuss the meanings of the words in the Examples column with a partner. Can you guess the meaning of the word by looking at the meaning of the suffix?

Suffix	Part of Speech	Meaning	Examples
-en	verb	cause to become	thick**en**, strength**en**
-ful	adjective	having	boast**ful**, thank**ful**
-ward	adverb	direction or manner	west**ward**, back**ward**
-ance	noun	action or state	disturb**ance**, griev**ance**

Practice

Work with a partner. As you read "The Parrot Who Wouldn't Say 'Cataño,'" look for words with the suffixes -*en*, -*ful*, -*ward*, or -*ance*. Make a list of the words you find. Discuss the meaning of each word, using a dictionary if necessary. Write a sentence for each word.
Hint: *There are seven words in the story for you to find.*

READING STRATEGY   CONNECT IDEAS

Connecting ideas in a text helps you understand what the author is trying to convey. To connect ideas, follow these steps as you read:

- What are the most important events in the story?
- How are the story events connected?
- How do the characters affect one another?
- What is the theme of the story? What story ideas support this theme?

As you read "The Parrot Who Wouldn't Say 'Cataño,'" look for important ideas. Ask yourself how the ideas might be connected.

333

Set a purpose for reading Read this story to find out about a sentimental old man and his pet parrot. What makes this parrot amazing?

The Parrot Who Wouldn't Say "Cataño"

Pura Belpré

Across the bay from San Juan in Puerto Rico is a town called Cataño. Here, long ago, lived a retired sailor called Yuba. His only possession and sole companion was a parrot—a beautiful, talkative bird, known to all the town. Much as the parrot talked, there was one thing she refused to say. That was the name of the town. No matter how hard Yuba tried to teach her, she would never say the word. This saddened Yuba who loved his town very much.

"You are an ungrateful bird," Yuba told the parrot. "You repeat everything you hear, yet refuse to say the name of the town where you have lived most of your life." But all the parrot would do was to blink her beady eyes and talk of other things.

One day as Yuba sat on his balcony with the parrot on his knee, arguing as usual, who should come by but Don Casimiro, the rich poultry fancier from San Juan. He stopped and listened. In all his years he had never heard such a parrot. What a wonderful addition to his poultry yard she would make! The more he listened to her conversation, the more he wanted to own her.

"Would you sell me that parrot?" he said at last. "I will pay you well for her."

"Neither silver nor gold can buy her, Señor," said Yuba.

---

retired, no longer working
poultry, birds kept on farms for supplying
    eggs and meat

334

Don Casimiro was surprised. To all appearances this man looked as if he could use some money. "What else would you take for her, my good man?" he asked.

"Nothing. But I will make a bargain with you," replied Yuba.

"A bargain? What kind of bargain?" Don Casimiro wanted to know.

"I have been trying to teach her to say 'Cataño.' But for reasons of her own she refuses to say it. Well, take her with you. If you can make her say it, the bird is yours and I will be grateful to you for the rest of my life. If you fail, bring her back to me."

"Agreed," said Don Casimiro delightedly. He took the parrot, thanked Yuba, and left.

Late that afternoon he returned home. He sat in the spacious corridor facing the courtyard filled with fancy fowls and potted plants. "Now," he said to the parrot, "repeat after me: *Ca-ta-ño!*" And he took great care to say each syllable clearly and slowly. The parrot flapped her wings, but said not a word.

"Come, come," said Don Casimiro. "Say *Ca-ta-ño.*" The parrot blinked her beady eyes at him, but said not a word.

"But you can say anything you want. I have heard you speak. Let's try it again. *Ca-ta-ño.*" Don Casimiro waited, but the parrot sauntered down the corridor as if she were deaf.

Now Don Casimiro was a man of great wealth but little patience. His temper was as hot as the chili peppers he grew in his vegetable patch. He strode after the parrot who had stopped beside a large potted fern at the end of the corridor. He grabbed the bird and shook her. "Say *CA-TA-ÑO!*" he commanded through clenched teeth.

---

bargain, an agreement to do something in return for something else
fowls, birds kept for their meat and eggs
sauntered, walked in a slow, proud way

✔ **LITERARY CHECK**
*What **archetype** is Yuba an example of?*

✔ **LITERARY CHECK**
*In what way is Don Casimiro a **foil** for Yuba?*

BEFORE YOU GO ON

1 Why does Yuba want his parrot to say "Cataño"?

2 What bargain does Yuba make with Don Casimiro?

On Your Own
Do you think Yuba will regret the bargain he has made? Why or why not?

The parrot blinked and quickly wriggled herself out of his hands. But Don Casimiro picked her up again and held her fast. "Say *Ca-ta-ño*, or I will wring your neck and throw you out of the window!"

The parrot said not a word.

Blinded with anger, Don Casimiro hurled her out of the window, forgetting to wring her neck. The parrot landed in the chicken coop.

That night a strange noise rose from the courtyard. Don Casimiro awoke with a start. "Thieves!" he cried. Thinking they were after his fowls he rushed out of the house and headed for the chicken coop. What a turmoil! Chicken feathers flew every which way. Pails of water and chicken feed were overturned. Squawking chickens ran hither and thither; others lay flat on the ground as though they were dead.

Suddenly, from the far end of the coop rose a voice saying: "Say *Ca-ta-ño*, or I will wring your neck and throw you out of the window!"

There, perched on a rafter, was the parrot, clutching one of the most precious fowls. Don Casimiro rushed to the spot and pulled the parrot down.

---

wring, twist tightly
turmoil, state of confusion and excitement
hither and thither, here and there

336

Before the sun had risen he was aboard the ferry boat on the way to Yuba's home. The parrot sat on his knees as if she had forgotten the happenings of the night before. He found Yuba sitting on his balcony sipping a cup of black coffee.

"So you failed too," said Yuba sadly.

"Oh, no, no!" Don Casimiro replied. "She said 'Cataño' all right! But the bargain is off. I want you to take her back."

Yuba was puzzled.

Don Casimiro noticed his confusion and quickly added: "You see, she played havoc in my chicken house before she said 'Cataño.'"

Yuba's face shone with happiness. He took the parrot and held her close. He watched Don Casimiro hurrying down the street toward the ferry boat station.

"Say *Ca-ta-ño*," he whispered to the parrot.

"Cataño, Cataño," the parrot replied.

And since that day no one was happier, in all of Cataño, than Yuba the retired sailor.

---

ferry boat, boat that carries people across a river or a bay
havoc, situation in which there is a lot of confusion
or damage

ABOUT THE **AUTHOR**

Pura Belpré was born in Puerto Rico. In 1921, she came to New York City for a visit but decided to stay. She studied library science at Columbia University and later became the first Latina librarian at the New York Public Library. Her passion for Puerto Rican folklore and storytelling made her popular among children and adults alike. In 1996 the Pura Belpré Award was established in her honor. It is given to writers and illustrators whose work celebrates the Latino cultural experience in excellent literature for young people.

BEFORE YOU GO ON

1 In what context did the parrot first say "Cataño"?

2 Why did Don Casimiro give the parrot back to Yuba?

On Your Own
Do you think parrots are amazing animals? Explain.

337

READER'S THEATER

Speaking TIP

Practice your lines in front of a mirror a few times before your performance.

Act out the following scene between Yuba and Don Casimiro.

Don Casimiro: Excuse me. That is a wonderful bird! I must have her. How much money would you like for your beautiful parrot?

Yuba: The parrot is not for sale, Señor. All the money in the world is not equal to her value.

Don Casimiro: You look as though you could use some money, my friend. There must be something I can give you for this talented bird.

Yuba: I do not want money, but I will make a deal with you. The bird will not say "Cataño," which is painful to me. If you can teach her to say "Cataño," you can keep her with my compliments. How I long to hear her say the name of my beloved hometown.

Don Casimiro: And if I can't teach her to say "Cataño"? What then?

Yuba: Then, alas, you must return her to me.

COMPREHENSION

Workbook Page 165

▲ A scarlet macaw

Right There

1. Where is Cataño? What upsets Yuba?

2. What is Don Casimiro's response to seeing Yuba's parrot for the first time?

Think and Search

3. Why does the parrot finally say "Cataño"?

4. What does Yuba think when he sees Don Casimiro returning the parrot?

5. Do you think Don Casimiro recognizes that the parrot is mimicking him when it first says "Cataño"? Why or why not?

6. What contrasts are there between Yuba and Don Casimiro?

7. Do you think it is important for a person who works with animals to have patience? Why or why not?

8. Is there a place you like as much as Yuba likes Cataño? Explain.

DISCUSSION

Discuss in pairs or small groups.

1. Would you have accepted Yuba's challenge? Why or why not?

2. Parrots are very intelligent animals. They can be great pets, but they require a lot of attention. Would you like to own a pet parrot? Explain.

Q **What makes animals so amazing?** Why do you think people get so attached to their pets? Have you ever been attached to an animal? If so, what was amazing about the animal?

RESPONSE TO LITERATURE

Workbook Page 165

The main character of this story, Yuba, is very proud of his town. Cataño must be a very beautiful place. Puerto Rico is located in the tropical zone, so average temperatures there are around 26° Celsius (80°F). The sun is out almost every day, shining on turquoise water, brightly colored flowers, and warm sandy beaches. Look at the picture of Puerto Rico shown below. Pretend you are Yuba. Write a paragraph explaining why you love your home.

Reduction of Adjective Clauses to Adjective Phrases

A clause is a group of related words that has a subject and a verb. A phrase is a group of related words that does not have a subject and a verb. Both an adjective clause and an adjective phrase modify nouns. You can reduce an adjective clause to an adjective phrase to say the same thing with fewer words. In the examples below, the clause is reduced to a phrase by omitting the relative pronoun (*who, that,* or *which*) and the verb *be.*

adjective clause

The parrot was a beautiful, talkative bird, **who was known to all the town**.

adjective phrase

The parrot was a beautiful, talkative bird, **known to all the town**.

adjective clause

He sat in the courtyard **which was filled with fancy fowls and potted plants**.

adjective phrase

He sat in the courtyard **filled with fancy fowls and potted plants**.

Practice  **Workbook** **Page 166**

Work with a partner. For each sentence below, reduce the adjective clause to an adjective phrase and write the new sentence in your notebook. Read your sentences aloud to check for mistakes.

1. In Cataño, long ago, lived a retired sailor who was called Yuba.

2. Don Casimiro, who was one of the richest men in San Juan, wanted to own Yuba's parrot.

3. The parrot landed in the chicken coop that was behind the house.

4. On the rafter was the parrot, who was clutching one of Don Casimiro's most precious fowls.

5. Don Casimiro took the ferry boat from San Juan to Cataño, which was the town across the bay.

WRITING A RESEARCH REPORT

Write an Introductory Paragraph

At the end of this unit, you'll write a research report. Here you'll learn how to begin one. You will select and narrow a topic. Then you'll do research and write an introductory paragraph.

Suppose your topic was animals. A narrower topic would be a type of animal—birds. An even narrower topic would be a type of bird—parrots. To narrow your topic even further, ask a question to direct your research. Here is an example: *Can parrots answer questions?* Once you write a question, choose your resources and begin your research.

After you have completed your research and have organized your ideas, you can begin writing. The introductory paragraph should engage the reader in your topic with an interesting fact or a quote.

Below is a model of an introductory paragraph. Before writing, the writer narrowed his topic using a graphic organizer.

Very broad topic
↓
Narrower topic
↓
Question to direct research

Micah Cowher

Alex, the African Grey

Everyone knows that parrots can repeat human speech. But can they answer questions? This research paper will show that parrots can make up sentences in response to questions. Alex, an African Grey parrot, was famous for his ability to answer questions. Trained by Dr. Irene Pepperberg, a psychologist studying avian intelligence, Alex understood the meaning of more than 50 words. He could name colors and shapes, count to six, and understand concepts such as similarity and difference. This amazing bird, about as intelligent as a five-year-old child, opened the door to many scientific discoveries. When Alex died suddenly in September, 2007, Dr. Pepperberg was asked to speak about Alex's contribution to science. She explained that Alex disproved the idea that birds are not intelligent creatures.

Practice

Workbook
Page 167

Select a topic related to animals. Use a graphic organizer to narrow your topic, and write a question to direct your research. Then do some research. Write an introductory paragraph for a research report on the topic. Use adjective phrases correctly.

Writing Checklist

ORGANIZATION:
☑ I introduced the question that directed my research in my first paragraph.

SENTENCE FLUENCY:
☑ I reduced awkward clauses to phrases.

341

What You Will Learn

Reading
- Vocabulary building: *Context, dictionary skills, word study*
- Reading strategy: *Evaluate new information*
- Text type: *Informational text (science)*

Grammar, Usage, and Mechanics
Relative pronouns as subjects

Writing
Write classifying paragraphs

THE BIG QUESTION

What makes animals so amazing? What do you know about bats? Copy the K-W-L-H chart into your notebook. Work in small groups to complete the first two columns. As you read "Getting to Know Real Bats," complete the third and fourth columns of the chart.

K What do I **know**?	**W** What do I **want** to know?	**L** What did I **learn**?	**H** **How** did I learn it?

BUILD BACKGROUND

This reading is a science article about bats. Bats are flying mammals. Some eat insects and some eat fruit. Bats live everywhere in the world except Antarctica and certain remote islands.

Some people believe that bats are aggressive and even dangerous. In **"Getting to Know Real Bats,"** you will learn that bats are shy creatures that can be very helpful to human beings.

A swarm of bats emerging from a cave ▶

Learn Key Words

Read these sentences. Use the context to figure out the meaning of the **red** words. Use a dictionary to check your answers. Then write each word and its meaning in your notebook.

Key Words

attitudes
echolocation
mammals
nocturnal
portray
wingspan

1. Many people used to think that bats were dangerous, but over the years their **attitudes** have changed. Now most people understand that bats are gentle.

2. By using **echolocation**, or by bouncing sounds off objects and listening to the echoes, bats can fly around in the dark without crashing into things.

3. Snakes are not **mammals**. They do not have hair on their bodies, and they do not nurse their young.

4. Many forest animals are **nocturnal**. They sleep or hide during the day and hunt for food at night.

5. Some pictures **portray** bats as scary and aggressive. But the bats in such pictures are actually frightened themselves.

6. The scientist measured the bat's **wingspan**; it was six feet from one wing tip to the other wing tip.

Practice

Workbook Page 168

Work with a partner to complete these sentences. Include the **red** word in your sentence. Then write the sentence in your notebook.

1. After scientists discovered that the animal was harmless . . . (**attitudes**)
2. Bats use a radar-like system . . . (**echolocation**)
3. Whales are . . . (**mammals**)
4. The owl is a . . . (**nocturnal**)
5. The photos did not . . . (**portray**)
6. The eagle's . . . (**wingspan**)

▲ A lesser long-nosed bat pollinates a saguaro cactus.

Learn Academic Words

Study the **red** words and their meanings. You will find these words useful when talking and writing about informational texts. Write each word and its meaning in your notebook. After you read "Getting to Know Real Bats," try to use these words to respond to the text.

Academic Words

accurate
beneficial
features
ignorance

accurate = exactly correct	➡	The scientists took special care to make sure the information was **accurate**.
beneficial = good or useful	➡	Bats are **beneficial** because they eat insects, keeping insect populations in check, or pollinate plants, helping plants reproduce.
features = parts of something that stand out because they seem important, interesting, or typical	➡	The most impressive **features** of the school were a new computer lab, a sports arena, and an art studio.
ignorance = lack of knowledge or information about something	➡	The man showed his **ignorance** of the city when he gave some tourists the wrong directions to the art museum.

Practice  Workbook Page 169

Work with a partner to answer these questions. Try to include the **red** word in your answer. Write the sentences in your notebook.

1. How can you get an **accurate** measurement of your height?

2. How is scientific research **beneficial** to human beings?

3. What **features** of dogs make them good choices for pets?

4. How can human **ignorance** endanger the lives of animals?

▲ A Waterhouse's leaf-nosed bat with a katydid it has caught

Word Study: Hyphenated Words

Spelling hyphenated words can be confusing. The best way to see if you have spelled a hyphenated word correctly is to look it up.

Hyphenated words can modify nouns. Use a hyphen between two words before the modified word. Study the chart below.

	Hyphenated Words	Example
make + believe =	make-believe	These are **make-believe** bats.
high + pitched =	high-pitched	The bat made a **high-pitched** noise.
warm + blooded =	warm-blooded	The bats looked for **warm-blooded** prey.
disease + carrying =	disease-carrying	Bats are not **disease-carrying** creatures.

Practice

Work with a partner to complete these sentences. Include the hyphenated word in your sentence. Then write the sentence in your notebook.

1. Many birds, bats, and frogs are . . . (insect-eating)
2. The police followed . . . (high-speed)
3. The salad was made . . . (cut-up)
4. To kill mosquitoes, we use . . . (all-natural)
5. The ice cream shop had . . . (forty-two)

READING STRATEGY   EVALUATE NEW INFORMATION

Evaluating new information helps you understand a text as it broadens your knowledge. To evaluate new information, follow these steps:

- Before you read, ask yourself what you already know about the subject.
- As you read, make a note of the new facts and ideas you find.
- Compare the new information to what you already know.
- How does the new information broaden your knowledge of the subject?

Before you read "Getting to Know Real Bats," think about what you already know about bats. As you read, make a note of new and interesting facts and ideas.

Set a purpose for reading Read this science article to find out some surprising information about bats. What amazing abilities do bats have?

GETTING TO KNOW REAL

Bats

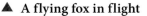

▲ A flying fox in flight

Laurence Pringle

Bats. To some people, this word means scary, ugly, disease-carrying creatures that are almost blind and sometimes fly into and become entangled in women's hair. These are make-believe bats. Real bats are quite different.

Bats make up nearly a quarter of all mammals on earth and live on all continents except Antarctica. They are the only mammals that fly. "Just as dolphins have mastered the sea," says Merlin Tuttle, "bats have mastered the sky."

There are two main groups of bats. About two hundred species—the megabats—are large, fruit-eating bats called flying foxes. They live in the tropics of Asia and Africa. Some have wingspans of nearly six feet, and others fly about in the daytime, not at night. Flying foxes have big eyes and see very well.

Nearly eight hundred species of small, insect-eating bats make up the second group—the microbats—with forty-two kinds living in Canada and the United States. The smallest mammal on earth is a bat: the bumblebee bat of Thailand. It weighs less than a penny.

Also in this group is a species of bat that catches frogs, one that scoops fish out of the water, others that catch birds and rats, and three species that lap blood from

A close-up of a flying fox ▶

---

entangled, twisted and caught in

▲ A bat with a moth it has caught

little bites they nip in the skin of cattle and other warm-blooded prey. These vampire bats live in the warmest regions of South and Central America.

Microbats have small eyes, but they can probably see as well as mice and other small mammals. Their food is mostly flying insects, which they catch in the air at night. To accomplish this, a bat flies with its mouth open, emitting high-pitched squeaks that humans cannot hear. Some of the sounds echo off flying insects as well as tree branches and other obstacles that lie ahead. The bat listens to the echoes and gets an instantaneous picture in its brain of the objects in front of it.

From this echolocation, or sonar, as it is called, a bat can tell a great deal about a mosquito or another flying insect. "With

extreme precision," Merlin Tuttle says, "bats can perceive motion, distance, speed, trajectory, and shape. They can detect and avoid obstacles no thicker than a human hair, and millions of bats sometimes fly at the same time in a large cave without jamming each other's sonar. Their abilities far surpass our present understanding."

Some people still shudder at the thought of being face-to-face with a bat. Most of this fear is a result of ignorance about bats and of seeing only images of bats looking their worst, with mouths open and teeth bared.

instantaneous, immediate

precision, accuracy, exactness
trajectory, curved path of a flying object

BEFORE YOU GO ON

1 What can bats do that no other mammal can do?

2 What are the two main groups of bats?

On Your Own
Do you like bats? Why or why not?

347

In 1978 Merlin Tuttle began to think about the image that many people have of bats. He was asked to write a chapter about bats for a book on mammals to be published by the National Geographic Society. Then he saw the photographs that were going to illustrate his words.

Merlin recalls, "I had never considered the impact of the bat pictures that were then typical; most showed bats snarling in self-defense. Because of their shy nature and nocturnal habits, bats are exceptionally difficult to portray photographically as they really are in the wild. When first captured, they either try to fly away, bare their teeth in a threat display, or hunker down, eyes closed, expecting the worst. Impatient photographers typically held a bat by its wings, blew into its face, and snapped a quick picture when the bat tried to defend itself with a snarl."

---

hunker down, crouch, keep low to
    the ground

▲ A big brown bat baring its teeth in self-defense

Photos like these, enlarged and published in books and magazines, reinforced the notion that bats were vicious and fearsome. Merlin wanted his chapter to show bats accurately, and the book editors agreed to try. A *National Geographic* staff photographer, Bates Littlehales, was assigned to take bat photos, under Merlin's direction. After several weeks, however, only a few good photos were taken, despite their best efforts.

Merlin was an amateur photographer when he met Bates Littlehales, who generously shared his knowledge. After Littlehales left to return to *National Geographic*, Merlin began to experiment with the high-speed photography needed to capture bats in flight. When an editor tried to arrange for Littlehales and Tuttle to travel to Mexico to take photos of fishing bats, Littlehales said that Merlin

---

notion, idea
amateur, someone who does something for
    pleasure or interest, not as a job

▲ A big brown bat with a normal, calm expression

▲ A fisherman bat with a minnow in its feet

had learned enough about photography to try it alone.

From other mammalogists, Merlin learned where to look in Mexico for fishing bats. After several nights of great effort, he and his assistants caught seven of the bats in nets. The bats became docile after several hours of gentle care but refused to take food.

After much frustration, Merlin was about to give up and release the bats, but first he tried tucking bits of cut-up minnow under their lips. Eventually one bat ate a piece of minnow. "Then," Merlin recalls, "to our great elation, he grabbed a whole minnow from my hand, eating it with gusto. The others continued to refuse even small pieces, but we perched them on each side of the feeding bat until, one by one, each succumbed to the

temptation. An hour later, all seven bats were eagerly eating from our hands and allowing themselves to be photographed with their meals, some in flight.

"When I returned from the trip and had the film developed, I was amazed to see the spectacular photographs that resulted. Even more impressive, when I showed the photographs to others, I soon saw that most people's negative attitudes about bats could be changed in minutes. They simply needed an opportunity to see bats as they really are. Bats that are not afraid can be just as curious, winsome, and even comical as any household pet."

---

mammalogists, scientists who study mammals
docile, quiet, calm, easy to control
succumbed, gave in

---

winsome, pleasant and attractive

BEFORE YOU GO ON

1 Why are bats difficult to portray accurately?

2 How were the photos of the fishing bats different?

On Your Own
Do you think you would like to photograph wild animals? Why or why not?

349

▲ Merlin Tuttle photographing a bat

People who acknowledge that bats are appealing may still fear them because they believe that bats commonly carry the disease rabies. This idea originated in the early 1960s, when research seemed to show that bats were not harmed by rabies, yet passed the deadly disease on to other animals. Further study showed that this was not true, but most people and health officials heard about only the first, erroneous research.

Merlin Tuttle notes that "bats can get rabies, the same as dogs and cats can, but when they do get it they die quickly, just as other animals do. Anyway, less than half of one percent of bats contract rabies, and, unlike most mammals, even when bats are rabid they rarely become aggressive."

---

rabies, disease that kills animals, including people

---

erroneous, incorrect or wrong
rabid, infected with rabies

◄ A pallid bat perched on a limb

▲ A male great fruit bat guards a female and a baby.

The greatest threat posed by bats is an indirect one: the actions of unscrupulous or uninformed pest control companies using poisons to kill bats in attics of homes. One widely used poison, chlorophacinone (Rozel), has been clearly shown to pose a serious health threat to people. At least fifteen states still allow its use, and some pest control operators in other states use it illegally.

There are simple, non-chemical ways to keep bats out of houses. Besides, some people are pleased to have a colony of insect-eating bats in or near their homes. "Just leave bats alone," Merlin concludes, "and the odds of being harmed are infinitesimally small."

unscrupulous, behaving in an unfair or dishonest way

ABOUT THE **AUTHOR**

Laurence Pringle has written over one hundred books for young readers. Although his focus is mainly on animals and nature, he does write an occasional work of fiction or a book about a social studies topic. Before he became a writer, he studied wildlife biology at Cornell University and the University of Massachusetts. He also worked as a teacher and an editor. Pringle grew up in New York, where he still lives with his wife and children.

BEFORE YOU GO ON

1 Why do some people fear bats?

2 Why might people be pleased to have bats near their homes?

On Your Own
In what ways are bats amazing?

COMPREHENSION

Workbook
Page 172

Right There

1. What are megabats? What are microbats?
2. What is sonar, or echolocation? What do bats use echolocation for?

Think and Search

3. Why were bats usually portrayed as frightening creatures?
4. How are bats different from other mammals?

Author and You

5. How did the author and Merlin Tuttle fight against ignorance?
6. In what ways do you think bats are beneficial to people?

On Your Own

7. Have you ever seen a bat? What time of day did you see it? Were you afraid of it?
8. Has this article changed your attitude toward bats? Why or why not?

▲ A Peter's dwarf epauletted bat eats a fig.

IN YOUR OWN WORDS

Imagine you are telling a friend or family member about bats. What would you say to help change their attitudes about bats? Use the words in the chart below to describe bats as they really are. Explain why bats have been misunderstood and unjustly feared for so long.

Speaking TIP

Ask listeners if they have any questions.

Types of Bats	megabats, microbats, flying foxes, vampire bats
Features of Bats	echolocation, high-pitched squeak, small eyes, wingspan
Nature of Bats	nocturnal, docile, comical, gentle, timid

A Gambian epauletted fruit bat with her young ▶

352

DISCUSSION

Discuss in pairs or small groups.

1. What do people do to harm bats? How can this be prevented?
2. Has the author proven to you that bats are gentle creatures? Why or why not?

🔵 **What makes animals so amazing?** Many cultures have myths or tales about bats. Have you ever heard any? In what ways are the bats in the stories amazing?

 Listening TIP

Give each speaker your full attention. Be quiet while the speaker is talking.

READ FOR FLUENCY

It is often easier to read a text if you understand the difficult words and phrases. Work with a partner. Choose a paragraph from the reading. Identify the words and phrases you do not know or have trouble pronouncing. Look up the difficult words in a dictionary.

Take turns pronouncing the words and phrases with your partner. If necessary, ask your teacher to model the correct pronunciation. Then take turns reading the paragraph aloud. Give each other feedback on your reading.

EXTENSION

Workbook Page 172

Bats eat thousands of mosquitoes every night. Many people encourage bats to nest around their homes by building bat boxes. Bat boxes are flat wooden structures where bats roost. Do research at the library or on the Internet to find out more information about bat boxes. Share your findings with the class.

▲ Bat boxes give bats safe places to live.

GRAMMAR, USAGE, AND MECHANICS

Relative Pronouns as Subjects

Adjective clauses describe, or modify, nouns or noun phrases. Adjective clauses begin with relative pronouns. Relative pronouns used as the subject of adjective clauses are *who, that, which,* and *whose.* Relative pronouns relate to a noun in the first part of the sentence. In the first example below, *they* relates to *the photographs* in the first sentence. In the second example, *that,* the relative pronoun replacing *they,* also relates to *the photographs.*

> subject
> Then he saw *the photographs.* **They** were going to illustrate his words.
>
> subject
> Then he saw *the photographs* **that** were going to illustrate his words.

Use *who* for people. *Who* relates to *the people.*

> Tuttle was grateful to the people, **who** generously shared their knowledge.

Use *which* or *that* for things and animals. *Which* relates to *bats,* and *that* relates to *a species.*

> *Bats* **which** lap blood from cattle are called vampire bats.
> Also in this group is *a species of bat* **that** catches frogs.

Use *whose* to show possession. *Whose* relates to *the photographer.*

> *The photographer* **whose** pictures we liked was Merlin Tuttle.

Practice

With a partner, rewrite each pair of sentences as one sentence, using a relative pronoun to join them. Write the new sentence in your notebook.

1. I read the article by the scientist. He knows about bats.
2. Chlorophacinone is a poison. It kills bats.
3. The photos show bats. The bats were frightened.
4. Megabats are large bats. The bats eat fruit.
5. They built the bat box. It was in the tree.

354

WRITING A RESEARCH REPORT

Write Classifying Paragraphs

One way to organize your ideas in a research report is by categories; this is also called classifying. When you classify, you discuss one category at a time, pointing out how the categories are similar and different. For example, suppose you were writing about flying animals. You might discuss birds in one part of the report and bats in another. You might say that birds and bats are similar in that they both can fly. They are different in that bats are mammals and birds are not.

Here is a model of paragraphs that classify bats. Before writing, the writer listed her ideas in a T-chart.

Megabats	Microbats

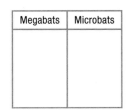

Leah Morales

Two Kinds of Bats

There are two major groups of bats: megabats and microbats. In general, megabats are larger than microbats. Because of their long noses, megabats are often called flying foxes. Their large eyes can see well during the day and at night, and they use their senses of sight and smell to find the fruit and nectar that they eat. They have small ears but can hear well. Megabats live in the tropics of Africa, Asia, and Australia.

Microbats are generally smaller than megabats. They have small eyes that see well, but not as well as megabats. Because microbats are active at night, they rely on echolocation to find food and to avoid obstacles in the dark. Most microbats eat insects. While flying, they hunt by sending out high-pitched sounds and listening for echoes. There are many more species of microbats than megabats, but both kinds of bats play an important part in keeping nature in balance.

Practice **Workbook Page 174**

Write two paragraphs that classify a group of animals. For example, you may choose to classify cats, such as lions and cheetahs. Use a T-chart to organize your ideas. Use relative pronouns correctly.

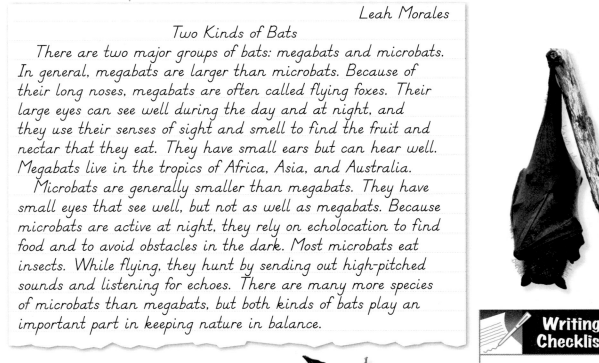

 **Writing Checklist**

ORGANIZATION:
☑ I organized my ideas and information by categories.

IDEAS:
☑ I chose a topic that interested me.

What You Will Learn

Reading
- Vocabulary building:
  Literary terms
  word study
- Reading strategy:
  Read aloud
- Text type:
  Literature (poetry)

Grammar, Usage, and Mechanics
Typical and atypical word order

Writing
Support the main idea

THE BIG QUESTION

What makes animals so amazing? Animals have been the subject of paintings and poetry since prehistoric times. Why do you think people are so fascinated by animals? Discuss with a partner.

BUILD BACKGROUND

You are about to read four poems about animals: **"The Bat," "A Narrow Fellow in the Grass," "Daybreak,"** and **"Birdfoot's Grandpa."** For each poem, think about the speaker's attitude toward the animal being described. Is the animal described in a humorous way? A loving way? A respectful way? Asking these questions will help you understand and appreciate the poems.

▲ A painting of a horse in the Cave of Lascaux, in France

Learn Literary Words

Similes and metaphors are types of figurative language, or language that is not meant to be interpreted literally. **Similes** are comparisons that use the words *like* or *as*. Read these lines from the poem "The Blood Horse" by Barry Cornwall. What similes can you find?

> His mane is like a river flowing,
> And his eyes like embers glowing
> In the darkness of the night,
> And his pace as swift as light

There are three similes in the lines above. The first one compares the horse's mane to a flowing river. The second one compares the horse's eyes to red-hot embers glowing in the darkness. The third simile compares his pace to the speed of light.

    Metaphors are implied comparisons in which one thing is spoken about as though it were something else. Read these lines from a poem by Emily Dickinson.

> "Hope" is the thing with feathers—
> That perches in the soul—
> And sings the tune without the words—
> And never stops—at all—

In the lines above, the idea of hope is said to be a bird that perches in our souls. This bird never stops singing, just as we never give up hope.

Practice

Workbook Page 175

With a partner, read the lines below. Tell whether each line is a simile or a metaphor. Identify the two things that are being compared.

1. The skinny cat was like a scarecrow covered with fur.
2. He bounced as he walked, as though he had springs under his feet.
3. The road was a ribbon of moonlight.
4. Her eyes were pools of hopefulness.
5. The lake was like a sheet of glass.

Learn Academic Words

Study the **red** words and their meanings. You will find these words useful when talking and writing about literature. Write each word and its meaning in your notebook. After you read "The Bat," "A Narrow Fellow in the Grass," "Daybreak," and "Birdfoot's Grandpa," try to use these words to respond to the text.

Academic Words

appreciation
explicit
implicit
invisible

appreciation = an understanding of the importance, meaning, or beauty of something	➡	Daniel's visit to the museum gave him a better **appreciation** of the work of Pablo Picasso.
explicit = expressed in a way that is very clear and direct	➡	The teacher's instructions were **explicit**; the students understood immediately what they were expected to do.
implicit = suggested or understood but not stated directly	➡	My dad and I have an **implicit** agreement not to talk about certain issues.
invisible = not able to be seen	➡	The window glass was so clean that it was almost **invisible**.

Practice  Workbook Page 176

Work with a partner to complete these sentences. Include the **red** word in your sentence. Then write the sentence in your notebook.

1. Pam's night at the opera . . . (**appreciation**)
2. The warning notice . . . (**explicit**)
3. The theme of the poem . . . (**implicit**)
4. The still water was so clean . . . (**invisible**)

▲ The coyote blends in so well with its surroundings that it is almost invisible.

Word Study: Words with Double Letters

Knowing when to spell words with double letters can be difficult. Copy the following rule and chart into your notebook to help you memorize when to use double letters.

Use double letters when you add -ed, -er, -est, and -ing to words ending in b, d, g, l, m, n, p, r, and t if the words follow a consonant-vowel-consonant pattern. Here are some examples:

Base Word	Add -ed, -er, -est, or -ing	Double Letter Spelling
mad	mad + -er, mad + -est	madder, maddest
big	big + -er, big + -est	bigger, biggest
pop	pop + -ed, pop + -ing	popped, popping
wrap	wrap + -ed, wrap + -ing	wrapped, wrapping

Practice

Copy the sentences into your notebook. Complete each sentence by adding the correct ending to the word in parentheses. If the word follows a consonant-vowel-consonant pattern, use double letters.

1. The young man is _____ at the store on his way home. (stop)
2. I am _____ for a new place to study. (look)
3. My older sister is the _____ of all the girls. (slim)
4. We _____ our car in the back of the parking lot. (spot)
5. She is _____ before the big game. (rest)

READING STRATEGY | READ ALOUD

Reading aloud brings literature to life. It can make reading more meaningful and enjoyable, especially in the case of poetry. When you read poetry aloud, keep these ideas in mind:

- Pay close attention to the sounds of the words.
- Think about the structure of the poem. Many poets use rhyme, but not all do. Which words in the poem rhyme with one another?
- Notice the rhythm of the language the poet has used.
- Use your voice as expressively as you can while you are reading.

As you read the poems aloud, notice the similarities and differences among them. Which one do you enjoy reading aloud the most?

Set a purpose for reading Read these poems to discover new ways of thinking about and appreciating four animals. In what ways are they amazing?

ABOUT THE
POET

Theodore Roethke (1908–1963) was an American poet who often wrote about the natural world. He spent much of his youth working in a greenhouse, where he developed a lifelong love of nature. He won the Pulitzer Prize in 1954 for his collection of poetry *The Waking: Poems, 1933–1953.*

THE BAT

By day the bat is cousin to the mouse.
He likes the attic of an aging house.

His fingers make a hat about his head.
His pulse beat is so slow we think him dead.

He loops in crazy figures half the night
Among the trees that face the corner light.

But when he brushes up against a screen,
We are afraid of what our eyes have seen:

For something is amiss or out of place
When mice with wings can wear a human face.

—*Theodore Roethke*

---

figures, shapes; patterns
amiss, wrong

✔ **LITERARY CHECK**
*What **metaphor** can you find in the last line?*

A Narrow Fellow in the Grass

A narrow Fellow in the Grass
Occasionally rides—
You may have met Him—did you not,
His notice sudden is—

The Grass divides as with a Comb—
A spotted shaft is seen—
And then it closes at your feet
And opens further on—

He likes a Boggy Acre,
A Floor too cool for Corn—
Yet when a Boy, and Barefoot,
I more than once, at Noon

Have passed, I thought, a Whip lash
Unbraiding in the Sun—
When, stooping to secure it,
It wrinkled, and was gone—

Several of Nature's People
I know, and they know me—
I feel for them a transport
Of cordiality—

But never met this Fellow
Attended or alone
Without a tighter breathing,
And Zero at the Bone—

—*Emily Dickinson*

---

notice, warning
shaft, long, thin object
boggy acre, wet and muddy ground
unbraiding, becoming straight
transport of cordiality, sudden feeling
   of friendliness

ABOUT THE POET

Emily Dickinson
(1830–1886) was one of the greatest American poets. She wrote over 1,700 poems, but only ten were published in her lifetime. She says in one of her poems: *This is my letter to the world/That never wrote to me.* Many of her poems explore love, death, and nature.

BEFORE YOU GO ON

1 How do a bat's fingers "make a hat about his head"?

2 How does the "narrow fellow" affect the grass as he moves?

On Your Own
Do you agree with the poets' attitudes toward their subjects? Explain.

Daybreak

On the tidal mud, just before sunset,
dozens of starfishes
were creeping. It was
as though the mud were a sky
and enormous, imperfect stars
moved across it as slowly
as the actual stars cross heaven.
All at once they stopped,
and, as if they had simply
increased their receptivity
to gravity, they sank down
into the mud, faded down
into it and lay still, and by the time
pink of sunset broke across them
they were as invisible
as the true stars at daybreak.

—*Galway Kinnell*

---

tidal, relating to the rise and fall of
the ocean
receptivity, readiness to give in to

✔ **LITERARY CHECK**
*What is the mud
being compared
to in this **simile**?*

ABOUT THE POET

Galway Kinnell
is a well-known
American poet.
Many of his
poems describe
connections between human beings
and other creatures. Some of his
most famous poems, such as "The
Bear," "The Porcupine," and "St.
Francis and the Sow," use sensory
details to describe an animal.

Birdfoot's Grandpa

The old man
must have stopped our car
two dozen times to climb out
and gather into his hands
the small toads blinded
by our lights and leaping,
live drops of rain.

The rain was falling,
a mist about his white hair
and I kept saying
you can't save them all,
accept it, get back in
we've got places to go.

But, leathery hands full
of wet brown life,
knee deep in the summer
roadside grass,
he just smiled and said
they have places to go, too.

—Joseph Bruchac

ABOUT THE **POET**

Joseph Bruchac writes poems, short stories, and novels. Both his writing and his style of storytelling reflect his Native-American heritage. The author of more than seventy books, he has won many awards, including Writer of the Year and Storyteller of the Year in 1998. Bruchac grew up in New York, near the Adirondack Mountains, where he lives with his wife, Carol.

BEFORE YOU GO ON

1. In what ways are the starfishes like real stars?

2. How is the old man's attitude toward the toads different from the speaker's?

On Your Own
Have you ever seen beauty or dignity in ordinary creatures? Explain.

DRAMATIC READING

Work in groups to reread, discuss, and interpret "The Bat," "A Narrow Fellow in the Grass," "Daybreak," and "Birdfoot's Grandpa." Read each poem line by line and talk about the images that come to mind. Identify similes, metaphors, and other types of figurative language. Discuss how each poem makes you feel. Try to figure out difficult words or phrasing from context. Consult a dictionary or your teacher for help if necessary.

After you analyze the poems, choose one to memorize. Have each student learn a few lines. Then recite the poem within your group. Comment on one another's reading and make suggestions for improvements. You may wish to hold a contest with the class in which each group competes for the best oral reading.

🔊 *Speaking* TIP

Match the tone of your voice to the tone of the poem. Speak slowly and with feeling.

COMPREHENSION

Workbook
Page 179

Right There

1. Where and when does "Daybreak" take place?
2. In "The Bat," what does the bat do during the day? What does the bat do at night?

Think and Search

3. Why is the old man concerned about the toads in the poem "Birdfoot's Grandpa"?
4. Who is the "narrow fellow in the grass"? How does the speaker of the poem feel whenever she meets him?

Author and You

5. What do you think Kinnell felt about the starfishes?
6. Why does Roethke find the bat's face so disturbing?

On Your Own

7. Why do you think people write poems about animals?
8. If you were to write a poem about an animal, which animal would you choose to write about? Why?

DISCUSSION

Discuss in pairs or small groups.

1. What lesson does the old man teach in "Birdfoot's Grandpa"?
2. Were the images in the poems implicit or explicit? Give details.

Q **What makes animals so amazing?** How do you think the poets whose work you just read would answer this question?

Listening TIP

Try to be open-minded as you consider other people's ideas.

RESPONSE TO LITERATURE

Workbook
Page 179

Each of the poems you have read is about an animal. Think about an animal that you find especially interesting. Write a paragraph telling what is special about this animal. Explain what makes the animal interesting to you. When you are finished writing, read your paragraph to the class.

GRAMMAR, USAGE, AND MECHANICS

Typical and Atypical Word Order

Typical word order, or usual word order, in English is *subject/verb/object*.
The typical word order for an adjective is before the noun it modifies
or after the verb *be*. A prepositional phrase typically appears after the
verb or the object. Look at the examples showing typical word order.

subject	verb	adjective	object
Emily Dickinson	writes	beautiful	poetry.

subject	verb	adjective
Emily Dickinson's poetry	is	beautiful.

subject	verb	prepositional phrase
The poem	comes	from her first collection.

subject	verb	object	prepositional phrase
Grandpa	saved	the toads	from certain death.

Poets often use atypical word order in their poetry. There are different
reasons why a poet would choose to use atypical word order.

In the following example from "A Narrow Fellow in the Grass," Emily
Dickinson uses atypical word order to give the poem a certain rhythm
and to create a rhyme (although irregular) between *rides* and *is*.

Atypical Word Order	Typical Word Order
A narrow Fellow in the Grass Occasionally rides— You may have met Him—did you not, His notice sudden is.	A narrow Fellow occasionally Rides in the Grass— You may have met Him—didn't you? His notice is sudden.

Practice
Workbook Page 180

Work with a partner. Choose one of the four poems you just finished
reading or another poem you know. Rewrite the poem using
typical word order (*subject/verb/object*), putting the adjectives and
prepositional phrases in the correct place. Discuss how typical word
order changes the rhythm and rhyming pattern of the poem.

WRITING A RESEARCH REPORT

Support the Main Idea

At the end of this unit, you will write a research report. One skill you'll need to know in order to write a research report is how to support your main idea with details, including facts and examples.

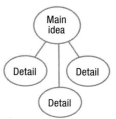

Using a main-idea-and-details web can help you organize your main idea and facts and examples that support it. List your ideas in the web as you do your research. Suppose the main idea of your report was the following: *Pet snakes are not easy to care for.* Your supporting details might be these: *Snakes eat live mice, which can be expensive and hard to find. Snakes need a cage that is kept warm at all times.*

Here is a model of a paragraph that supports a main idea with supporting facts and examples. The writer used a main-idea-and-details web to organize his notes.

Dylan Bishop

Snakes' Senses

Snakes have unique senses, unlike the senses of most other animals. They do not have a good sense of sight or hearing, so they rely mostly on their acute senses of smell and touch. Snakes do not have external ears. Instead, they have inner ears inside the head. They can hear by feeling vibrations through the ground. The vibrations pass through the snake's sensitive underbelly and travel through the body to reach a bone connected to the inner ear, which senses the vibrations. This is one way snakes can tell when other animals are moving toward them. Snakes also don't have an external nose. They use their tongue to take in particles from the air and analyze them in their mouth. By doing this, they can tell if a predator or a potential meal is nearby. Some snakes can sense body heat in other animals, which helps them detect warm-blooded prey such as mammals and birds.

Practice

Workbook Page 181

Write a paragraph about animals with a main idea supported by facts and examples. You might choose to write about a pet, animals in the wild, or how animals are important in your life. List your ideas in a main-idea-and-details web. Be sure to use typical word order.

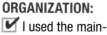

Writing Checklist

ORGANIZATION:
☑ I used the main-idea-and-details web to organize my notes.

SENTENCE FLUENCY:
☑ I used typical word order.

4

What You Will Learn

Reading
- Vocabulary building: *Context, dictionary skills, word study*
- Reading strategy: *Make generalizations*
- Text type: *Informational text (science)*

Grammar, Usage, and Mechanics
Gerunds and infinitives

Writing
Include quotations and citations

THE BIG QUESTION

What makes animals so amazing? Look at the photo below. Have you ever seen chimpanzees? Where did you see them? What did you observe about them? Discuss with a partner.

BUILD BACKGROUND

This reading is an excerpt from the book ***The Chimpanzees I Love*** by Jane Goodall. Goodall was born in 1934 in London, England. She was interested in animals from a young age. As an adult, she became a primatologist— a scientist who works with primates, or animals such as chimpanzees and gorillas. Goodall has written books, made documentary films, and won awards for her work with chimpanzees and other primates.

Chimpanzees playing in a tree ▶

Learn Key Words

Read these sentences. Use the context to figure out the meaning of the **red** words. Use a dictionary to check your answers. Then write each word and its meaning in your notebook.

1. Biologically speaking, **chimpanzees** are more similar to human beings than they are to gorillas.

2. The hunters used the meat for **commercial** purposes; they sold it to restaurants and grocery stores.

3. Animals that live in a well-designed zoo can enjoy a peaceful and pleasant **existence**.

4. Scientists spend much of their time in **laboratories**, rooms with equipment for doing experiments or research.

5. Last summer my friends and I volunteered to work at various animal **sanctuaries**, where sick and mistreated animals were recovering before being released back into the wild.

6. Because it is illegal to export elephant tusks, people **smuggle** the tusks out of Africa and take them to other countries.

Practice
Workbook Page 182

Write the sentences in your notebook. Choose a **red** word from the box above to complete each sentence. Then take turns reading the sentences aloud with a partner.

1. Poachers _____ illegal goods from one place to another.

2. All the workers at the zoo were excited when two new _____ arrived.

3. There are many _____ for endangered animals around the world.

4. Scientists test animal behavior in _____.

5. The _____ interests of the government were more important than the animals' lives.

6. What kind of _____ do you think circus animals have?

369

Learn Academic Words

Study the **red** words and their meanings. You will find these words useful when talking and writing about informational texts. Write each word and its meaning in your notebook. After you read the excerpt from *The Chimpanzees I Love*, try to use these words to respond to the text.

committed = used all of the time and energy that you could in order to achieve something	⇒	The woman **committed** all of her time to studying animals. She worked so hard that she rarely saw her friends.
inadequate = not good enough for a particular purpose	⇒	The animals received **inadequate** care. They were often hungry, unclean, and upset.
intelligent = having a high level of ability to learn, understand, and think about things	⇒	Chimpanzees are very **intelligent**. They can make and use tools and are capable of reasoned thought.
project = a carefully planned piece of work	⇒	We worked on a **project** with the local zoo to help build new homes for the animals.

Practice

Workbook Page 183

Work with a partner to answer these questions. Try to include the **red** word in your answer. Write the sentences in your notebook.

1. What is something you are very **committed** to?
2. What is an example of an **inadequate** meal for your lunch?
3. Who is the most **intelligent** person you know?
4. What was your favorite school **project** this year?

▲ A chimpanzee mom and her baby

Word Study: Frequently Misspelled Words

Spelling can be difficult in English. Some words are particularly tricky.
Learning how to spell these words correctly can save you time looking
up words in a dictionary. Look at the examples below.

Frequently Misspelled Words	Spelling Errors
piece	Mixing up letters, such as *peice*
existence	Confusing endings, such as *existance*
vicious	Mixing up sound-spellings, such as *viscious*
disappearing	Missing double letters, such as *disapearing*
until	Adding double letters, such as *untill*
grateful	Confusing homophones, such as *greatful*

Practice  Workbook Page 184

Work with a partner. Correct the spelling errors in the following words.
Write the words in your notebook. Check your work in a dictionary.
Then write a sentence with each word.

diffrent	disipline	inteligent	intimmidate	labratories

READING STRATEGY | **MAKE GENERALIZATIONS**

Making generalizations helps you learn from the information in a text.
A generalization is a broad statement. Here is an example: "Chimpanzees
need our help." To make generalizations, follow these steps:

- Look for important, broad statements or ideas in the text.
- Look for examples that support the broad statements or ideas.
- Use the information in the text and what you already know
  about a topic to make a generalization.

As you read the excerpt from *The Chimpanzees I Love,* look for
information and ideas about which you can make generalizations.

 Workbook Page 185

Set a purpose for reading Read this excerpt to learn about the amazing abilities of chimpanzees. Why are they in danger and why do they need our help?

from

Jane Goodall

The Mind of the Chimpanzee

The more we have learned about chimpanzees, the clearer it is that they have brains very like ours and can, in fact, do many things that we used to think only humans could do. The Gombe chimps use grass stems and twigs to fish termites from their nests. The chimps also use long smooth sticks to catch vicious biting army ants. They use crumpled leaves to soak up water from hollows in trees that they cannot reach with their lips, then suck the homemade sponge. They wipe dirt from their bodies with leaf napkins. They use stout sticks to open up holes in trees to get at birds' nests or honey and as clubs to intimidate one another or other animals. It seems that infant chimps learn these behaviors by watching the adults, and then imitating and practicing what they have seen. So the chimps have their own primitive culture.

Many scientists are finding out more about the chimpanzee mind from tests in captive situations. For example, chimps will go and find sticks to pull in food that has been placed outside the cage, beyond their reach. They can join two short sticks together to make one long tool. They have excellent memories—after eleven years' separation, a female named Washoe recognized the two humans who had brought her up. A chimp can plan what he or she is going to do. Often I've watched a chimp wake up, scratch himself slowly, gaze around in different directions, then suddenly get up, walk over to a clump of grass, carefully select a stem, trim it, and then travel quite a long way to a termite mound that was out of sight when he made his tool.

---

captive situations, situations in which they are kept in cages

---

termites, insects that eat and destroy wood
intimidate, frighten
primitive, simple

◀ A young chimp concentrating on fishing termites out of their nest

▲ Chimpanzees love to draw.

Chimpanzees can be taught to do many of the things that we can do, such as riding bicycles and sewing. Some love to draw or paint. Chimps can also recognize themselves in mirrors. But they cannot learn to speak words because their vocal cords are different. Two scientists, the Hayeses, brought up a little chimp named Vicky and tried to teach her to talk. After eight years she could say only four words, and only people who knew her could understand even those.

The Gardners had another idea. They got an infant chimpanzee, named her Washoe, and began teaching her American Sign Language (ASL) as used by deaf people. Then other infant chimps were taught this language. Chimps can learn 300 signs or more. They can also invent signs. The chimp Lucy, wanting a Brazil nut but not knowing its name, used two signs she knew and asked for a "rock berry." A fizzy soda became "listen drink," a duck on a pond, "water bird," and a piece of celery, "pipe food." Washoe's adopted son learned fifty-eight signs from Washoe and three other signing chimps by the time he was eight years old. He was never taught these signs by humans. These experiments have taught us, and continue to teach us, more and more about the chimpanzee mind.

Chimpanzees in Captivity

Unfortunately chimpanzees, so like us in many ways, are often very badly treated in many captive situations. Chimpanzees were first brought to Europe from Africa in the middle of the seventeenth century. People were amazed by these humanlike creatures. They dressed them up and taught them tricks.

Since then we have often treated chimpanzees cruelly, shooting their mothers in Africa, shipping them around the world, caging them in zoos, training them to perform, selling them as pets, and imprisoning them in medical research laboratories. A young male called Ham was sent up into space. He was shot up in a Mercury Redstone rocket in January 1961, and because he survived the ordeal (he was terrified), it was decided that it was safe for the first human astronauts. Ham was taught his routine by receiving an electric shock every time he pressed the wrong button.

Infant chimpanzees are adorable and, for the first two or three years, are gentle and easy to handle. People buy them and treat them like human children. But as they grow older they become more and more difficult. They are, after all, chimpanzees, and they want to behave like chimpanzees. They resent discipline. They can—and do—bite. And by the time they are six years old they are already as strong as a human male. What will happen to them then? Zoos don't want them, for they have not been able to learn chimpanzee social behavior and they do not mix well with others of their kind. Often they end up in medical research labs.

BEFORE YOU GO ON

1 How do infant chimps learn to use tools?

2 Why don't chimpanzees make good pets?

On Your Own
Why do you think people are so fascinated by chimpanzees?

▲ A chimpanzee in a cage at a zoo

It is because their bodies are so like ours that scientists use chimps to try to find out more about human diseases and how to cure and prevent them. Chimpanzees can be infected with almost all human diseases. It is very unfair that, even though chimpanzees are being used to try to help humans, they are almost never given decent places to live. Hundreds of them are shut up in 5' × 5' × 7' bare, steel-barred prisons, all alone, bored, and uncomfortable.

I shall never forget the first time I looked into the eyes of an adult male chimpanzee in one of these labs. For more than ten years he had been living in his tiny prison. The sides, floor, and ceiling were made of thick steel bars. There was a car tire on the floor. His name, I read on the door, was JoJo. He lived at the end of a row of five cages, lined up along a bare wall. Opposite were five more cages. At either end of the room was a metal door. There was no window. JoJo could not touch any of his fellow prisoners— only the ends of his fingers fitted between the bars. He had been born in an African forest, and for the first couple of years he lived in a world of greens and browns, leaves and vines, butterflies and birds. Always his mother had

been close to comfort him, until the day when she was shot and he was snatched from her dead or dying body. The young chimpanzee was shipped away from his forest world to the cold, bleak existence of a North American research lab. JoJo was not angry, just grateful that I had stopped by him. He groomed my fingers, where the ridges of my cuticles showed through the surgical gloves I had to wear. Then he looked into my eyes and with one gentle finger reached to touch the tear that rolled down into my mask.

In the United States, several hundred chimpanzees have been declared "surplus"— they are no longer needed for medical research. Animal welfare groups are trying to raise the money to build them sanctuaries so that they can end their lives with grass and trees, sunshine and companionship. Some lucky ones—including JoJo—have already been freed from their laboratory prisons. Many others are waiting.

Zoos are getting better, but there are still many chimps in small concrete and metal cages with no soft ground and nothing to occupy them. Good zoos keep their chimpanzees in groups and provide them with all kinds of stimulating things to do, different things each day, so that they don't get bored. Many zoos now have artificial termite mounds. Chimps use sticks or straws to poke into holes for honey or other foods. These innovations make a world of difference.

---

cuticles, the hard edge of skin around
   your fingernails
surplus, more than is wanted, needed, or used
artificial, not real but made to look real
innovations, new ideas, methods, or inventions

Protecting the Chimpanzees

One hundred years ago we think there were about two million chimpanzees in Africa; now there may be no more than 150,000. They are already extinct in four of the twenty-five countries where they once lived. They are disappearing for various reasons:

1 All over Africa, their forest homes are being destroyed as human populations grow and need ever more land for their crops and wood for their homes.

2 In many places chimpanzees are caught in snares set for bushpigs or antelopes. Some chimps die; others lose a hand or a foot, after months of agony.

3 There are still dealers who are trying to smuggle chimpanzees out of Africa for the live animal trade. Mothers are shot so that hunters can steal their infants for entertainment or medical research. The dealers pay the hunters only a few dollars while they themselves can sell an infant chimp for $2,000 or more.

4 The greatest threat to chimpanzees in the great Congo basin is commercial hunting for food. Logging companies have made roads deep into the heart of the last remaining forests. Hunters ride the trucks to the end of the road and shoot everything—chimps, gorillas, bonobos, elephants, antelopes—even quite small birds. The meat is smoked or even loaded fresh onto the trucks and taken for sale in the big towns. The trouble is that so many people living there prefer the taste of meat from wild animals, and they will pay more for it than for that from domestic animals. If this trade (known as the "bushmeat" trade) cannot be stopped, there will soon be no animals left.

---

extinct, no longer in existence
snares, traps using a wire or rope to catch an animal by its foot
agony, very severe pain

▲ Chimpanzee orphans in a sanctuary in the Republic of Congo

BEFORE YOU GO ON

1 Why do scientists use chimps to learn more about human diseases?

2 What are four serious threats to chimpanzees?

On Your Own
Would you like to work with chimpanzees? Why or why not?

375

It is easy to feel depressed when you think about all the problems in the world. When I think of all that humans have done to spoil our planet during the sixty-six years of my own life, I feel very sad—and ashamed of our own species. But I am full of hope, too. That is why I started a program called Roots & Shoots.

Roots & Shoots is the education program of the Jane Goodall Institute. I'd love you to be part of it. It began in Tanzania, but now there are groups in more than fifty countries. Every group chooses at least one hands-on activity in each of three areas to show care and concern: 1) for animals, including dogs, cats, cows, and so on; 2) for the human community; 3) for the environment we all share. The projects you choose depend on whether you live in the inner city or in a rural area, in the United States or Africa or China or wherever. People of all ages, from kindergarten to college, have joined Roots & Shoots. It's growing very fast.

I get so excited when I hear what all the Roots & Shoots groups are doing to make the world a better place. Everywhere more and more people have begun to understand that their own lives *do* matter, that we are all here for a purpose, and we can each of us make a difference. We shall not let the chimpanzees become extinct in Africa, and we shall not let them go on being cruelly treated in captivity. Chimpanzees make us realize that there is not, after all, a sharp line dividing humans from the rest of the animal kingdom. So we think of all animals with new respect and greater compassion.

---

animal kingdom, a main classification of living organisms that include all animals
compassion, strong feeling of sympathy for those who are suffering

▲ A chimpanzee in a metal cage

▲ Jane Goodall plants a kiss on the forehead of an infant chimpanzee.

ABOUT THE **AUTHOR**

Jane Goodall is best known for her work with chimpanzees. Her many trips to Tanzania and other African countries to study these animals in the wild have made her one of the world's leading chimpanzee experts. In 1977, she founded the Jane Goodall Institute for Wildlife Research, Education, and Conservation. Goodall has received many awards for her efforts, including the highly esteemed Kyoto Prize from Japan. Today, she speaks to groups all over the world about her experiences and her conservation efforts.

BEFORE YOU GO ON

1 What is Roots & Shoots?

2 What has Roots & Shoots helped people understand?

On Your Own
What will you do to help protect the chimpanzees?

377

COMPREHENSION  Workbook Page 186

Right There

1. What have scientists used chimpanzees for?
2. What happened when the Gardners taught Washoe ASL?

Think and Search

3. What do good zoos provide for their chimpanzees?
4. In what ways are chimpanzees like humans?

Author and You

5. What is significant about the fact that the chimp Lucy invented signs?
6. How do chimpanzees make us realize that there is not a sharp line dividing humans from the rest of the animal kingdom?

On Your Own

7. Would you join Roots & Shoots? Why or why not?
8. Does this article make you feel depressed or hopeful? Why?

▲ An infant chimpanzee held captive in a private zoo in Monrovia, Liberia

IN YOUR OWN WORDS

In the excerpt from *The Chimpanzees I Love,* Jane Goodall gives four reasons to explain why chimpanzees are disappearing. Work with a partner. Copy the cause-and-effect chart below into your notebook and fill it in. Then use the chart to explain in your own words why chimpanzees are disappearing.

> 🔊 *Speaking* TIP
>
> Communicate your belief in what you are saying, so the audience will believe it, too.

Cause	Effect
growing human population	
animal traps	
live animal trade	
commercial hunting	

DISCUSSION

Discuss in pairs or small groups.

1. In what ways does helping to protect chimpanzees benefit humans as well as chimpanzees?

2. Do you think animals should be used for medical testing? Why or why not?

 **What makes animals so amazing?** What special abilities do chimpanzees have? Do you think they have feelings? Why or why not?

READ FOR FLUENCY

Reading with feeling helps make what you read more interesting. Work with a partner. Choose a paragraph from the reading. Read the paragraph. Ask each other how you felt after reading the paragraph. Did you feel happy or sad?

Take turns reading the paragraph aloud to each other with a tone of voice that represents how you felt when you read it the first time. Give each other feedback.

EXTENSION

Workbook Page 186

Do research at the library or on the Internet to find out more information about Roots & Shoots or another organization committed to making the world a better place. Take notes and write a brief paragraph about one of the organizations. Then share what you have found with the class.

GRAMMAR, USAGE, AND MECHANICS

Gerunds and Infinitives

Gerunds and infinitives are verb forms that function as nouns. A gerund is the base form of the verb + -ing. An infinitive is to + the base form of the verb. Gerunds or gerund phrases can be the subject of a sentence, a subject complement, the object of a verb, or the object of a preposition.

> **Protecting the chimpanzees** has been Goodall's life's work. [subject]
> The greatest threat to chimps is **commercial hunting**. [subject complement]
> Goodall will keep **studying chimps**. [object of verb *keep*]
> Chimps learn these behaviors by **watching the adults**. [object of preposition *by*]

Infinitives or infinitive phrases can be the subject of a sentence or the object of a verb. They can express a purpose. They can also follow certain adjectives.

> **To protect chimpanzees** is our goal. [subject]
> Animal welfare groups are trying **to raise money**. [object of verb *are trying*]
> Chimps are being used **to help humans**. [expresses purpose]
> Infant chimpanzees are easy **to handle**. [follows adjective *easy*]

Practice

Copy the sentences below into your notebook. Circle the gerund or infinitive in each sentence. Then use the examples on this page to identify how the gerund or infinitive is used in the sentence.

1. Chimpanzees use crumpled leaves to soak up water.
2. Young chimps learn by imitating what they have seen.
3. Chimpanzees cannot learn to speak words.
4. Studying chimpanzees has taught us a lot about ourselves.
5. Lonely and bored, Jojo was happy to see Jane Goodall.

Include Quotations and Citations

One effective way to support your ideas in a research report is to use quotations. Whenever you quote text word for word, you must place the text within quotation marks. After the quotation, you must also provide a citation, information telling the source of the quote. There are many ways to cite sources. See pages 449–450 for some common methods.

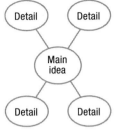

This paragraph from a research report includes a quotation and a citation. Before writing, the writer listed his ideas in a graphic organizer.

Adrian Perez

Amazing Chimpanzees

Chimpanzees are like humans in many ways. They can make and use simple tools. They can use reason to solve problems. They feel emotions such as joy and grief. At one time, scientists believed that learning and using language were abilities that separated human beings from other animals. But a chimpanzee named Washoe changed all that. Washoe was a forty-two-year-old chimpanzee who learned American Sign Language from her trainers, Allen and Beatrice Gardner. Washoe knew about 250 signs. Even more remarkably, Washoe taught her son over 50 signs all on her own. Washoe was part of the Chimpanzee and Human Communication Institute, an organization that studies chimpanzee behavior and communication. The institute is dedicated to educating people about the need to protect chimpanzees in the wild and in captivity. As Jane Goodall asks, "Don't they deserve to be treated with the same sort of consideration we accord to other highly sensitive beings: ourselves?" ("Chimpanzee Central")

Works Consulted List

"Chimpanzee Central." *The Jane Goodall Institute*. September 2007 27 September 2009. <http://www.janegoodall.org/chimpcentral/default.asp>

Practice

Write a paragraph that includes a quotation and a citation. List your ideas in a graphic organizer. Use gerunds and infinitives correctly.

Writing Checklist

SENTENCE FLUENCY:
☑ My paragraph flows naturally.

CONVENTIONS:
☑ I used gerunds and infinitives correctly.

381

Link the Readings

Critical Thinking

Look back at the readings in this unit. Think about what they have in common. They all tell about amazing animals. Yet they do not all have the same purpose. The purpose of one reading might be to inform, while the purpose of another might be to entertain or persuade. In addition, the content of each reading relates to amazing animals differently. Now copy the chart below into your notebook and complete it.

Title of Reading	Purpose	Big Question Link
"The Parrot Who Wouldn't Say 'Cataño'"		
"Getting to Know Real Bats"	*to inform*	
"The Bat" "A Narrow Fellow in the Grass" "Daybreak" "Birdfoot's Grandpa"		*Each animal is amazing in its own way.*
From *The Chimpanzees I Love*		

Discussion

Discuss in pairs or small groups.

- What do "Getting to Know Real Bats" and the excerpt from *The Chimpanzees I Love* have in common?

- **Q** **What makes animals so amazing?** What do you think is amazing about the animals you studied in this unit?

Fluency Check

Work with a partner. Choose a paragraph from one of the readings. Take turns reading it for one minute. Count the total number of words you read. Practice saying the words you had trouble reading. Take turns reading the paragraph three more times. Did you read more words each time? Copy the chart below into your notebook and record your speeds.

	1st Speed	2nd Speed	3rd Speed	4th Speed
Words Per Minute				

Projects

Work in pairs or small groups. Choose one of these projects.

1 Many poets have written about animals. For example, T. S. Eliot wrote a book of poetry about cats called *Old Possum's Book of Practical Cats*. Write a poem about a pet or an animal you saw at the zoo. Read your poem to the class.

2 Animal rights groups—such as People for the Ethical Treatment of Animals (PETA)—fight to stop the use of animals for fur and leather and animal testing for cosmetics and medicine. Call your local PETA group and interview a member to find out more about the organization. Share your findings with the class.

3 Almost all communities have animal shelters or sanctuaries. Go to your local animal shelter or sanctuary and find out how you can become a volunteer. Make a poster to recruit volunteers. Then share your poster with the class.

4 Changes to an animal's habitat can have a great impact on the animal. Do research to find out how changes in a particular animal's habitat are affecting the animal. Present your findings in a poster.

Further Reading

To find out more about the theme of this unit, choose from these reading suggestions.

Jim Smiley and His Jumping Frog and Other Stories, Mark Twain
This Penguin Reader® collection includes Twain's humorous story of a jumping-frog contest during California's Gold Rush days.

Never Cry Wolf, Farley Mowat
The author, an animal behaviorist, lived alone on the frozen tundra, learning about the arctic wolves and caribou.

The Compassion of Animals: True Stories of Animal Courage and Kindness, Kristin Von Kreisler
This collection of true stories tells about animals who risked their lives to keep the humans they love out of danger.

LISTENING & SPEAKING WORKSHOP

TV Documentary

A TV documentary is a show that provides information about something in the real world. It is longer and more detailed than a TV news report. Documentaries usually include narration, interviews, film clips, photos, and other visuals. With a group, you will present a documentary about an animal, animal species, or organization that works with animals.

1 **THINK ABOUT IT** Work in small groups. Discuss what you have learned about animals in this unit. Which animals did you find most interesting? What animals would you like to learn more about? Make a list of possible topics for your documentary. Here are some examples:

- How elephants communicate
- The importance of bees
- Manatees: what they are and why they're endangered
- Koko the gorilla/The Gorilla Language Project

Work with your group members to choose a topic for your documentary.

2 **GATHER AND ORGANIZE INFORMATION** As a group, list facts you already know about your topic and questions you want to have answered. You can look at an encyclopedia or a website for ideas. Remember to ask *Who*, *What*, *When*, *Where*, and *Why* questions.

Research Research your topic at the library or on the Internet. Coordinate your efforts with other group members to avoid duplicating work. Take notes and look for useful visuals as you read.

Order Your Notes Share your notes with the group members. Together, decide which information to include in your documentary, and arrange it in an order that makes sense. Make an outline for your presentation, and work with your group members to assign tasks. Prepare questions to ask in real or role-played interviews. Make note cards to use during your part of the documentary.

Use Visuals List the visuals you'll need. Decide who will find or make each one. Use a variety of images, including photos and maps. If a video recorder is available, you can film interviews with people. You can also role-play an interview during your presentation, letting one student play an expert.

3 PRACTICE AND PRESENT

Practice your part until you know it well. Use your note cards only as a memory aid. Then practice your documentary with your group members. Listen carefully to each other, and give suggestions to help make the presentation clearer and more interesting. If you plan to show video clips, make sure you have the necessary equipment and know how to use it. Practice as a group until the whole presentation runs smoothly.

Deliver Your TV Documentary Present your documentary to the class. When it's your turn to speak, face the audience (or imaginary TV camera) and speak loudly and clearly. Hold up your visuals and/or pass them around the class at appropriate times.

4 EVALUATE THE PRESENTATION

You will improve your skills as a speaker and a listener by evaluating each presentation you give and hear. Use this checklist to help you judge your documentary and the documentaries of your classmates.

- ☑ Was the topic of the documentary interesting? Was it well researched?
- ☑ Did the visuals illustrate the most important points clearly?
- ☑ Did the documentary answer the 5Ws: *who, what, when, where,* and *why*?
- ☑ Was the group well prepared?
- ☑ What suggestions do you have for improving the documentary?

WRITING WORKSHOP
Research Report

In a research report, writers explain a topic they have studied in detail. They include information gathered from different sources. A good research report begins with a paragraph that introduces the writer's topic and main ideas. Each body paragraph focuses on a main idea. Facts, details, and examples support each main idea. A concluding paragraph summarizes the writer's main points. The report includes a complete list of the writer's sources.

Your assignment for this workshop is to write a five-paragraph research report about an idea, issue, or event related to animals.

1 **PREWRITE** Select a topic that interests you. Make sure the topic is narrow enough to cover in five paragraphs. Then write a question to direct your research. Possible research sources include books about your topic, newspapers, magazines, encyclopedias, and websites. Take notes and list your sources.

List and Organize Ideas and Details Use your notes to create an outline. A student named Evan decided to write about endangered species. Here is the outline he prepared:

I. Introduce the problem of species endangerment
    A. Animals slow to adapt to surroundings
    B. Humans quick to alter environment
II. How many endangered species are in the world today?
    A. Total amount of endangered species: 16,118
    B. Recent addition of lichens and mushrooms
III. What are some reasons for animal endangerment associated with human interaction?
    A. Deforestation
    B. Poaching
    C. Toxic chemicals
IV. What are some organizations and activities that promote wildlife protection?
    A. Wildlife Conservation Society
    B. Endangered Species Act passed in 1973 in U.S.
V. Conclude on species endangerment
    A. Enforcement of laws needed to preserve wildlife
    B. Combined efforts of lawmakers, experts, and public

2 **DRAFT** Use the model on pages 388–389 and your outline to help you write a first draft. Remember to begin with a paragraph that clearly presents your topic. Be sure to use your own words when you write your report. If you use exact words from a source, punctuate the quotation correctly. List all your sources accurately at the end of your report.

Citing Sources Look at the style, punctuation, and order of information in the following sources. Use these examples as models.

Book
Stanchak, John. Civil War. New York: Dorling Kindersley, 2000.

Magazine article
Kirn, Walter. "Lewis and Clark: The Journey That Changed America Forever." [Time 8 July 2002]: 36–41.

Internet website
Smith, Gene. "The Structure of the Milky Way." Gene Smith's Astronomy Tutorial. 28 April 1999. Center for Astrophysics & Space Sciences, University of California, San Diego. 20 July 2009 <http://casswww.ucsd.edu/public/tutorial/MW.html>.

Encyclopedia article
Siple, Paul A. "Antarctica." World Book Encyclopedia. 1991 ed.

---

3 **REVISE** Read over your draft. As you do so, ask yourself the questions in the writing checklist. Use the questions to help you revise your report.

SIX TRAITS OF WRITING CHECKLIST

- ☑ **IDEAS:** Does my first paragraph introduce my topic in an engaging way?
- ☑ **ORGANIZATION:** Do facts, examples, and details support the main idea in each paragraph?
- ☑ **VOICE:** Are my tone and style appropriately formal?
- ☑ **WORD CHOICE:** Do I use transitions to connect ideas?
- ☑ **SENTENCE FLUENCY:** Do my sentences vary in length and rhythm?
- ☑ **CONVENTIONS:** Does my writing follow the rules of grammar, usage, and mechanics?

Here are the changes Evan plans to make when he revises his first draft:

Endangered Species

Over the last couple of centuries, steadily advancing technology has greatly improved the lives of people at the expense of plant and animal species. The endangerment of plants and animals, along with the fragile ecosystems on which they depend, is a widespread problem that is. It has sparked much debate. Plants and animals adapt to changes in their surroundings only over an extended period of time, while humans can change their environment very quickly to suit their needs.

Data for the number of endangered species is published yearly in a pamphlet called the <u>Red Data Book</u> by the International Union for the Conservation of Nature and Natural Resources (IUCN). According to the IUCN's statistics the total number of endangered species was 16,118 in the year 2006. It is also interesting to see that the <u>Others</u> category, which is composed of mushrooms and lichens, has been added recently ("Table 1").

One human activity that has a negative effect on wildlife is deforestation. Each day thousands of acres of rainforest are cleared, land which is known to nourishes more than half the world's plant and animal species on only seven percent of the earth's surface (Collins). Hunting also extremely damaging is, especially illegal hunting by poachers. A third activity that threatens many species is the use of

388

toxic chemicals such as DDT. ~~It~~ works by "hitching a ride on the food chain, first getting into plants, then the animals that eat plants, then animals that eat animals (Lampton 50).

Several international groups have been formed to raise awareness of endangered animal and plant life, such as the Wildlife Conservation Society. Laws have been passed ~~for protecting~~ endangered species. An example is the endangered species act of 1973, which officially prohibited any endangered or potentially threatened species from being brought into the united States (Stefoff 97).

Wildlife endangerment has received much attention but many protections have not been enforced, making them useless. If action is not taken now, tropical rainforests may all disappear within the next century (Collins). With the help of lawmakers, scientific experts, and the public, the idea of a peaceful coexistence between humans and other living things could become closer to a reality.

Works Consulted List

Collins, Jocelyn. "Biodiversity." <u>EnviroFacts</u>. 1 Feb. 2001. 23 May 2009
   <http://www.bcb.uwc.ac.za/Envfacts/facts/biodiversity.htm>.

Lampton, Christopher. <u>Endangered Species</u>. New York: Franklin Watts, 1988.

Stefoff, Rebecca. <u>Extinction</u>. New York: Chelsea House Publishers, New York, 1992.

"Table 1: Numbers of threatened species by major groups of organisms."
   <u>The IUCN Red List of Threatened Species</u>. 13 Dec. 2006. International Union
   for Conservation of Nature and Natural Resources. 23 May 2009
   <http://www.iucnredlist.org/info/tables/table1>.

Copy your revised draft onto a clean sheet of paper. Read it again. Correct any errors in grammar, word usage, mechanics, and spelling. Here are the additional changes Evan plans to make when he prepares his final draft.

Evan Arbogast

Endangered Species

Over the last couple of centuries, steadily advancing technology has greatly improved the lives of people at the expense of plant and animal species. Plants and animals adapt to changes in their surroundings only over an extended period of time, while humans can change their environment very quickly to suit their needs. The endangerment of plants and animals, along with the fragile ecosystems on which they depend, is a widespread problem that has sparked much debate.

Data for the number of endangered species is published yearly in a pamphlet called the <u>Red Data Book</u> by the International Union for the Conservation of Nature and Natural Resources (IUCN). According to the IUCN's statistics the total number of endangered species was 16,118 in the year 2006. It is also interesting to see that the <u>Others</u> category, composed of mushrooms and lichens, has been added recently ("Table 1").

One human activity that has a negative effect on wildlife is deforestation. Each day thousands of acres of rainforest are cleared, land that nourishes more than half the world's plant and animal species on only seven percent of the earth's surface (Collins). Hunting is also extremely damaging, especially illegal hunting by poachers. A third activity that threatens many species is the use of toxic chemicals such as DDT, which works by "hitching a ride on the food chain," first getting into plants, then the animals that eat plants, then animals that eat animals (Lampton 50).

Several international groups have been formed to raise awareness of endangered animal and plant life, such as the Wildlife Conservation Society. In addition to the efforts of conservation groups, laws have been passed to protect endangered species. An example is the Endangered Species Act of 1973, which officially prohibited any endangered or potentially threatened species from being brought into the united States (Stefoff 97).

Wildlife endangerment has received much attention but many protections have not been enforced, making them useless. If action is not taken now, tropical rainforests may all disappear within the next century (Collins). However, with the help of lawmakers, scientific experts, and the public, the idea of a peaceful coexistence between humans and other living things could become closer to a reality.

Works Consulted List

Collins, Jocelyn. "Biodiversity." <u>EnviroFacts</u>. 1 Feb. 2001. 23 May 2009
    <http://www.bcb.uwc.ac.za/Envfacts/facts/biodiversity.htm>.

Lampton, Christopher. <u>Endangered Species</u>. New York: Franklin Watts, 1988.

Stefoff, Rebecca. <u>Extinction</u>. New York: Chelsea House Publishers, New York, 1992.

"Table 1: Numbers of threatened species by major groups of organisms."
    <u>The IUCN Red List of Threatened Species</u>. 13 Dec. 2006. International Union
    for Conservation of Nature and Natural Resources. 23 May 2009
    <http://www.iucnredlist.org/info/tables/table1>.

5 **PUBLISH** Prepare your final draft. Share your essay with your teacher and classmates.

Workbook
Page 190

391

Animals in Human Society

*A*rtists have captured the animal world in many different ways. Some try to reproduce every detail so the creature seems alive and about to jump off the canvas. Others use fantastic colors and shapes to capture the essence or spirit of an animal. All want to celebrate or understand the other life forms that share planet Earth with us.

John Steuart Curry, *Ajax* (1936–37)

In *Ajax*, John Steuart Curry painted a lifelike portrait of an all-American bull. He deliberately placed the animal on a growing field, because so many farmers in the United States had lost their farms during the terrible economic depression of the 1930s. He wanted to capture hope and success, not failure.

Curry placed his bull on the crest of a hill in the center of the painting. The animal's huge brown side seems grand against the big, white clouds in the sky. Two small birds fly around the bull and eat insects off of its back. Their tiny size highlights the bull's enormous size. Fertile green fields stretch into the distance in the background. Curry's American landscape is one of energy, power, and bounty.

▲ John Steuart Curry, *Ajax*, 1936–37, oil, 36 × 48¼ in., Smithsonian American Art Museum

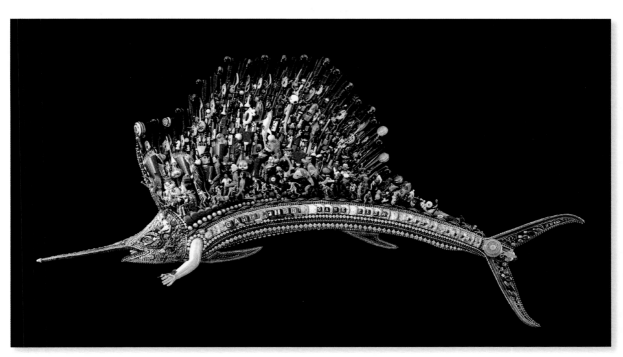

▲ Larry Fuente, *Game Fish*, 1988, mixed media, 51½ x 112½ x 10¾ in., Smithsonian American Art Museum

Larry Fuente, *Game Fish* (1988)

In *Game Fish*, Larry Fuente combines the real with the imaginary. He attached brightly colored beads, buttons, coins and game-related items onto a swordfish frame. He is making fun using the traditional trophy fish that fishermen often hang on the walls of their homes. On the fin he added dozens of plastic statues of some children's favorite play figures: Mickey Mouse, Superman, even monkeys from a popular game called Barrel of Monkeys. The work's title is repeated in individual letters from children's building blocks or word games and mounted on the curving arch of the fish's side.

A human arm pops out of the side of the fish near the head. The hand holds a red-tipped dart. The armed fish now becomes the hunter instead of the hunted!

Both of these artists focus on a single animal. But they use that animal to make different statements about people's relationship with nature.

Apply What You Learned

1 Which of these artworks do you think tries to capture the essence or spirit of the animal? Explain.

2 Do you think these two artists have similar feelings about animals? Why or why not?

Q Big Question
In what way does each of these artworks make a statement about animals in human society?

Workbook
Pages 191–192

393

Contents
Handbooks and Resources

Study Skills and Language Learning

HOW TO LEARN LANGUAGE

Learning a language takes time, but, just like learning to swim, it can be fun. Whether you're learning English for the first time or adding to your knowledge of English by learning academic or content-area words, you're giving yourself a better chance of success in your studies and in your everyday life.

Learning any language is a skill that requires you to be active. You listen, speak, read, and write when you learn a language. Here are some tips that will help you learn English more actively and efficiently.

Listening

1. Set a purpose for listening. Think about what you hope to learn from today's class. Listen for these things as your teacher and classmates speak.

2. Listen actively. You can think faster than others can speak. This is useful because it allows you to anticipate what will be said next. Take notes as you listen. Write down only what is most important, and keep your notes short.

3. If you find something difficult to understand, listen more carefully. Do not give up and stop listening. Write down questions to ask afterward.

4. The more you listen, the faster you will learn. Use the radio, television, and Internet to practice your listening skills.

Speaking

1. Pay attention to sentence structure as you speak. Are you saying the words in the correct order?

2. Think about what you are saying. Don't worry about speaking fast. It's more important to communicate what you mean.

3. Practice speaking as much as you can, both in class and in your free time. Consider reading aloud to improve your pronunciation. If possible, record yourself speaking.

4. Do not be afraid of making mistakes. Everyone makes mistakes!

Reading

1. Read every day. Read as many different things as possible: Books, magazines, newspapers, and websites will all help you improve your comprehension and increase your vocabulary.

2. Try to understand what you are reading as a whole, rather than focusing on individual words. If you find a word you do not know, see if you can figure out its meaning from the context of the sentence before you look it up in a dictionary. Make a list of new vocabulary words and review it regularly.

3. Read texts more than once. Often your comprehension of a passage will improve if you read it twice or three times.

4. Try reading literature, poems, and plays aloud. This will help you understand them. It will also give you practice pronouncing new words.

Writing

1. Write something every day to improve your writing fluency. You can write about anything that interests you. Consider keeping a diary or a journal so that you can monitor your progress as time passes.

2. Plan your writing before you begin. Use graphic organizers to help you organize your ideas.

3. Be aware of sentence structure and grammar. Always write a first draft. Then go back and check for errors before you write your final version.

HOW TO BUILD VOCABULARY

1. Improving Your Vocabulary
Listening and Speaking

The most common ways to increase your vocabulary are listening, reading, and taking part in conversations. One of the most important skills in language learning is listening. Listen for new words when talking with others, joining in discussions, listening to the radio or audio books, or watching television.

You can find out the meanings of the words by asking, listening for clues, and looking up the words in a dictionary. Don't be embarrassed about asking what a word means. It shows that you are listening and that you want to learn. Whenever you can, use the new words you learn in conversation.

Reading Aloud

Listening to texts read aloud is another good way to build your vocabulary. There are many audio books available, and most libraries have a collection of them. When you listen to an audio book, you hear how new words are pronounced and how they are used. If you have a printed copy of the book, read along as you listen so that you can both see and hear new words.

Reading Often

Usually, people use a larger variety of words when they write than when they speak. The more you read, the more new words you'll find. When you see new words over and over again, they will become familiar to you and you'll begin to use them. Read from different sources—books, newspapers, magazines, Internet websites—in order to find a wide variety of words.

2. Figuring Out What a Word Means
Using Context Clues

When you come across a new word, you may not always need to use a dictionary. You might be able to figure out its meaning using the context, or the words in the sentence or paragraph in which you found it. Sometimes the surrounding words contain clues to tell you what the new word means.

Here are some tips for using context clues:
- Read the sentence, leaving out the word you don't know.
- Find clues in the sentence to figure out the new word's meaning.
- Read the sentence again, but replace the word you don't know with another possible meaning.
- Check your possible meaning by looking up the word in the dictionary. Write the word and its definition in your vocabulary notebook.

398

3. Practicing Your New Words

To make a word part of your vocabulary, study its definition, use it in your writing and speaking, and review it to make sure that you really understand its meaning.

Use one or more of these ways to remember the meanings of new words.

Keep a Vocabulary Notebook

Keep a notebook for vocabulary words. Divide your pages into three columns: the new words; hint words that help you remember their meanings; and their definitions. Test yourself by covering either the second or third column.

Word	Hint	Definition
zoology	zoo	study of animals
fortunate	fortune	lucky
quizzical	quiz	questioning

Make Flashcards

On the front of an index card, write a word you want to remember. On the back, write the meaning. You can also write a sentence that uses the word in context. Test yourself by flipping through the cards. Enter any hard words in your vocabulary notebook. As you learn the meanings, remove these cards and add new ones.

Say the Word Aloud

A useful strategy for building vocabulary is to say the new word aloud. Do not worry that there is no one to say the word to. Just say the word loud and clear several times. This will make you feel more confident and help you to use the word in conversation.

Record Yourself

Record your vocabulary words. Leave a ten-second space after each word, and then say the meaning and a sentence using the word. Play the recording. Fill in the blank space with the meaning and a sentence. Replay the recording until you memorize the word.

HOW TO USE REFERENCE BOOKS

The Dictionary

When you look up a word in the dictionary, you find the word and information about it. The word and the information about it are called a dictionary entry. Each entry tells you the word's spelling, pronunciation, part of speech, and meaning. Many English words have more than one meaning. Some words, such as *handle*, can be both a noun and a verb. For such words, the meanings, or definitions, are numbered. Sometimes example sentences are given in italics to help you understand how the word is used.

Here is part of a dictionary page with its important features labeled.

Pronunciation   **Part of Speech**

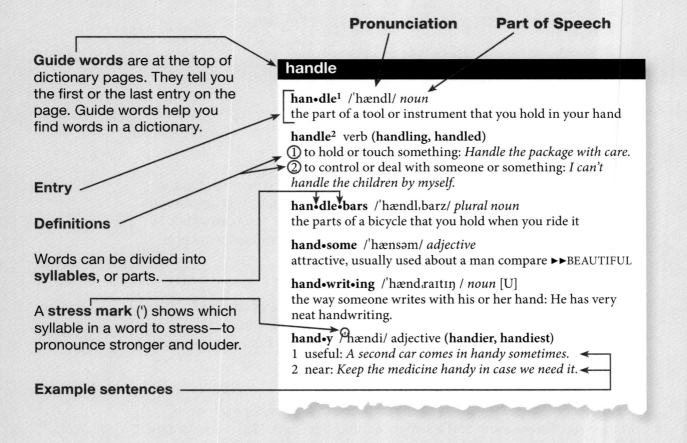

Guide words are at the top of dictionary pages. They tell you the first or the last entry on the page. Guide words help you find words in a dictionary.

Entry

Definitions

Words can be divided into **syllables**, or parts.

A **stress mark** (') shows which syllable in a word to stress—to pronounce stronger and louder.

Example sentences

handle

han·dle¹ /ˈhændl/ *noun*
the part of a tool or instrument that you hold in your hand

handle² verb (**handling, handled**)
① to hold or touch something: *Handle the package with care.*
② to control or deal with someone or something: *I can't handle the children by myself.*

han·dle·bars /ˈhændlˌbarz/ *plural noun*
the parts of a bicycle that you hold when you ride it

hand·some /ˈhænsəm/ *adjective*
attractive, usually used about a man compare ►►BEAUTIFUL

hand·writ·ing /ˈhændˌraɪtɪŋ/ *noun* [U]
the way someone writes with his or her hand: *He has very neat handwriting.*

hand·y /ˈhændi/ *adjective* (**handier, handiest**)
1 useful: *A second car comes in handy sometimes.*
2 near: *Keep the medicine handy in case we need it.*

400

The Thesaurus

A thesaurus is a kind of dictionary. It is a specialized dictionary that lists synonyms, or words with similar meanings, for words. You can use a print thesaurus (a book) or an online thesaurus on the Internet.

A thesaurus is a useful writing tool because it can help you avoid repeating the same word. It can also help you choose more precise words. Using a thesaurus regularly can help build your vocabulary by increasing the number of words you know that are related by an idea or concept.

In a thesaurus, words may either be arranged alphabetically or be grouped by theme. When the arrangement is by theme, you first have to look up the word in the index to find out in which grouping its synonyms will appear. When the thesaurus is arranged alphabetically, you simply look up the word as you would in a dictionary.

The entry below is from a thesaurus that is arranged alphabetically.

sad *adjective* Tending to cause sadness or low spirits : blue, cheerless, depressed, depressing, dismal, dispiriting, downcast, gloomy, heartbreaking, joyless, melancholy, miserable, poignant, sorrowful, unhappy. See **happy** (antonym) in index.
—See also **depressed, sorrowful**.

Choose synonyms carefully. You can see from the thesaurus entry above that there are many synonyms for the word *sad*. However, not all of these words may be the ones you want to use. For example, *depressed* can mean that you have an illness called depression, but it can also mean that you feel sad. If you are not sure what a word means, look it up in a dictionary to check that it is, in fact, the word you want to use.

HOW TO TAKE TESTS

In this section, you will learn some ways to improve your test-taking skills.

1. Taking Tests

Objective tests are tests in which each question has only one correct answer. To prepare for these tests, you should study the material that the test covers.

Preview the Test

1. Write your name on each sheet of paper you will hand in.
2. Look over the test to get an idea of the kinds of questions being asked.
3. Find out whether you lose points for incorrect answers. If you do, do not guess at answers.
4. Decide how much time you need to spend on each section of the test.
5. Use the time well. Give the most time to questions that are hardest or worth the most points.

Answer the Questions

1. Answer the easy questions first. Put a check next to harder questions and come back to them later.
2. If permitted, use scratch paper to write down your ideas.
3. Read each question at least twice before answering.
4. Answer all questions on the test (unless guessing can cost you points).
5. Do not change your first answer without a good reason.

Proofread Your Answers

1. Check that you followed the directions completely.
2. Reread questions and answers. Make sure you answered all the questions.

2. Answering Different Kinds of Questions

This section tells you about different kinds of test questions and gives you specific strategies for answering them.

True-or-False Questions

True-or-false questions ask you to decide whether or not a statement is true.

1. If a statement seems true, make sure that it is *all* true.
2. Pay special attention to the word *not*. It often changes the meaning of a statement entirely.
3. Pay attention to words that have a general meaning, such as *all*, *always*, *never*, *no*, *none*, and *only*. They often make a statement false.
4. Pay attention to words that qualify, such as *generally*, *much*, *many*, *most*, *often*, *sometimes*, and *usually*. They often make a statement true.

Multiple-Choice Questions

This kind of question asks you to choose from four or five possible answers.

1. Try to answer the question before reading the choices. If your answer is one of the choices, choose that answer.
2. Eliminate answers you know are wrong. Cross them out if you are allowed to write on the test paper.

Matching Questions

Matching questions ask you to match items in one group with items in another group.

1. Count each group to see whether any items will be left over.
2. Read all the items before you start matching.
3. Match the items you know first, and then match the others. If you can write on the paper, cross out items as you use them.

Fill-In Questions

A fill-in question asks you to give an answer in your own words.

1. Read the question or exercise carefully.
2. If you are completing a sentence, look for clues in the sentence that might help you figure out the answer. If the word *an* is right before the missing word, this means that the missing word begins with a vowel sound.

Short-Answer Questions

Short-answer questions ask you to write one or more sentences in which you give certain information.

1. Scan the question for key words, such as *explain*, *compare*, and *identify*.
2. When you answer the question, give only the information asked for.
3. Answer the question as clearly as possible.

Essay Questions

On many tests, you will have to write one or more essays. Sometimes you are given a choice of questions that you can answer.

1. Look for key words in the question or questions to find out exactly what information you should give.
2. Take a few minutes to think about facts, examples, and other types of information you can put in your essay.
3. Spend most of your time writing your essay so that it is well planned.
4. Leave time at the end of the test to proofread and correct your work.

STUDY SKILLS AND LEARNING STRATEGIES

1. Understanding the Parts of a Book
The Title Page
Every book has a **title page** that states the title, author, and publisher.

The Table of Contents and Headings
Many books have a **table of contents**. The table of contents can be found in the front of the book. It lists the chapters or units in the book. Beside each chapter or unit is the number of the page on which it begins. A **heading** at the top of the first page of each section tells you what that section is about.

The Glossary
While you read, you can look up unfamiliar words in the **glossary** at the back of the book. It lists words alphabetically and gives definitions.

The Index
To find out whether a book includes particular information, use the **index** at the . back of the book. It is an alphabetical listing of names, places, and subjects in the book. Page numbers are listed beside each item.

The Bibliography
The **bibliography** is at the end of a nonfiction book or article. It tells you the other books or sources where an author got information to write the book. The sources are listed alphabetically by author. The bibliography is also a good way to find more articles or information about the same subject.

2. Using the Library
The Card Catalog
To find a book in a library, use the **card catalog**—an alphabetical list of authors, subjects, and titles. Each book has a **call number**, which tells you where to find a book on the shelf. Author cards, title cards, and subject cards all give information about a book. Use the **author card** when you want to find a book by an author but do not know the title. The **title card** is useful if you know the title of a book but not the author. When you want to find a book about a particular subject, use the **subject card**.

The Online Library Catalog
The **online library catalog** is a fast way to find a book using a computer. Books can be looked up by author, subject, or title. The online catalog will give you information on the book, as well as its call number.

3. Learning Strategies

Strategy	Description and Examples
Organizational Planning	Setting a learning goal; planning how to carry out a project, write a story, or solve a problem
Predicting	Using parts of a text (such as illustrations or titles) or a real-life situation and your own knowledge to anticipate what will occur next
Self-Management	Seeking or arranging the conditions that help you learn
Using Your Knowledge and Experience	Using knowledge and experience to learn something new, brainstorm, make associations, or write or tell what you know
Monitoring Comprehension	Being aware of how well a task is going, how well you understand what you are hearing or reading, or how well you are conveying ideas
Using/Making Rules	Applying a rule (phonics, decoding, grammar, linguistic, mathematical, scientific, and so on) to understand a text or complete a task; figuring out rules or patterns from examples
Taking Notes	Writing down key information in verbal, graphic, or numerical form, often as concept maps, word webs, timelines, or other graphic organizers
Visualizing	Creating mental pictures and using them to understand and appreciate descriptive writing
Cooperation	Working with classmates to complete a task or project, demonstrate a process or product, share knowledge, solve problems, give and receive feedback, and develop social skills
Making Inferences	Using the context of a text and your own knowledge to guess meanings of unfamiliar words or ideas
Substitution	Using a synonym or paraphrasing when you want to express an idea and do not know the word(s)
Using Resources	Using reference materials (books, dictionaries, encyclopedias, videos, computer programs, the Internet) to find information or complete a task
Classification	Grouping words, ideas, objects, or numbers according to their attributes; constructing graphic organizers to show classifications
Asking Questions	Negotiating meaning by asking for clarification, confirmation, rephrasing, or examples
Summarizing	Making a summary of something you listened to or read; retelling a text in your own words
Self-evaluation	After completing a task, judging how well you did, whether you reached your goal, and how effective your problem-solving procedures were

Grammar Handbook

In English there are eight **parts of speech**: nouns, pronouns, adjectives, verbs, adverbs, prepositions, conjunctions, and interjections.

Nouns

Nouns name people, places, or things. There are two kinds of nouns: **common nouns** and **proper nouns**.

A **common noun** is a general person, place, or thing.

> person   thing   place
> The **student** brings a **notebook** to **class**.

A **proper noun** is a specific person, place, or thing. Proper nouns start with a capital letter.

> person   place   thing
> **Joseph** went to **Paris** and saw the **Eiffel Tower**.

A noun that is made up of two words is called a **compound noun**. A compound noun can be one word or two words. Some compound nouns have hyphens.

> One word: **newspaper, bathroom**
> Two words: **vice president, pet shop**
> Hyphens: **sister-in-law, grown-up**

Articles identify nouns. *A, an,* and *the* are articles.

A and *an* are called **indefinite articles**. Use the article *a* or *an* to talk about one general person, place, or thing.

Use *an* before a word that begins with a vowel sound.

> I have **an** idea.

406

Use *a* before a word that begins with a consonant sound.

> May I borrow **a** pen?

The is called a **definite article**. Use *the* to talk about one or more specific people, places, or things.

> Please bring me **the** box from your room.
> **The** books are in my backpack.

Pronouns

Pronouns are words that take the place of nouns or proper nouns. In this example, the pronoun *she* replaces, or refers to, the proper noun *Angela*.

> proper noun   pronoun
> **Angela** is not home. **She** is babysitting.

Pronouns can be subjects or objects. They can be singular or plural.

	Subject Pronouns	Object Pronouns
Singular	I, you, he, she, it	me, you, him, her, it
Plural	we, you, they	us, you, them

A **subject pronoun** replaces a noun or proper noun that is the subject of a sentence. A **subject** is who or what a sentence is about. In these sentences, *He* replaces *Daniel*.

> subject   subject pronoun (singular)
> **Daniel** is a student. **He** goes to school every day.

In these sentences, *We* replaces *Heather* and *I*.

> subject   subject pronoun (plural)
> **Heather** and **I** like this movie. **We** think it's great.

An **object pronoun** replaces a noun or proper noun that is the object of a verb. A verb tells the action in a sentence. An **object** receives the action of a verb.

In these sentences the verb is *gave*. *Him* replaces *Ed*, which is the object of the verb.

Lauren gave **Ed** the notes. Lauren gave **him** the notes.

An object pronoun can also replace a noun or proper noun that is the **object of a preposition**. Prepositions are words like *for, to,* or *with*. In these sentences, the preposition is *with*. *Them* replaces *José* and *Yolanda*, which is the object of the preposition.

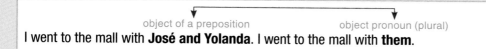

I went to the mall with **José and Yolanda**. I went to the mall with **them**.

Pronouns can also be possessive. A **possessive pronoun** replaces a noun or proper noun. It shows who owns something.

	Possessive Pronouns
Singular	mine, yours, hers, his
Plural	ours, yours, theirs

In these sentences, *hers* replaces the words *Kyoko's coat*. It shows that Kyoko owns the coat.

It is **Kyoko's coat**. It is **hers**.

Adjectives

Adjectives describe nouns. An adjective usually comes before the noun it describes.

tall grass　　　　　**big** truck　　　　　**two** kittens

An adjective can also come *after* the noun it describes.

The bag is **heavy**. The books are **new**.

Do not add -*s* to adjectives that describe plural nouns.

the **red** houses　　　　　the **funny** jokes　　　　　the **smart** teachers

Verbs

Verbs express an action or a state of being.

subject　verb　　　　　　　　subject　verb Jackie **walks** to school. The school **is** near her house.

An **action verb** tells what someone or something does or did. You cannot always see the action of an action verb.

Verbs That Tell Actions You Can See		Verbs That Tell Actions You Cannot See	
dance	swim	know	sense
play	talk	remember	name
sit	write	think	understand

A **linking verb** shows no action. It links the subject with another word that describes the subject.

Linking Verbs		
look	is	appear
smell	are	seem
sound	am	become
taste	were	
feel		

In this sentence, the adjective *tired* tells something about the subject, *dog*. *Seems* is the linking verb.

> Our dog **seems** tired.

In this sentence, the noun *friend* tells something about the subject, *brother*. *Is* is the linking verb.

> Your brother **is** my friend.

A **helping verb** comes before the main verb. It adds to the main verb's meaning. Helping verbs can be forms of the verbs *be*, *do*, or *have*.

	Helping Verbs
Forms of *be*	am, was, is, were, are
Forms of *do*	do, did, does
Forms of *have*	have, had, has
Other helping verbs	can, must, could, have (to), should, may, will, would

In this sentence, *am* is the helping verb; *walking* is the action verb.

> helping action
> verb   verb
> I **am walking** to my science class.

In this sentence, *has* is the helping verb; *completed* is the action verb.

> helping   action
> verb   verb
> He **has completed** his essay.

In questions, the subject comes between a helping verb and a main verb.

> person
> **Did** Liang **give** you the CD?

Adverbs

Adverbs describe the action of verbs. They tell *how* an action happens. Adverbs answer the question *Where? When? How? How much?* or *How often?*

Many adverbs end in *-ly.*

easily	slowly	carefully

Some adverbs do not end in *-ly.*

seldom	fast	very

In this sentence, the adverb *everywhere* modifies the verb *looked.* It answers the question *Where?*

> verb   adverb
> Nicole looked **everywhere** for her cell phone.

In this sentence, the adverb *quickly* modifies the verb *walked.* It answers the question *How?*

> verb   adverb
> They walked home **quickly**.

Adverbs also modify adjectives. They answer the question *How much?* or *How little?*

In this sentence, the adjective *dangerous* modifies the noun *road.* The adverb *very* modifies the adjective *dangerous.*

> adverb adjective noun
> This is a **very** dangerous road.

Adverbs can also modify other adverbs. In this sentence, the adverb *fast* modifies the verb *runs.* The adverb *quite* modifies the adverb *fast.*

> verb adverb adverb
> John runs **quite** fast.

Prepositions

Prepositions can show time, place, and direction.

Time	Place	Direction
after	above	across
before	below	down
during	in	into
since	near	to
until	under	up

In this sentence, the preposition *above* shows where the bird flew. It shows place.

> preposition
> A bird flew **above** my head.

In this sentence, the preposition *across* shows direction.

> preposition
> The children walked **across** the street.

A **prepositional phrase** starts with a preposition and ends with a noun or pronoun.

In this sentence, the preposition is *near* and the noun is *school*.

> prepositional phrase
> The library is **near the new school**.

Conjunctions

A **conjunction** joins words, groups of words, and whole sentences.

Conjunctions			
and	for	or	yet
but	nor	so	

In this sentence, the conjunction *and* joins two proper nouns: *Jonah*
and *Teresa*.

> noun   noun
> Jonah **and** Teresa are in school.

In this sentence, the conjunction *or* joins two prepositional phrases: *to the movies*
and *to the mall*.

> prepositional   prepositional
> ┌─ phrase ─┐ ┌ phrase ┐
> They want to go to the movies **or** to the mall.

In this sentence, the conjunction *and* joins two independent clauses: *Amanda
baked the cookies*, and *Eric made the lemonade*.

> ┌─ independent clause ─┐   ┌─ independent clause ─┐
> Amanda baked the cookies, **and** Eric made the lemonade.

Interjections

Interjections are words or phrases that express emotion.

Interjections that express strong emotion are followed by an exclamation point.

> **Wow!** Did you see that catch?
> **Hey!** Watch out for that ball.

Interjections that express mild emotion are followed by a comma.

> **Gee,** I'm sorry that your team lost.
> **Oh,** it's okay. We'll do better next time.

CLAUSES

Clauses are groups of words with a subject and a verb. Some clauses form complete sentences; they tell a complete thought. Others do not.

This clause is a complete sentence. Clauses that form complete sentences are called **independent clauses**.

> subject verb
> The dog's **tail wagged**.

This clause is not a complete sentence. Clauses that don't form complete sentences are called **dependent clauses**.

> subject verb
> when the **boy patted** him.

Independent clauses can be combined with dependent clauses to form a sentence.

In this sentence, *The dog's tail wagged* is an independent clause. *When the boy patted him* is a dependent clause.

> ┌—independent clause—┐ ┌—independent clause—┐
> The dog's tail wagged when the boy patted him.

SENTENCES

Sentences have a subject and a verb, and tell a complete thought. A sentence always begins with a capital letter. It always ends with a period, question mark, or exclamation point.

> subject action verb
> The **cheetah runs** very fast.
>
> helping
> verb subject action verb
> **Do you play** soccer?
>
> subject linking verb
> **I am** so late!

Simple Sentences and Compound Sentences

Some sentences are called simple sentences. Others are called compound sentences. A **simple sentence** has one independent clause. Here is an example.

> ┌──── independent clause ────┐
> The dog barked at the mail carrier.

Compound sentences are made up of two or more simple sentences, or independent clauses. They are joined together by a **conjunction** such as *and* or *but*.

> ┌──── independent clause ────┐ ┌── independent clause ──┐
> The band has a lead singer, **but** they need a drummer.

Sentence Types

Sentences have different purposes. There are four types of sentences: declarative, interrogative, imperative, and exclamatory.

Declarative sentences are statements. They end with a period.

> We are going to the beach on Saturday.

Interrogative sentences are questions. They end with a question mark.

> Will you come with us?

Imperative sentences are commands. They usually end with a period. If the command is strong, the sentence may end with an exclamation point.

> Put on your life jacket. Now jump into the water!

Exclamatory sentences express strong feeling. They end with an exclamation point.

> I swam all the way from the boat to the shore!

End Marks

End marks come at the end of sentences. There are three kinds of end marks: periods, question marks, and exclamation points.

Use a **period** to end a statement (declarative sentence).

The spacecraft *Magellan* took pictures of Jupiter.

Use a **period** to end a command or request (imperative sentence) that isn't strong enough to need an exclamation point.

Please change the channel.

Use a **question mark** to end a sentence that asks a question. (interrogative sentence).

Where does Mrs. Suarez live?

Use an **exclamation point** to end a sentence that expresses strong feeling (exclamatory sentence).

That was a great party!
Look at that huge house!

Use an **exclamation point** to end an imperative sentence that gives an urgent command.

Get away from the edge of the pool!

Periods are also used after initials and many abbreviations.

Use a **period** after a person's initial or abbreviated title.

Ms. Susan Vargas	Mrs. Fiske	J. D. Salinger
Gov. Lise Crawford	Mr. Vargas	Dr. Sapirstein

Use a **period** after the abbreviation of streets, roads, and so on.

Avenue	Ave.	Road	Rd.
Highway	Hwy.	Street	St.

Use a **period** after the abbreviation of many units of measurement. Abbreviations for metric measurements do *not* use periods.

inch	in.	centimeter	cm
foot	ft.	meter	m
pound	lb.	kilogram	kg
gallon	gal.	liter	l

Commas

Commas separate, or set off, parts of a sentence, or phrase.

Use a comma to separate two independent clauses linked by a conjunction. In this sentence, the comma goes before the conjunction *but*.

┌─independent clause ─┐   ┌─independent clause ─┐
We went to the museum, **but** it is not open on Mondays.

Use commas to separate the parts in a series. A series is a group of three or more words, phrases, or very brief clauses.

Commas in Series	
To separate words	Lucio's bike is red, white, and silver.
To separate phrases	Today, he rode all over the lawn, down the sidewalk, and up the hill.
To separate clauses	Lucio washed the bike, his dad washed the car, and his mom washed the dog.

Use a comma to set off an introductory word, phrase, or clause.

Commas with Introductory Words	
To separate words	Yes, Stacy likes to go swimming.
To set off a phrase	In a month, she may join the swim team again.
To set off a clause	If she joins the swim team, I'll miss her at softball practice.

Use commas to set off an interrupting word, phrase, or clause.

	Commas with Interrupting Words
To set off a word	We left, finally, to get some fresh air.
To set off a phrase	Carol's dog, a brown pug, shakes when he gets scared.
To set off a clause	The assignment, I'm sorry to say, was too hard for me.

Use a comma to set off a speaker's quoted words in a sentence.

Jeanne asked, "Where is that book I just had?"
"I just saw it," said Billy, "on the kitchen counter."

In a direct address, one speaker talks directly to another. Use commas to set off the name of the person being addressed.

Thank you, Dee, for helping to put away the dishes.
Phil, why are you late again?

Use a comma between the day and the year.

My cousin was born on September 9, 2003.

If the date appears in the middle of a sentence, use a comma before and after the year.

Daria's mother was born on June 8, 1969, in New Jersey.

Use a comma between a city and a state and between a city and a nation.

My father grew up in Bakersfield, California.
We are traveling to Acapulco, Mexico.

If the names appear in the middle of a sentence, use a comma before *and* after the state or nation.

> My friend Carl went to Mumbai, India, last year.

Use a comma after the greeting in a friendly letter. Use a comma after the closing in both a friendly letter and formal letter. Do this in e-mail letters, too.

> Dear Margaret,   Sincerely,   Yours truly,

Semicolons and Colons

Semicolons can connect two independent clauses. Use them when the clauses are closely related in meaning or structure.

> The team won again; it was their ninth victory.
> Ana usually studies right after school; Rita prefers to study in the evening.

Colons introduce a list of items or important information.

Use a colon after an independent clause to introduce a list of items. (The clause often includes the words *the following, these, those,* or *this.*)

> The following animals live in Costa Rica: monkeys, lemurs, toucans, and jaguars.

Use a colon to introduce important information. If the information is in an independent clause, use a capital letter to begin the first word after the colon.

> There is one main rule: Do not talk to anyone during the test.
> You must remember this: Stay away from the train tracks!

Use a colon to separate hours and minutes when writing the time.

> 1:30   7:45   11:08

Quotation Marks

Quotation Marks set off direct quotations, dialogue, and some titles. A **direct quotation** is the exact words that somebody said, wrote, or thought.

Commas and periods *always* go inside quotation marks. If a question mark or exclamation point is part of the quotation, it is also placed *inside* the quotation marks.

> "Can you please get ready?" Mom asked.
> My sister shouted, "Look out for that bee!"

If a question mark or exclamation point is *not* part of the quotation, it goes *outside* the quotation marks. In these cases there is no punctuation before the end quotation marks.

> Did you say, "I can't do this"?

Conversation between two or more people is called **dialogue**. Use quotation marks to set off spoken words in dialogue.

> "What a great ride!" Pam said. "Let's go on it again."
> Julio shook his head and said, "No way. I'm feeling sick."

Use quotation marks around the titles of short works of writing or other art forms. The following kinds of titles take quotation marks:

Chapters	"The Railroad in the West"
Short Stories	"The Perfect Cat"
Articles	"California in the 1920s"
Songs	"This Land Is Your Land"
Single TV episodes	"Charlie's New Idea"
Short poems	"The Bat"

Titles of all other written work and artwork are underlined or set in italic type. These include books, magazines, newspapers, plays, movies, TV series, and paintings.

Apostrophes

Apostrophes can be used with singular and plural nouns to show ownership or possession. To form the possessive, follow these rules:

For singular nouns, add an apostrophe and an *s*.

Maria's eyes	hamster's cage	the sun's warmth

For singular nouns that end in *s*, add an apostrophe and an *s*.

her boss's office	Carlos's piano	the grass's length

For plural nouns that do not end in *s*, add an apostrophe and an *s*.

women's clothes	men's shoes	children's books

For plural nouns that end in *s*, add an apostrophe.

teachers' lounge	dogs' leashes	kids' playground

Apostrophes are also used in **contractions**. A contraction is a shortened form of two words that have been combined. The apostrophe shows where a letter or letters have been taken away.

I will
I'll be home in one hour.

do not
We **don't** have any milk.

Capitalization

There are five main reasons to use capital letters:

1. To begin a sentence and in a direct quotation
2. To write the word *I*
3. To write a proper noun (the name of a specific person, place, or thing)
4. To write a person's title
5. To write the title of a work (artwork, written work, magazine, newspaper, musical composition, organization)

Use a capital letter to begin the first word in a sentence.

Cows eat grass. They also eat hay.

Use a capital letter for the first word of a direct quotation. Use the capital letter even if the quotation is in the middle of a sentence.

Carlos said, "We need more lettuce for the sandwiches."

Use a capital letter for the word *I*.

How will I ever learn all these things? I guess I will learn them little by little.

Use a capital letter for a proper noun: the name of a specific person, place, or thing. Capitalize the important words in names.

Robert E. Lee   Morocco   Tuesday   Tropic of Cancer

Capital Letters in Place Names	
Streets	Interstate 95, Center Street, Atwood Avenue
City Sections	Greenwich Village, Shaker Heights, East Side
Cities and Towns	Rome, Chicago, Fresno
States	California, North Dakota, Maryland
Regions	Pacific Northwest, Great Plains, Eastern Europe
Nations	China, Dominican Republic, Italy
Continents	North America, Africa, Asia
Mountains	Mount Shasta, Andes Mountains, Rocky Mountains
Deserts	Mojave Desert, Sahara Desert, Gobi Desert
Islands	Fiji Islands, Capri, Virgin Islands
Rivers	Amazon River, Nile River, Mississippi River
Lakes	Lake Superior, Great Bear Lake, Lake Tahoe
Bays	San Francisco Bay, Hudson Bay, Galveston Bay
Seas	Mediterranean Sea, Sea of Japan
Oceans	Pacific Ocean, Atlantic Ocean, Indian Ocean

Capital Letters for Specific Things	
Historical Periods, Events	Renaissance, Battle of Bull Run
Historical Texts	Constitution, Bill of Rights
Days and Months	Monday, October
Holidays	Thanksgiving, Labor Day
Organizations, Schools	Greenpeace, Central High School
Government Bodies	Congress, State Department
Political Parties	Republican Party, Democratic Party
Ethnic Groups	Chinese, Latinos
Languages, Nationalities	Spanish, Canadian
Buildings	Empire State Building, City Hall
Monuments	Lincoln Memorial, Washington Monument
Religions	Hinduism, Christianity, Judaism, Islam
Special Events	Boston Marathon, Ohio State Fair

Use a capital letter for a person's title if the title comes before the name. In the second sentence below, a capital letter is not needed because the title does not come before a name.

I heard Senator Clinton's speech about jobs. The senator may come to our school.

Use a capital letter for the first and last word and all other important words in titles of books, newspapers, magazines, short stories, plays, movies, songs, paintings, and sculptures.

Lucy wants to read The Lord of the Rings.
The newspaper my father reads is The New York Times.
Did you like the painting called Work in the Fields?
This poem is called "The Birch Tree."

Reading Handbook

People often think of reading as a passive activity—that you don't have to do much, you just have to take in words—but that is not true. Good readers are active readers.

Reading comprehension involves these skills:

1. Understanding what you are reading.
2. Being part of what you are reading, or engaging with the text.
3. Evaluating what you are reading.
4. Making connections between what you are reading and what you already know.
5. Thinking about your response to what you have read.

Understanding What You Are Reading

One of the first steps is to recognize letters and words. Remember that it does not matter if you do not recognize all the words. You can figure out their meanings later. Try to figure out the meaning of unfamiliar words from the context of the sentence or paragraph. If you cannot figure out the meaning of a word, look it up in a dictionary. Next, you activate the meaning of words as you read them. That is what you are doing now. If you find parts of a text difficult, stop and read them a second time.

Engaging with the Text

Good readers use many different skills and strategies to help them understand and enjoy the text they are reading. When you read, think of it as a conversation between you and the writer. The writer wants to tell you something, and you want to understand his or her message.

Practice using these tips every time you read:

- Predict what will happen next in a story. Use clues you find in the text.
- Ask yourself questions about the main idea or message of the text.
- Monitor your understanding. Stop reading from time to time and think about what you have learned so far.

Evaluating What You Are Reading

The next step is to think about what you are reading. First, think about the author's purpose for writing. What type of text are you reading? If it is an informational text, the author wants to give you information about a subject, for example, about science, social science, or math. If you are reading literature, the author's purpose is probably to entertain you.

When you have decided what the author's purpose is for writing the text, think about what you have learned. Use these questions to help you:

- Is the information useful?
- Have you changed your mind about the subject?
- Did you enjoy the story, poem, or play?

Making Connections

Now connect the events or ideas in a text to your own knowledge or experience. Think about how your knowledge of a subject or your experience of the world can help you understand a text better.

- If the text has sections with headings, notice what these are. Do they give you clues about the main ideas in the text?
- Read the first paragraph. What is the main idea?
- Now read the paragraphs that follow. Make a note of the main ideas.
- Review your notes. How are the ideas connected?

Thinking about Your Response to What You Have Read

You read for a reason, so it is a good idea to think about how the text has helped you. Ask yourself these questions after you read:

- What information have I learned? Can I use it in my other classes?
- How can I connect my own experience or knowledge to the text?
- Did I enjoy reading the text? Why or why not?
- Did I learn any new vocabulary? What was it? How can I use it in conversation or in writing?

WHAT ARE READING STRATEGIES?

Reading strategies are specific things readers do to help them understand texts. Reading is like a conversation between an author and a reader. Authors make decisions about how to effectively communicate through a piece of writing. Readers use specific strategies to help them understand what authors are trying to communicate. Ten of the most common reading strategies are Previewing, Predicting, Skimming, Scanning, Comparing and Contrasting, Identifying Problems and Solutions, Recognizing Cause and Effect, Distinguishing Fact from Opinion, Identifying Main Idea and Details, and Identifying an Author's Purpose.

HOW TO IMPROVE READING FLUENCY

1. What Is Reading Fluency?

Reading fluency is the ability to read smoothly and expressively with clear understanding. Fluent readers are better able to understand and enjoy what they read. Use the strategies that follow to build your fluency in these four key areas: accuracy and rate, phrasing, intonation, expression.

2. How to Improve Accuracy and Rate

Accuracy is the correctness of your reading. Rate is the speed of your reading.
- Use correct pronunciation.
- Emphasize correct syllables.
- Recognize most words.

3. How to Read with Proper Rate

- Match your reading speed to what you are reading. For example, if you are reading a mystery story, read slightly faster. If you are reading a science textbook, read slightly slower.
- Recognize and use punctuation.

4. Test Your Accuracy and Rate

- Choose a text you are familiar with, and practice reading it multiple times.
- Keep a dictionary with you while you read, and look up words you do not recognize.
- Use a watch or clock to time yourself while you read a passage.
- Ask a friend or family member to read a passage for you so you know what it should sound like.

5. How to Improve Intonation

Intonation is the rise and fall in the pitch of your voice as you read aloud. Pitch means the highness or lowness of the sound. Follow these steps:
- Change the sound of your voice to match what you are reading.
- Make your voice flow, or sound smooth, while you read.
- Make sure you are pronouncing words correctly.
- Raise the pitch of your voice for words that should be stressed, or emphasized.
- Use proper rhythm and meter.
- Use visual clues.

Visual Clue and Meaning	Example	How to Read It
Italics: draw attention to a word to show special importance	He is *serious*.	Emphasize "serious."
Dash: shows a quick break in a sentence	He is—serious.	Pause before saying "serious."
Exclamation point: can represent energy, excitement, or anger	He is serious!	Make your voice louder at the end of the sentence.
All capital letters: can represent strong emphasis or yelling	HE IS SERIOUS.	Emphasize the whole sentence.
Boldfacing: draws attention to a word to show importance	He is **serious**.	Emphasize "serious."
Question mark: shows curiosity or confusion	Is he serious?	Raise the pitch of your voice slightly at the end of the sentence.

6. How to Improve Phrasing

Phrasing is how you group words together. Follow these steps:

- Use correct rhythm and meter by not reading too fast or too slow.
- Pause for key words within the text.
- Make sure your sentences have proper flow and meter, so they sound smooth instead of choppy.
- Make sure you sound like you are reading a sentence instead of a list.
- Use punctuation to tell you when to stop, pause, or emphasize.

7. How to Improve Expression

Expression in reading is how you express feeling. Follow these steps:

- Match the sound of your voice to what you are reading. For example, read louder and faster to show strong feeling. Read slowly and more quietly to show sadness or seriousness.
- Match the sound of your voice to the genre. For example, read a fun, fictional story using a fun, friendly voice. Read an informative, nonfiction article using an even tone and a more serious voice.
- Avoid speaking in monotone, or using only one tone in your voice.
- Pause for emphasis and exaggerate letter sounds to match the mood or theme of what you are reading.

Viewing and Representing

Viewing

Viewing is something you do every day. Much of what you read and watch includes visuals that help you understand information. These visuals can be maps, charts, diagrams, graphs, photographs, illustrations, and so on. They can inform you, explain a topic or an idea, entertain you, or persuade you.

Websites use visuals, too. It is important for you to be able to view visuals critically in order to evaluate what you are seeing or reading.

Representing

Representing is creating a visual to convey an idea. It is important for you to be able to create and use visuals in your own written work and presentations. You can use graphic organizers, diagrams, charts, posters, and artwork to illustrate and explain your ideas. Following are some examples of visuals.

HOW TO READ MAPS AND DIAGRAMS

Maps

Maps help us learn more about our world. They show the location of places such as countries, states, and cities. Some maps show where mountains, rivers, and lakes are located.

Many maps have helpful features. For example, a **compass rose** shows which way is north. A **scale** shows how miles or kilometers are represented on the map. A **key** shows what different colors or symbols represent.

◀ Three trails on which cowboys drove cattle north from Texas

Diagrams

Diagrams are drawings or plans used to explain things or show how things work. They are often used in social studies and science books. Some diagrams show pictures of how objects look on the outside or on the inside. Others show the different steps in a process.

This diagram shows what a kernel of corn looks like on the inside.

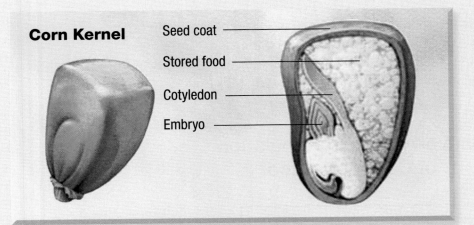

Corn Kernel

Seed coat

Stored food

Cotyledon

Embryo

A **flowchart** is a diagram that uses shapes and arrows to show a step-by-step process. The flowchart below shows the steps involved in baking chicken fingers. Each arrow points to the next step.

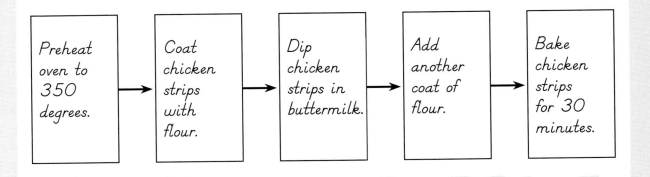

Preheat oven to 350 degrees. → Coat chicken strips with flour. → Dip chicken strips in buttermilk. → Add another coat of flour. → Bake chicken strips for 30 minutes.

Graphs organize and explain information. They show how two or more kinds of information are related, or how they are alike. Graphs are often used in math, science, and social studies books. Three common kinds of graphs are **line graphs**, **bar graphs**, and **circle graphs**.

Line Graphs

A line graph shows how information changes over a period of time. This line graph explains how, over a period of about 100 years, the Native-American population of Central Mexico decreased by more than 20 million people. Can you find the population in the year 1540? What was it in 1580?

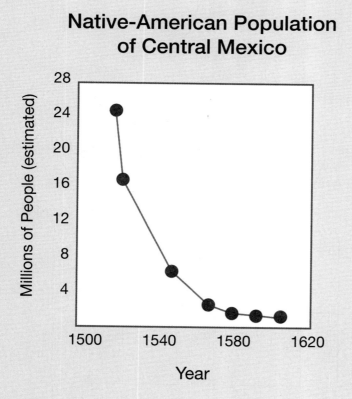

Native-American Population of Central Mexico

Bar Graphs

We use bar graphs to compare information. For example, this bar graph compares the populations of the thirteen United States in 1790. It shows that, in 1790, Virginia had over ten times as many people as Delaware.

Population of the 13 United States, 1790

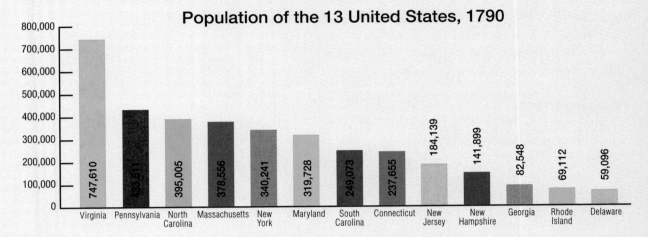

Virginia 747,610 — Pennsylvania 433,611 — North Carolina 395,005 — Massachusetts 378,556 — New York 340,241 — Maryland 319,728 — South Carolina 249,073 — Connecticut 237,655 — New Jersey 184,139 — New Hampshire 141,899 — Georgia 82,548 — Rhode Island 69,112 — Delaware 59,096

Circle Graphs

A circle graph is sometimes called a pie chart because it looks like a pie cut into slices. Circle graphs are used to show how different parts of a whole thing compare to one another. In a circle graph, all the "slices" add up to 100 percent. This circle graph shows that only 29 percent of the earth's surface is covered by land. It also shows that the continent of Asia takes up 30 percent of the earth's land.

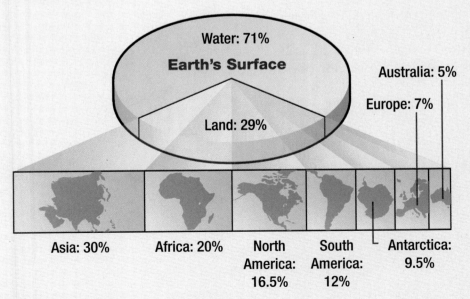

Earth's Surface — Water: 71% — Land: 29%

Australia: 5%
Europe: 7%

Asia: 30% — Africa: 20% — North America: 16.5% — South America: 12% — Antarctica: 9.5%

HOW TO USE GRAPHIC ORGANIZERS

A graphic organizer is a diagram that helps you organize information and show relationships among ideas. Because the information is organized visually, a graphic organizer tells you—in a quick snapshot—how ideas are related. Before you make a graphic organizer, think about the information you want to organize. How are the ideas or details related? Choose a format that will show those relationships clearly.

Venn diagrams and word webs are commonly used graphic organizers. Here is an example of each.

Venn Diagrams

A Venn diagram shows how two thing are alike and different. The diagram below compares oranges and bananas.

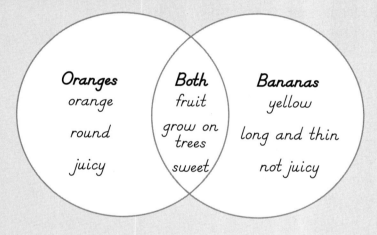

Word Webs

A word web is often used to help a writer describe something. The word web below lists five sensory details that describe popcorn.

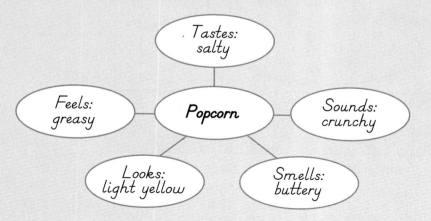

Writing Handbook

Narration

When writers tell a story, they use narration. There are many kinds of narration. Most include characters, a setting, and a sequence of events. Here are some types of narration.

A **short story** is a short, creative narrative. Most short stories have one or more characters, a setting, and a plot. A few types of short stories are realistic stories, fantasy stories, science-fiction stories, and adventure stories.

Autobiographical writing is a factual story of a writer's own life, told by the writer, usually in the first-person point of view. An autobiography may tell about the person's whole life or only a part of it.

Biographical writing is a factual story of a person's life told by another person. Most biographies are written about famous or admirable people.

Description

Description, or descriptive writing, is writing that gives the reader a mental picture of whatever is being described. To do this, writers choose their words carefully. They use figurative language and include vivid sensory details.

Persuasion

Writers use persuasion to try to persuade people to think or act in a certain way. Forms of persuasive writing include advertisements, essays, letters, editorials, speeches, and public-service announcements.

Exposition

Exposition, or expository writing, is writing that gives information or explains something. The information that writers include in expository writing is factual. Here are some types of expository writing.

A **compare-and-contrast essay** analyzes the similarities and differences between or among things.

A **cause-and-effect essay** explains causes or effects of an event. For example, a writer might examine several causes of a single effect or several effects of a single cause.

Writers use a **problem-and-solution essay** to describe a problem and offer one or more solutions to it.

A **how-to essay** explains how to do or make something. The process is broken down into steps, which are explained in order.

A **summary** is a brief statement that gives the main ideas of an event or a piece of writing. One way to write a summary is to read a text and then reread each paragraph or section. Next put the text aside and write the main ideas in your own words in a sentence or two.

Research Writing

Writers often use research to gather information about topics, including people, places, and things. Good research writing does not simply repeat information. It guides the readers through a topic, showing them why each fact matters and creating a complete picture of the topic. Here are some types of research writing.

Research report A research report presents information gathered from reference books, interviews, or other sources.

Biographical report A biographical report includes dates, details, and main events in a person's life. It can also include information about the time in which the person lived.

Multimedia report A multimedia report presents information through a variety of media, including text, slides, photographs, prerecorded music and sound effects, and digital imaging.

Responses to Literature

A **literary essay** is one type of response to literature. In a literary essay, a writer discusses and interprets what is important in a book, short story, essay, article, or poem.

Literary criticism is another type of response to literature. Literary criticism is the result of a careful examination of one or more literary works. The writer makes a judgment by looking carefully and critically at various important elements in the work.

A book **critique** gives readers a summary of a book, encouraging the reader either to read it or to avoid reading it. A movie critique gives readers a summary of a movie, tells if the writer enjoyed the movie, and then explains the reasons why or why not.

A **comparison of works** compares the features of two or more works.

Creative Writing

Creative writing blends imagination, ideas, and emotions, and allows the writer to present a unique view of the world. Poems, plays, short stories, dramas, and even some cartoons are examples of creative writing.

Practical and Technical Documents

Practical writing is fact-based writing that people do in the workplace or in their day-to-day lives. A business letter, memo, school form, job application, and a letter of inquiry are a few examples of practical writing.

Technical documents are fact-based documents that identify a sequence of activities needed to design a system, operate machinery, follow a procedure, or explain the rules of an organization. You read technical writing every time you read a manual or a set of instructions.

In the following descriptions, you'll find tips for tackling several types of practical and technical writing.

Business letters are formal letters that follow one of several specific formats.

News releases, also called press releases, announce factual information about upcoming events. A writer might send a news release to a local newspaper, local radio station, TV station, or other media that will publicize the information.

Guidelines give information about how people should act or how to do something.

Process explanations are step-by-step explanations of how to do something. The explanation should be clear and specific and can include diagrams or other illustrations. Below is an example.

KEYSTONE
CD-ROM

Usage Instructions
1. Insert the *Keystone* CD-ROM into your CD drive.
2. Open "My Computer."
3. Double-click on your CD-ROM disk drive.
4. Click on the *Keystone* icon. This will launch the program.

THE WRITING PROCESS

The **writing process** is a series of steps that can help you write effectively.

Step 1: Prewrite

During **prewriting**, you collect topic ideas, choose a topic, plan your writing, and gather information.

A good way to get ideas for a topic is to **brainstorm**. Brainstorming means writing a list of all the topic ideas you can think of.

Look at your list of topic ideas. Choose the one that is the most interesting to you. This is your **topic**, the subject you will write about.

Plan your writing by following these steps:

- First, decide on the **type** of writing that works best with your topic. For example, you may want to write a description, a story, or an essay.
- The type of writing is called the **form** of writing.
- Then think about your **audience**. Identifying your audience will help you decide whether to write formally or informally.
- Finally, decide what your reason for writing is. This is your **purpose**. Is your purpose to inform your audience? To entertain them?

How you gather information depends on what you are writing. For example, for a report, you need to do research. For a description, you might list your ideas in a graphic organizer. A student named Becca listed her ideas for a description of her week at art camp in the graphic organizer below.

Main Idea:
My summer at art camp.

Detail:
Why I went

Detail:
What I did

Detail:
What I learned

Step 2: Draft

In this step, you start writing. Don't worry too much about spelling and punctuation. Just put your ideas into sentences.

Here is the first paragraph that Becca wrote for her first draft.

> I saw an art contest advertised in the newspaper last spring. I entered my best drawing. I have always loved art. The prize was a week at an art camp in June with 9 other kids. I was very happy when I won.

Step 3: Revise

Now it's time to revise, or make changes. Ask yourself these questions:
- Are my ideas presented in the order that makes the most sense?
- Does my draft have a beginning, a middle, and an end?
- Does each paragraph have a main idea and supporting details?

If you answered *no* to any of these questions, you need to revise. Revising can mean changing the order of paragraphs or sentences. It can mean changing general words for specific words. It can mean correcting errors.

Once you decide what to change, you can mark the corrections on your draft using editing marks. Here's how Becca marked up her first paragraph.

> When I saw an art contest advertised in the newspaper last spring, I entered my best drawing. (I have always loved art.) The prize was a week at an art camp in June with nine 9 other kids. I was very happy excited when I won.

Step 4: Edit and Proofread

In this step, you make a second draft that includes the changes you marked on your first draft. You can also add details you may have thought of since writing your first draft. Now you're ready to **proofread**, or check your work for errors and make final corrections.

Here's Becca's first draft after she finished proofreading.

My Week at Art Camp

I have always loved art. When I saw an art contest advertised in the newspaper last spring, I entered my best drawing. The prize was a week at an art camp in June with nine other students. I was very excited when I won.

The camp was located at the Everson museum of art. On the first day, we looked at paintings by different artists. My favorite was by a painter named Monet. He painted colorful land scapes of boats and gardens. On the second day we began our own paintings. I choose to paint a picture of the duck pond on the campus. I worked hard on my painting because we were going to have an art show of all our work at the end of the week.

I learned alot about painting at camp. I especially liked learning to use watercolors. For example I found out that you can make interesting designs by sprinkling salt on a wet watercolor painting.

I had a great time at art camp. The show at the end of the week was a big success, and I made some new friends. I hope to go again next year.

Step 5: Publish

Prepare a final copy of your writing to **publish**, or share with your audience. Here are some publishing tips.

- Photocopy and hand out your work to your classmates.
- Attach it to an e-mail and send it to friends.
- Send it to a school newspaper or magazine for possible publication.

Here is the final version of Becca's paper.

My Week at Art Camp

I have always loved art. When I saw an art contest advertised in the newspaper last spring, I entered my best drawing. The prize was a week at an art camp in June with nine other students. I was very excited when I won.

The camp was located at the Everson Museum of Art. On the first day, we looked at paintings by different artists. My favorite was by a painter named Monet. He painted colorful landscapes of boats and gardens. On the second day, we began our own paintings. I chose to paint a picture of the duck pond on the campus. I worked hard on my painting because we were going to have an art show of all our work at the end of the week.

I learned a lot about painting at camp. I especially liked learning to use watercolors. For example, I found out that you can make interesting designs by sprinkling salt on a wet watercolor painting.

I had a great time at art camp. The show at the end of the week was a big success, and I made some new friends. I hope to go again next year.

Once you have shared your work with others, you may want to keep it in a **portfolio**, a folder or envelope with your other writing. Each time you write something, add it to your portfolio. Compare recent work with earlier work. See how your writing is improving.

RUBRICS FOR WRITING

What Is a Rubric?

A **rubric** is a tool, often in the form of a chart or a grid, that helps you assess your work. Rubrics are helpful for writing and speaking assignments.

To help you or others assess your work, a rubric offers several specific criteria to be applied to your work. Then the rubric helps you indicate your range of success or failure according to those specific criteria. Rubrics are often used to evaluate writing for standardized tests.

Using a rubric will save you time, focus your learning, and improve your work. When you know the rubric beforehand, you can keep the specific criteria for the writing in your mind as you write. As you evaluate the essay before giving it to your teacher, you can focus on the specific criteria that your teacher wants you to master—or on areas that you know present challenges for you. Instead of searching through your work randomly for any way to improve or correct it, you will have a clear and helpful focus.

How Are Rubrics Structured?

Rubrics can be structured in several different ways:

1. Your teacher may assign a rubric for a specific assignment.
2. Your teacher may direct you to a rubric in your textbook.
3. Your teacher and your class may structure a rubric for a particular assignment together.
4. You and your classmates may structure a rubric together.
5. You can create your own rubric with your own specific criteria.

How Will a Rubric Help Me?

A rubric will help you assess your work on a scale. Scales vary from rubric to rubric but usually range from 6 to 1, 5 to 1, or 4 to 1, with 6, 5, or 4 being the highest score and 1 being the lowest. If someone else is using the rubric to assess your work, the rubric will give your evaluator a clear range within which to place your work. If you are using the rubric yourself, it will help you improve your work.

What Are the Types of Rubrics?

A **holistic rubric** has general criteria that can apply to a variety of assignments. An **analytic rubric** is specific to a particular assignment. The criteria for evaluation address the specific issues important in that assignment. The following pages show examples of both types of rubrics.

440

Holistic Rubrics

Holistic rubrics such as this one are sometimes used to assess writing assignments on standardized tests. Notice that the criteria for evaluation are focus, organization, support, and use of conventions.

Points	Criteria
6 Points	• The writing is focused and shows fresh insight into the writing task. • The writing is marked by a sense of completeness and coherence and is organized with a logical progression of ideas. • A main idea is fully developed, and support is specific and substantial. • A mature command of the language is evident. • Sentence structure is varied, and writing is free of fragments. • Virtually no errors in writing conventions appear.
5 Points	• The writing is focused on the task. • The writing is organized and has a logical progression of ideas, though there may be occasional lapses. • A main idea is well developed and supported with relevant detail. • Sentence structure is varied, and the writing is free of fragments. • Writing conventions are followed correctly.
4 Points	• The writing is focused on the task, but unrelated material may intrude. • Clear organizational pattern is present, though lapses occur. • A main idea is adequately supported, but development may be uneven. • Sentence structure is generally fragment free but shows little variation. • Writing conventions are generally followed correctly.
3 Points	• Writing is focused on the task, but unrelated material intrudes. • Organization is evident, but writing may lack a logical progression of ideas. • Support for the main idea is present but is sometimes illogical. • Sentence structure is free of fragments, but there is almost no variation. • The work demonstrates a knowledge of conventions, with misspellings.
2 Points	• The writing is related to the task but generally lacks focus. • There is little evidence of an organizational pattern. • Support for the main idea is generally inadequate, illogical, or absent. • Sentence structure is unvaried, and serious errors may occur. • Errors in writing conventions and spellings are frequent.
1 Point	• The writing may have little connection to the task. • There has been little attempt at organization or development. • The paper seems fragmented, with no clear main idea. • Sentence structure is unvaried, and serious errors appear. • Poor diction and poor command of the language obscure meaning. • Errors in writing conventions and spelling are frequent.
Unscorable	• The response is unrelated to the task or is simply a rewording of the prompt. • The response has been copied from a published work. • The student did not write a response. • The response is illegible. • The words in the response are arranged with no meaning. • There is an insufficient amount of writing to score.

Analytic Rubrics

This analytic rubric is an example of a rubric to assess a persuasive essay. It will help you assess presentation, position, evidence, and arguments.

Presentation	Position	Evidence	Arguments
6 Points Essay clearly and effectively addresses an issue with more than one side.	Essay clearly states a supportable position on the issue.	All evidence is logically organized, well presented, and supports the position.	All reader concerns and counterarguments are effectively addressed.
5 Points Most of essay addresses an issue that has more than one side.	Essay clearly states a position on the issue.	Most evidence is logically organized, well presented, and supports the position.	Most reader concerns and counterarguments are effectively addressed.
4 Points Essay adequately addresses issue that has more than one side.	Essay adequately states a position on the issue.	Many parts of evidence support the position; some evidence is out of order.	Many reader concerns and counterarguments are adequately addressed.
3 Points Essay addresses issue with two sides but does not present second side clearly.	Essay states a position on the issue, but the position is difficult to support.	Some evidence supports the position, but some evidence is out of order.	Some reader concerns and counterarguments are addressed.
2 Points Essay addresses issue with two sides but does not present second side.	Essay states a position on the issue, but the position is not supportable.	Not much evidence supports the position, and what is included is out of order.	A few reader concerns and counterarguments are addressed.
1 Point Essay does not address issue with more than one side.	Essay does not state a position on the issue.	No evidence supports the position.	No reader concerns or counterarguments are addressed.

Friendly Letters

A friendly letter is less formal than a business letter. It is a letter to a friend, a family member, or anyone with whom the writer wants to communicate in a personal, friendly way. Most friendly letters are made up of five parts: the **date**, the **greeting** (or salutation), the **body**, the **closing**, and the **signature**. The greeting is followed by a comma, and the paragraphs in the body are indented.

The purpose of a friendly letter is usually to share personal news and feelings, to send or to answer an invitation, or to express thanks.

In this letter, Maité tells her friend Julio about her new home.

Greeting

Date

March 2, 2009

Dear Julio,

I was so happy to receive your letter today. I am feeling much better. My mom and I finally finished decorating my room. We painted the walls green and the ceiling pink. At first, my mom was nervous to paint the ceiling something other than white, but I knew it would look good. Now that my bedroom is finished, Manhattan is starting to feel more like home.

Over the weekend I went to the Museum of Natural History. The whale exhibit made me think of back home and how you and I would spend hours at the beach. I am starting to adjust to city life, but I miss the smell of salt in the air and collecting sea glass on the shore.

My parents said I can spend the summer with my grandparents at their beach house. They said I could invite you for a couple of weeks. We'll go swimming every day. I can't wait!

Body

Your friend, ← **Closing**

Maité ← **Signature**

Business Letters

Business letters follow one of several formats. In **block format**, each part of the letter begins at the left margin. A double space is used between paragraphs. In **modified block format**, some parts of the letter are indented to the center of the page. No matter which format is used, all letters in business format have a date, an inside address, a greeting (or salutation), a body, a closing, and a signature. These parts are shown on the model business letter below, formatted in block style.

June 11, 2009 ←————————— **Date**

Edward Sykes, Vice President
Animal Rights Group ←————————— **Inside Address**
154 Denver Street
Syosset, NY 11791

Dear Mr. Sykes: ←————————— **Greeting**

Many students at Bellevue High School would like to learn about animal rights for a project we're starting next fall. We've read about your program on your website and would like to know more about your activities.

Would you send us some information about your organization? We're specifically interested in learning what we as students can do to help protect animals. About 75 students have expressed interest so far—I think we'll have the people power to make the project a success and have an impact.   ←— **Body**

Please help us get started. Thank you for your time and consideration.

Sincerely, ←——— **Closing**

Pedro Rodriguez ←——— **Signature**

Pedro Rodriguez

The **inside address** shows where the letter will be sent. The **greeting** is punctuated with a colon. The **body** of the letter states the writer's purpose. The **closing** "Sincerely" is common, but "Yours truly" or "Respectfully yours" are also acceptable. The writer types his or her name and writes a **signature**.

FILLING IN FORMS

Forms are preprinted documents with spaces for the user to enter specific information. Some include directions; others assume that users will follow the labels and common conventions. Two common forms in the workplace are fax cover sheets and applications. When you fill out forms, it is important to do the following:

- Fill them out accurately and completely.
- Write neatly in blue or black ink.
- Include only information that is asked for on the form.

Forms usually have limited space in which to write. Because space is limited, you can use standard symbols and abbreviations, such as *$10/hr.* to mean "10 dollars per hour."

FAX COVER SHEET

To: *Mr. Robert Thompson* **From:** *Laura Rivas*

Fax: *(001) 921-9833* **Pages:** *2 (including cover sheet)*

Date: *12/04/09*

Re: *Job Application*

Message:

Dear Mr. Thompson:

Thank you for meeting with me today about the sales associate position at Story Land Bookshop. The following page is my completed application form.

Sincerely,

Laura Rivas

Filling in an Application for Employment

Story Land Bookshop

PRE-EMPLOYMENT QUESTIONNAIRE
EQUAL OPPORTUNITY EMPLOYER
Date: 12/04/2009

PERSONAL INFORMATION

Name (last name first)
Rivas, Laura

Social Security No.
145-53-6211

Present Address	**City**	**State**	**Zip Code**
351 Middleton Road	Osborne	TX	78357

Permanent Address	**City**	**State**	**Zip Code**
Same			

Phone No.
(001) 661-1567

Referred by
Josh Logan

EMPLOYMENT DESIRED

Position	**Start Date**	**Salary Desired**
Sales associate	Immediately	$10/hr.

Are you presently employed? ☐ Yes ☑ No
May we contact your former employer? ☑ Yes ☐ No
Were you ever employed by this company? ☐ Yes ☑ No

EDUCATION

Name and Location of School	**Yrs Attended**	**Did you graduate?**
Osborne High School, Osborne, TX	3	Expect to graduate 2010

FORMER EMPLOYERS

Name and Address of Employer	**Salary**	**Position**
Blue River Summer Camp 127 Horse Lane Millwood, TX 78721	$195 per week	Junior camp counselor

Date Month and Year	**Reason for Leaving**
6/20/09 to 9/20/09	Summer ended

CONDUCTING RESEARCH

Reference Skills
There is a wide range of print and electronic references you can use to find many different kinds of information.

Encyclopedias
Encyclopedias contain facts on a great many subjects. They provide basic information to help you start researching a topic. Use encyclopedias for basic facts, background information, and suggestions for additional research.

Periodicals
Periodicals are magazines and journals. Once you've used a periodical index to identify the articles you want to read, ask a librarian to help you locate the periodicals. Often, past issues of magazines are stored electronically on microfilm, a database, or CD-ROMs. The librarian can help you use these resources. Use the table of contents, the titles, and other magazine features to help you find information.

Biographical References
These books provide brief life histories of famous people in many different fields. Biographical references may offer short entries similar to those in dictionaries or longer articles more like those in encyclopedias. Most contain an index to help you locate entries.

Nonfiction Books
Nonfiction books about your topic can also be useful reference tools. Use titles, tables of contents, prefaces, chapter headings, glossaries, indexes, and appendixes to locate the information you need.

Almanacs
Almanacs are published annually. They contain facts and statistics about many subjects, including government, world history, geography, entertainment, business, and sports. To find a subject in a printed almanac, refer to the index in the front or back. In an electronic almanac, you can usually find information by typing a subject or key word.

Electronic Databases
Available on CD-ROMs or online, electronic databases provide quick access to a wealth of information on a topic. Using a search feature, you can easily access any type of data, piece together related information, or look at the information in a different way.

PROOFREADING

All forms of writing—from a letter to a friend to a research paper—are more effective when they are error-free. Once you are satisfied with the content of your writing, polish the grammar, usage, and mechanics.

Challenge yourself to learn and apply the skills of proofreading to everything you write. Review your writing carefully to find and correct all errors. Here are the broad categories that should direct your proofreading:

☑ **CHECK YOUR SPELLING:** Use a dictionary or an electronic spelling checker to check any spelling of which you are unsure.

☑ **CHECK YOUR GRAMMAR AND USAGE:** Use a writing handbook to correct problems in grammar or usage.

☑ **REVIEW CAPITALIZATION AND PUNCTUATION:** Review your draft to be sure you've begun each sentence with a capital letter and used proper end punctuation.

☑ **CHECK THE FACTS:** When your writing includes facts gathered from outside sources, confirm the accuracy of your work. Consult reference materials. Check names, dates, and statistics.

Editing Marks		
To:	**Use This Mark:**	**Example:**
add something	∧	We ate rice, bean^s and corn.
delete something	ℯ	We ate rice, beans, and corns.
start a new paragraph	¶	¶We ate rice, beans, and corn.
add a comma	∧	We ate rice, beans and corn.
add a period	⊙	We ate rice, beans, and corn⊙
switch letters or words	∼	We ate rice, baens, and corn.
change to a capital letter	a̲	we ate rice, beans, and corn.
change to a lowercase letter	⧸A	WE ate rice, beans, and corn.

CITING SOURCES

Proofreading and Preparing Manuscript
Before preparing a final copy, proofread your manuscript.
- Choose a standard, easy-to-read font.
- Type or print on one side of unlined 8 1/2" x 11" paper.
- Set the margins for the side, top, and bottom of your paper at approximately one inch. Most word-processing programs have a default setting that is appropriate.
- Double-space the document.
- Indent the first line of each paragraph.
- Number the pages in the upper right corner.

Follow your teacher's directions for formatting formal research papers. Most papers will have the following features: Title page, Table of Contents or Outline, Works Consulted List.

Crediting Sources
When you credit a source, you acknowledge where you found your information and you give your readers the details necessary for locating the source themselves. Within the body of the paper, you provide a short citation, a footnote number linked to a footnote, or an endnote number linked to an endnote reference. These brief references show the page numbers on which you found the information. Prepare a reference list at the end of the paper to provide full bibliographic information on your sources. These are two common types of reference lists:

A **bibliography** provides a listing of all the resources you consulted during your research. A **works consulted list** lists the works you have referenced in your paper.

The chart on the next page shows the Modern Language Association format for crediting sources. This is the most common format for papers written in the content areas in middle school and high school. Unless instructed otherwise by your teacher, use this format for crediting sources.

MLA Style for Listing Sources

Book with one author	Pyles, Thomas. *The Origins and Development of the English Language*. 2nd ed. New York: Harcourt Brace Jovanovich, Inc., 1971.
Book with two or three authors	McCrum, Robert, William Cran, and Robert MacNeil. *The Story of English*. New York: Penguin Books, 1987.
Book with an editor	Truth, Sojourner. *Narrative of Sojourner Truth*. Ed. Margaret Washington. New York: Vintage Books, 1993.
Book with more than three authors or editors	Donald, Robert B., et al. *Writing Clear Essays*. Upper Saddle River, NJ: Prentice Hall, Inc., 1996.
Single work from an anthology	Hawthorne, Nathaniel. "Young Goodman Brown." *Literature: An Introduction to Reading and Writing*. Ed. Edgar V. Roberts and Henry E. Jacobs. Upper Saddle River, NJ: Prentice-Hall, Inc., 1998. 376–385. [Indicate pages for the entire selection.]
Introduction in a published edition	Washington, Margaret. Introduction. *Narrative of Sojourner Truth*. By Sojourner Truth. New York: Vintage Books, 1993, pp. v–xi.
Signed article in a weekly magazine	Wallace, Charles. "A Vodacious Deal." *Time* 14 Feb. 2000: 63.
Signed article in a monthly magazine	Gustaitis, Joseph. "The Sticky History of Chewing Gum." *American History* Oct. 1998: 30–38.
Unsigned editorial or story	"Selective Silence." Editorial. *Wall Street Journal* 11 Feb. 2000: A14. [If the editorial or story is signed, begin with the author's name.]
Signed pamphlet or brochure	[Treat the pamphlet as though it were a book.]
Pamphlet with no author, publisher, or date	*Are You at Risk of Heart Attack?* n.p. n.d. "n.p. n.d." indicates that there is no known publisher or date.]
Filmstrips, slide programs, videocassettes, DVDs, and other audiovisual media	*The Diary of Anne Frank*. Dir. George Stevens. Perf. Millie Perkins, Shelly Winters, Joseph Schildkraut, Lou Jacobi, and Richard Beymer. Twentieth Century Fox, 1959.
Radio or television program transcript	"Nobel for Literature." Narr. Rick Karr. *All Things Considered*. National Public Radio. WNYC, New York. 10 Oct. 2002. Transcript.
Internet	*National Association of Chewing Gum Manufacturers*. 19 Dec. 1999 <http://www.nacgm.org/consumer/funfacts.html> [Indicate the date you accessed the information. Content and addresses at websites change frequently.]
Newspaper	Thurow, Roger. "South Africans Who Fought for Sanctions Now Scrap for Investors." *Wall Street Journal* 11 Feb. 2000: A1+ [For a multipage article, write only the first page number on which it appears, followed by a plus sign.]
Personal interview	Smith, Jane. Personal interview. 10 Feb. 2000.
CD (with multiple publishers)	Simms, James, ed. *Romeo and Juliet*. By William Shakespeare. CD-ROM. Oxford: Attica Cybernetics Ltd.; London: BBC Education; London: HarperCollins Publishers, 1995.
Signed article from an encyclopedia	Askeland, Donald R. "Welding." *World Book Encyclopedia*. 1991 ed.

Technology Handbook

Technology is a combination of resources that can help you do research, find information, and write. Good sources for research include the Internet and your local library. The library contains databases where you can find many forms of print and nonprint resources, including audio and video recordings.

The Internet

The Internet is an international network, or connection, of computers that share information with each other. It is a popular source for research and finding information for academic, professional, and personal reasons. The World Wide Web is a part of the Internet that allows you to find, read, and organize information. Using the Web is a fast way to get the most current information about many topics.

Words or phrases can be typed into the "search" section of a search engine, and websites that contain those words will be listed for you to explore. You can then search a website for the information you need.

Information Media

Media is all the organizations, such as television, radio, and newspapers that provide news and information for the public. Knowing the characteristics of various kinds of media will help you to spot them during your research. The following chart describes several forms of information media.

Types of Information Media	
Television News Program	• Covers current news events • Gives information objectively
Documentary	• Focuses on one topic of social interest • Sometimes expresses controversial opinions
Television Newsmagazine	• Covers a variety of topics • Entertains and informs
Commercial	• Presents products, people, or ideas • Persuades people to buy or take action

Other Sources of Information

There are many other reliable print and nonprint sources of information to use in your research. For example: magazines, newspapers, professional or academic journal articles, experts, political speeches, press conferences.

Most of the information from these sources is also available on the Internet. Try to evaluate the information you find from various media sources. Be careful to choose the most reliable sources for this information.

451

HOW TO USE THE INTERNET FOR RESEARCH

Keyword Search

Before you begin a search, narrow your subject to a keyword or a group of **keywords**. These are your search terms, and they should be as specific as possible. For example, if you are looking for information about your favorite musical group, you might use the band's name as a keyword. You might locate such information as band member biographies, the group's history, fan reviews of concerts, and hundreds of sites with related names containing information that is irrelevant to your search. Depending on your research needs, you might need to narrow your search.

How to Narrow Your Search

If you have a large group of keywords and still don't know which ones to use, write out a list of all the words you are considering. Then, delete the words that are least important to your search, and highlight those that are most important.

Use search connectors to fine-tune your search:

AND: narrows a search by retrieving documents that include both terms.
       For example: *trumpets AND jazz*

OR: broadens a search by retrieving documents including any of the terms.
       For example: *jazz OR music*

NOT: narrows a search by excluding documents containing certain words.
       For example: *trumpets NOT drums*

Good Search Tips

1. Search engines can be case-sensitive. If your first try at searching fails, check your search terms for misspellings and search again.
2. Use the most important keyword first, followed by the less important ones.
3. Do not open the link to every single page in your results list. Search engines show pages in order of how close it is to your keyword. The most useful pages will be located at the top of the list.
4. Some search engines provide helpful tips for narrowing your search.

Respecting Copyrighted Material

The Internet is growing every day. Sometimes you are not allowed to access or reprint material you find on the Internet. For some text, photographs, music, and fine art, you must first get permission from the author or copyright owner. Also, be careful not to plagiarize while writing and researching. Plagiarism is presenting someone else's words, ideas, or work as your own. If the idea or words are not yours, be sure to give credit by citing the source in your work.

HOW TO EVALUATE THE QUALITY OF INFORMATION

Since the media presents large amounts of information, it is important to learn how to analyze this information critically. Analyzing critically means you can evaluate the information for content, quality, and importance.

How to Evaluate Information from Various Media

Sometimes the media tries to make you think a certain way instead of giving all the facts. These techniques will help you figure out if you can rely on information from the media.

✔ Ask yourself if you can trust the source, or if the information you find shows any bias. Is the information being given in a one-sided way?

✔ Discuss the information you find from different media with your classmates or teachers to figure out its reliability.

✔ Sort out facts from opinions. Make sure that any opinions given are backed up with facts. A fact is a statement that can be proved true. An opinion is a viewpoint that cannot be proved true.

✔ Be aware of any loaded language or images. Loaded language and images are emotional words and visuals used to persuade you.

✔ Check surprising or questionable information in other sources. Are there instances of faulty reasoning? Is the information adequately supported?

✔ Be aware of the kind of media you are watching. If it's a program, is it a documentary? A commercial? What is its purpose? Is it correct?

✔ Read the entire article or watch the whole program before reaching a conclusion. Then develop your own views on the issues, people, and information presented.

How to Evaluate Information from the Internet

There is so much information available on the Internet that it can be hard to understand. It is important to be sure that the information you use as support or evidence is reliable and can be trusted. Use the following checklist to decide if a Web page you are reading is reliable and a credible source.

- ☑ The information is from a well-known and trusted website. For example, websites that end in **.edu** are part of an educational institution and usually can be trusted. Other cues for reliable websites are sites that end in **.org** for "organization" or **.gov** for "government." Sites with a **.com** ending are either owned by businesses or individuals.

- ☑ The people who write or are quoted on the website are experts, not just everyday people telling their ideas or opinions.

- ☑ The website gives facts, not just opinions.

- ☑ The website is free of grammatical and spelling errors. This is often a hint that the site was carefully made and will not have factual mistakes.

- ☑ The website is not trying to sell a product or persuade people. It is simply trying to give correct information.

- ☑ If you are not sure about using a website as a source, ask your teacher for advice. Once you become more aware of the different sites, you will become better at knowing which sources to trust.

HOW TO USE TECHNOLOGY IN WRITING

Personal Computers

A personal computer can be an excellent writing tool. It enables a writer to create, change, and save documents. The cut, copy, and paste features are especially useful when writing and revising.

Organizing Information

Create a system to organize the research information you find from various forms of media, such as newspapers, books, and the Internet.

Using a computer and printer can help you in the writing process. You can change your drafts, see your changes clearly, and keep copies of all your work. Also, consider keeping an electronic portfolio. This way you can store and organize copies of your writing in several subject areas. You can review the works you have completed and see your improvement as a writer.

It is easy to organize electronic files on a computer. The desktop is the main screen, and holds folders that the user names. For example, a folder labeled "Writing Projects September" might contain all of the writing you do during that month. This will help you find your work quickly.

As you use your portfolio, you might think of better ways to organize it. You might find you have several drafts of a paper you wrote, and want to create a separate folder for these. Every month, take time to clean up your files.

Computer Tips

1. Rename each of your revised drafts using the SAVE AS function. For example, if your first file is "essay," name the first revision "essay2" and the next one "essay3."
2. If you share your computer with others, label a folder with your name and keep your files separate by putting them there.
3. Always back up your portfolio on a server or a CD.

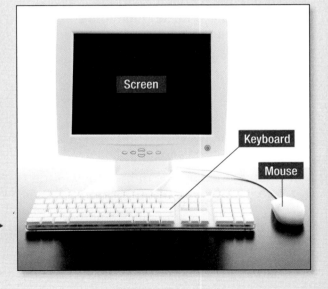

Personal computer ▶

Glossary

abstract existing only as an idea or quality rather than as something concrete you can see and touch

accurate exactly correct

achievement something important you succeed in doing as a result of your actions

affect make someone feel strong emotions

alliance a union of countries or groups formed by agreement for some special purpose

analyze examine or think about something carefully in order to understand it

anticipation a feeling of excitement because something good or fun is going to happen

appreciation an understanding of the importance, meaning, or beauty of something

approached moved closer to

archetype a type of character that appears in literature often enough to be considered universal

armistice an agreement to stop fighting, usually for a specific period

arteries blood vessels that carry blood from the heart to the rest of the body

assassination the murdering of an important person, especially for political reasons

astronomy the science of the study of the sun, moon, and stars

attached feeling connected to someone or something

attitudes the ways people think or feel about something or someone

auditorium a large room, especially in a school, where people sit to watch a performance

author someone who writes a book, story, article, or play

beneficial good or useful

biased unfair because of a preference or dislike of something

bitterness deep resentment; intense anger

blood vessels tubes through which blood flows in your body

capillaries very small, narrow blood vessels

celestial relating to the sky or heaven

challenge something new, exciting, or difficult that needs a lot of skill and effort to do

characterization the creation and development of a character in a story

chimpanzees African apes that are very intelligent

circulatory relating to the circulation of blood through the body

civilians people who are not members of any of the armed forces

commercial related to buying and selling goods

committed used all of the time and energy that you could in order to achieve something

communicate express your thoughts and feelings so that other people understand them

concave curved inward like a bowl

concept idea

concert performance given by musicians or singers

conditions the situation in which people live or work

conduct the way someone behaves

conflict a struggle between opposing forces

congregation a group of people gathered in a church for a religious service, or the people who usually go to a particular church

consequence something that happens as a result of a particular action

constantly always or regularly

consulate the official building where a consul lives and works

consult ask for advice from someone who might have the answer

context situation and conditions that surround something

contract become smaller or tighter

contrast a large difference between people or things that are compared

convex curved outward like the surface of a ball

create make

creative original and inventive

culture the art, literature, music, beliefs, and practices of a particular group of people

debate formal discussion of a subject in which people express differing opinions

declined became less in number or quality

defects faults or imperfections

define clearly show what something is or means

despite in spite of; regardless of

determination a strong desire to succeed even when it is difficult

develop grow or change into something

devoted giving someone or something a lot of love, concern, or attention

dialogue a conversation in a book, play, or movie

diction choice and use of words and phrases to express meaning, especially in literature and poetry

diplomat someone who officially represents his/her government in a foreign country

discrimination the practice of treating one group of people differently from another in an unfair way

distribution scattering or spreading of something over an area

document a piece of paper that has official information written on it

dramatic exciting and impressive

eccentric deviating from a circular path; not quite round

echolocation the system used by animals such as dolphins and bats to locate objects by emitting usually high-pitched sounds

embryo the part of a seed that becomes the plant

energy usable power

environment the land, water, and air in which plants and animals live

equipment the things that you need for a particular activity

equivalent something that has the same value or importance

establish begin or set in motion

estimate guess the value, size, number, etc., of something

ethical having to do with right and wrong

eventful full of events

existence state of being alive

explicit expressed in a way that is very clear and direct

exploits brave and exciting actions

expose give people information that was previously hidden

factors things that influence or cause a situation

fantasy an imaginative story that usually includes characters, settings, or events not found in real life

features parts of something that stand out because they seem important, interesting, or typical

figurative language language that expresses more than a literal meaning

foil a character, who, by contrast, highlights the qualities of another character

function the usual purpose of a thing

germination the stage at which the embryo inside a seed starts to grow

heroism very great courage

honor do something to show publicly that someone is respected and admired

ignorance lack of knowledge or information about something

ignore pay no attention to someone or something

imagery the use of vivid language to describe objects, ideas, or actions

imitate copy; make or do something like someone else

immigrants people from another country who come to your country to live

impact the effect that an event or situation has on someone or something

implicit suggested or understood but not stated directly

inactive not doing anything

individual a person considered separately from other people in the same group

industrial relating to industry

inhumanity cruel behavior or acts of extreme cruelty

injustice a specific unjust act; a wrong

instruct officially tell someone what to do or how to do something

integrity the quality of being honest and having high moral principles

internal conflict a struggle that takes place in a character's mind

interpret explain or decide what something means

invisible not able to be seen

isolated far away from other things

issue a subject, problem, or question that people discuss

justify give a reasonable or acceptable explanation for something

labor work, especially work using much physical or mental effort

laboratories rooms with equipment for doing experiments or research

lecture a talk given to a group of people about a particular subject

mammals animals such as cats and humans that drink their mothers' milk when they are young

manual having to do with the hand or hands

metaphor an implied comparison in which one thing is spoken about as though it were something else

migration action of a large group of animals, including people, moving from one place to another

miserable very unhappy or uncomfortable

moral a lesson about what is right and wrong that you learn from a story

motivation the reason for a character's actions

mutual felt by two or more people toward one another

network a system of lines or tubes that cross one another and are connected to one another

neutral not supporting either side in an argument, competition, or war

nocturnal active at night

objectively in a way that is not influenced by a person's feelings, beliefs, or ideas

onomatopoeia the use of words that imitate sounds

opaque unable to be seen through

percent one part—five, ten, etc.—in every hundred

persistence the act of continuing firmly in some state, purpose, or course of action

personification a figure of speech in which something nonhuman is given human characteristics

plot the sequence of events that make up a story

point of view the perspective from which a story is written

portray describe or show something in a particular way

potential possible

principle a moral set of ideas that makes you behave in a certain way

process a series of actions, developments, or changes that happen in a sequence

property something that someone owns

proposed suggested that something be done

protective used or intended for keeping someone or something safe from harm, damage, or illness

pulmonary relating to the lungs

pursue continue doing an activity or trying to achieve something over a long time

reaction something you say or do because of what has happened or been said to you

refugees people who have to leave their country, especially because of war

region a fairly large area of a state or country, usually without exact limits

regulate adjust things within a system to keep the system operating well

relocate move to a new place

reluctance unwillingness to do something

repetition the act of saying or doing something again

residents people who live in a place

resources all the money, property, and other goods that are available for use

response something that is said, written, or done as a reply to something else

reveal make something known that was previously hidden or unseen

revolution one complete circular movement around a certain point

rural relating to the country

sanctuaries areas for birds and other animals where they are protected and cannot be hunted

sensation a feeling

setting the time and place of a story's action

significance importance or meaning of something

similar almost the same

simile an expression that compares two things using the words *like* or *as*

smuggle to take something secretly and illegally from one place to another

source the cause of something or the place where it starts

spirituals religious folk songs of African-American origin

stage directions instructions that tell the actors what they should do and how they should do it

straighten become straight

surrendered gave up fighting; admitted defeat

survival the state of continuing to live, especially after a difficult time or a dangerous situation

symbol something that stands for or represents something else

sympathetic showing that you understand how sad, hurt, lonely, etc., someone feels

tangible able to be perceived through the sense of touch

technology the combination of all the latest knowledge, equipment, and methods used in scientific or industrial work

temporary existing or happening only for a limited period of time

tension the emotionally charged relationship between people or groups of people

terrestrial describing any of the four planets that are nearest to the sun and made mostly of rock

text the words in a printed piece of writing

theme the central idea or message of a work of literature

tone general feeling or attitude expressed in a piece of writing, activity, etc.

tradition a belief, custom, or way of doing something that has existed for a long time

translucent able to allow some light to pass through

transmit pass something through

transparent clear, able to be seen through

transport move or carry from one place
     to another

trenches long narrow holes dug in the earth
     to protect soldiers

trend a general tendency in the way a
     situation is changing or developing

unique being the one and only of its kind

urban relating to a town or city

vehicles machines such as cars, buses, or
     trucks used for carrying people or things
     from one place to another

veins blood vessels that carry blood to
     your heart

version a reworking of an existing work

virtual able to be seen but not real

visible able to be seen

visual relating to seeing or sight

wavelength the distance between two
     waves of light

welfare health, comfort, and happiness

wingspan the distance from the end of one
     wing to the end of the other

Index of Skills

moral, 137
motivation, 137
onomatopoeia, 5
personification, 281
plot, 85
point of view, 85
repetition, 5
setting, 33
simile, 357
stage directions, 213
symbol, 243
theme, 163
tone, 305

Word Study
Antonyms, 35
Borrowed words, 307
Compound words, 7
Contractions, 215
Frequently misspelled words, 371
Homographs, 87
Homophones, 283
Hyphenated words, 345
Idioms, 113
Irregular plurals, 139
Long *a, i, o,* 101
Long and short vowels, 165
Prefixes, 153
Related words, 231, 75
Roots, 269
Sound /z/, 245
Suffixes, 47, 333
Suffix *-ful,* 201
Suffix *-ness,* 295
Synonyms, 177
Words with double letters, 359
Words with /əl/ spelled *-le* and *-el,* 21

Writing
Applications
  Descriptive writing
  essay, 64–67
    of character, 17
    of experience, 59
    of object, 31
    of place, 43
  Expository writing
    essay, 258–261, 322–324
    cause-and-effect paragraph, 279
    compare and contrast, 291
    critical analysis, 253
    critique, 211
    instructions, 241
    news article, 303
    problem-and-solution paragraph, 317
    summary, 227
  Narrative writing
    fictional narrative, 128–131
    personal letter, 109
    personal narrative, 123
    rewriting a familiar story, 97
    story with starter, 83
  Persuasive writing
    advertisement, 185
    letter to the editor, 161
    persuasive paragraph, 173
    review, 149
    speech, 190–192
  Research report
    classifying paragraphs, 355
    introductory paragraph, 341
    main idea support, 367
    quotations and citations, 381
    report, 386–391

Organization
  ask and answer a question, 303
  cause and effect, 279
  chronological order, 59, 83
  classify, 355
  compare and contrast, 97, 291, 355
  gather and organize information, 109, 123, 253, 386
  graphic organizers, 17, 31, 43, 59, 64, 83, 97, 109, 123, 128, 149, 161, 190, 211, 227, 241, 253, 257, 279, 291, 303, 317, 322, 355, 367, 381, 388
  logical order, 258
  outline, 386
  problem and solution, 317
  spatial order, 43
  step-by-step instructions, 241
  story chart, 128
Skills and strategies
  Description
    character traits, 17
    physical traits, 17
    sensory details, 31, 59, 64–67
    spatial order, 43
  Expository
    5Ws, 303, 322–325
    cause and effect, 279
    compare and contrast, 291
    personal response, 253
    sequence of steps, 241
    standards, 211
    supporting main idea with details, 227, 258–261
    supporting reasons and examples, 317

Index of Authors, Titles, Art, and Artists

Acknowledgments

UNIT 1

"Grandmother Spider Brings the Sun" by Geri Keams. Copyright © 1995 by Geri Keams. Reprinted by permission of Northland Publishing, Flagstaff, AZ.

"Light" adapted from *Prentice Hall Science Explorer Focus on Physical Science* by M. J. Padilla, Ph.D., I. Miaoulis, Ph.D., and & M. Cyr, Ph.D. Copyright © 2001 by Pearson Education Inc., publishing as Prentice Hall. Used by permission.

Excerpt from "A Game of Light and Shade" from *Run to the Waterfall* by Arturo Vivante. Reprinted by permission of Curtis Brown.

Excerpt from *The Eye of Conscience* by Milton Meltzer and Bernard Cole. Copyright © 1974 by Milton Meltzer and Bernard Cole. Reprinted by permission of Harold Ober Associates Incorporated.

UNIT 2

"How Seeds and Plants Grow." Copyright © Pearson Longman, 10 Bank Street, White Plains, NY 10606.

"Two Brothers and the Pumpkin Seeds" from *Good as Gold: Stories of Values from Around the World* by Barbara Baumgartner. Copyright © 1998, Dorling Kindersley Limited. Reprinted by permission of Barbara Baumgartner.

Excerpt from *Roll of Thunder, Hear My Cry* by Mildred D. Taylor. Copyright © 1976 by Mildred D. Taylor. Used by permission of Dial Books for Young Readers, a Division of Penguin Young Readers Group, a Member of Penguin Group (U.S.A.) Inc., 345 Hudson Street, New York, NY 10014. All rights reserved. Reprinted by permission of Penguin Books Ltd.

"Migration Patterns." Copyright © Pearson Longman, 10 Bank Street, White Plains, NY 10606.

"Abuela Invents the Zero" from *An Island Like You* by Judith Ortiz Cofer. Copyright © 1995 by Judith Ortiz Cofer. Reprinted by permission of Orchard Books, an Imprint of Scholastic Inc.

UNIT 3

"The Golden Serpent' by Walter Dean Myers. Copyright © 1980 by Walter Dean Myers. Reprinted by permission of Miriam Altshuler Literary Agency, on behalf of Walter Dean Myers.

Adaptation of "I ♥ Pluto" by Tim Kreider. Copyright © 2006 by The New York Times Company. Reprinted by permission.

Excerpt from *A Single Shard* by Linda Sue Park. Copyright © 2001 by Linda Sue Park. First appeared in *A Single Shard*, published by Clarion Books. Reprinted by permission of Clarion Books, an Imprint of Houghton Mifflin Company and Curtis Brown, Ltd. All rights reserved.

"Marian Anderson: A Voice for Change." Copyright © Pearson Longman, 10 Bank Street, White Plains, NY 10606.

UNIT 4

Excerpt from *The Story of My Life* by Helen Keller. Public domain.

Excerpt from *The Little Prince* by Rick Cummins and John Scoullar. Dramatic Publishing Co.

Excerpt from *The Heart: Our Circulatory System* by Seymour Simon. Copyright © 1996 by Seymour Simon. Reprinted by permission of HarperCollins Publishers.

"Heart-Healthy Recipe" Copyright © Pearson Longman, 10 Bank Street, White Plains, NY 10606.

"Ginger from the Heart" from *Tales from Gold Mountain: Stories of the Chinese in the New World* by Paul Yee. Copyright © 1989 by Paul Yee. Reprinted by permission of Groundwood Books Ltd.

"Love Poem" by Michael Hannon. Reprinted by permission of Michael Hannon.

Credits

Smithsonian American Art Museum List of Artworks

UNIT 1 Capturing the Power of Contrasts
Page 68
Edward Hopper
Ryder's House
1933
oil on canvas
36⅛ x 50 in.
Smithsonian American Art Museum, Bequest of Henry Ward
Ranger through the National Academy of Design

Page 69
Arthur Dove
Sun
1943
wax emulsion on canvas
24 x 32 in.
Smithsonian American Art Museum, Bequest of Suzanne M. Smith

Robert Sperry
Plate #753
1986
stoneware, white slip over black glaze
4 x 27⅝ in. diam.
Smithsonian American Art Museum, Gift of the James Renwick Alliance

UNIT 2 Cycles of Nature
Page 132
Thomas Hart Benton
Wheat
1967
oil on wood
20 x 21 in.
Smithsonian American Art Museum, Gift of Mr. and Mrs. James A. Mitchell and museum purchase

Page 133
Mary Vaux Walcott
Untitled (Mixed Flowers)
1876
watercolor on paper
5⅛ x 2⅜ in.
Smithsonian American Art Museum, Gift of the artist

Heikki Seppä
Lupin Wedding Crown
1982
18k gold, sterling silver, and diamond
4 x 8 x 8 in.
Smithsonian American Art Museum, Gift of the James Renwick Alliance

UNIT 3 That's Art?
Page 194
Deborah Butterfield
Monekana
2001
bronze
96 x 129½ x 63½ in.
Smithsonian American Art Museum, Gift of the American Art Forum, Mr. and
Mrs. Frank O. Rushing, Shelby and Frederick Gans and museum purchase
© 2001 Deborah Butterfield

Page 195
Sam Gilliam
Swing
1969
acrylic and aluminum on canvas
119⅝ x 283½ in.
Smithsonian American Art Museum, Gift of Mr. Edwin Janss Jr.

Man Ray
Cadeau (Serie II)
1970
flat iron
6⅛ x 4⅛ x 3½ in.
Smithsonian American Art Museum, Gift of Juliet Man Ray

UNIT 4 Bonding or Breaking?
Page 262
William T. Wiley
Love Poem—Poem by Michael Hannon
1997
watercolor on paper
41 x 27 in.
Smithsonian American Art Museum, Gift of the artist
© 1997 William T. Wiley

Page 263
Washington Allston
Hermia and Helena
before 1818
oil on canvas
30⅜ x 25¼ in.
Smithsonian American Art Museum, Museum purchase through the Smithsonian
Institution Collections Acquisition Program and made possible by Ralph Cross
Johnson, the Catherine Walden Myer Fund, and the National Institute

UNIT 5 Citizens on the Home Front
Page 326
Norman Rockwell
Publisher: Office of War Information
Printer: Government Printing Office
Save Freedom of Speech
1943
color lithograph on paper
56 x 48 in.
Smithsonian American Art Museum, Gift from the Steven L. Block Collection
©1943 The Norman Rockwell Family Trust

Page 327
Roger Shimomura
Diary: December 12, 1941
1980
acrylic on canvas
50¼ x 60 in.
Smithsonian American Art Museum, Gift of the artist
© Smithsonian American Art Museum

UNIT 6 Animals in Human Society
Page 392
John Steuart Curry
Ajax
1936–37
oil on canvas
36 x 48¼ in.
Smithsonian American Art Museum, Gift of Peter and Paula Lunder

Page 393
Larry Fuente
Game Fish
1988
mixed media
51½ x 112½ x 10¾ in.
Smithsonian American Art Museum, Gift of the James Renwick Alliance and museum
purchase through the Smithsonian Institution Collections Acquisition Program
© 1988 Larry Fuente